THE
SACRED BOOKS OF THE EAST

Translated by
VARIOUS ORIENTAL SCHOLARS

Edited by
F. MAX MÜLLER

VOLUME 38

SACRED BOOKS OF THE EAST

(50 Volumes)

Ed. *F. Max-Müller*

ISBN: 978-93-5676-187-2 (Set)

These volumes of the Sacred Books of the East series include translations of all the most important works of the seven non-Christian religions that have exercised a profound influence on the civilisations of the continent of Asia. The Vedic Brahmanic system claims 21 volumes, Buddhism 10, and Jainism 2; 8 volumes comprise Sacred Books of the Parsees; 2 volumes represent Islam; and 6 the two main indigenous systems of China. Translated by twenty leading authorities in their respective fields, the volumes have been edited by the late F. Max Müller. The inception, publication and the compilation of these books cover 34 years.

BUDDHISM

Vol. 49: Buddhist Mahayana Texts (2 Parts)
Vol. 11: Buddhist Suttas
Vol. 10: The Dhammapada and Sutta Nipata
Vols. 35 & 36: The Questions of King Milinda (2 Parts)
Vol. 21: The Saddharma Pundarika or the Lotus of the True Law
Vols. 13, 17 & 20: Vinaya Texts (3 Parts)

CHINESE

Vols. 3, 16, 27, 28, 39 & 40: The Sacred Books of China (6 Parts)
Vol. 19: The Fo-Sho-Hing-Tsan-King

ISLAM

Vols. 6 & 9: The Qur'an (2 Parts)

JAINISM

Vols. 22 & 45: The Jaina Sutras (2 Parts)

PARSIS

Vols. 5, 18, 24, 37 & 47: Pahlavi Texts (5 Parts)
Vols. 4, 23 & 31: The Zend-Avesta (3 Parts)
Vol. 50: A General Index to the Names and Subject-matter of the Sacred Books of the East

VEDIC-BRAHMANIC SYSTEM

Vol. 8: The Bhagavadgita with the Sanatsujatiya and the Anugita
Vols. 29 & 30: The Grihya-Sutras: Rules of Vedic Domestic Ceremonies (2 Parts)
Vol. 42: Hymns of the Atharva Veda together with Extracts from the Ritual Books and the Commentaries
Vol. 7: The Institutes of Vishnu
Vol. 25: The Laws of Manu
Vol. 33: The Minor Law Books
Vols. 2 & 14: The Sacred Laws of the Aryas as Taught in the Schools of Apastamba, Gautama, Vasishtha and Baudhayana (2 Parts)
Vols. 12, 26, 41, 43 & 44: The Satapatha Brahmana According to the Text of the Madhyandina School (5 Parts)
Vols. 1 & 15: The Upanishads (2 Parts)
Vols. 34 & 38: The Vedanta Sutras (2 Parts)
Vol. 48: The Vedanta-Sutras (with the commentary by Ramanuja)
Vols. 32 & 46: Vedic Hymns (2 Parts)

THE VEDÂNTA-SÛTRAS

Translated by
GEORGE THIBAUT

PART V
WITH THE COMMENTARY OF ŚANKARĀCĀRYA

MOTILAL BANARSIDASS
PUBLISHING HOUSE • DELHI
Email: naraina@mlbd.in • Website: www.mlbd.in
@mlbdofficial

*10th Reprint Delhi : **2023***
First Edition : Oxford University Press, 1962

ISBN: 978-93-5676-068-4 (Hardcover)
ISBN: 978-93-5676-069-1 (Paperback)

UNESCO COLLECTION OF REPRESENTATIVE WORKS—*Indian Series*
This book has been accepted in the Indian Translation Series of the UNESCO Collection of Representative Works, jointly sponsored by the United Nations Educational, Scientific and Cultural Organization (UNESCO) and the Government of India

Printed & Published by
Rajendra P Jain *for*
Motilal Banarsidass Publishing House
A-44, Naraina Industrial Area, Phase I,
New Delhi–110 028 (INDIA)
Email: naraina@mlbd.in Website: www.mlbd.in
Tel.: (+91-11)4751 1592
Showroom:
4637/20, F-2, Hari Sadan, First Floor, Ansari Road, Daryaganj
Delhi–110 002 (Opp. Fire Station) ***Tel.*** : (+91-11)4559 7999

RASHTRAPATI BHAVAN,
NEW DELHI-4
June 10, 1962

I am very glad to know that the Sacred Books of the East, published years ago by the Clarendon Press, Oxford, which have been out-of-print for a number of years, will now be available to all students of religion and philosophy. The enterprise of the publishers is commendable and I hope the books will be widely read.

S. RADHAKRISHNAN

PUBLISHERS' NOTE

First, the man distinguished between eternal and perishable. Later he discovered within himself the germ of the Eternal. This discovery was an epoch in the history of the human mind and the *East was the first to discover it.*

To watch in the Sacred Books of the East the dawn of this religious consciousness of man, must always remain one of the most inspiring and hallowing sights in the whole history of the world. In order to have a solid foundation for a comparative study of the Religions of the East, we must have before all things, complete and thoroughly faithful translation of their Sacred Books in which some of the ancient sayings were preserved because they were so true and so striking that they could not be forgotten. They contained eternal truths, expressed for the first time in human language.

With profoundest reverence for Dr. S. Radhakrishnan, President of India, who inspired us for the task; our deep sense of gratitude for Dr. C. D. Deshmukh & Dr. D. S. Kothari, for encouraging assistance; esteemed appreciation of UNESCO for the warm endorsement of the cause ; and finally with indebtedness to Dr. H. Rau, Director, Max Müller Bhawan, New Delhi, in procuring us the texts of the Series for reprint, we humbly conclude.

PREFATORY NOTE TO THE NEW EDITION

Since 1948 the United Nations Educational, Scientific and Cultural Organization (UNESCO), upon the recommendation of the General Assembly of the United Nations, has been concerned with facilitating the translation of the works most representative of the culture of certain of its Member States, and, in particular, those of Asia.

One of the major difficulties confronting this programme is the lack of translators having both the qualifications and the time to undertake translations of the many outstanding books meriting publication. To help overcome this difficulty in part, UNESCO's advisers in this field (a panel of experts convened every other year by the International Council for Philosophy and Humanistic Studies), have recommended that many worthwhile translations published during the 19th century, and now impossible to find except in a limited number of libraries, should be brought back into print in low-priced editions, for the use of students and of the general public. The experts also pointed out that in certain cases, even though there might be in existence more recent and more accurate translations endowed with a more modern apparatus of scholarship, a number of pioneer works of the greatest value and interest to students of Eastern religions also merited republication.

This point of view was warmly endorsed by the Indian National Academy of Letters (Sahitya Akademi), and the Indian National Commission for UNESCO.

It is in the spirit of these recommendations that this work from the famous series "Sacred Books of the East" is now once again being made available to the general public as part of the UNESCO Collection of Representative Works.

CONTENTS.

VEDÂNTA-SÛTRAS WITH THE COMMENTARY BY *S*AṄKARÂ*K*ÂRYA.

VEDÂNTA-SÛTRAS

WITH

*S*AṄKARA BHÂSHYA.

SECOND ADHYÂYA.

THIRD PÂDA.

REVERENCE TO THE HIGHEST SELF!

1. Ether[1] (does) not (originate), on account of the absence of scriptural statement.

In the Vedânta-texts we meet in different places with different statements concerning the origination of various things. Some of those passages declare that ether originated; some do not. Some record the origination of air; others do not. Other passages again make analogous statements concerning the individual soul and the vital airs.—Similarly we observe that other scriptural texts contradict one another concerning order of succession and the like.—Now, as we ourselves have inferred the worthlessness of other philosophical doctrines from their mutual contradictions, a suspicion might arise that our doctrine is equally worthless, owing to its intrinsic contradictions. Hence a new discussion is begun in order to clear from all doubt the sense of all those Vedânta-texts which refer to creation, and thus to remove the suspicion alluded to.

Here we have to consider in the first place the question

---

[1] Here, as generally in the preceding parts of this translation, âkâsa is rendered by 'ether.' There is no doubt that occasionally the appropriate—and in some cases the only possible—rendering is not 'ether' but 'space;' but the former rendering, after all, best agrees with the general Vedântic view of âkâsa. The Vedântins do not clearly distinguish between empty space and an exceedingly fine matter filling all space, and thus it happens that in many cases where we speak of the former they speak of âkâsa, i.e. the all-pervading substratum of sound; which howsoever attenuated is yet one of the material elements, and as such belongs to the same category as air, fire, water, and earth.

B 2

whether ether has an origin or not.—The pûrvapakshin maintains that ether does not originate, since there is no scriptural statement to that effect. For in the chapter which treats of the origin (of the world) ether is not mentioned at all. In the passage 'In the beginning there was that only which is, one only, without a second' the *Kh*ândogya at first introduces Brahman as the general subject-matter, by means of the clause 'that which is,' and thereupon (in the passages 'It thought,' 'It sent forth fire,' &c.) records the origin of three elements, viz. fire, water, and earth; giving the first place to fire which (ordinarily) occupies the middle place among the five elements[1]. Now, as scriptural statement is our (only) authority in the origination of the knowledge of supersensuous things, and as there is no scriptural statement declaring the origin of ether, ether must be considered to have no origin.

2. But there is (a scriptural statement of the origination of ether).

The conjunction 'but' indicates the adoption of another alternative.—The origin of ether may not be stated in the *Kh*ândogya; but it *is* stated in other scriptural passages. For the text of the Taittirîyakas, after having introduced Brahman as the general subject-matter,—in the words, 'The true, knowledge, without end is Brahman,'—goes on to say, 'From that Self sprang ether' (Taitt. Up. II, 1).—Hence there arises a conflict of scriptural passages, the creation sometimes being said to begin with fire, sometimes with ether.—But may we not appropriately assume the two scriptural passages to form one syntactical whole?—It would be well indeed if we could do so, but a unity of the kind desired cannot be admitted, because the creator who is mentioned only once—in the passage 'he sent forth fire'—cannot be connected with two things to be created, as if the construction were 'He sent forth fire, he sent forth ether.'—But—an objection may be raised—we see that sometimes an agent, although mentioned once only, is yet

[1] The usual order being ether, air, fire, water, earth.

connected with two objects; as when we say 'after having cooked broth he now cooks rice.' We therefore may combine the two scriptural sentences into one, 'Brahman having created ether created fire.'—Such a combination of sentences, we reply, is not admissible here, because the *Kh*ândogya intimates that fire was created first, while the Taittirîyaka assigns the samc position to ether, and because it is impossible that both should have been created first.—The same remarks apply to a further contradiction involved in the other scriptural passage, 'From that Self sprang ether,' &c.; for there also the material cause and the fact of origination, being mentioned only once, cannot be connected with fire as well as ether, so as to effect a sentence of the following kind, 'from that there sprang ether, from that there sprang fire.' Moreover the Taittirîyaka states separately that 'fire (sprang) from air [1].'—With regard to this conflict of statements somebody now maintains the following view.

3. (The Vedic statement concerning the origination of ether) has a secondary sense, on account of the impossibility (of the origination of ether).

The ether does not originate on account of the absence of scriptural statement.—That other passage which (apparently) declares the origination of the ether must be taken as having a secondary (figurative) meaning.—Why?—On account of the impossibility. The origination of ether cannot be shown to be possible as long as there exist followers of the opinion of the reverend Ka*n*abhu*g* (Ka*n*âda). For the latter deny the origination of ether on the ground that it is impossible to demonstrate the existence of the required apparatus of causes. Whatever is originated, they say, is originated from inherent causes, non-inherent causes, and operative causes. Of a substance the inherent causes are substances belonging to the same class and more than one in number. But for ether there are no such originating substances, belonging to the same

[1] While the *Kh*ând. says that fire sprang from the Self.

class and more than one in number, from which, as its inherent cause, it could originate, and consequently there also exists no non-inherent cause of ether; for the latter would have to be looked for in the conjunction of the primary substances. And as thus there exist no inherent cause and no non-inherent cause, there is absolutely no room for an operative cause; for the only function of the latter is to assist the two other causes. Those elements moreover which have an origin, as fire and the like, we may conceive to exist in different conditions at an earlier and a later time; we may conceive e.g. that fire, previously to its origination, did not give light or produce any other effects, while it does do so subsequently to its origination. Of the ether, on the other hand, no such difference between an earlier and a later period can be conceived; for, we ask, would it be possible to maintain that before its alleged origination there were no large, minute, and atomic spaces?—That ether is without an origin further follows from its characteristic qualities, such as all-pervadingness and so on, which altogether distinguish it from earth and the other elements.—Hence, as the word 'ether' (âkâ*s*a) is used in a secondary sense in such phrases as 'make room' (âkâ*s*a), 'there is room,' and as space although one only is designated as being of different kinds when we speak of the space of a jar, the space of a house, &c.—a form of expression met with even in Vedic passages such as 'he is to place the wild animals in the spaces' (âkâ*s*eshu)'—we conclude that those Vedic passages also which speak of its origination must be supposed to have a secondary meaning.

4. And on account of the word (of the Veda).

The word of the Veda also proclaims the non-originatedness of ether; for it declares that 'air and ether (antariksha) are immortal' (B*ri*. Up. II, 3, 3), and what is immortal cannot have an origin. Another scriptural passage ('omnipresent and eternal like ether'), by comparing two attributes of Brahman, viz. omnipresence and eternity with the other, intimates that those qualities belong to the ether also; in which case no beginning can be attributed to it. Other passages to be quoted in this connexion are, 'As this ether is infinite, so the Self is to be known as infinite;' and 'Brahman has the ether for its body, the ether is the Self.' For if the ether had a beginning, it could not be predicated of Brahman (as is done in the last passage), as we predicate blueness of a lotus ('the lotus is blue'). Hence we understand that the eternal Brahman is of the same nature as ether.

5. The one (word 'sprang') may be (taken in its secondary as well as in its primary sense), like the word 'Brahman.'

This Sûtra contains the reply to a doubt.—If we admit the opinion maintained hitherto, how can one and the same word 'sprang' ('from that Self sprang the ether') be used in the same chapter, in its primary (real) meaning with regard to fire and so on, and in a secondary meaning with regard to ether?—The answer to this objection is that the one word 'sprang' may, according to the nature of the things to which it refers, be used in its primary as well as its secondary sense, just as the word 'Brahman' is used. For the one word 'Brahman' is, in the passage Taitt. Up. III, 2–6 ('Try to know Brahman by penance, for penance is Brahman'), used in a secondary sense with regard to food, &c., and in its primary sense with regard to bliss; and the same word Brahman is, in the way of figurative identification (bhakti), applied to penance, which is merely the means of knowing Brahman, and again directly to Brahman as the object of knowledge.—But how—to raise another question—can we, on the supposition of ether having no beginning, uphold the validity of the statement made in the clause 'one only, without a second?' For if ether is a second entity (co-existing with Brahman from eternity), it follows that Brahman has a second. And if so, how can it be said that when Brahman is known everything is known? (*Kh.* Up. VI, 1).—The word 'one,' the pûrvapakshin replies, may be used with reference to (the absence of) effects. As in ordinary life a person, who on a certain day sees in a potter's house a lump of clay, a staff, a wheel and so on, and on the following day a number of finished vessels, might say, 'Yesterday there was only clay,' meaning thereby only that on the preceding day there were no things made of clay, not that there were no staff, wheel and the like; so the passage under discussion also is to be understood.—The term 'without a second' (does not exclude the existence from eternity of ether, but) excludes the existence of any other superintending being (but Brahman). While there is a superintending potter in addition to the material cause of the vessels, i. e. the clay, there is no other superintendent in addition to Brahman, the material cause of the world. Nor does the existence of ether as a second entity involve Brahman's being associated with a second (and therefore not being of a simple nature). For diversity is founded on difference of characteristic attributes, and before the origin (of the creation) no difference of attributes separating Brahman and ether exists; the two being mixed like water and milk, and having the common attributes of all-pervadingness, immateriality and so on. At the time of creation however a certain diversity of the two determines itself, Brahman putting forth energy in order to produce the world, while the ether remains immoveable.—And also from the passages quoted above—such as 'Brahman has the ether for its body'—it follows that the two are identical. Thence again it follows that through the knowledge of Brahman everything is known.—Moreover every effect, which is produced, is produced in such a way as not to be separated from ether in place as well as in time, and ether itself is non-separated in place and time from Brahman; hence, if there are known Brahman and its effects, the ether also is known. The case is similar to that of a few drops of water poured into a jug full of milk. Those drops are taken when the milk is taken; the taking of the drops does not constitute something additional to the taking of the milk. Analogously the ether, as being non-separate in place and time from Brahman and its effects, is comprised within Brahman, and consequently we have to understand the passages about the origin of the ether in a secondary sense.—To this argumentation we make the following reply.

6. The non-abandonment of the promissory statements (results only) from the non-difference (of the entire world from Brahman), according to the words of the Veda.

In all the Vedânta-texts we meet with promissory statements of the following nature:—'That by which we hear what is not heard, perceive what is not perceived, know what is not known' (*Kh.* Up. VI, 1, 3); 'When the Self has been seen, heard, perceived, and known, then all this is known' (B*ri*. Up. IV, 5, 6); 'Sir, what is that through which if it is known everything else becomes known?' (Mu. Up. I, 1, 3); 'Outside that which is there is no knowledge.' These promissory statements are not abandoned, i.e. not stultified, only if the entire aggregate of things is non-different from Brahman, the object of knowledge; for if there were any difference, the affirmation that by the knowledge of one thing everything is known, would be contradicted thereby. Non-difference again of the two is possible only if the whole aggregate of things originates from the one Brahman. And we understand from the words of the Veda that that affirmation can be established only through the theory of the non-difference of the material cause and its effects. For the affirmation contained in the clause 'That by which we hear what is not heard,' &c., is proved by the analogous instances of clay, &c., which all aim at showing the identity of effect and cause. In order to establish this, the subsequent clauses also ('Being only, my dear, this was in the beginning, one only, without a second; it thought; it sent forth fire,' &c.) at first state that the aggregate of effects belongs to Brahman, and then declare its identity with Brahman, viz. from the passage 'In it all that exists has its Self' (VI, 8, 7), up to the end of the prapâ*th*aka.—If, now, the ether were not one of the effects of Brahman, it could not be known by Brahman being known, and that would involve an abandonment of a (previous) affirmation; an alternative which, as invalidating the authoritativeness of the Veda, is of course altogether unacceptable.—Similarly in all the Vedânta-texts certain passages are to be found which, by means of various instances, make the same affirmation, so e.g. 'This everything, all is that Self' (B*ri*. Up. II, 4, 6); 'Brahman alone is that Immortal before' (Mu. Up. II, 2, 11).—Hence, like fire and the other substances, the ether also is a product.—The averment made by the pûrvapakshin that on account of the absence of scriptural statements the ether is not a product is unfounded, since a scriptural passage referring to the origin of ether has already been pointed out, viz. 'from that Self sprang ether.'—True,—the pûrvapakshin may reply,—such a statement has indeed been pointed out, but it is contradicted by another statement, viz. 'It sent forth fire,' &c. Should it be alleged that there can be no contradiction, because all scriptural passages form one whole, the reply is that all non-contradictory passages form a whole; in the present case, however, a contradiction has been shown to exist, because the creator, who is mentioned only once, cannot be connected with two things created; because two things cannot both be created first; and because an option is, in that case, inadmissible [1].—This reply, we rejoin, is without force. It is indeed true that it is impossible to explain the passage of the Taittirîyaka in any modified sense; for it distinctly declares that fire was produced in the third place, 'From that Self sprang the ether, from ether air, from air fire.' But, on the other hand, it is possible to give a different turn to the passage from the *Kh*ândogya, which may be explained to mean that 'Brahman, after having created ether and air, created fire.' For as the purport of this passage is to relate the origin of fire, it cannot at the same time impugn the account of the origin of ether given in another passage; according to the principle that to one and the same sentence a double purport must not be ascribed. As, on the

[1] For we cannot maintain that optionally either the one or the other was created first.

other hand, one creator may successively create more than one thing, and as on that ground the combination of the two passages into one syntactical whole is possible, we are not obliged to disregard any scriptural statement on account of its meaning being contradicted (by other scriptural passages). Nor do we mean to say that a creator mentioned only once is to be connected with two created things; for the other (second) created thing is supplied from another scriptural passage. And, in the same way as the fact of the whole aggregate of things being produced from Brahman—which is stated directly in the passage 'Let a man meditate with calm mind on that as beginning, ending and breathing in it' (*Kh.* Up. III, 14, 1)—does not impugn the order of creation stated elsewhere to begin with fire; so also the statement as to fire being produced from Brahman has no force to impugn the order of creation which, in another scriptural passage, is said to begin with ether.

But, it may be objected, the passage 'Let a man meditate with calm mind,' &c. has the purpose of enjoining calmness, and does not state anything with regard to creation; it need not therefore adapt itself to the order (of creation) established by another passage[1]. On the other hand, the passage 'It sent forth fire' refers to the creation, and we must therefore accept the order exactly as stated there.—This objection we refute by the remark that it is not legitimate to abandon, from deference to the circumstance of fire occupying the first place (in the *Kh.* Up.), the thing, viz. the ether which is known (to have been created) from another passage; for order of succession is a mere attribute of things (and therefore subordinate to the latter). Moreover, in the passage 'It sent forth fire' we meet with no word directly indicating the order of succession; but we merely infer the latter from the sense, and this (merely inferred) order is impugned by the order established by another direct scriptural state-

[1] Yatpara*h* *s*abda*h* sa *s*abdârtho na *k*âya*m* *s*abda*h* s*ri*sh*t*iparo*-*tô na prasiddha*m* kramam bâdhitum alam iti. Ân. Gi.

ment, viz. 'From air there sprang fire.' Now with regard to the question whether ether or fire were created first, neither option nor addition are permissible, because the former is impossible in itself, and the latter non-admitted by the texts[1]. Hence the two scriptural passages are not contradictory.—Moreover, in order to justify the promise made in the *Kh*ândogya in the beginning of the chapter ('That instruction by which we hear what is not heard'), we have to count the ether, although 'not heard' (i. e. not mentioned in the text) among the things produced; how much more impossible then is it for us not to accept the statement actually made about the ether in the Taittirîyaka!—To the assertion, made above by the pûrvapakshin, that the ether as occupying the same space with everything is known together with Brahman and its effects, and that thus the assertion (of everything being known through Brahman) is not contradicted; and that moreover the scriptural passage 'one only, without a second' is not contradicted, because Brahman and the ether may be considered as non-separate, like milk and water, we make the following reply. That knowledge of everything through the knowledge of one thing (of which scripture speaks) cannot be explained through the analogy of milk mixed with water, because we understand from the parallel instance of a piece of clay being brought forward (*Kh*. Up. VI, 1, 4) that the knowledge of everything has to be explained through the relation of the material cause and the material effect (the knowledge of the cause implying the knowledge of the effect). Moreover, the knowledge of everything, if assumed to be analogous to the case of the knowledge of milk and water, could not be called a perfect knowledge (samyag-vi*gñ*âna), because the water which is

[1] An optional proceeding, i.e. the doctrine that either ether or fire was the first product is impossible because only actions to be done, not existing things, fall within the sphere of option; addition, i.e. the fact of fire and ether together being the first creation is not admitted by scripture, which teaches a successive creation of the elements.

apprehended only through the knowledge of the milk (with which it is mixed) is not grasped by perfect knowledge[1]. Nor can Vedic affirmations about things be viewed, like ordinary human statements, as mixed up with error, untruth, and deceit[2]. And we should do violence to the emphatic assertion made in the passage 'one only, without a second,' if we explained it according to the analogy of milk mixed with water.—Nor must we explain the cognition of everything (through one thing), and the assertion as to the one without a second, as referring only to a part of existing things, viz. the avowed effects of Brahman (to the exclusion of ether), on the ground that such is the case in the parallel instances of clay and the like. For what is said about clay and the like is not something altogether new and independent; but has to be understood in connexion with the previous passage 'Svetaketu, as you are so conceited,' &c. We therefore must conclude that the 'knowledge of everything' has all things whatever for its objects, and is here introduced with a view to showing that everything is the effect of Brahman.

The next Sûtra replies to the assertion, made by the pûrvapakshin, that the passage which speaks of the origin of ether is to be understood in a secondary sense, on account of the impossibility (of ether having an origin).

7. But wherever there are effects, there is division; as in ordinary life.

The conjunction 'but' is meant to exclude the suspicion of impossibility.—We must not imagine the origin of ether to be impossible, because wherever we observe effects (modifications of a substance), such as jars, pots and urns, or bracelets, armlets and earrings, or needles, arrows and swords, we also observe division; while, on the other hand,

[1] For the water, although mixed with the milk, yet is different from it.

[2] But the promise that through the knowledge of one thing everything becomes known is to be taken in its full literal meaning.

nothing which is not an effect is seen to be divided [1]. Now, we apprehend ether as divided from earth and so on; hence ether also must be an effect. Thereby (i. e. by the circumstance of their being divided) place (dis), time, mind (manas) and the atoms also are shown to be effects.

But—an objection may be raised—the Self also is divided from ether and so on, and hence it follows that it is an effect like jars and the like.—This objection we refute by pointing to the scriptural statement that 'ether sprang from the Self' (Taitt. Up. II, 1). For if the Self also were a mere modification (of something else), it would follow that all effects such as the ether and so on are without a Self [2]; for scripture mentions nothing beyond the Self, and that Self itself would (on the supposition stated) be a mere effect. And thus we should be driven to the hypothesis of a general void (sûnyavâda). Just because it is the Self, it is impossible for us to entertain the idea even of its being capable of refutation. For the (knowledge of the) Self is not, in any person's case, adventitious, not established through the so-called means of right knowledge; it rather is self-established. The Self does indeed employ perception and the other means of right knowledge for the purpose of establishing previously non-established objects of knowledge; for nobody assumes such things as ether and so on to be self-established independently of the means of right knowledge. But the Self, as being the abode of the energy that acts through the means of right knowledge, is itself established previously to that energy. And to refute such a self-established entity is impossible. An adventitious thing, indeed, may be refuted, but not that which is the essential nature (of him who attempts the refutation); for it is the essential nature of him who refutes. The heat of a fire is not refuted (i. e. sublated) by the fire itself.—Let us further consider the relation expressed in the following clauses: 'I know at the present moment whatever is present; I knew (at former moments) the nearer and the remoter past; I shall know

[1] Whatever is divided, is an effect, as jars, pots, &c. Whatever is not an effect, is not divided, as the Self.

[2] I. e. without a material cause.

(in the future) the nearer and the remoter future.' Here the object of knowledge changes according as it is something past or something future or something present; but the knowing agent does not change, since his nature is eternal presence. And as the nature of the Self is eternal presence, it cannot undergo destruction even when the body is reduced to ashes; nay we cannot even conceive that it ever should become something different from what it is.—It thus follows from the essential irrefutability of its nature that the Self is not an effect. The ether, on the other hand, falls under the category of effected things.

To the objection, raised above by the pûrvapakshin, that there is no plurality of homogeneous substances out of which the ether could originate, we reply that it is not an absolute law that effects should originate only from things belonging to the same genus, not from such as belong to different genera. Threads for instance and the conjunctions of threads[1] do not belong to the same genus, the former being admitted to belong to the genus 'substance,' the latter to the genus 'quality.' Nor again is there a binding rule that the operative causes such as the shuttle, the loom and so on should belong to the same genus.—Well then let the doctrine that the causes must belong to the same genus extend to the inherent causes only, not to the other causes[2].—But here also there is no absolute rule. For we see that one and the same rope is made of things belonging to different genera, such as threads and cow-hair, and several kinds of cloth are woven of vegetable thread and wool.—If it were assumed that the postulate of the inherent causes belonging to the same genus refers only to the genera of essentiality, substantiality, &c., the rule would be a superfluous one; for in that sense every inherent cause belongs to the same genus as every other[3].

[1] Threads are the inherent cause of a piece of cloth; the conjunction of the threads constitutes the non-inherent cause; the loom, shuttle, &c. are the operative causes.

[2] So much only was in fact insisted upon by the pûrvapakshin, II, 3, 3.

[3] An inherent cause is always a substance (dravya), and as such

—Nor again is there an absolute rule that only a plurality of inherent causes, not one such cause, is able to originate an effect. For it is admitted that an atom as well as the mind (manas) originate their first activity; i. e. one atom by itself, and also the mind by itself, give rise to their primary actions, without being in conjunction with other substances.—And, should it be said that there is an absolute rule as to several causes only having originating power in the case of the origination of substances only (not in the case of the origination of actions, &c.), we again deny that, because it is admitted that there is such a thing as change (transformation). An absolute rule, such as maintained by you, would exist if substances did originate other substances, only when assisted by conjunction (a non-inherent cause). But, as a matter of fact, one and the same substance, when passing over into a different state distinguished by peculiar characteristic marks, is admitted to be an effect. In some cases more substances than one undergo the change, as when a young plant springs from seed and earth; in other cases one substance only changes, as when milk turns into curds.—In short it is none of the Lord's laws that only several causes in conjunction should produce an effect. We therefore decide, on the authority of scripture, that the entire world has sprung from the one Brahman, ether being produced first and later on the other elements in due succession. A statement to that effect has already been made above (II, 1, 24).

The further assertion made by the pûrvapakshin, that on the assumption of ether having had an origin it is impossible to conceive a difference between the former and later periods (the time before and after the origination of ether) is likewise unfounded; for we have to understand that that very specialising difference [1], from which we ascertain at present that there is a thing such as ether, different from earth and the other elements, did not exist before the

---

always falls under the notion of essentiality (sattâ), which constitutes the summum genus for substances, qualities, and actions.

[1] Viz. the quality of sound.

origination of ether. And just as Brahman's nature does not participate in the nature of earth and the other elements characterised by grossness and similar qualities,—according to such scriptural passages as 'It is not gross, it is not subtle,'—so also it does not participate in the nature of ether, as we understand from the passage 'it is without ether' (B*ri*. Up. III, 8, 8). It therefore remains a settled conclusion that, before ether was produced, Brahman existed without ether.

The inference, drawn by the pûrvapakshin, that ether has no beginning, because it differs in nature from those substances which avowedly have a beginning, such as earth and so on, is without any value; for, as it is contradicted by scripture, it must be considered fallacious. We, on our part, have brought forward arguments showing that ether is an originated thing; and we may moreover reason as follows: Ether is non-eternal, because it is the substratum of a non-eternal quality, viz. sound, just as jars and other things, which are the substrata of non-eternal qualities, are themselves non-eternal.—Nor is there any danger of this latter reasoning being extended to the Self also, for the philosopher who takes his stand on the Upanishads does not admit that the Self is the substratum of non-eternal qualities. Moreover, those who teach ether to have an origin do not consider it proved that it is all-pervading and so on.

In reply to the remarks made under II, 3, 4 we point out that those scriptural passages which speak of the 'immortality of ether' are to be understood in the same way as the analogous statements about the immortality of the gods [1], since the origin and destruction of the ether have been shown to be possible. And if it is said of Brahman that 'it is omnipresent and eternal like ether,' Brahman is there compared to ether, whose greatness is well known, merely in order to indicate its supereminent greatness, not in order to maintain its being equal to ether. Similarly, when we say that the sun moves with the speed of an

[1] I.e. as referring to a relative immortality only.

arrow, we merely mean that he moves fast, not that he moves at the same rate as an arrow. This remark explains that scriptural passage also in which Brahman is declared to be infinite like ether.—On the other hand, such passages as 'It is greater than ether' prove that the extent of ether is less than that of Brahman; passages like 'there is no image of him' (*S*ve. Up. IV, 19) show that there is nothing to compare Brahman to; and passages like 'Everything else is of evil' (B*ri*. Up. III, 4, 2) show that everything different from Brahman such as ether, &c. is of evil.—All which serves to refute the assertion that the passage which declares ether to have originated has to be taken in a secondary sense, as the word Brahman actually has to be taken in some passages. Scripture and reasoning in combination rather show that ether has an origin, and the final conclusion therefore is that ether is an effect of Brahman.

8. Hereby air (also) is explained.

The present Sûtra extends the reasoning concerning ether to the air of which the ether is the abode.—The different views about air also are to be arranged in an analogous manner. The pûrvapakshin maintains that the air is not a product, because it is not mentioned in that chapter of the *Kh*ândogya which treats of the origination of things.—The opposite opinion is. that the air is mentioned in the parallel chapter of the Taittirîyaka ('from the ether sprang the air').—The two scriptural passages being of a conflicting nature, the pûrvapakshin maintains that the passage which declares the air to have originated must be taken in a secondary sense; firstly on account of the impossibility (of the literal sense being adopted), as shown (in the adhikara*n*a treating of the ether); secondly on account of that passage which denies that it ever sets, 'Vâyu (the air) is the deity that never sets' (B*ri*. Up. I, 5, 22); and thirdly on account of those passages which declare it to be immortal. The final opinion on the other hand is, that air is a product; in the first place because this conclusion is conformable to the general tendency of scripture; and, in the second place, because it is generally admitted that whatever is divided is an effect.—The denial of its ever setting refers to the lower knowledge (aparâ vidyâ [1]) and is merely a relative one, Vâyu not setting in the same way as fire, &c. The statement as to the immortality, &c. of air has already received its reply (in the adhikara*n*a treating of the ether).—Here it may be asked why, ether and air being equally mentioned and not mentioned in the chapters treating of the origin of the world, one adhikara*n*a is not considered to suffice for both, and why instead of that there is made a formal extension of the former reasoning to the latter case, although there is no difference between the two cases.—To this we reply that there is indeed some reason for the question; that, however, the formal extension is made for the purpose of removing any doubts which might possibly be engendered in the minds of slow-witted people by mere words [2]. For as, in the Sa*m*vargavidyâ and other passages, the glory of Vâyu is referred to as an object of worship; and as scripture says that he never sets, &c., some men might think that he is eternal.

9. But there is no origin of that which is (i.e. of Brahman), on account of the impossibility (of such an origin).

Somebody, who has learned from scripture that ether and air, although not in themselves likely to have originated, yet actually are things with a beginning, might feel inclined to suspect that Brahman itself has sprung from something else.—And further somebody, who has learned from scripture that from ether and the other elements which are themselves mere effects further effects are produced, might think that also Brahman, from which ether has sprung, is a mere effect.—In order to remove this doubt the Sûtra declares that Brahman, whose Self is Being, must not be suspected to have sprung from anything else 'on account of the impossibility.' Brahman which is mere Being cannot spring from mere

[1] In which Brahman is spoken of as to be meditated upon under the form of Vâyu.

[2] *S*abdânurodhiny eva *s*a*n*kâ na vastvanurodhinîti. Ân. Gi.

being, since the relation of cause and effect cannot exist without a certain superiority (on the part of the cause). Nor again can Brahman spring from that which is something particular, since this would be contrary to experience. For we observe that particular forms of existence are produced from what is general, as, for instance, jars and pots from clay, but not that what is general is produced from particulars. Nor again can Brahman spring from that which is not (asat), for that which is not is without a Self[1], and moreover scripture expressly rejects that view, in the passage 'How could that which is spring from that which is not?' (*Kh*. Up. VI, 2, 2). Another passage, moreover, expressly denies that Brahman has any progenitor, 'He is the cause, the lord of the lords of the organs, and there is of him neither progenitor nor lord' (*S*ve. Up. VI, 9).—With regard to ether and air the possibility of an origin has been shown; but in Brahman's case there is no such possibility; hence the cases are not parallel. Nor does the fact of other effects springing from effects imply that Brahman also must be an effect; for the non-admission of a fundamental causal substance would drive us to a retrogressus in infinitum. And that fundamental causal substance which as a matter of fact is generally acknowledged to exist, just that is our Brahman.—Thus there is not any contradiction.

10. Fire (is produced) thence (i.e. from air); for thus (the text) declares.

In the *Kh*ândogya it is said that fire has for its source that which is (Brahman), in the Taittirîyaka that it has the air for its source. There being thus a conflict of scriptural passages with regard to the origin of fire, the pûrvapakshin maintains that fire has Brahman for its source. —Why?—Because the text, after having stated at the outset that there existed only that which is, teaches that it sent forth fire; and because the assertion of everything being known through Brahman is possible only in case of every-

[1] And cannot therefore constitute a cause; for a cause is the Self of its effects.

thing being produced from Brahman; and because the scriptural statement as to the 'Taggalân' (*Kh.* Up. III, 14, 1) specifies no difference[1]; and because another scriptural passage (Mu. Up. II, 1, 3) teaches that everything without exception is born from Brahman. The Taittirîyaka also makes a statement about the entire world without any exception, 'after having brooded he sent forth all whatever there is' (Taitt. Up. II, 6). Hence the statement that 'fire was produced from air' (Taitt. Up. II, 1) must be considered to teach the order of succession only 'fire was produced subsequently to air.'

To this the Sûtra replies that fire was produced thence, i.e. from air, because the text declares it to be so—'from air sprang fire.' For if fire had sprung directly from Brahman and not from air, the scriptural statement that 'fire sprang from air' would be contradicted thereby. That that statement should intimate the order of succession merely, as maintained by the pûrvapakshin, we cannot admit. For as in the preceding sentence ('from that Self sprang ether') the fifth case (âtmana*h*) denotes the Self as that from which the origination proceeds, and as the same verb ('sprang') governs our sentence also, and as in the following sentences also—such as 'from earth the herbs'—the fifth case (p*ri*thivyâ*h*) denotes that from which something proceeds, we understand that in our sentence also the fifth case (vâyo*h*) denotes that from which fire proceeds. Moreover, if we should explain our sentence to mean 'after air fire was produced,' we should have to supply some preposition (or adverb as 'after,' 'subsequently'), while that construction which rests on the proper sense of the fifth case-affix is ready made at hand and does not require anything to be supplied. The passage therefore intimates that fire springs from air.—But, it may be said, the other scriptural passage ('it sent forth fire') intimates that fire springs from Brahman. —Not so, we reply; for this latter passage remains uncontradicted, even if we assume that fire sprang from Brahman only through intermediate links (not directly).

[1] But implies the whole world to have sprung from Brahman.

Even the supposition that Brahman, after having created ether and air, assumed the form of air and thus created fire would not be opposed to fire having sprung from Brahman; for we may say equally that milk comes from the cow, that curds come from the cow, that cheese comes from the cow. There is, moreover, a scriptural passage declaring that Brahman abides as the Self of its effects, viz. Taitt. Up. II, 7, 'That made itself its Self.' And analogously Sm*ri*ti—in the passage beginning 'Cognition, knowledge, steadiness of mind' (Bha. Gî. X, 4)—says about the Lord, 'From me only spring the manifold states of the beings.' For although cognition and so on are observed to spring directly from their immediate causes, yet (the assertion made in the passage quoted holds good), since the entire aggregate of beings is, directly or indirectly, derived from the Lord.—Thereby those scriptural passages are accounted for which speak of the creation (on the whole) without specifying the order of succession[1]; for they may be explained anyhow, while on the other hand the passages specifying the order of creation cannot be turned in any other way (i.e. not away from their direct sense). The general assertion, moreover, of everything springing from Brahman requires only that all things should ultimately proceed from that which is, not that they should be its immediate effects.—Thus there remains no difficulty.

11. Water (is produced from fire).

We have to supply from the preceding Sûtra the words 'thence' and 'for thus the text declares.'—Water is produced from fire; for the text says, 'it sent forth water' (*Kh*. Up. VI, 2, 3), and 'from fire (sprang) water' (Taitt. Up. II, 1). These explicit statements allow no room for doubt[2]. The Sûtrakâra, however, having explained the creation of fire, and being about to explain the creation of

[1] I.e. it appears from the preceding discussion that those passages have to be explained in such a way as to agree with those other passages which state the order of the created beings.

[2] So that the Sûtra might possibly be looked upon as no called for.

earth, propounds this Sûtra in order to insert water (and thus to point out its position in the *sri*sh*t*ikrama).

12. The earth (is meant by the word 'anna'), on account of the subject-matter, the colour, and other passages.

We read, 'Water thought, may I be many, may I grow forth. It sent forth food (anna)' (*Kh*. Up. VI, 2, 4).—Here a doubt arises, whether the word 'anna' denotes things fit to be used as food, such as rice, barley and the like; or cooked food; or else the earth.

The pûrvapakshin maintains that the word is to be understood in the former sense; for, he says, the word 'anna' means 'food' in ordinary language, and is moreover confirmed in that sense by the complementary passage, 'Therefore whenever it rains anywhere, most food is then produced;' for when it rains, rice, barley and the like, but not earth, are produced in abundance.

To this we reply that by the word 'anna' we have to understand earth as being produced from water.—Why?—On account of the subject-matter, on account of the colour, and on account of other passages.—The subject-matter, in the first place, is clearly connected with the elements, as we see from the preceding passages, 'it sent forth fire, it sent forth water.' It would therefore be improper to pass over a further element, viz. earth, when its turn has come, and to assume without reason that rice and the like are meant by the word 'anna.'—In the second place, we find that in a complementary passage there is mentioned a colour which agrees with earth, 'the black colour (of fire) is the colour of anna.' Eatable things on the other hand, such as cooked dishes, and rice, barley and the like, are not necessarily black.—But earth too is not necessarily black; for the soil of some fields has a whitish colour like milk, and that of others looks red like glowing coals!—True, but that does not affect our argument, since what we have to look to is the predominant colour. Now the predominant colour of earth is black, not either white or red. The Paurâ*n*ikas also designate the colour of the earth by the term 'night' (*s*arvarî); now the night is black, and we therefore conclude that black is the colour of earth also.—In the third place other scriptural passages also, which refer to the same subject, declare that 'from water (sprang) earth' (Taitt. Up. II, 1), and that 'what was there as the froth of the water, that was hardened and became the earth' (B*ri*. Up. I, 2, 2). On the other hand the text declares that rice and the like were produced from the earth, 'From earth sprang herbs, from herbs food' (Taitt. Up. II, 1).—As, thus, the general subject-matter as well as other arguments clearly proves that the word 'anna' here denotes earth, we can in no way accept the view that rice and the like are referred to. The common use of language to which the pûrvapakshin appeals is of no avail against the arguments favouring our interpretation. The complementary passage also ('whenever it rains,' &c.) is to be viewed as pointing out that, owing to the earthy nature of food (rice, &c.), earth itself mediately springs from water.—For all these reasons the word 'anna' denotes this earth.

13. But on account of the indicatory mark supplied by their reflecting (i.e. by the reflection attributed to the elements), he (i.e. the Lord is the creative principle abiding within the elements).

A doubt here arises whether ether and the other elements do themselves send forth their effects, or if the highest Lord abiding within certain Selfs produces, after reflection, certain effects.

Here the pûrvapakshin maintains that the elements themselves send forth, because the texts speak of them as acting independently; compare, for instance, 'from ether sprang air, from air fire,' &c. The objection that non-intelligent beings cannot enter on independent activity is invalidated by the fact that the elements also are spoken of in the sacred texts as endowed with intelligence, cf. for instance, 'fire thought,' 'water thought' (*Kh*. Up. VI, 2, 3; 4).

To this we reply that the highest Lord himself abiding within certain Selfs sends forth, after reflection, certain effects.—Why?—On account of the indicatory marks. For texts such as 'he who dwells in the earth, and within the earth, whom the earth does not know, whose body the earth is and who rules the earth within' show that the elements enter on their activity only if presided over by an intelligent principle. Texts such as 'He became sat and tyat' (which occurs in the passage, 'he wished may I be many, may I grow forth,' Taitt. Up. II, 6) and 'It made itself its Self' (i.e. the Self of everything which exists; II, 7) show that he (the highest Lord) is the Self of everything. The thinking and hearing which the texts attribute to water and fire must be viewed as due to the fact of the highest Lord having entered them; for the passage, 'there is no other seer but he,' denies there being any other seer (thinker), and that which is (i.e. Brahman), in the character of seer (or thinker), constitutes the subject-matter of the whole chapter; as we conclude from the introductory passage, 'It thought, may I be many, may I grow forth' (*Kh.* Up. VI, 2, 3).

14. The order (in which the elements are retracted into Brahman) is the reverse of that (i.e. the order in which they are created); this is proved (by its agreement with observation).

Having considered the order of the creation of the elements we now proceed to consider the order of their retractation.—The question here is whether their retractation takes place in an indefinite order, or in the order of the creation, or in the inverse order. That the origin, the subsistence and the retractation of the elements all depend on Brahman, scripture declares 'That from whence these beings are born, that by which when born they live, that into which they enter at their death.'

The pûrvapakshin maintains that the retractation of the elements is not bound to any definite order, because scripture contains no specific information on the point. Or else, he says, let him who wishes to know the order of the retractation accept the order of creation, since the latter is expressly mentioned in the texts.

To this we reply that the order of retractation must be viewed as the reverse of the order of creation. For we see in ordinary life that a man who has ascended a stair has, in descending, to take the steps in the reverse order. Moreover we observe that things made of clay, such as jars, dishes, &c., on being destroyed pass back into clay, and that things which have originated from water, such as snow and hailstones, again dissolve into water. Hence we rightly assume that earth which has (according to scripture) sprung from water passes back into water when the period of its subsistence comes to an end, and that water which has sprung from fire passes back into fire. In this way each particular effect passes back into its immediately antecedent cause—each cause being of a subtler nature than its effect—until in the end the last cause is refunded into Brahman, the ultimate and most subtle of all causes. It certainly would be irrational to assume that an effect, passing over its immediate cause, should at once refund itself into the cause of the cause. Sm*ri*ti also declares that the order of retractation is the order of origination inverted, 'The earth, the basis of the world, is dissolved into water, O divine *Ri*shi, the water into fire, the fire into air.' The order of creation is indeed stated in the sacred texts, but that statement refers to creation only, and can therefore not be extended to retractation. We, moreover, cannot even desire to apply the order in which the elements are created to their retractation also since it is clearly unsuitable in the latter case. For, as long as an effect subsists, it is impossible to assume the dissolution of the cause, since on the dissolution of the latter the effect also cannot exist. On the other hand, we may assume a continued existence of the cause although the effect be destroyed; for that is actually observed in the case of clay (and the things made of it).

15. If it be said that between (Brahman and the elements) the intellect and mind (are mentioned; and that therefore their origination and retractation are to be placed) somewhere in the series, on account of there being inferential signs (whereby the order of the creation of the elements is broken); we

deny that, on account of the non-difference (of the organs and the elements).

In what precedes we have said that the creation and the retractation of the elements take place in direct and reverse order; further that the creation proceeds from the Self, and that the retractation terminates in the Self.—Now *S*ruti as well as Sm*ri*ti enlightens us concerning the existence of the mind (manas) together with the senses, and of the intellect (buddhi); compare, for instance, the indicatory marks contained in the passage, Ka. Up. I, 3, 3. 4, 'Know the intellect to be the charioteer and the mind the reins; the senses they call the horses,' &c. And as the whole aggregate of beings avowedly springs from Brahman, we must assume that the mind, the intellect and the senses also originate from it and are again merged in it in due order, occupying a definite place among the things created and retracted. Moreover the Âtharva*n*a (Mu*nd*aka), in the chapter treating of the creation, mentions the organs between the Self and the elements, 'From him is born breath, mind and all organs of sense, ether, air, light, water and the earth the support of all' (II, 1, 3). And from this there results a break in the previously stated order of the creation and the retractation of the elements.

This we deny, on account of the non-difference (of the organs from the elements). If the organs themselves are of the nature of the elements, their origination and retractation are the same as those of the elements, and we therefore have not to look out in their case for a different order. And that the organs are of the nature of the elements, for that we have inferential marks, in passages such as the following, 'for mind, my child, consists of earth, breath of water, speech of fire' (*Kh.* Up. VI, 6, 5). That the organs (although in reality belonging to the elements) are sometimes mentioned separately from them, is to be understood in the same way as when the Parivrâ*g*akas (mendicant Brâhma*n*as) are spoken of separately from the Brâhma*n*as. And supposing even that the organs are not of the nature of the elements, still the order of the origin of the elements would not be interfered with by the organs; for we might assume either that the organs are produced first and the elements last; or else that the elements are produced first and the organs last. In the Âtharva*n*a-upanishad quoted above we have merely a serial enumeration of the organs and the elements, not a statement as to the order of their origination. Similarly in other places also the series of the organs is recorded apart from the series of the elements; so, for instance, in the following passage. 'Pra*g*âpati indeed was all this in the beginning, he reflected on himself; he sent forth mind; there was mind only; mind reflected on itself; it sent forth speech,' &c.—Hence the origination of the organs does not cause a break in the order of the origination of the elements.

16. But the designation (as being born and dying) abides in the (bodies of beings) moving and non-moving; it is secondary (metaphorical) if applied to the soul, as the existence (of those terms) depends on the existence of that (i.e. the body).

On account of certain popular modes of expression such as 'Devadatta is born,' 'Devadatta has died, and the like, and on account of certain ceremonies such as the *G*âtaka-karman, some people might fall into the error of thinking that the individual soul has a beginning, and in the end undergoes destruction. This error we are going to dispel.—The individual soul has no beginning and is not subject to dissolution, since thus only it can be connected with the results of actions, as the *S*âstra teaches. If the individual soul perished after the body, there would be no sense in the religious injunctions and prohibitions referring to the enjoyment and avoidance of pleasant and unpleasant things in another body (another birth). And scripture says, 'This body indeed dies when the living soul has left it, the living soul does not die' (*Kh*. Up. VI, 11, 3).—But it has been pointed out above that ordinary language speaks of the birth and the death of the individual soul!—True; but the terms 'birth' and 'death,' if applied to the soul, have to be taken in a secondary sense.—What then is that thing to which those words apply in their primary sense, and with reference to which we can speak of a secondary sense?—They apply, we answer, to whatever moves and whatever does not move. The words 'birth' and 'death' have reference to the bodies of moving and non-moving beings; for such beings are born (produced) and die. To them the terms 'birth' and 'death' apply in their primary sense; while they are used metaphorically only with reference to the soul dwelling in them. For their existence (i. e. their being used) depends on the existence of the body; i. e. the words 'birth' and 'death' are used where there take place the manifestation and disappearance of bodies, not where they are absent. For nobody ever observes a soul being born or dying, apart from its connexion with a body. That the words 'birth' and 'death' have reference to the conjunction with—and separation from—a body merely, is also shown by the following passage: 'On being born that person assuming his body, &c.; when he passes out (of the body) and dies,' &c. (B*ri*. Up. IV, 3, 8). The *g*âta-ceremony also is to be viewed as having reference to the manifestation of the body only; for the soul is not manifested.—Whether the individual soul is produced from the highest Self like ether, &c. or not, will be discussed in the next Sûtra; the present Sûtra merely states that the gross origination and dissolution which belong to the body do not affect the soul.

17. The (living) Self is not (produced) as there is no scriptural statement, and as it is eternal according to them (i. e. scriptural passages).

There is a Self called the living one (the individual soul), which rules the body and the senses, and is connected with the fruits of actions. With regard to that Self the conflict of scriptural passages suggests the doubt, whether it is produced from Brahman like ether and the other elements, or if, like Brahman itself, it is unproduced. Some scriptural passages, by comparing it to sparks proceeding from a fire and so on, intimate that the living soul is produced from Brahman; from others again we learn that the highest Brahman, without undergoing any modification, passes, by entering into its effects (the elements), into the condition of the individual soul. These latter passages do not thus record an origination of the individual soul.

The pûrvapakshin maintains that the individual soul is produced, because on that view the general promissory statement is not contradicted. For the general assertion that 'by one thing being known all this is known' is not contradicted, only if the entire aggregate of things springs from Brahman; while it would be contradicted by the assumption of the individual soul being a thing of a different kind. Nor can the individual soul be conceived as mere unmodified highest Self, on account of the difference of their respective characteristics. For the highest Self is characterised by freedom from sin and so on, while the individual soul possesses the opposite attributes. That it is an effect, follows moreover from its being divided. For ether and all other things, in so far as divided, are effects, and we have concluded therefrom that they have an origin. Hence the soul also, which is distributed through all the bodies, doing good and evil and experiencing pleasure and pain, must be considered to originate at the time when the entire world is produced. We have moreover the following scriptural passage, 'As small sparks come forth from fire, thus from that Self all vital airs,' &c. (B*ri*. Up. II, 1, 20). This text teaches first the creation of the aggregate of objects of fruition, beginning with the vital airs, and then (in the words, 'all the Selfs') separately teaches the creation of all the enjoying souls. Again we have the passage, 'As from a blazing fire sparks, being of the same nature as fire, fly forth a thousandfold, thus are various beings brought forth from the Imperishable, my friend, and return hither also' (Mu. Up. II, 1, 1); a passage descriptive of the origin and the retractation of the souls, as we infer from the statement about the sameness of nature[1].

[1] That the word bhâvâ*h* 'beings' here means 'individual souls,' we conclude from their being said to have the same nature as the Imperishable.

For the individual souls are of the same nature as Brahman, because they are endowed with intelligence. Nor can the fact that in some places (as, for instance, in the accounts of the creation of the elements) the creation of the soul is not mentioned, invalidate what is stated about it in other places; it being a general principle of interpretation that whatever new, and at the same time non-contradictory, matter is taught in some scriptural passage has to be combined with the teaching of all other passages. Hence that passage also which speaks of the Self entering (into its effects and thus becoming *g*iva) must be explained as stating the Self's passing over into an effect (viz. the soul), analogously to such passages as 'that made itself its Self,' &c. (Taitt. Up. II, 7).—From all which it follows that the individual soul is a product.

To all this we reply, that the individual soul is not a product.—Why?—On account of the absence of scriptural statement. For in the chapters which treat of the creation, the production of the soul is, in most cases, not mentioned. —But, it was admitted above that the circumstance of something not being stated in some places does not invalidate the statements made about it elsewhere.—True, that was admitted; but we now declare that the production of the soul is not possible.—Why?—'On account of the eternity, &c., resulting from them' (i.e. the scriptural passages). The word '&c.' implies non-originatedness and similar attributes. For we know from scriptural passages that the soul is eternal, that it has no origin, that it is unchanging, that what constitutes the soul is the unmodified Brahman, and that the soul has its Self in Brahman. A being of such a nature cannot be a product. The scriptural passages to which we are alluding are the following:—'The living Self dies not' (*Kh*. Up. VI, 11, 3); 'This great unborn Self undecaying, undying, immortal, fearless is indeed Brahman' (B*ri*. Up. IV, 4, 25); 'The knowing Self is not born, it dies not' (Ka. Up. I, 2, 18); 'The Ancient is unborn, eternal, everlasting' (Ka. Up. I, 2, 18); 'Having sent forth that he entered into it' (Taitt. Up. II, 6); 'Let me now enter those with this living Self and let me then evolve names and forms' (*Kh.* Up. VI, 3, 2); 'He entered thither to the very tips of the finger-nails' (B*ri.* Up. I, 4, 7); 'Thou art that' (*Kh.* Up. VI, 8, 7); 'I am Brahman' (B*ri.* Up. I, 4, 10); 'This Self is Brahman knowing all' (B*ri.* Up. II, 5, 19).—All these texts declare the eternity of the soul, and thus militate against the view of its having been produced.—But it has been argued above that the soul must be a modification because it is divided, and must have an origin because it is a modification!—It is not, we reply, in itself divided; for scripture declares that 'there is one God hidden in all beings, all-pervading, the Self within all beings' (*S*ve. Up. VI, 11); it only appears divided owing to its limiting adjuncts, such as the mind and so on, just as the ether appears divided by its connexion with jars and the like. Scripture (viz. B*ri.* Up. IV, 4, 5, 'that Self is indeed Brahman, made up of knowledge, mind, life, sight, hearing,' &c.) also declares that the one unmodified Brahman is made up of a plurality of intellects (buddhi), &c. By Brahman being made up of mind and so on is meant, that its nature is coloured thereby, while the fact of its being entirely separate from it is non-apparent. Analogously we say that a mean, cowardly fellow is made up of womanishness.—The casual passages which speak of the soul's production and dissolution must therefore be interpreted on the ground of the soul's connexion with its limiting adjuncts; when the adjunct is produced or dissolved, the soul also is said to be produced or dissolved. Thus scripture also declares, 'Being altogether a mass of knowledge, having risen from out of these elements it again perishes after them. When he has departed there is no more knowledge' (B*ri.* Up. IV, 5, 13). What is meant there, is only the dissolution of the limiting adjuncts of the Self, not the dissolution of the Self itself[1]. The text itself explains this, in reply to Maitreyî's ques-

[1] Hence the phrase, 'there is no more knowledge,'—which seems to contradict the term 'a mass of knowledge,'—only means that, on the limiting adjuncts being dissolved, there is no longer any knowledge of distinctions.

tion ('Here, Sir, thou hast landed me in utter bewilderment. Indeed I do not understand him, that when he has departed there is no more knowledge'), in the words, 'I say nothing that is bewildering. Verily, beloved, that Self is imperishable and of an indestructible nature. But it enters into contact with the sense organs.'—Non-contradiction moreover of the general assertion (about everything being known through one) results only from the acknowledgment that Brahman is the individual soul. The difference of the attributes of both is also owing to the limiting adjuncts only. Moreover the words 'Speak on for the sake of final deliverance' (uttered by *G*anaka with reference to the instruction he receives from Yâ*gñ*avalkya about the vi*gñ*ânamaya âtman) implicitly deny that the Self consisting of knowledge (i.e. the individual soul) possesses any of the attributes of transitory existence, and thus show it to be one with the highest Self.—From all this it follows that the individual soul does not either originate or undergo destruction.

18. For this very reason (the individual soul is) intelligent.

Owing to the conflicting views of the philosophical schools there arises a doubt whether, as the followers of Ka*n*âda think, the soul is in itself non-intelligent, so that its intelligence is merely adventitious; or if, as the Sâṅkhyas think, eternal intelligence constitutes its very nature.

The pûrvapakshin maintains that the intelligence of the Self is adventitious, and is produced by the conjunction of the Self with the mind (manas), just as, for instance, the quality of redness is produced in a jar by the conjunction of the jar with fire. For if the soul were of eternal (essential) intelligence, it would remain intelligent in the states of deep sleep, swoon, and possession, while as a matter of fact, men when waking from sleep and so on declare in reply to questions addressed to them that they were not conscious of anything. Men in their ordinary state, on the other hand, are seen to be (actively) intelligent. Hence, as intelligence is clearly intermittent, we conclude that the Self's intelligence is adventitious only.

To this we reply that the soul is of eternal intelligence, for that very reason that it is not a product but nothing else but the unmodified highest Brahman which, owing to the contact with its limiting adjuncts, appears as individual soul. That intelligence constitutes the essential nature of the highest Brahman, we know from scriptural passages such as 'Brahman is knowledge and bliss' (B*ri*. Up. III, 9, 28, 7); 'Brahman is true, knowledge, infinite' (Taitt. Up. II, 1); 'Having neither inside nor outside, but being altogether a mass of knowledge' (B*ri*. Up. IV, 5, 13). Now, if the individual soul is nothing but that highest Brahman, then eternal intelligence constitutes the soul's essential nature also, just as light and heat constitute the nature of fire. In the chapter treating of that which consists of knowledge, there are, moreover, passages (directly declaring that the individual soul is of the nature of self-luminous intelligence), 'He not asleep himself looks down upon the sleeping (senses)' (B*ri*. Up. IV, 3, 11); 'That person is self-illuminated' (B*ri*. Up. IV, 3, 14); 'For there is no intermission of the knowing of the knower' (B*ri*. Up. IV, 3, 30). That the soul's nature is intelligence, follows moreover from the passage (*Kh*. Up. VIII, 12, 4) where it is represented as connected with knowledge through all sense-organs, 'He who knows let me smell this, he is the Self,' &c. &c.—From the soul's essential nature being intelligence it does not follow that the senses are useless; for they serve the purpose of determining the special object of each sense, such as smell and so on. This is expressly declared by scripture, 'Smell is for the purpose of perceiving odour' (*Kh*. Up. VIII, 12, 4).—The objection that sleeping persons are not conscious of anything is refuted by scripture, where we read concerning a man lying in deep sleep, 'And when there he does not see, yet he is seeing though he does not see. For there is no intermission of the seeing of the seer, because it cannot perish. But there is then no second, nothing else different from him that he could see' (B*ri*. Up. IV, 3, 23). That means:

The absence of actual intelligising is due to the absence of objects, not to the absence of intelligence; just as the light pervading space is not apparent owing to the absence of things to be illuminated, not to the absence of its own nature. —The reasoning of the Vaiseshikas and others is, as contradicting scripture, merely fallacious, and we therefore decide that eternal intelligence is the essential nature of the soul.

19. (On account of the scriptural declarations) of (the soul's) passing out, going and returning, (the soul is of atomic size).

We now have to consider of what size the soul is, whether of atomic size or of a medium size, or of great (infinite) size.—But, it has been shown above that the soul is not a product and that eternal intelligence constitutes its nature, whence it follows that it is identical with the highest Self. Now the infinity of the highest Self is clearly stated in scripture; what need then is there of a discussion of the soul's size?—True, we reply; but certain scriptural passages which speak of the soul's passing out, going and returning, establish the primâ facie view that the soul is of limited size, and moreover in some places scripture expressly declares it to be of atomic size. The present discussion is therefore begun for the purpose of clearing up this doubtful point.

The pûrvapakshin maintains that, on account of its being said to pass out, go and return, the soul must be held to be of limited, atomic size. Its passing out is mentioned (Kau. Up. III, 3), 'And when he passes out of this body he passes out together with all these;' its going (Kau. Up. I, 2), 'All who depart from this world go to the moon;' its returning (B*ri*. Up. IV, 4, 6), 'From that world he returns again to this world of action.' From these statements as to the soul's passing out, going and returning it follows that it is of limited size. For motion is impossible in the case of an all-pervading being. And a limited size being once admitted, we have to conclude more especially that the size is atomic, since the hypothesis of the soul being of the same size as the body has already been refuted in our examination of the Ârhata-system.

20. And on account of the two latter (i.e. going and returning) being connected with their Self (i.e. the agent), (the soul is of atomic size).

We admit that 'passing out' might possibly be attributed to the soul even if it does not move, viz. if that expression be taken to mean the soul's ceasing to be the ruler of the body, in consequence of the results of its former actions having become exhausted; just as somebody when ceasing to be the ruler of a village may be said to 'go out.' But the two latter activities, viz. going and returning, are not possible in the case of something which does not move; for they are both connected with the own Self (of the agent), going (and coming back) being activities abiding in the agent[1]. Now going and coming are possible for a being that is not of medium size, only if it is of atomic size. And as going and coming must be taken in their literal sense, we conclude that the passing out also means nothing but the soul's actual moving out of the body. For the soul cannot go and return without first having moved out of the body. Moreover certain parts of the body are mentioned as the points from which the soul starts in passing out, viz. in the following passage, 'Either from the eye or from the skull or from other places of the body (the Self passes out)' (B*ri*. Up. IV, 4, 2). Other passages mention that the embodied soul goes and comes within the body also; so, for instance, 'He taking with him those elements of light descends into the heart' (B*ri*. Up. IV, 4, 1); 'Having assumed light he again goes to his place' (B*ri*. Up. IV, 3, 11).—Thereby the atomic size of the soul is established as well.

21. If it be said that (the soul is) not atomic, on account of scriptural statements about what is not that (i.e. what is opposed to atomic size); we deny

[1] Going is known to be an activity inherent in the agent, from the fact of its producing effects inherent in him, such as his conjunction with—or disjunction from—other things.

that, on account of the other one (the highest Self) being the subject-matter (of those passages).

Nevertheless, it may be objected, the soul cannot be of atomic size, because there are scriptural statements of what is not that, i.e. because there are scriptural statements of its size being the opposite of atomic size. So that by accepting the alternative of atomic size we should place ourselves in opposition to scriptural passages such as the following, 'He is that great unborn Self who consists of knowledge, is surrounded by the Prâ*n*as, the ether within the heart' (B*ri*. Up. IV, 4, 22); 'Like the ether he is omnipresent, eternal;' 'Truth, knowledge, infinite is Brahman' (Taitt. Up. II. 1).

This objection, the pûrvapakshin replies, is not valid 'on account of the other one forming the subject of discussion.' For those statements about a size different (from the atomic one) occur under the heading of the highest Self which on account of its pre-eminence constitutes the general object of knowledge in all Vedânta-texts; and moreover the passage, 'It is spotless, beyond the ether' (B*ri*. Up. IV, 4, 20), specially proves that the highest Self constitutes the subject-matter (in the passage quoted above from the B*ri*. Up.). Thus with regard to the other passages also.—But from the expressions, 'consisting of knowledge, surrounded by the prâ*n*as,' it appears that the embodied Self only (not the highest Self) is designated as connected with greatness.—That designation, the pûrvapakshin replies, is founded on an intuition, vouched for by scripture, as in the case of Vâmadeva[1].—As therefore the statements of a different size refer to the highest Self (prâ*gñ*a), they do not militate against the view of the individual soul being of atomic size.

22. And also on account of direct statement, and of inference.

The soul is of atomic size for that reason also that scripture contains a direct statement to that effect, 'By

[1] Who 'paramârthad*r*ish*t*yâ' identifies himself with everything in the universe. (*Ri*g-veda Sa*m*hita IV, 26. 1 ff.).

thought is to be known that atomic Self into which breath has entered fivefold' (Mu. Up. III, 1, 9). That the Self spoken of there as atomic is the living Self, i.e. the individual soul, we see from its connexion with breath.—Inference also favours the conclusion that the soul is of atomic size; i.e. we infer that from such passages as 'That living soul is to be known as part of the hundredth part of the point of a hair divided a hundred times' (*S*ve. Up. V, 9), and, 'That lower one also is seen small even like the point of a goad.'—But, an objection may here be raised, if the soul is assumed to be of atomic size, and therefore to occupy one point of the body only, the fact of sensation extending over the whole body would appear contrary to reason. And yet it is a matter of experience that men bathing in the Ganges or in a pond experience the sensation of cold over their whole bodies, and again that in summer people feel hot all over the body.—To this objection the following Sûtra replies.

23. There is no contradiction, as in the case of sandal-ointment.

Just as a drop of sandal-ointment, although in actual contact with one spot of the body only, yet produces a refreshing sensation extending over the whole body; so the soul, although abiding in one point of the body only, may be the cause of a perception extending over the entire body. And as the soul is connected with the skin (which is the seat of feeling), the assumption that the soul's sensations should extend over the whole body is by no means contrary to reason. For the connexion of the soul and the skin abides in the entire skin, and the skin extends over the whole body.

24. If it be said (that the two cases are not parallel), on account of the specialisation of abode (present in the case of the sandal-ointment, absent in the case of the soul); we deny that, on account of the acknowledgment (by scripture, of a special place of the soul), viz. within the heart.

Here it may be objected that the argumentation relied upon in the last Sûtra is not admissible, because the two cases compared are not parallel. If it were a settled matter that the soul dwells in one point of the body, the drop of sandal-ointment might be adduced as a parallel instance. But, as a matter of fact, we know from perception that the drop of sandal-ointment is in contact with one spot of the body only, just as we know that it refreshes the whole body; while in the case of the soul observation tells us only that it is percipient all over the body, but not that it abides in one spot.—Should it be said that the latter point must be settled by inference, we reply that inference is here of no use, because it is not capable of removing the doubt whether the perception extending over the whole body belongs to a soul which extends over the whole body like the skin and the sense of touch inhering in it, or to a soul which is all-pervading like ether, or to a soul which, like a drop of ointment, is minute and abides in one spot only [1].

This objection, the pûrvapakshin replies, is unfounded 'on account of the acknowledgment of a speciality of abode,' an abiding in one spot of the body being admitted in the case of the soul no less than in the case of a drop of ointment. For we read in the Vedânta-texts that the soul abides within the heart; cp. for instance, the information given (in Pr. Up. III, 6), 'The Self is in the heart;' (*Kh.* Up. VIII, 3, 3), 'That Self abides in the heart;' (B*ri*. Up. IV, 3, 7), 'Who is that Self?—He who is within the heart, surrounded by the Prâ*n*as, the person of light, consisting of knowledge.'—As therefore the two cases compared are not devoid of parallelism, the argumentation resorted to in Sûtra 23 is unobjectionable.

25. Or on account of (its) quality (viz. intelligence), as in cases of ordinary experience.

---

[1] We cannot reason as follows, 'The soul is atomic because it produces effects extending (over the whole body), like a drop of sandal-ointment;' for that reasoning would apply to the sense of touch (the skin) also, which we know not to be of atomic size.

That the soul although atomic produces effects extending over the whole body, is not contrary to reason, on account of the pervadingness of intellect which is its quality. From ordinary experience we know that luminous things, such as lamps or gems, although occupying only one spot of a chamber, produce, by means of their light which fills the chamber, an effect in every part of the chamber.—This Sûtra has the purpose of removing the doubts of those who might object that sandal-ointment, because consisting of parts, may perhaps refresh the entire body by the diffusion of imperceptible particles; that, however, the soul as a mere atom does not possess any parts by means of which it could diffuse itself through the whole body.—But how can a quality extend beyond that in which it inheres, and abide elsewhere? We certainly do not see that the whiteness which is the quality of a piece of cloth extends beyond that piece of cloth to other places. Nor must you say that the case of the soul is analogous to that of the light diffused from a lamp; for that light itself is admitted to be (not a quality but) a substance. The flame of a lamp is substantial light with its particles crowded close to one another; the light diffused from that flame is substantial light whose particles are thin and scattered.—The reply to this objection is given in the next Sûtra.

26. The extending beyond is as in the case of odour.

Just as odour, although a quality, extends beyond the odorous substance—as appears from the fact of our perceiving odour even without actually grasping flowers which are the seat of odour—so the quality of intelligence also may extend beyond the soul although the latter be atomic. It therefore is an undue stretch of inference to maintain that a quality, such as colour and the like, cannot separate itself from the substratum in which it inheres, because it is a quality; for we see that odour although a mere quality does separate itself from its substratum.—The objection that odour also separates itself from its substance only with the substance (i. e. parts of the substance) we do not admit, because that would involve the dwindling away of the fundamental substance from which the separation of parts takes place. But that it does not so dwindle away, we conclude from its remaining in its former condition; otherwise it would lose the heaviness and other qualities belonging to it in its former state.—Well, but perhaps the separation of the particles in which odour resides is not noticed on account of their minuteness. Nevertheless the fact may be that minute odorous atoms spreading in all directions enter the cavity of the nose and there produce the sensation of smell.—This we cannot admit, because the atoms are suprasensible, and because in some cases, as, for instance, from the blossoms of the nâgakesara-tree, a very strong odour is perceived [1]. According to the generally prevailing idea, moreover, it is not the odorous substance which is smelled, but ordinary people rather think that they smell the odour only.—The objection that, because we do not perceive colour and so on to extend beyond their substratum, we have no right to assume that odour does so, we cannot admit, because there is no room for that conclusion [2], on account of the (actually existing) perception (of the smell apart from the odorous substance). Logicians must shape their inferences in such a way as to make them agree with ordinary observation, not in any other way. For, to quote another instance, the circumstance that one of the qualities, viz. taste, is perceived by the tongue, certainly does not entitle us to draw the general inference that colour and the other qualities also are perceived by means of the tongue.

27. And thus (scripture also) declares.

Scripture also, after having signified the soul's abiding in the heart and its atomic size, declares by means of such

[1] Single atoms could not produce any sensations; trasare*n*us, i.e. combinations of three atoms even could not produce lively sensations.

[2] Viz. that smell cannot exist apart from the odorous substance, because it is a quality like colour.

passages as 'Up to the hairs, up to the tips of the nails' (Kau. Up. IV, 20; B*ri*. Up. I. 4, 7), that the soul pervades the entire body by means of intelligence which is its quality.

28. On account of the separate statement (of soul and intelligence).

From the passage 'Having by knowledge taken possession of the body' which represents the soul and intelligence as separate, viz. as respectively the agent and the instrument of action, we understand that the soul pervades the body only by means of intelligence, its quality. Again the passage 'Then (the intelligent person) having through the intelligence of the senses absorbed within himself all intelligence' (B*ri*. Up. II, 1, 17) shows intelligence to be different from the agent, i.e. the embodied soul, and so likewise confirms our view.—The reply to all this is as follows.

29. But it is designated thus (i.e. as atomic), on account of its having for its essence the qualities of that (i.e. the buddhi); as in the case of the intelligent Self (i.e. Brahman).

The word 'but' is meant to set aside the opinion maintained hitherto.—The soul is not of atomic size, since scripture does not declare it to have had an origin. On the contrary, as scripture speaks of the highest Brahman entering into the elements and teaches that it is their Self, the soul is nothing else but the highest Brahman. And if the soul is the highest Brahman, it must be of the same extent as Brahman. Now scripture states Brahman to be all-pervading. Therefore the soul also is all-pervading.—On that view all the statements about the all-pervadingness of the soul made in *S*ruti and Sm*ri*ti are justified, so, for instance, the passage, 'He is that great unborn Self who consists of knowledge, is surrounded by the prâ*n*as &c.' (B*ri*. Up. IV, 4, 22). Nor again could the soul, if it were of atomic size, experience sensations extending over the whole body. If it be said that that is possible owing to the soul's connexion with the sense of touch (the skin), we deny that assertion. For from that it would follow that, when we tread on a thorn, the sensation extends over the whole body, since the connexion of the thorn and the skin abides in the entire skin, and the skin extends over the whole body. While as a matter of fact, when treading on a thorn we experience a sensation in the sole of the foot only.—Nor again is it possible that a quality of an atom should diffuse itself beyond the atom. For qualities occupy the same place with the substances of which they are qualities, and a quality not abiding in its substance would no longer be a quality. Concerning the light emitted from a lamp we have already shown that it is, not a quality, but rather a different kind of substance. Hence odour also, being avowedly a quality, can exist in so far only as it inheres in its substance; otherwise it would cease to be odour. Thus the reverend Dvaipâyana also says, 'Having perceived odour in water some unthinking people ascribe it to the latter; but know that it is in the earth only, and (merely) passes over into air and water.' If the intelligence of the soul pervades the whole body, the soul cannot be atomic; for intelligence constitutes the soul's proper nature, just as heat and light constitute that of fire. A separation of the two as quality and that which is qualified does not exist. Now it has already been shown (II, 2, 34) that the soul is not of the same size as the body; the only remaining alternative therefore is that it is all-pervading (infinite). But why then, our opponent asks, is the soul designated (in some scriptural passages) as being of atomic size, &c.?—It is designated as such 'on account of being of the nature of the essence of that (i.e. the buddhi)'—The Self is here said to be of the nature of the essence of the mind's (buddhi) qualities, because those qualities, such as desire, aversion, pleasure, pain and so on, constitute the essence, i.e. the principal characteristics of the Self as long as it is implicated in transmigratory existence. Apart from the qualities of the mind the mere Self does not exist in the sa*m*sâra state; for the latter, owing to which the Self appears as an agent and enjoyer, is altogether due to the circumstance of the qualities of the buddhi and the other limiting adjuncts being wrongly superimposed upon the Self. That the non-transmigrating eternally free Self which neither acts nor enjoys is declared to be of the same size as the buddhi, is thus due only to its having the qualities of the buddhi for its essence (viz. as long as it is in fictitious connexion with the buddhi). Moreover we have the scriptural passage, 'That living soul is to be known as part of the hundredth part of the point of a hair, divided a hundred times, and yet it is to be infinite' (*S*ve. Up. V, 9), which at first states the soul to be atomic and then teaches it to be infinite. Now this is appropriate only in the case of the atomicity of the soul being metaphorical while its infinity is real; for both statements cannot be taken in their primary sense at the same time. And the infinity certainly cannot be understood in a metaphorical sense, since all the Upanishads aim at showing that Brahman constitutes the Self of the soul.—The other passage also (*S*ve. Up. V, 8) which treats of the measure of the soul, 'The lower one, endowed with the quality of mind and the quality of body, is seen small even like the point of a goad,' teaches the soul's small size to depend on its connexion with the qualities of the buddhi, not upon its own Self. The following passage again, 'That small (a*n*u) Self is to be known by thought' (Mu. Up. III, 1, 9), does not teach that the soul is of atomic size, since the subject of the chapter is Brahman in so far as not to be fathomed by the eye, &c., but to be apprehended by the serene light of knowledge, and since moreover the soul cannot be of atomic size in the primary sense of the word. Hence the statement about a*n*utva (smallness, subtlety) has to be understood as referring either to the difficulty of knowing the soul, or else to its limiting adjuncts. Similarly such passages as 'Having by knowledge taken possession of the whole body' (Kau. Up. III, 6), which mention a difference (between the soul and knowledge), must be understood to mean that the soul takes possession of the whole body through the buddhi, its limiting adjunct; or else they must be considered as mere modes of expression, as when we speak of the body of a stone statue. For we have already shown that the distinction of quality and thing qualified does not exist in the case of the soul.—The statements as to the soul abiding in the heart are likewise to be explained on the ground of the buddhi abiding there.—That also the soul's passing out and so on depend on the limiting adjuncts, is shown by the passage, 'What is it by whose passing out I shall pass out, and by whose staying I shall stay? He sent forth prâ*n*a,' &c. (Pr. Up VI, 3, 4). For where there is no passing out, no going and returning are known; for what has not left the body cannot go and return[1].—As thus the soul (as long as involved in the sa*m*sâra) has for its essence the qualities of its limiting adjuncts. it is spoken of as minute. The case is analogous to that of Brahman (prâ*g*ña). Just as in those chapters whose topic is the meditation on the qualified Brahman, the highest Self is spoken of as possessing relative minuteness and so on, because it has the qualities of its limiting adjuncts for its essence (cp. 'Smaller than a grain of rice or barley;' 'He who consists of mind, whose body is prâ*n*a,' &c., *Kh*. Up. III, 14, 2; 3); so it is also with the individual soul.—Very well, let us then assume that the transmigratory condition of the soul is due to the qualities of the buddhi forming its essence. From this, however, it will follow that, as the conjunction of buddhi and soul—which are different entities—must necessarily come to an end, the soul when disjoined from the buddhi will be altogether undefinable and thence non-existing or rather non-existing in the sa*m*sâra state[2].—To this objection the next Sûtra replies.

30. The objection (raised above) is not valid, since (the connexion of the soul with the buddhi) exists as long as the soul; it being thus observed (in scripture).

We need not fear that the objection formulated above can be proved.—Why?—'On account of the existence of the connexion of the soul with the buddhi, as long as the

[1] So that the distinction insisted on in Sûtra 20 is not valid.

[2] Katham asattva*m* svarûpena sattvâd ity âsaṅkhyâha sa*m*sâritva*m* veti. Ân. Gi.

soul exists.' That means: as long as this Self is in the sa*m*sâra-state, as long as the sa*m*sâra-state is not brought to an end by means of perfect knowledge, so long the connexion of the soul with the buddhi does not cease. And as long as its connexion with the buddhi, its limiting adjunct, lasts, so long the individual soul remains individual soul, implicated in transmigratory existence. In reality, however, there is no individual soul but in so far as it is fictitiously hypostatized by the buddhi, its limiting adjunct. For in attempting to determine the object of the Vedânta-texts we meet with no other intelligent substance but the one omniscient Lord whose nature is eternal freedom. This appears from innumerable texts, such as the following:—'There is no other seer but he, there is no other hearer but he, there is no other perceiver but he, there is no other knower but he' (B*ri*. Up. III, 7, 23); 'There is nothing that sees, hears, perceives, knows but it' (B*ri*. Up. III, 8, 11); 'Thou art that' (*Kh*. Up. VI, 8, 7); 'I am Brahman' (B*ri*. Up. I, 4, 10).—How again is it known that the soul is connected with the buddhi as long as it exists?—We reply: because that is seen (viz. in scripture). For scripture makes the following declaration: 'He who is within the heart, consisting of knowledge, surrounded by the prâ*n*as, the person of light, he remaining the same wanders along the two worlds as if thinking, as if moving' (B*ri*. Up. IV, 3, 7). Here the term 'consisting of knowledge' means 'consisting of buddhi,' as we infer from another passage, viz. 'The Self consisting of knowledge, mind, life, sight, hearing' (B*ri*. Up. IV, 4, 5), where knowledge is enumerated among mind and so on[1]. By 'being made up of buddhi' is meant 'having for one's essence the qualities of buddhi.' Similarly a phrase like 'Devadatta is made up of womanishness,' which may be made use of in ordinary language, means that in Devadatta feminine attributes such as softness of voice and the like prevail. Moreover, the passage, 'He remaining the same wanders along the two worlds,' declares that the Self, even

[1] And therefore has to be understood in the sense of buddhi.

when going to another world, is not separated from the buddhi, &c. For if we ask whereby it does remain the same, the answer, based on proximity[1], is 'by means of the buddhi.'—Further, such modes of expression, 'as if thinking,' 'as if moving,' lead us to the same conclusion; for they mean that the Self does not think and move on its own account, but thinks as it were and moves as it were, because the buddhi to which it is joined really moves and thinks.—Moreover, the connexion of the Self with the buddhi, its limiting adjunct, depends on wrong knowledge, and wrong knowledge cannot cease except through perfect knowledge; hence as long as there does not rise the cognition of Brahman being the universal Self, so long the connexion of the soul with the buddhi and its other limiting adjuncts does not come to an end. Thus scripture also says, 'I know that great person of sunlike lustre beyond the darkness. A man who knows him passes over death; there is no other path to go' (Sve. Up. III, 8).

But, an objection is raised, in the states of deep sleep and retractation (pralaya) no connexion of the Self with the buddhi can be acknowledged, since scripture declares that 'then he becomes united with the True, he is gone to his own' (*Kh*. Up. VI, 8, 1), and as then all modifications have avowedly passed away. How then can it be said that the connexion with the buddhi exists as long as the Self?—To this objection the following Sûtra replies.

31. On account of the appropriateness of the manifestation of that (connexion) which exists (potentially); like virile power.

As in ordinary life virile power and so on, existing potentially only in young children, and being then looked upon as non-existing, become manifest at the time of puberty—and do not originate at that time from previous non-existence, because in that case they might originate in eunuchs also—; so the connexion of the soul with the

[1] I.e. on the proximity of terms clearly indicating the buddhi, viz. vig*ñ*âna-maya*h* prâ*n*eshu.

buddhi exists potentially merely during deep sleep and the period of general retractation, and again becomes manifest at the time of waking and the time of creation.—This explanation is appropriate, because nothing can be assumed to spring up unless from something else; otherwise we should have to suppose that effects spring up without causes. That the rising from deep sleep is due to the existence of potential avidyâ, scripture also declares, 'Having become merged in the True they know not that they are merged in the True. Whatever these creatures are here, whether a lion or a wolf,' &c. (*Kh.* Up. VI, 9, 2; 3).—It is therefore a proved matter that the connexion of the soul with the buddhi and the other adjuncts lasts as long as the soul (in its sa*m*sâra-state).

32. Otherwise (if no manas existed) there would result either constant perception or constant non-perception, or else a limitation of either of the two (i.e. of the soul or of the senses).

The internal organ which constitutes the limiting adjunct of the soul is called in different places by different names, such as manas (mind), buddhi (intelligence), vig*ñ*âna (knowledge), *k*itta (thought). This difference of nomenclature is sometimes made dependent on the difference of the modifications of the internal organ which is called manas when it is in the state of doubt, &c., buddhi when it is in the state of determination and the like.—Now we must necessarily acknowledge the existence of such an internal organ; because otherwise there would result either perpetual perception or perpetual non-perception. There would result perpetual perception whenever there is a conjunction of the soul, the senses and the objects of sense—the three together constituting the instruments of perception; or else, if on the conjunction of the three causes the effect did not follow, there would take place perpetual non-perception. But neither of these two alternatives is actually observed.—Or else we should have to assume that there are obstacles in the way of the energy either of the Self or the sense-organs. But the former is not possible, as the

Self is not capable of any modification; nor the latter, as we cannot assume that the energy of the sense-organ which is non-obstructed in the preceding and the following moment should, without any cause, be obstructed (in the intervening moment). Hence we have to acknowledge the existence of an internal organ through whose attention and non-attention perception and non-perception take place. Thus scripture declares, 'My mind was elsewhere, I did not see; my mind was elsewhere, I did not hear; for a man sees with his mind and hears with his mind' (B*ri*. Up. I, 5, 3). Scripture moreover shows that desire and similar states are modifications of the mind, 'Desire, representation, doubt, faith, want of faith, memory, forgetfulness, shame, reflection, fear, all this is mind.' The explanation given in Sûtra 29 is therefore an appropriate one.

33. (The soul is) an agent, on account of scripture having a purport (thereby).

In connexion with the doctrine that the soul possesses for its essence the qualities of the buddhi, another attribute of the soul is set forth.—The individual soul is an agent, because thus scripture has a purport. For only on that assumption scriptural injunctions (such as 'He is to sacrifice,' 'He is to make an oblation into the fire,' 'He is to give,' &c.) acquire a purport; otherwise they would be purportless. For they all teach special acts to be done by agents; which would not be possible if the soul did not possess the quality of being an agent.—On that supposition a meaning belongs to the following passage also, 'For it is he who sees, hears, perceives, conceives, acts, he the person whose Self is knowledge' (Pr. Up. IV, 9).

34. And on account of (the text) teaching its wandering about.

The quality of being an agent has to be attributed to the soul for that reason also, that, in a chapter treating of the soul, the text declares it to wander about in the state of sleep, 'The immortal one goes wherever he likes' (B*ri*. Up.

IV, 3, 12); and again, 'He moves about, according to his pleasure, within his own body' (B*ri*. Up. II, 1, 18).

35. On account of its taking.

The quality of being an agent has to be attributed to the soul for that reason also that in the same chapter treating of the soul the text speaks of the soul taking its instruments, 'Having taken, through the intelligence of the senses, intelligence,' and 'having taken the senses' (B*ri*. Up. II, 1, 18; 17).

36. (The soul is an agent) also because it is designated as such with regard to actions; if it were not such, there would be a change of designation.

The quality of being an agent belongs to the soul for that reason also that the sacred texts speak of its agency in sacred and secular actions, 'Understanding performs the sacrifice, it performs all acts' (Taitt. Up. II, 5).—But, an objection may here be raised, we have seen that the word 'understanding' applies to the buddhi; how then can it indicate the circumstance of the soul being an agent? —The soul only, we reply, is designated there, not the buddhi. If the soul were not meant to be designated. there would be a change in the designation, i. e. the passage would run, 'through understanding it performs,' &c. For we see that in another passage where the buddhi is meant the word 'understanding' is exhibited in the instrumental form, 'Having through the understanding (intelligence) of these senses taken all understanding' (B*ri*. Up. II, 1, 17). In the passage under discussion, on the other hand, the word 'understanding' is given in the case characteristic of the agent (viz. the nominative), and therefore indicates the Self which is distinct from the buddhi. Hence your objection is not valid.—Another objection is raised. If the soul in so far as distinct from the buddhi were the agent, it would, because it is independent, bring about exclusively what is pleasant and useful to itself, not the opposite. We, however, observe that it does bring about the opposite also. But such an unrestricted proceeding does not become the independent Self.—To this objection the following Sûtra replies.

37. The absence of restriction is as in the case of perception.

Just as this Self, although free with regard to perception, yet perceives unrestrictedly what is unpleasant as well as what is pleasant, so we assume that it also brings about what is unpleasant as well as what is pleasant.—The objection that in the act of perception also the soul is not free because it depends on the employment of the causes of perception (i.e. the sense-organs), we invalidate by the remark that the use of the causes of perception is merely to present the objects of perception, that however in the act of perception the soul because endowed with intelligence does not depend on anything else[1].—Moreover in actions also the soul is not absolutely free, as it depends on differences of place, time, and efficient causes. But an agent does not cease to be so because he requires assistance. A cook remains the agent in the action of cooking although he requires fuel, water, and so on. The presence of a plurality of co-operating factors is therefore not opposed to the activity of the soul unrestrictedly extending to actions productive of pleasant as well as unpleasant results.

38. On account of the reversal of power.

The soul distinct from 'understanding' has to be viewed as an agent for the following reason also. If the buddhi which is denoted by the term 'understanding' were the agent, there would take place a reversal of power, i.e. the instrumental power which appertains to the buddhi would have to be set aside, and to be replaced by the power of an agent. But if the buddhi has the power of an agent, it must be admitted that it is also the object of self-conscious-

[1] *K*akshurâdînâ*m* vishayopanâyakatvât tadupalabdhau *k*âtmanas *k*etanatvena svâtantryâd udâhara*n*asiddhir ity âha neti. Ân. Gi.

ness (ahampratyaya)[1], since we see that everywhere activity is preceded by self-consciousness, '*I* go, *I* come, *I* eat, *I* drink,' &c. But if the buddhi is endowed with the power of an agent and effects all things, we have to assume for it another instrument by means of which it effects everything. For we see that agents although themselves capable of acting yet become really active only through making use of instruments.—Hence the whole dispute is about a name only, and there is no real difference, since in either case that which is different from the instrument of action is admitted to be the agent.

39. And on account of the impossibility of meditation (samâdhi).

Moreover the meditation taught in the Vedânta-texts, whose aim is the realisation of the Self as represented by the Upanishads, is possible only if the Self is the agent[2]. Compare the following passages, 'Verily, the Self is to be seen, to be heard, to be perceived, to be marked' (B*ri*. Up. II, 4, 5); 'The Self we must seek out, we must try to understand' (*Kh*. Up. VIII, 7, 1); 'Meditate on the Self as Om' (Mu. Up. II, 2, 6).—Therefrom also it follows that the Self is an agent.

40. And as the carpenter, in double fashion.

That the embodied Self is an agent, has been proved by the reasons set forth in Sûtra 33, &c. We now have to consider whether this agency depends on the fundamental nature of the Self, or is due to its limiting adjuncts.—If here it be maintained that for the same reasons which were employed to prove the Self's being an agent its agency must be held to be natural, there being no reasons to the contrary, we reply as follows.

---

[1] And that would virtually identify the buddhi with the *g*îva, the individual soul.

[2] The Self which enjoys the fruit of final release must be the agent in the meditation which is instrumental in bringing about final release.

The Self's being an agent cannot be founded on its real nature, because (if it were so) the impossibility of final release would follow. For if being an agent belongs to the soul's nature, it can never free itself from it—no more than fire can divest itself of heat.—and as long as man has not freed himself from activity he cannot obtain his highest end, since activity is essentially painful.—But, an objection will be raised, the end of man may be obtained, even as long as the potentiality of activity remains, viz. by man avoiding the effects of activity, and this he may accomplish by avoiding its occasions, just as fire, for instance, although endowed with the potentiality of burning, does, if fuel is withheld from it, not produce its natural effect, i.e. burning.—This objection we invalidate by the remark that the occasions, because connected (with the soul) by means of the peculiar connexion called 'potentiality' (power), cannot be avoided absolutely[1].—Nor can it be said that release will be obtained through the means effecting it being employed, because whatever depends on means to be employed is non-eternal. Scripture moreover declares that release results from the instruction about the eternally pure, intelligent, free Self. Now instruction of this nature would not be possible, if the agentship of the Self formed part of its nature. The agentship of the Self is therefore due to the attributes of its adjuncts being ascribed to it, and does not form part of its nature. Hence scripture says of the Self, 'As if thinking, as if moving' (B*ri*. Up. IV, 3, 7), and 'He (the Self) when in union with the body, the senses, and the mind, is called the enjoyer by wise people' (Ka. Up. I, 3, 4); which passages show that the Self passes into the special condition of being an enjoyer, &c., only through its

[1] Kart*ri*tvasya dharmâdîni nimittâni teshâ*m* g*ñ*ânânivartyatve muktâv api sambhavât kart*ri*tva*m* syât g*ñ*ânena tanniv*ri*ttau teshâm ag*ñ*ânakâryatvât k*ri*ta*m* kart*ri*tvam api tathâ syât, *s*aktes *k*a *s*akta*s*akyasâpekshatayâ sanimittakriyâlaksha*n*a*s*akyâpekshakatvâd. anirmokshas tasmân nimittaparihârasya duranush*th*ânatvân na *s*aktivâde muktir iti. Ân. Gi.

*S*akta*s*akyâ*s*rayâ *s*akti*h* svasattayâva*s*ya*m* *s*akyam âkshipati. Bhâ.

connexion with the limiting adjuncts. For to the discerning there is no Self called the living Self and being either agent or enjoyer, apart from the highest Self; according to the scriptural passage 'There is no other seer but he,' &c. (B*ri*. Up. III. 7, 23). Nor must we suppose that, if there were no intelligent individual Soul, different from the highest Self and distinct from the aggregate consisting of buddhi, &c., it would follow that the highest Self is involved in the sa*m*sâra-state as agent and enjoyer. For the conditions of being agent and enjoyer are presented by Nescience merely. Scripture also, after having declared (in the passage, 'For where there is duality, as it were, there one sees the other,' &c., B*ri*. Up. IV, 5, 15) that the conditions of being an agent and an enjoyer belong to the state of Nescience only, excludes them from the state of knowledge, 'But where the Self only is all this, how should he see another?' And again, after having declared that the Self, in the states of waking and of dreaming, suffers weariness owing to the contact with its limiting adjuncts, like a falcon flying about in the air, scripture teaches that that fatigue ceases in deep sleep when the soul is embraced by the intelligent (highest) Self. 'This indeed is his true form in which his wishes are fulfilled, in which the Self only is his wish, in which no wish is left,—free from any sorrow'—up to 'This is his highest goal, this is his highest success, this is his highest world, this is his highest bliss' (B*ri*. Up. IV, 3, 21–32).—This the teacher intimates in the Sûtra, 'and as the carpenter in both ways.' 'And' is here used in the sense of 'but.' It is not to be supposed that the agentship of the Self belongs to its true nature, as heat belongs to the nature of fire. But just as in ordinary life a carpenter as long as working with his axe and other tools undergoes pain, while on the other hand he enjoys ease and leisure after having finished his work, laid his tools aside and returned to his home; so the Self also, as long as it is joined with duality presented by Nescience and is an agent in the states of waking and dreaming, undergoes pain; but as soon as, for the purpose of shaking off its weariness, it enters into its own highest Self, it frees itself from the complex of effects and instruments, and enjoys full ease in the state of deep sleep. And in the state of final release also, the Self, having dispelled the darkness of ignorance by the light of knowledge, and having reached the state of absolute isolation and rest, enjoys full ease.—The case of the carpenter must be considered as being parallel to the following extent. The carpenter is, in certain kinds of work, such as cutting wood, &c., an agent with regard to certain definite tools, such as the axe and so on, but a non-agent with his mere body; so this Self also is an agent in all its functions with regard to its instruments, such as the mind, &c., but is a non-agent by its own Self. On the other hand, the Self has no parts corresponding to the hands and other limbs of the carpenter, by means of which it could take up or put aside its instruments, as the carpenter takes up and puts aside his tools.

In reply to the reasons brought forward in favour of the soul's agentship being natural, as, for instance, the reason based on scripture having a purport, we remark that the scriptural injunctions in prescribing certain acts presuppose an agentship established somehow, but do not themselves aim at establishing the (direct) agentship of the Self. Now we have shown that the agentship of the Self does not constitute part of its real nature because scripture teaches that its true Self is Brahman; we therefore conclude that the Vedic injunctions are operative with reference to that agentship of the soul which is due to Nescience. Such scriptural passages also as 'The agent, the person whose Self is understanding' (Pr. Up. IV, 9), must be assumed, because being of the nature of anuvâdas [1], to refer to an agentship already established elsewhere, and being the product of Nescience.

The preceding remarks refute also the reasons founded on 'the wandering about' and the 'taking' (Sûtras 34, 35), as the statements about them also are mere anuvâdas.—But, an objection may be raised, the passage which teaches that the soul while its instruments are asleep, 'moves about,

[1] I.e. being only incidental remarks about matters established or taught elsewhere.

according to its pleasure, within its own body' (Bri. Up. II, 1, 18), clearly implies that the pure Self is an agent. And in the passage relative to the taking ('(the purusha) having through the intelligence of the senses absorbed all intelligence'), the fact of the instruments appearing in the objective and instrumental cases likewise intimates that the pure Self is the agent.—To this we reply that even in the state of dream the instruments of the Self are not altogether at rest; for scripture states that even then it is connected with the buddhi, 'Having become a dream, together with buddhi it passes beyond this world.' Smriti also says, 'When, the senses being at rest, the mind not being at rest is occupied with the objects, that state know to be a dream.' And scripture says that desire, &c., are modifications of the mind (cp. Bri. Up. I, 5, 3). Now these are observed in dreams; therefore the Self wanders about in dreams together with the mind only. That wandering about moreover is founded on the mental impressions (vâsanâ) only, is not real. Thus scripture also in describing our doings in dreams qualifies them by an 'as it were:' 'As it were rejoicing together with women, or laughing as it were, or seeing terrible sights' (Bri. Up. IV, 3, 13). Ordinary people also describe their dreams in the same manner, 'I ascended as it were the summit of a mountain,' 'I saw a tree as it were.'—And although it is true that, in the statement about the taking, the instruments are exhibited in the objective and instrumental cases, still the agentship of the Self must be considered as connected with those instruments, since we have shown that the pure Self cannot be an agent.

In ordinary language also we meet with similar variations of expression; the two sentences, for instance, 'the warriors fight' and 'the king fights by means of his warriors,' really have the same meaning. Moreover, the statement about the taking means to express only the cessation of activity on the part of the instruments, not the independent activity of any one.—The passage referred to above, 'understanding performs the sacrifice,' establishes the agentship of the buddhi merely, as the word 'understanding' is known to have that sense, and as the mind is mentioned close by, and as in the passage, 'Faith is its head,' &c., faith and so on are declared to be the members of the Self which consists of understanding, and as faith, &c., are known to be attributes of the buddhi. Another reason is furnished by the complementary sentence, 'All gods worship understanding as the oldest, as Brahman' (Taitt. Up. II, 5), for buddhi is known to be the oldest, i. e. the first produced [1]. Another scriptural passage also avers that that sacrifice is accomplished by means of speech and buddhi, 'The sacrifice is what results from speech and mind.' Nor can it rightly be maintained (cp. Sûtra 38) that to view the instruments as agents would lead to an exchange of power on the part of the buddhi; for all instruments must necessarily be considered as agents in regard of their special functions [2]. But with reference to perception (upalabdhi) those instruments are (not agents, but) mere instruments, and perception belongs to the Self. Nor can agentship be ascribed to the Self on account of perception, since permanent perception constitutes its nature (and hence cannot be viewed as a mere transitory activity). Nor can the agentship which has self-consciousness for its antecedent belong to the perceiving principle (upalabdh*ri*); for self-consciousness itself is an object of perception (on the part of the upalabdh*ri*, i. e. the pure, isolated, intelligent Self). And on this doctrine there is no occasion for assuming a further instrument, as we maintain the buddhi itself to be the instrument.

The objection founded on the impossibility of meditation (Sûtra 39) is already refuted by the fact, pointed out above, of scripture having a purport, meditation being enjoined by scripture with reference to such agentship as is already established by other passages.—The result of all this is

[1] According to the *s*ruti: mahad yaksham prathamaga*m* veda yo ha vai *g*yesh*th*a*m k*a *s*resh*th*a*m k*a veda.

[2] Wood, for instance, is an 'agent' in regard of the function of burning, while it is a mere instrument with reference to the action of cooking.

that the agentship of the Self is due to its limiting adjuncts only.

41. But from the highest (Lord there result sa*m*sâra and moksha), because scripture teaches that.

We now enter on the discussion whether the agentship, characterising the individual soul in the state of Nescience and founded on its limiting adjuncts, is independent of the Lord or dependent on him.

The pûrvapakshin maintains that the soul as far as it is an agent does not depend on the Lord, because the assumption of such a dependence would serve no purpose. For as the individual soul has motives in its own imperfections, such as passion, aversion, and so on, and is furnished with the whole apparatus of the other constituents of action[1], it is able to occupy on its own account the position of an agent; and what then should the Lord do for it? Nor does ordinary experience show that in addition to the oxen which are required for such actions as ploughing and the like the Lord also is to be depended upon. Moreover (if all activity depended on the Lord) it would follow that the Lord is cruel because imposing on his creatures activity which is essentially painful, and at the same time unjust because allotting to their activities unequal results.—But it has already been shown (II, 1, 34) that the Lord cannot be taxed with cruelty and injustice, on account of his dependence.—True, that has been shown, but only on the condition of the dependence on the Lord being possible. Now such dependence is possible only if there exist religious merit and demerit on the part of the creatures, and these again exist if the soul is an agent; if then the agentship of the soul again depends on the Lord, whereupon will the Lord's dependence depend? And (if we should assume the Lord to determine the souls without reference to their merits and demerits) it would follow that the souls have to undergo

[1] I.e. the constituents of action such as instrument, object, &c., exclusive of the agent.

consequences not due to their actions.—Hence the soul's activity is independent.

Setting aside this primâ facie view by means of the word 'but,' the Sûtrakâra asserts 'from the highest.' For the soul which in the state of Nescience is blinded by the darkness of ignorance and hence unable to distinguish itself from the complex of effects and instruments, the sa*m*sâra-state in which it appears as agent and enjoyer is brought about through the permission of the Lord who is the highest Self, the superintendent of all actions, the witness residing in all beings, the cause of all intelligence; and we must therefore assume that final release also is effected through knowledge caused by the grace of the Lord.

Why so?—'Because scripture teaches that.' For although the soul has its own imperfections, such as passion and so on, for motives, and is furnished with the whole apparatus of action, and although ordinary experience does not show that the Lord is a cause in occupations such as ploughing and the like, yet we ascertain from scripture that the Lord is a causal agent in all activity. For scripture says, 'He makes him whom he wishes to lead up from these worlds do a good deed; and the same makes him whom he wishes to lead down from these worlds, do a bad deed' (Kau. Up. III, 8); and again, 'He who dwelling within the Self pulls the Self within' (*S*at. Br. XIV, 6, 7, 30).

But if causal agency thus belongs to the Lord, it follows that he must be cruel and unjust, and that the soul has to undergo consequences of what it has not done.—This objection the following Sûtra refutes.

42. But with a view to the efforts made (by the soul) (the Lord makes it act), on account of the (otherwise resulting) purportlessness of the injunctions and prohibitions, &c.

The word 'but' removes the objections started.—The Lord makes the soul act, having regard to the efforts made by it, whether meritorious or non-meritorious. Hence there is no room for the objections raised. Having regard to the inequality of the virtuous and vicious actions of the souls, the Lord, acting as a mere occasional cause, allots to them corresponding unequal results. An analogous case is furnished by rain. As rain constitutes the common occasional cause for shrubs, bushes, corn, and so on, which belong to different species and spring each from its particular seed—for the inequality of their sap, flowers, fruits, and leaves results neither when rain is absent nor when the special seeds are absent—; so we also must assume that the Lord arranges favourable or unfavourable circumstances for the souls with a view to their former efforts.—But if the activity of the soul is dependent on something else, this having regard (on the part of the Lord) to former effort is inappropriate.—By no means, we reply; for although the activity of the soul is not independent, yet the soul does act. The Lord indeed causes it to act, but it acts itself. Moreover, the Lord in causing it to act now has regard to its former efforts, and he caused it to act in a former existence, having regard to its efforts previous to that existence; a regressus against which, considering the eternity of the sa*m*sâra, no objections can be raised.—But how is it known that the Lord has regard to the efforts made (in former existences)?—The Sûtra replies: from the purportlessness, &c., of injunctions and prohibitions. For thus (i.e. if the Lord has regard to former actions) injunctions such as 'he who is desirous of the heavenly world is to sacrifice,' and prohibitions such as 'a Brâhma*n*a must not be killed,' are not devoid of purport. On the other alternative they would be without purport, and the Lord would in fact be enjoined in the place of injunctions and prohibitions [1], since the soul would be absolutely dependent. And then the Lord might requite with good those who act according to the injunctions, and with evil men doing what is forbidden; which would

[1] Î*s*vara eva vidhinishedhayo*h* sthâne niyugyeta yad vidhinishedhayo*h* phala*m* tad î*s*vare*n*a tatpratipâditadharmâdharmanirapekshe*n*a k*ri*tam iti. Bhâ.

subvert the authoritativeness of the Veda. Moreover, if the Lord were absolutely without any regard, it would follow that also the ordinary efforts of men are without any purport; and so likewise the special conditions of place, time, and cause. And also the difficulty mentioned above[1] would present itself.—All these latter difficulties the Sûtrakâra comprises in his '&c.'

43. (The soul is) a part of the Lord, on account of the declarations of difference, and (because) in a different way also some record that (Brahman) is of the nature of slaves, fishers, and so on.

We have shown that the individual soul and the Lord stand to each other in the relation of what is being acted upon and what is acting upon. This relation is observed in ordinary life to exist only between things connected, such as a master and a servant, or a fire and its sparks. Now as the soul and the Lord also are acknowledged to stand in the relation of what is acted upon and what is acting, a doubt arises whether their connexion is analogous to that of a master and a servant, or to that of a fire and its sparks.

The pûrvapakshin maintains that either the matter is to be considered as undetermined, or that the connexion is like that of master and servant, because that connexion only is well known to be the relation of ruler (Lord) and subject ruled.

To this the Sûtra replies that the soul must be considered a part of the Lord, just as a spark is a part of the fire. By 'part' we mean 'a part as it were,' since a being not composed of parts cannot have parts in the literal sense.—Why, then, do we not view the Lord, who is not composed of parts, as identical with the soul?—'On account of the declarations of difference.' For such scriptural passages as 'That (self) it is which we must search out, that it is which we must try to understand' (*Kh.* Up.

[1] I.e. the objectionable assumption that men have to undergo consequences not resulting from their own former actions.

VIII, 7); 'He who knows him becomes a muni' (B*ri*. Up. IV, 4, 22); 'He who dwelling within the Self pulls the Self within' (B*ri*. Up. III, 7, 23); which all of them refer to a difference (between the highest and the individual Self) would be inappropriate, if there were no difference.—But, it may be said, these statements of difference would agree better with a relation similar to that of master and servant.—Hence the sûtrakâra adds, 'and otherwise also.' That the soul is a part (of the Lord) we learn not only from the passages declaring their difference, but there are other statements also which teach their non-difference. The members of a certain *s*âkhâ of the Atharva-veda record in a Brahma-sûkta that 'Brahman are the fishermen, Brahman the slaves, Brahman these gamblers,' &c. Here low creatures such as fishermen, and slaves depending on their masters, and gamblers are called Brahman; whence it appears that all individual souls which have entered into aggregates of effects and instruments (i.e. bodies) depending on name and form are Brahman. The same view is set forth in other passages such as 'Thou art woman, thou art man; thou art youth, thou art maiden; thou as an old man totterest along on thy staff, thou art born with thy face turned everywhere' (*S*ve. Up. IV, 3), and 'The wise one who, having produced all forms and made all names, sits calling (the things by their names)' (Taitt. Âr. III, 12, 7). Passages such as 'There is no other seer but he' and other similar ones establish the same truth.—Non-differenced intelligence belongs to the soul and the Lord alike, as heat belongs to the sparks as well as the fire.—From these two views of difference and non-difference there results the comprehensive view of the soul being a part of the Lord.—The following Sûtra supplies a further reason.

44. And on account of the mantra.

A mantra also intimates the same view. 'Such is the greatness of it; greater than it is the Person. One foot of it are all beings, three feet of it are the Immortal in heaven' (*Kh*. Up. III, 12, 6). Here the word 'beings' denotes all moving and non-moving things, among which the souls occupy the first place; in accordance with the use of the word in the following passage, 'Not giving pain to any being (bhûta) except at the tîrthas' (*Kh.* Up. VIII, 15). Herefrom also we conclude that the individual soul is a part of the Lord.—And again from the following reason.

45. Moreover it is so stated in Sm*ri*ti.

In the Î*s*varagîtâs (Bhagavad-gîtâ) also it is said that the soul is a part of the Lord, 'an eternal part of me becomes the individual soul in the world of life' (Bha. Gî. XV, 7). With regard to the assertion made above, viz. that in ordinary life the relation of ruler and ruled is known to hold good in the case of master and servant &c. only, we remark that, although that may be the case in ordinary life, we ascertain from scripture that the relation of part and whole and that of ruler and ruled may go together. Nor is there anything contradictory in assuming that the Lord who is provided with superexcellent limiting adjuncts rules the souls which are connected with inferior adjuncts only.

Here the pûrvapakshin raises another objection. If we admit that the souls are parts of the Lord, it follows that the Lord also, whose part the soul is, will be afflicted by the pain caused to the soul by its experience of the sa*m*sâra-state; as we see in ordinary life that the entire Devadatta suffers from the pain affecting his hand or foot or some other limb. Herefrom it would follow that they who obtain Brahman obtain a greater pain[1]; so that the former sa*m*sâra-condition would be preferable, and complete knowledge be devoid of purpose.—To this the following Sûtra replies.

46. (As the soul is affected by pleasure and pain) not so the highest (Lord); as in the case of light and so on.

We maintain that the highest Lord does not feel the pain of the sa*m*sâra-state in the same way as the soul does. The soul being engrossed by Nescience identifies itself as it were

[1] Viz. by participating in all pain.

with the body and so on, and imagines itself to be affected by the experience of pain which is due to Nescience, 'I am afflicted by the pain due to the body;' the highest Lord, on the other hand, neither identifies himself with a body, nor imagines himself to be afflicted by pain. The pain of the individual soul also is not real, but imaginary only, caused by the error consisting in the non-discrimination of (the Self from) the body, senses, and other limiting adjuncts which are due to name and form, the effects of Nescience. And as a person feels the pain of a burn or cut which affects his body by erroneously identifying himself with the latter, so he feels also the pain affecting others, such as sons or friends, by erroneously identifying himself with them, entering as it were into them through love, and imagining 'I am the son, I am the friend.' Wherefrom we infer with certainty that the feeling of pain is due merely to the error of false imagination. At the same conclusion we arrive on the ground of negative instances. Let us consider the case of many men, each of whom possesses sons, friends, &c., sitting together, some of them erroneously imagining that they are connected with their sons, friends, &c., while others do not. If then somebody calls out 'the son has died,' 'the friend has died,' grief is produced in the minds of those who are under the imagination of being connected with sons and friends, but not in the minds of religious mendicants who have freed themselves from that imagination. From this it appears that perfect knowledge is of use even to an ordinary man; of how much greater use then will it be to him (i.e. the Lord) whose nature is eternal pure intelligence, who sees nothing beside the Self for which there are no objects. Hence it follows that perfect knowledge is not purposeless. —To illustrate this view the Sûtra introduces a comparison 'like light,' &c. Just as the light of the sun or the moon which pervades the entire space becomes straight or bent as it were when the limiting adjuncts with which it is in contact, such as a finger, for instance, are straight or bent, but does not really become so; and just as the ether, although imagined to move as it were when jars are being moved, does not really move; and as the sun does not tremble, although its image trembles when you shake the cup filled with water in which the sun's light is reflected; thus the Lord also is not affected by pain, although pain be felt by that part of him which is called the individual soul, is presented by Nescience, and limited by the buddhi and other adjuncts. That also the soul's undergoing pain is due to Nescience only, we have already explained. Accordingly the Vedânta-texts teach that, when the soul's individual state, due to Nescience, is sublated, it becomes Brahman, 'Thou art that &c.'—Thus there is no occasion to conclude that the highest Self is affected by the pain of the individual soul.

47. And the Smritis state (that).

Vyâsa and others state in their smritis that the highest Self is not afflicted by the pain of the individual soul, 'That highest Self is said to be eternal, devoid of qualities, nor is it stained by the fruits of actions any more than a lotus leaf by water. But that other Self whose essence is action is connected with bondage and release; again and again it is joined with the seventeenfold aggregate[1].'—On the ground of the particle 'and' (in the Sûtra) we have to supply 'and scripture also records that.' So, for instance, 'One of them eats the sweet fruit, the other looks on without eating' (Mu. Up. III, 1, 1), and 'The one Self within all things is never contaminated by the misery of the world, being himself without' (Ka. Up. II, 5, 11).

Here the pûrvapakshin raises a new objection.—If there is only one internal Self of all beings, what room is there for permissions and prohibitions, worldly as well as Vedic? You must not reject this objection on the ground of your having proved that the individual soul is a part of the Lord, and that thus injunctions and prohibitions may, without any mutual interference, apply to the soul which is different from the Lord. For there are other scriptural passages which teach that the soul is not different from the Lord, and therefore not a part of him, as, for instance, the following ones:

[1] I. e. the subtle body consisting of the ten sense-organs, the five prânas, manas, and buddhi.

Having sent forth that he entered into it' (Taitt. Up. II, 6); There is no other seer but he' (B*ri*. Up. III, 7, 23); 'From death to death goes he who perceives therein any diversity' (B*ri*. Up. IV, 4, 19); 'Thou art that' (*Kh*. Up. VI, 8, 7); 'I am Brahman' (B*ri*. Up. I, 4, 10). Should you say that just from this concurrence of intimations of difference on the one hand and non-difference on the other hand it follows that the soul is a part of the Lord, we reply that such might be the case if the intention of the texts were to teach difference as well as non-difference. But the fact is that the texts aim solely at teaching non-difference, because through the knowledge of Brahman being the universal Self the highest end of man is obtained. About difference on the other hand mere occasional statements (anuvâda) are made as about something already established naturally (i.e. apart from scripture). Moreover, we have already maintained that Brahman as not composed of parts can have no parts. Hence it follows that the one highest Self which is within all beings appears as individual soul, and it therefore remains to show how injunctions and prohibitions are possible.

48. (The possibility of) injunctions and prohibitions (results) from the connexion (of the Self) with bodies; as in the case of light and so on.

Passages such as 'He is to approach his wife at the proper time,' and 'he is not to approach the wife of his guru,' are examples of permissions (or injunctions) and prohibitions; or again passages such as 'He is to kill the animal devoted to Agnîshomau,' and 'He is not to hurt any being.' Corresponding examples from ordinary life are: A friend is to be served,' and 'Enemies are to be shunned.' Permissions and prohibitions of this kind are possible, because the Self although one only is connected with various bodies.—Of what kind then is that connexion?—It consists in the origination in the Self of the erroneous notion that the Self is the aggregate consisting of the body and so on. This erroneous notion is seen to prevail in all living beings, and finds its expression in thoughts such as the following: *I* go,' '*I* come,' '*I* am blind,' '*I* am not blind,' '*I* am confused,' '*I* am not confused.' That erroneous notion cannot be removed by anything but perfect knowledge, and before the latter supervenes, it remains spread among all living beings. And thus, although the Self must be admitted to be one only, injunctions and prohibitions are possible owing to the difference effected by its connexion with bodies and other limiting adjuncts, the products of Nescience.—It then follows that for him who has obtained perfect knowledge, injunctions and prohibitions are purportless.—No, we reply, (they are not purportless for him, but they do not refer to him), since to him who has obtained the highest aim no obligation can apply. For obligations are imposed with reference to things to be avoided or desired; how then should he, who sees nothing, either to be wished or avoided, beyond the universal Self, stand under any obligation? The Self certainly cannot be enjoined on the Self.—Should it be said that injunctions and prohibitions apply to all those who discern that the soul is something different from the body (and therefore also to him who possesses perfect knowledge), we reply that (such an assertion is too wide, since) obligation depends on a man's imagining his Self to be (actually) connected with the body. It is true that obligation exists for him only who views the soul as something different from the body; but fundamentally all obligation is an erroneous imagination existing in the case of him only who does not see that his Self is no more connected with a body than the ether is with jars and the like. For him, on the other hand, who does not see that connexion no obligation exists, much less, therefore, for him who discerns the unity of the Self.—Nor does it result from the absence of obligation, that he who has arrived at perfect knowledge can act as he likes; for in all cases it is only the wrong imagination (as to the Self's connexion with a body) that impels to action, and that imagination is absent in the case of him who has reached perfect knowledge.—From all this it follows that injunctions and prohibitions are based on the Self's connexion with the body; 'as in the case of light.' The case under discussion is analogous to cases such as the following: Light is one only, and yet we shun a fire which has consumed dead bodies, not any other fire. The sun is one only; yet we shun only that part of his light which shines on unholy places, not that part which falls on pure ground. Some things consisting of earth are desired, e.g. diamonds and beryls; other things likewise consisting of earth are shunned, e.g dead bodies. The urine and dung of cows are considered pure and used as such; those of other animals are shunned. And many similar cases.

49. And on account of the non-extension (of the individual soul), there is no confusion (of the results of actions).

Well, let it be granted that injunctions and prohibitions are valid, because the Self although one is joined with particular bodies.—From the admission, however, of the unity of the Self it follows that there must be a confusion of the fruits of actions, there being only one master (i.e. one soul to enjoy the fruits of action).—This is not so, we reply, because there is no extension of the acting and enjoying Self, i.e. no connexion on its part with all bodies. For, as we have shown, the individual soul depends on its adjuncts, and owing to the non-extension of those adjuncts there is also non-extension of the soul. Hence there is no confusion of actions or fruits of actions.

50. And (the individual soul is) an appearance (reflection) only.

And that individual soul is to be considered a mere appearance of the highest Self, like the reflection of the sun in the water; it is neither directly that (i.e. the highest Self), nor a different thing. Hence just as, when one reflected image of the sun trembles, another reflected image does not on that account tremble also; so, when one soul is connected with actions and results of actions, another soul is not on that account connected likewise. There is therefore no confusion of actions and results. And as that 'appearance' is the effect of Nescience, it follows that the sa*m*sâra which is based on it (the appearance) is also the effect of Nescience, so that from the removal of the latter there results the cognition of the soul being in reality nothing but Brahman.

For those, on the other hand, who maintain that there are many Selfs and all of them all-pervading, it follows that there must be a confusion of actions and results.—In what way?—According to the opinion of the Sâṅkhyas there exist many all-pervading Selfs, whose nature is pure intelligence, devoid of qualities and of unsurpassable excellence. For the common purpose of all of them there exists the pradhâna, through which the souls obtain enjoyment and release.—According to the followers of Kaṇâda there exist many all-pervading Selfs, but they are, like so many jars or stools, mere substances and unintelligent in themselves. With those Selfs there co-operate the internal organs (manas), atomic and also unintelligent. From the conjunction of these two classes of substances, viz. the Selfs and the internal organs, there spring the nine special qualities of the Selfs, viz. desire, &c.[1] These qualities inhere in the individual Selfs separately, without any confusion, and that constitutes the saṁsâra-state. Final release, on the other hand, consists in the absolute non-origination of those nine qualities.

With regard to these opinions we remark that, as far as the Sâṅkhyas are concerned, their doctrine that all Selfs are of the nature of intelligence, and that there is no difference between them in the point of proximity (to the pradhâna), &c.[2], implies that, if one Self is connected with pleasure and pain, all Selfs will be so connected.—Well but, the Sâṅkhya might reply, a difference (in the connexion of the individual Selfs with pleasure and pain) may result from the circumstance that the activity of the pradhâna aims at the isolation (emancipation) of the Selfs[3]. Other-

---

[1] Cognition, pleasure, pain, desire, aversion, endeavour, merit, demerit, and bhâvanâ.

[2] The &c. implies the non-activity (audâsînya) of the Selfs.

[3] And therefore proceeds in a special definite direction capable of effecting in the end the emancipation of some particular Self.

wise the activity of the pradhâna would serve no other end but to manifest the pradhâna's power, in consequence whereof no final release would ever take place.—This argumentation, we reply, is not sound. For we have no right to assume a difference which has for its only motive the accomplishment of an end desirable (to us, viz. the emancipation of the Selfs), but we must rather bring forward some proof for that difference. If no such proof can be brought forward, the desired end, i.e. the emancipation of the soul, must be supposed not to take place; while at the same time the absence of any cause of difference establishes the confusion of actions and their results.—Against the Kâ*n*âdas we urge that if, on their theory, the internal organ is connected with one soul, it must in the same way be connected with all other souls as well, as there is no difference in the point of proximity, &c.[1] Hence, there being no difference of cause and consequently no difference of effect, it follows that, when one soul is connected with pleasure and pain, all souls are thus connected.—But may not the limitation (of actions and their results) be caused by the unseen principle (ad*r*ish*t*a)? By no means, the following Sûtra replies.

51. On account of the unseen principle being non-limitative.

While there are many souls, all-pervading like ether, and in equal proximity to all bodies from within as well as without, the so-called unseen principle (ad*r*ish*t*a), which is of the nature of religious merit or demerit, is acquired through mind, speech, and body (i.e. thoughts, words, and actions).—Now, according to the Sâṅkhyas, that principle inheres not in the Self, but abides in the pradhâna and cannot, on account of the pradhâna being the same (for all souls), be the limitative cause of the enjoyment of pleasure and pain for each individual Self.—And according to the Kâ*n*âdas also the unseen principle is due to the non-particular conjunction of the Selfs with the internal

[1] The '&c.' implies substantiality and so on.

organs, and as thus there is no limitative reason for any particular ad*ri*sh*t*a belonging to any particular soul, the doctrine is open to the same objection.—Well, but there are at work in every particular Self resolutions, &c., such as, 'I wish to obtain that result,' 'I wish to avoid that other result,' 'I am striving for that purpose,' 'I wish to act in that way,' &c. &c., and these may, we assume, define the relation of ownership in which particular Selfs stand to particular ad*ri*sh*t*as.—This objection is negatived in the following Sûtra.

52. And this is also the case in resolutions, &c.

The objection pointed out before applies also to resolutions, &c., for they also are made through the non-particular conjunction of the internal organ and the Self, in proximity to all Selfs. Hence they also cannot furnish a reason for limitation.

53. (Should it be said that distinction of pleasure, pain, &c., results) from (difference of) place; we say no, on account of the (Self's) being within (all things).

Here it might be objected that, although all Selfs are all-pervading, yet their conjunction with the internal organ which is seated in the body must take place in that part of each Self which is limited by the body; and that thus there may result from difference of locality a limitative distinction of resolutions, &c., of the ad*ri*sh*t*a, and of pleasure and pain.—This also, we reply, is not possible 'on account of the being within.' For, as being equally infinite, all Selfs are within all bodies. Thus the Vai*s*eshikas have no right whatever to assume any part of the Self to be limited by the body. And if they do assume such a part of the Self which in reality is without any parts, that part because merely assumptive will be incapable of limiting a real effect. Moreover, it is impossible to limit the body which originates in proximity to all (omnipresent) Selfs to one particular Self to the exclusion of all others. Moreover, on the doctrine of limitation due to difference of place, it would follow that sometimes two Selfs enjoying the same pleasure or pain might effect their fruition by one and the same body, since it may happen that the unseen principle of two Selfs occupies the same place. For we may observe, e. g. that after Devadatta's body has moved away from a certain spot in which Devadatta had enjoyed a certain amount of pleasure or pain, and the body of Ya*gñ*adatta has moved into that very same place, Ya*gñ*adatta enjoys an equal amount of pleasure or pain; a thing which (on the theory discussed) could not happen if the unseen principles of the two men did not occupy the same place. From the doctrine that the unseen principles occupy fixed places it would, moreover, follow that no enjoyment of the heavenly world, &c. can take place; for the ad*r*ish*t*a is effected in definite places such as e. g. the body of a Brâhma*n*a, and the enjoyment of the heavenly world is bound to a definite different place.—It further[1] is impossible to maintain that there exist many all-pervading Selfs[2], as there are no parallel instances. Mention if you can a plurality of other things occupying the same place!—You will perhaps bring forward colour and so on[3]. But we refuse to accept that instance as parallel, because colour, &c., although non-different in so far as they are attributes of one substance, yet differ through their essential characteristics. On the other hand there is no difference of characteristics between your (alleged) many Selfs. If you say that a difference of characteristics can be established on the ground of the ultimate special differences (of all substances), we point out that you implicate yourself in a logical circle as the assumption of difference of characteristics and the assumption of ultimate differences presuppose each other.

[1] And this is an attack on the basis of the position of the Sâṅkhyas as well as of the Vai*s*eshikas.

[2] Which being equally omnipresent would all occupy the same space.

[3] Many attributes such as colour, smell, touch, &c. reside in one place as belonging to one material object.

Should you adduce as parallel instances the all-pervadingness of ether, &c. (the '&c.' implying place and time), we reply that their all-pervadingness is not proved for him who holds the doctrine of Brahman and looks upon ether and so on as mere effects.

All which establishes the conclusion that the only doctrine not open to any objections is the doctrine of the unity of the Self.

FOURTH PÂDA.

Reverence to the highest Self!

1. Thus the vital airs.

In the third pâda it has been shown that a conflict of Vedic passages as to ether, &c., does not exist. The same is now done in this fourth pâda with regard to the vital airs. On the one hand the chapters treating of the origin of things do not record an origin of the vital airs; so e.g. (*Kh*. Up. VI, 2, 3) 'It sent forth fire,' &c.; and (Taitt. Up. II, 1) 'From that Self sprang ether,' &c. On the other hand it is said expressly in some places that the vital airs were not produced. The following passage, e.g. 'Non-being indeed was this in the beginning; they say: what was that non-being? those *ri*shis indeed were the non-being in the beginning; they say: who are those *ri*shis? the vital airs indeed are the *ri*shis' (*S*at. Br. VI, 1, 1, 1), states that the vital airs existed before the origin of things.—In other passages again we read of the origin of the vital airs also, so e.g. 'As small sparks come forth from fire, thus do all vital airs come forth from that Self' (B*ri*. Up. II, 1, 20); 'From that is born the vital air, mind, and all organs of sense' (Mu. Up. II, 1, 3); 'The seven vital airs also spring from him' (Mu. Up. II, 1, 8); 'He sent forth the vital air; from the vital air *s*raddhâ, ether, air, light, water, earth, sense, mind, food' (Pr. Up. VI, 4). Hence as there is a conflict of scriptural passages, and as no reason can be made out for deciding in favour of either alternative, the pûrvapakshin thinks that either no opinion can be formed, or that the passages relative to the origin of the vital airs must be taken in a metaphorical sense, since scripture expressly states the prâ*n*as to have existed before the creation.

In reply to this the author of the Sûtras says, 'thus the

prâ*n*as.'—What then, it will be asked, is the fitness of the word 'thus,' as there is no point of comparison with the matter under discussion? The matter under discussion at the conclusion of the preceding pâda was the refutation of those who maintain a plurality of omnipresent Selfs, and with this no comparison can be instituted because there is no similarity. For a comparison is possible only where there is similarity; as when we say, e.g. 'as a lion so is Balavarman.' Possibly it might be said that the comparison is meant to intimate similarity with the ad*ri*sh*t*a; the meaning being that as the ad*ri*sh*t*a is not limited because it is produced in proximity to all Selfs, so the prâ*n*as also are not limited with regard to all the different Selfs. But, on that explanation, the Sûtra would be an idle repetition, as it has already been explained that that absence of limitation is due to the non-limitation of bodies.—Nor can the prâ*n*as be compared with the individual soul, because that would be contrary to the conclusion about to be established. For it has been shown that the individual soul is without an origin, while the intention is to declare that the prâ*n*as have an origin. Hence it appears that the word 'so' is devoid of connexion.—Not so, we reply. A connexion may be established by means of a comparison based on the exemplifying passages. Under that category fall those passages which state the origin of the prâ*n*as, as e.g. 'From that Self come forth all prâ*n*as, all worlds, all gods, all beings' (B*ri*. Up. II, 1, 20); which passage means that as the worlds and so on are produced from the highest Brahman so the prâ*n*as also. Such passages also as (Mu. Up. II, 1, 3) 'From him are born prâ*n*a, mind and all organs of sense, ether, air, light, water, and the earth the support of all,' are to be considered as intimating that the origin of the prâ*n*as is analogous to that of the ether, &c.—Or else, as a connexion with a somewhat remote object of comparison is resorted to in such cases as the one treated of in Pû. Mî. Sû. III, 4, 32 ('and the accident in drinking Soma, in the same manner')[1], we may construe our Sûtra in the following

[1] The 'tadvat' in the quoted Sûtra refers not to the immediately preceding adhikara*n*a but to Sûtra III, 4, 28.

way: in the same way as ether and so on, which are mentioned in the beginning of the preceding pâda, are understood to be effects of the highest Brahman, so the prâ*n*as also are effects of the highest Brahman. And if it be asked what reason we have for assuming the prâ*n*as to be so, we reply: the fact of this being stated by scripture.—But it has been shown above that in some places the origin of the prâ*n*as is not mentioned.—That is of no weight, we reply, as it is mentioned in other places. For the circumstance of a thing not being stated in some places has no power to invalidate what is stated about it in other places. Hence, on account of equality of scriptural statement, it is proper to maintain that the prâ*n*as also are produced in the same way as ether and so on.

2. On account of the impossibility of a secondary (origin of the prâ*n*as).

Against the objection that the origin of the prâ*n*as must be understood in a secondary sense because the text states that they existed before the origin of the world, the Sûtrakâra declares 'on account of the impossibility of a secondary origin.' The statement as to the origin of the prâ*n*as cannot be taken in a secondary sense because therefrom would result the abandonment of a general assertion. For after the text has asserted that the knowledge of everything depends on the knowledge of one ('What is that through which when it is known everything else becomes known?' Mu. Up. I, 1, 3), it goes on to say, in order to prove that assertion, that 'From him is born prâ*n*a,' &c. (Mu. Up. II, 1, 3). Now the assertion is made good only if the whole world including the prâ*n*as is an effect of Brahman, because then there is no effect independent of the material cause; if on the other hand the statement as to the origin of the prâ*n*as were taken in a secondary sense, the assertion would thereby be stultified. The text, moreover, makes some concluding statements about the matter asserted, 'The Person is all this, sacrifice, penance, Brahman, the highest Immortal' (II, 1, 10), and 'Brahman alone is all this; it is the Best.'—That same assertion is to be connected with such passages as the following, 'When we see, hear, perceive, and know the Self, then all this is known' (B*ri*. Up. II, 4, 5).—How then have we to account for the statement that the prâ*n*as existed before the creation?—That statement, we reply, does not refer to the fundamental causal substance; for we ascertain from scriptural passages, such as Mu. Up. II, 1, 2 ('That heavenly Person is without breath and without mind, pure, higher than the high Imperishable'), that the fundamental causal substance is devoid of all distinctions such as breath and the like. We must rather view the statement about the existence of the prâ*n*as before the creation as having for its object a subordinate causal substance[1], and being made with reference to the effects of the latter only. For it is known from *S*ruti and Sm*ri*ti that even in the universe of evolved things many states of being may stand to each other in the relation of causal substance and effect. —In the adhikara*n*a treating of the ether there occurred a Sûtra (composed of the same syllables) 'gau*n*yasambhavât,' which as being the pûrvapaksha-sûtra had to be explained as 'gau*n*î asambhavât,' 'the statement about the origin of ether must be taken in a secondary sense on account of the impossibility (of the primary sense).' There the final conclusion was established by means of the abandonment of the general assertion. Here on the other hand the Sûtra is the Siddhânta Sûtra and we have therefore explained it as meaning 'on account of the impossibility of a secondary meaning.'—Those who explain the present Sûtra in the same way as the previous Sûtra overlook the fact of the general assertion being abandoned (viz. if the passages referring to the origin of the prâ*n*as were taken in a secondary sense).

3. On account of that (word which indicates origin) being enunciated at first (in connexion with the prâ*n*as).

That the scriptural statement about the origin of the

[1] Such as Hira*n*yagarbha.

prâ*n*as is to be taken in its literal sense just as the statements about the ether, &c., appears from that circumstance also that the one word which (in the passage from the Mu. Up.) indicates origination, viz. 'is born' (*g*âyate), is in the first place connected with the prâ*n*as and has afterwards to be joined with ether, &c., also ('from him is born breath, mind, and all organs of sense, ether, air,' &c.). Now as it is a settled matter that the phrase 'is born' must be taken in its primary sense with reference to ether and so on, it follows that the origin of the prâ*n*as also to which the same word is applied must be understood as a real origin. For it would be impossible to decide that a word enunciated once only in one chapter and one sentence, and connected with many other words, has in some cases to be taken in its primary sense, and in others in a secondary sense; for such a decision would imply want of uniformity.—So likewise in the passage, 'He sent forth prâ*n*a, from prâ*n*a *s*raddhâ,' &c. (Pr. Up. VI, 4), the phrase 'he sent forth' which the text exhibits in conjunction with the prâ*n*as has to be carried on to *s*raddhâ and the other things which have an origin.—The same reasoning holds good in those cases where the word expressing origination occurs at the end and has to be connected with the preceding words; as e.g. in the passage ending 'all beings come forth from the Self,' where the word 'come forth' must be connected with the prâ*n*as, &c., mentioned in the earlier part of the sentence.

4. Because speech is preceded by that (viz. fire and the other elements).

Although in the chapter, 'That sent forth fire,' &c., the origin of the prâ*n*as is not mentioned, the origin of the three elements, fire, water, and earth only being stated, nevertheless, the fact of the text declaring that speech, prâ*n*a, and mind presuppose fire, water, and earth—which in their turn have Brahman for their causal substance—proves that they—and, by parity of reasoning, all prâ*n*as—have sprung from Brahman. That speech, prâ*n*a, and mind presuppose fire, water, and earth is told in the same chapter, 'For truly, my child, mind consists of earth, breath of water, speech of fire' (*Kh.* Up. VI, 5, 4). If their consisting of earth and so on is taken literally, it follows at once that they have sprung from Brahman. And if it be taken in a metaphorical sense only, yet, as the sentence forms part of the chapter which treats of the evolution of names and forms effected by Brahman; and as the introductory phrase runs, 'That by which we hear what is not heard' (*Kh.* Up. VI, 1, 3); and as the concluding passage is 'In it all that exists has its Self' (*Kh.* Up. VI, 8, 7); and as the matter is moreover known from other scriptural passages; we understand that also the statement about mind and so on consisting of earth, &c., is meant to teach that they are products of Brahman.—It is therefore an established conclusion that the prâ*n*as also are effects of Brahman.

5. (The prâ*n*as are) seven, on account of this being understood (from scriptural passages) and of the specification (of those seven).

So far we have shown that there is in reality no conflict of scriptural passages regarding the origin of the prâ*n*as. It will now be shown that there is also no conflict regarding their number. The chief vital air (mukhya prâ*n*a) will be discussed later on. For the present the Sûtrakâra defines the number of the other prâ*n*as. A doubt arises here owing to the conflicting nature of the scriptural passages. In one place seven prâ*n*as are mentioned, 'The seven prâ*n*as spring from him' (Mu. Up. II, 1, 8). In another place eight prâ*n*as are mentioned as being grahas, 'Eight grahas there are and eight atigrahas' (B*ri*. Up. III, 2, 1). In another place nine, 'Seven are the prâ*n*as of the head, two the lower ones' (Taitt. Sa*m*h. V, 3, 2, 5). Sometimes ten, 'Nine prâ*n*as indeed are in men, the navel is the tenth' (Taitt. Sa*m*h. V, 3, 2, 3). Sometimes eleven, 'Ten are these prâ*n*as in man, and Âtman is the eleventh' (B*ri*. Up. III, 9, 4). Sometimes twelve, 'All touches have their centre in the skin,' &c. (B*ri*. Up. II, 4, 11). Sometimes thirteen, 'The eye and what can be seen,' &c. (Pr. Up. IV, 8).—Thus the scriptural passages disagree about the number of the prâ*n*as.

Here the pûrvapakshin maintains that the prâ*n*as are in reality seven in number, on account of understanding, i. e. because they are understood to be so many, from passages such as 'The seven prâ*n*as spring from him,' &c. These seven prâ*n*as are moreover specified in the other passage quoted above, 'Seven indeed are the prâ*n*as of the head. —But in the same passage we meet with the following reiteration, 'Resting in the cave they are placed there seven and seven,' which intimates that there are prâ*n*as in addition to the seven.—No matter, we reply; that reiteration is made with reference to the plurality of men, and means that each man has seven prâ*n*as; it does not mean that there are two sets of seven prâ*n*as each of different nature. —But, another objection will be raised, other scriptural passages speak of the prâ*n*as as eight in number; how then should they be seven?—True, we reply, the number of eight also is stated; but on account of the contradictory nature of the statements we have to decide in favour of either of the two numbers; hence we decide in favour of the number seven, in deference to the (simpler) assumption of a low number, and consider the statements of other numbers to refer to the difference of modifications (of the fundamental seven prâ*n*as).—To this argumentation the next Sûtra replies.

6. But (there are also, in addition to the seven prâ*n*as mentioned,) the hands and so on. This being a settled matter, therefore (we must) not (conclude) thus (viz. that there are seven prâ*n*as only).

In addition to the seven prâ*n*as scripture mentions other prâ*n*as also, such as the hands, &c., 'The hand is one graha and that is seized by work as the atigraha; for with the hands one does work' (B*ri*. Up. III, 2, 8), and similar passages. And as it is settled that there are more than seven, the number seven may be explained as being contained within the greater number. For wherever there is a conflict between a higher and a lower number, the higher number has to be accepted because the lower one is contained within it; while the higher is not contained within the lower. We therefore must not conclude that, in deference to the lower number, seven prâ*n*as have to be assumed, but rather that there are eleven prâ*n*as, in deference to the higher number. This conclusion is confirmed by one of the passages quoted, 'Ten are these prâ*n*as in man, and Âtman is the eleventh.' By the word Âtman we have to understand the internal organ, on account of its ruling over the organs. Should it be objected that scripture also mentions numbers higher than eleven, viz. twelve and thirteen, we admit that, but remark that there are no objective effects in addition to the eleven (well-known) objective effects on account of which additional organs would have to be assumed. There are five distinctions of buddhi having for their respective objects sound, touch, colour, taste, and smell, and on their account there are the five intellectual organs; again there are five classes of action, viz. speaking, taking, going, evacuation, and begetting, and on their account there are the five organs of action; finally there is the manas which has all things for its objects and extends to the past, the present, and the future; it is one only but has various functions. On account of the plurality of its functions we find it designated by different terms in different places, as manas or buddhi or aha*m*kâra or *k*itta. Thus scripture also after having enumerated the various functions such as desire, &c., says at the end, 'All this is manas only.'—That passage again which speaks of the prâ*n*as of the head as seven means four prâ*n*as only, which on account of the plurality of their places may be counted as seven; viz. the two ears, the two eyes, the two nostrils, and speech.—Nor can it be maintained that there are in reality only so many (i.e. seven), the other prâ*n*as being mere functions of the seven; for the functions of the hands and so on are absolutely different (from the functions of the seven senses admitted by the pûrvapakshin).—Again, in the passage 'Nine prâ*n*as indeed are in man, the navel is the tenth,' the expression 'ten prâ*n*as' is used to denote the different openings of the human body, not the difference of nature of the prâ*n*as, as we conclude from the navel being mentioned as the eleventh. For no prâ*n*a is known that bears the name of navel; but the navel as being one of the special abodes of the chief prâ*n*a is here enumerated as a tenth prâ*n*a.—In some places so and so many are counted for the purpose of meditation; in other places so and so many for the purpose of illustration [1]. As the statements concerning the number of the prâ*n*as are of so varying a nature we must therefore distinguish in each case what the object of the statement is. Meanwhile it remains a settled conclusion that that statement which makes the prâ*n*as to be eleven is authoritative, on account of the objective effects (being eleven also).

The two Sûtras (referring to the number of the prâ*n*as) may be construed in the following manner also. The prâ*n*as are seven because scripture mentions the going (gati) of seven only, 'When he thus departs life departs after him, and when life thus departs all the other prâ*n*as [2] depart after it' (B*ri*. Up. IV, 4, 2).—But, it may be objected, this passage says 'all the other prâ*n*as;' how then does it declare the going of seven only?—The Sûtra replies, 'on account of their being specified.' Seven senses only, from seeing up to feeling, are specified there because so many only are under discussion; as we see from the enumeration given in the passage, 'When that person in the eye turns away then he ceases to know any forms. He has become one they say, he does not see' &c. The word 'all' refers here only to what is under discussion, i.e. only to the seven prâ*n*as mentioned before, not to any other. Analogously when we say 'all the Brâhma*n*as have been fed,' we mean only those Brâhma*n*as who have been invited and concern us at the time, not any other.—If it be objected that the passage quoted mentions understanding (vi*gñ*âna) as the eighth thing departing, and that we therefore have no right to speak of the departing of seven only, we reply that manas and understanding differ not in essential nature but only in function, and that on this account we are entitled to speak of seven prâ*n*as only.—The answer to this

[1] Sapta prâ*n*â*h* prabhavantîty âder gatim âha kva*k*id iti, ash*t*au grahâ ityâder gati*m* sû*k*ayati gati*m* iti. Ân. Gi.

[2] I.e. seeing, smelling, tasting, speaking, hearing, feeling, and the manas.

pûrvapaksha is as follows.—In addition to the seven senses, other prâ*n*as also, such as the hands, are known to exist, as we see from such passages as 'The hands are one graha,' &c. (B*ri*. Up. III, 2, 8). By their being a graha (seizer) is meant that they are bonds by which the individual soul (kshetra*gñ*a) is tied. Now the individual soul is tied not in one body only, but is equally tied in other bodies also. Hence it follows that that bond called graha (i.e. among other things the hands) moves over into other bodies also. Sm*ri*ti also ('He—the Self—is joined with the aggregate of eight, comprising breath, &c.[1], as his mark; his bondage consists in being bound by it, his release in being freed from it') shows that the Self is, previous to final release, not freed from the bonds called grahas. And also in the enumeration of the senses and their objects given by the Atharva*n*a Upanishad ('The eye and what can be seen,' &c., Pr. Up. IV, 8), the organs of action such as the hands and so on, together with their objects, are specified as well, 'the hands and what can be grasped; the member and what can be delighted; the anus and what can be evacuated; the feet and what can be walked.' Moreover the passage, 'These ten vital breaths and âtman as the eleventh; when they depart from this mortal body they make us cry' (B*ri*. Up. III, 9, 4), shows that eleven prâ*n*as depart from the body. —Moreover the word 'all' (which occurs in the passage, B*ri*. Up. IV, 4, 2) must, because connected with the word 'prâ*n*as,' denote all prâ*n*as, and cannot, on the ground of general subject-matter, be limited to the seven prâ*n*as; for a direct statement has greater force than the subject-matter. Even in the analogous sentence, 'all Brâhma*n*as have been fed,' we have, on the ground of the words, to understand all Brâhma*n*as living on the earth; but because it is impossible to feed all Brâhma*n*as in the latter sense, we accept that meaning of

[1] The eightfold aggregate of which the Self is freed in final release only comprises the five prâ*n*as (vital airs), the pentad of the five subtle elements, the pentad of the organs of intellect, the pentad of the organs of action, the tetrad of internal organs (manas, &c.), avidyâ, desire (kâma), and karman.

'all,' according to which it denotes all invited Brâhma*n*as. In our case on the other hand there is no reason whatever for narrowing the meaning of 'all.'—Hence the word 'all' includes all prâ*n*as without exception. Nothing on the other hand prevents the enumeration of seven prâ*n*as being taken as illustrative only. It is therefore an established conclusion, resting on the number of the effects as well as on Vedic statement, that there are eleven prâ*n*as.

7. And (they are) minute.

The author of the Sûtras adds another characteristic quality of the prâ*n*as. The prâ*n*as under discussion must be viewed as minute. By their minuteness we have to understand subtilty and limited size; but not atomic size, as otherwise they would be incapable of producing effects which extend over the whole body. They must be subtle; for if they were big the persons surrounding a dying man would see them coming out from the body at the moment of death, as a snake comes out of its hole. They must be limited; for if they were all-pervading the scriptural statements as to their passing out of the body, going and coming, would be contradicted thereby, and it could not be established that the individual soul is 'the essence of the qualities of that' (i. e. the manas; cp. II, 3, 29). Should it be said that they may be all-pervading, but at the same time appear as functions (v*ri*tti) in the body only, we rejoin that only a function can constitute an instrument. Whatever effects perception, may it be a function or something else, just that is an instrument for us. The disagreement is therefore about a name only, and the assumption of the instruments (prâ*n*as) being all-pervading is thus purposeless.—Hence we decide that the prâ*n*as are subtle and of limited size.

8. And the best (i.e. the chief vital air).

The Sûtra extends to the chief vital air (mukhya prâ*n*a) a quality already asserted of the other prâ*n*as, viz. being an effect of Brahman.—But, an objection may be raised, it has already been stated of all prâ*n*as without difference that they are effects of Brahman; e.g. the passage, 'From him is born breath, mind, and all organs of sense' (Mu. Up. II, 1, 3), states the origin of prâ*n*a separately from the senses and the manas; and there are other passages also such as 'He sent forth prâ*n*a' (Pr. Up. VI, 4). Why then the formal extension?—We reply: For the purpose of removing further doubt. For in the Nâsadîya-sûkta whose subject is Brahman there occurs the following mantra: 'There was neither death nor the Immortal; nor manifestation of either night or day. By its own law the One was breathing without wind; there was nothing different from that or higher than it' (*Ri*. Sa*m*h. X, 129, 2). Here the words, 'was breathing,' which denote the proper function of breath, intimate that breath existed as it were before the creation. And therefrom it might be concluded that prâ*n*a is not produced; an idea which the Sûtrakâra discards by the formal extension (to prâ*n*a of the quality of having originated from Brahman).—Moreover the word 'breathed' does not intimate that prâ*n*a existed before the creation; for in the first place it is qualified by the addition 'without wind,' and in the second place scriptural passages—such as 'He is without breath, without mind, pure' (Mu. Up. II, 1, 2)—declare expressly that the causal substance is without any qualifications such as prâ*n*a and so on. Hence the word 'breathed' has merely the purpose of setting forth the existence of the cause.—The term 'the best' (employed in the Sûtra) denotes the chief vital air, according to the declaration of scripture, 'Breath indeed is the oldest and the best' (*Kh*. Up. V, 1, 1). The breath is the oldest because it begins its function from the moment when the child is conceived; the senses of hearing, &c., on the other hand, begin to act only when their special seats, viz. the ears, &c., are formed, and they are thus not 'the oldest.' The designation 'the best' belongs to the prâ*n*a on account of its superior qualities and on account of the passage, 'We shall not be able to live without thee' (B*ri*. Up. VI, 1, 13).

9. (The chief prâ*n*a is) neither air nor function, on account of its being mentioned separately.

An inquiry is now started concerning the nature of that chief prâ*n*a.—The pûrvapakshin maintains that the prâ*n*a is, according to *S*ruti, nothing but air. For *S*ruti says, 'Breath is air; that air assuming five forms is prâ*n*a, apâna, vyâna, udâna, samâna.'—Or else the pûrvapaksha may be formulated according to the view of another philosophical doctrine, and prâ*n*a may be considered as the combined function of all organs. For so the followers of another doctrine (viz. the Sâṅkhyas) teach, 'The five airs, prâ*n*a, &c., are the common function of the instruments[1].'

To this we reply that the prâ*n*a is neither air nor the function of an organ; for it is mentioned separately. From air prâ*n*a is distinguished in the following passage, 'Breath indeed is the fourth foot of Brahman. That foot shines as Agni with its light and warms.' If prâ*n*a were mere air, it would not be mentioned separately from air.—Thus it is also mentioned separately from the functions of the organs; for the texts enumerate speech and the other organs and mention prâ*n*a separately from them, and the function and that to which the function belongs (the organ) are identical. If it were a mere function of an organ, it would not be mentioned separately from the organs. Other passages also in which the prâ*n*a is mentioned separately from air and the organs are here to be considered so, e.g. 'From him is born breath, mind, and all organs of sense, ether, air,' &c. (Mu. Up. II, 1, 3). Nor is it possible that all the organs together should have one function (and that that function should be the prâ*n*a); for each organ has its own special function and the aggregate of them has no active power of its own.—But—an objection may be raised—the thing may take place in the manner of the moving bird-cage. Just as eleven birds shut up in one cage may, although each makes a separate effort, move the cage by the combination of their efforts; so the eleven

---

[1] Sâṅkhya Sû. II, 31; where, however, the reading is 'sâmânya-kara*n*av*ri*tti*h*,' explained by the Comm. as sâdhâra*n*î kara*n*asya anta*h*-kara*n*atrayasya v*ri*tti*h* pari*n*âmabhedâ iti. *S*aṅkara, on the other hand, understands by kara*n*a the eleven prâ*n*as discussed previously.

prâ*n*as which abide in one body may, although each has its own special function, by the combination of these functions, produce one common function called prâ*n*a.—This objection, we reply, is without force. The birds indeed may, by means of their separate subordinate efforts, which all favour the movement of the cage, move the cage by combination; that is a matter of observation. But we have no right to assume that the different prâ*n*as with their subordinate functions such as hearing &c. can, by combination, produce the function of vital breath; for there is no means to prove this, and the vital breath is in kind absolutely different from hearing and so on.—Moreover, if the vital breath were the mere function of an organ (or the organs) it could not be glorified as the 'best,' and speech and so on could not be represented as subordinate to it. Hence the vital breath is different from air and the functions (of the organs).—How then have we to understand the scriptural passage, 'The prâ*n*a is air,' &c.?—The air, we reply, passing into the adhyâtma-state, dividing itself fivefold and thus abiding in a specialized condition is called prâ*n*a. It therefore is neither a different being nor is it mere air. Hence there is room for those passages as well which identify it with air as those which do not.—Well, let this be granted. The prâ*n*a then also must be considered to be independent in this body like the individual soul, as scripture declares it to be the 'best' and the organs such as speech, &c., to be subordinate to it. For various powers are ascribed to it in scriptural passages. It is said, for instance, that when speech and the other (organs) are asleep the prâ*n*a alone is awake; that the prâ*n*a alone is not reached by death; that the prâ*n*a is the absorber, it absorbs speech, &c.; that the prâ*n*a guards the other senses (prâ*n*as) as a mother her sons[1]. Hence it follows that the prâ*n*a is independent in the same way as the individual soul.—This view is impugned in the next Sûtra.

---

[1] Cp. Ka. Up. II, 5, 8; B*ri*. Up. I, 5, 21; *Kh*. Up. IV, 3, 3; Pr. Up. II, 13.

10. But (the prâ*n*a is subordinate to the soul) like the eye, &c., on account of being taught with them (the eye, &c.), and for other reasons.

The word 'but' sets aside the independence of the prâ*n*a. As the eye and so on stand, like the subjects of a king, in mere subordinate relation to the acting and enjoying of the soul and are not independent, so the chief vital air also, occupying a position analogous to that of a king's minister, stands in an entirely subordinate relation to the soul and is not independent.—Why?—Because it is taught (spoken of) together with them, i. e. the eye and the other organs, in such passages as the colloquy of the prâ*n*as, &c. For to be mentioned together is appropriate only in the case of things with the same attributes, as e. g. the B*ri*hat-sâman and the Rathantara-sâman[1]. The words 'and so on' (in the Sûtra) indicate other reasons refuting the independence of the prâ*n*a, such as its being composed of parts, its being of a non-intelligent nature and the like.—Well, but if it be admitted that the prâ*n*a stands to the soul in the relation of an instrument as the eye and so on, it will follow that we must assume another sense-object analogous to colour and so on. For the eyes, &c., occupy their specific subordinate position with regard to the soul through their functions which consist in the seeing of colour and so on. Now we can enumerate only eleven classes of functions, viz. the seeing of colour and so on, on whose account we assume eleven different prâ*n*as, and there is no twelfth class of effects on account of which a twelfth prâ*n*a could be assumed.—To this objection the following Sûtra replies.

11. And on account of (its) not being an instrument the objection is not (valid); for thus (scripture) declares.

The objection urged, viz. that there would result another sense-object, is not valid; because the prâ*n*a is not an

[1] Which go together because they are both sâmans.

instrument. For we do not assume that the prâ*n*a is, like the eye, an organ because it determines a special sense-object. Nor is it on that account devoid of an effect; since scripture declares that the chief vital air has a specific effect which cannot belong to the other prâ*n*as. For in the so-called colloquies of the prâ*n*as we read in the beginning, 'The prâ*n*as quarrelled together who was best;' after that we read, 'He by whose departure the body seems worse than worst, he is the best of you;' thereupon the text, after showing how, on the successive departure of speech and so on, the life of the body, although deprived of one particular function, went on as before, finally relates that as soon as the chief prâ*n*a was about to depart all other prâ*n*as became loosened and the body was about to perish; which shows that the body and all the senses subsist by means of the chief prâ*n*a. The same thing is declared by another passage, 'Then prâ*n*a as the best said to them: Be not deceived; I alone dividing myself fivefold support this body and keep it' (Pr. Up. II, 3). Another passage, viz. 'With prâ*n*a guarding the lower nest' (B*ri*. Up. IV, 3, 12), shows that the guarding of the body depends on prâ*n*a. Again, two other passages show that the nourishing of the body depends on prâ*n*a, 'From whatever limb prâ*n*a goes away that limb withers' (B*ri*. Up. I, 3, 19), and 'What we eat and drink with it supports the other vital breaths.' And another passage declares that the soul's departing and staying depend on prâ*n*a, 'What is it by whose departure I shall depart, and by whose staying I shall stay?—The created prâ*n*a' (Pr. Up. VI, 3; 4).

12. It is designated as having five functions like mind.

The chief vital air has its specific effect for that reason also that in scripture it is designated as having five functions, prâ*n*a, apâna, vyâna, udâna, samâna. This distinction of functions is based on a distinction of effects. Prâ*n*a is the forward-function whose work is aspiration, &c.; apâna is the backward-function whose work is inspiration, &c.; vyâna is that which, abiding in the junction of the two, is the cause of works of strength[1]; udâna is the ascending function and is the cause of the passing out (of the soul); samâna is the function which conveys the juices of the food equally through all the limbs of the body. Thus the prâ*n*a has five functions just as the mind (manas) has. The five functions of the mind are the five well-known ones caused by the ear, &c., and having sound and so on for their objects. By the functions of the mind we cannot here understand those enumerated (in B*ri*. Up. I, 5, 3), 'desire, representation,' &c., because those are more than five.—But on the former explanation also there exists yet another function of the mind which does not depend on the ear, &c., but has for its object the past, the future, and so on; so that on that explanation also the number five is exceeded.—Well, let us then follow the principle that the opinions of other (systems) if unobjectionable may be adopted, and let us assume that the five functions of the manas are those five which are known from the Yoga*s*âstra, viz. right knowledge, error, imagination, slumber, and remembrance. Or else let us assume that the Sûtra quotes the manas as an analogous instance merely with reference to the plurality (not the fivefoldness) of its functions.—In any case the Sûtra must be construed to mean that the prâ*n*a's subordinate position with regard to the soul follows from its having five functions like the manas.

13. And it is minute.

And the chief vital air is to be considered as minute like the other prâ*n*as.—Here also we have to understand by minuteness that the chief vital air is subtle and of limited size, not that is of atomic size; for by means of its five functions it pervades the entire body. It must be viewed as subtle because when passing out of the body it is not perceived by a bystander, and as limited because scripture speaks of its passing out, going and coming.—But, it may be said, scripture speaks also of its all-pervadingness; so,

[1] Viz. the holding in of the breath; cp. *Kh*. Up. I, 3, 3-5.

e.g. 'He is equal to a grub, equal to a gnat, equal to an elephant, equal to these three worlds, equal to this Universe' (B*ri*. Up. I, 3, 22).—To this we reply that the all-pervadingness of which this text speaks belongs to the Self of the prâ*n*a in its adhidaivata relation, according to which it appears as Hira*n*yagarbha in his double—universal and individual—form, not in its adhyâtma relation. Moreover the statements of equality 'equal to a grub,' &c., just declare the limited size of the prâ*n*a which abides within every living being.—Thus there remains no difficulty.

14. But there is guidance (of the prâ*n*as) by fire, &c., on account of that being declared by scripture.

Here there arises a discussion whether the prâ*n*as of which we have been treating are able to produce their effects by their own power or only in so far as guided by divinities.—The pûrvapakshin maintains that the prâ*n*as being endowed with the capacity of producing their effects act from their own power. If we, moreover, admitted that the prâ*n*as act only in so far as guided by divinities, it would follow that those guiding divinities are the enjoyers (of the fruits of the actions), and the individual soul would thus cease to be an enjoyer. Hence the prâ*n*as act from their own power.—To this we reply as follows. 'But there takes place guidance by fire,' &c.—The word 'but' excludes the pûrvapaksha. The different classes of organs, speech, &c., the Sûtra says, enter on their peculiar activities, guided by the divinities animating fire, and so on. The words, 'on account of that being declared by scripture,' state the reason. For different passages declare this, cp. Ait. Âr. II, 4, 2, 4, 'Agni having become speech entered the mouth.' This statement about Agni (fire) becoming speech and entering the mouth is made on the assumption of Agni acting as a ruler with his divine Self (not as a mere element). For if we abstract from the connexion with the divinity we do not see that there is any special connexion of fire either with speech or the mouth. The subsequent passages, 'Vâyu having become breath entered into the nostrils,' &c., are to be explained in the same way.

—This conclusion is confirmed by other passages also, such as 'Speech is indeed the fourth foot of Brahman; that foot shines with Agni as its light and warms' (*Kh.* Up. IV, 18, 3), which passage declares that speech is made of the light of Agni. Other passages intimate the same thing by declaring that speech, &c., pass over into Agni, &c., cp. B*ri*. Up. I, 3, 12, 'He carried speech across first; when speech had become freed from death it became Agni.' Everywhere the enumeration of speech and so on on the one side and Agni and so on on the other side—wherein is implied a distinction of the personal and the divine element—proceeds on the ground of the same relation (viz. of that which is guided and that which guides). Sm*ri*ti-passages also declare at length that speech, &c., are guided by Agni and the other divinities, cp. for instance, 'Brâhma*n*as knowing the truth call speech the personal element, that which is spoken the natural element and fire (Agni) the divine element.'—The assertion that the prâ*n*as being endowed with the capability of producing their effects act from their own power is unfounded, as we see that some things which possess the capability of motion, e.g. cars, actually move only if dragged by bulls and the like. Hence, as both alternatives are possible[1], we decide on the ground of scripture that the prâ*n*as act under the guidance of the divinities.—The next Sûtra refutes the assertion that from the fact of the divinities guiding the prâ*n*as it would follow that they—and not the embodied soul—are the enjoyers.

15. (It is not so) (because the prâ*n*as are connected) with that to which the prâ*n*as belong (i.e. the individual soul), (a thing we know) from scripture.

Although there are divinities guiding the prâ*n*as, yet we learn from scripture that those prâ*n*as are connected with the embodied soul which is the Lord of the aggregate of

[1] Viz. that something should act by itself, and that it should act under guidance only.

instruments of action. The following passage, e.g. 'where the sight has entered into the void there is the person of the eye; the eye itself is the instrument of seeing. He who knows, let me smell this, he is the Self; the nose is the instrument of smelling,' declares that the prâ*n*as are connected with the embodied soul only. Moreover the plurality of the divinities guiding the organs renders it impossible that they should be the enjoyers in this body. For that there is in this body only one embodied enjoyer is understood from the possibility of the recognition of identity and so on[1].

16. And on account of the permanence of this (viz. the embodied soul).

This embodied soul abides permanently in this body as the enjoyer, since it can be affected by good and evil and can experience pleasure and pain. Not so the gods; for they exist in the state of highest power and glory and cannot possibly enter, in this wretched body, into the condition of enjoyers. So scripture also says, 'Only what is good approaches him; verily evil does not approach the devas' (B*ri*. Up. I, 5, 20).—And only with the embodied soul the prâ*n*as are permanently connected, as it is seen that when the soul passes out &c. the prâ*n*as follow it. This we see from passages such as the following: 'When it passes out the prâ*n*a passes out after it, and when the prâ*n*a thus passes out all the other prâ*n*as pass after it' (B*ri*. Up. IV, 4, 2). Hence although there are ruling divinities of the organs, the embodied soul does not cease to be the enjoyer; for the divinities are connected with the organs only, not with the state of the soul as enjoyer.

17. They (the prâ*n*as) are senses, on account of being so designated, with the exception of the best (the mukhya prâ*n*a).

We have treated of the mukhya prâ*n*a and the other

---

[1] Yo*ha*m* rûpam adrâksha*m* so*ha*m* *srin*omîty ekasyaiva pratyabhig*ñ*ânam pratisamdhânam. Go. Ân.

eleven prâ*n*as in due order.—Now there arises another doubt, viz. whether the other prâ*n*as are functions of the mukhya prâ*n*a or different beings.—The pûrvapakshin maintains that they are mere functions, on account of scriptural statement. For scripture, after having spoken of the chief prâ*n*a and the other prâ*n*as in proximity, declares that those other prâ*n*as have their Self in the chief prâ*n*a, 'Well, let us all assume his form. Thereupon they all assumed his form' (B*ri*. Up. I, 5, 21).—Their unity is moreover ascertained from the unity of the term applied to them, viz. prâ*n*a. Otherwise there either would result the objectionable circumstance of one word having different senses, or else the word would in some places have to be taken in its primary sense, in others in a derived sense. Hence, as prâ*n*a, apâna, &c. are the five functions of the one chief prâ*n*a, so the eleven prâ*n*as also which begin with speech are mere functions of the chief prâ*n*a.—To this we reply as follows. Speech and so on are beings different from the chief prâ*n*a, on account of the difference of designation.—Which is that difference of designation?—The eleven prâ*n*as remaining if we abstract from the best one, i.e. the chief prâ*n*a, are called the sense-organs (indriya), as we see them designated in *S*ruti, 'from him is born breath, mind, and all organs of sense' (Mu. Up. II, 1, 3). In this and other passages prâ*n*a and the sense-organs are mentioned separately.—But in that case the mind also would have to be excluded from the class of sense-organs, like the prâ*n*a; as we see that like the latter it is separately mentioned in the passage, 'The mind and all organs of sense.' True; but in Sm*ri*ti eleven sense-organs are mentioned, and on that account the mind must, like the ear, and so on, be comprised in the sense-organs. That the prâ*n*a on the other hand is a sense-organ is known neither from Sm*ri*ti nor *S*ruti.—Now this difference of designation is appropriate only if there is difference of being. If there were unity of being it would be contradictory that the prâ*n*a although one should sometimes be designated as sense-organ and sometimes not. Consequently the other prâ*n*as are different in being from the chief prâ*n*a.—For this conclusion the following Sûtra states an additional reason.

18. On account of the scriptural statement of difference.

The prâ*n*a is everywhere spoken of as different from speech, &c. The passage, e.g. beginning with 'They said to speech' (B*ri*. Up. I, 3, 2), enumerates speech, &c., which were overwhelmed by the evil of the Asuras, concludes thereupon the section treating of speech, &c., and then specially mentions the mukhya prâ*n*a as overcoming the Asuras, in the paragraph beginning 'Then they said to the breath in the mouth.'—Other passages also referring to that difference may be quoted, so, for instance, 'He made mind, speech, and breath for himself' (B*ri*. Up. I, 5, 3).—For this reason also the other prâ*n*as are different in being from the chief prâ*n*a.—Another reason follows.

19. And on account of the difference of characteristics.

There is moreover a difference of characteristics between the chief prâ*n*a and the other prâ*n*as. When speech &c. are asleep, the chief prâ*n*a alone is awake. The chief prâ*n*a alone is not reached by death, while the other prâ*n*as are. The staying and departing of the chief prâ*n*a—not that of the sense-organs—is the cause of the maintenance and the destruction of the body. The sense-organs, on the other hand, are the cause of the perception of the sense-objects, not the chief prâ*n*a. Thus there are manifold differences distinguishing the prâ*n*a from the senses, and this also shows the latter to be different in being from the prâ*n*a.—To infer from the passage, 'thereupon they all assumed his form,' that the sense-organs are nothing but prâ*n*a is wrong, because there also an examination of the context makes us understand their difference. For there the sense-organs are enumerated first ('Voice held, I shall speak,' &c.); after that it is said that speech, &c. were seized by death in the form of weariness ('Death having become weariness held them back; therefore speech grows weary'); finally prâ*n*a is mentioned separately as not having been overcome by death ('but death did not seize the central breath'), and is asserted to be the best ('he is the best of us'). The assuming of the form of prâ*n*a has therefore, in accordance with the quoted passages, to be understood to mean that the energizing of speech and so on depends on the prâ*n*a, but not that they are identical with it.—Hence it follows that the word 'prâ*n*a' is applied to the sense-organs in a secondary sense. Thus *S*ruti also says, 'Thereupon they all assumed his form, and therefore they are called after him prâ*n*as;' a passage declaring that the word prâ*n*a, which properly refers to the chief prâ*n*a, is secondarily applied to the sense-organs also. Speech and the other sense-organs are therefore different in being from the prâ*n*a.

20. But the fashioning of names and forms belongs to him who renders tripartite, on account of the teaching (of scripture).

In the chapter treating of the Being (sat), subsequently to the account of the creation of fire, water, and food (earth), the following statement is made, 'That divinity thought, let me now enter those three beings with this living Self (*g*îva âtmâ), and let me then evolve names and forms [1];—let me make each of these three tripartite' (*Kh.* Up. VI, 3, 2; 3).—Here the doubt arises whether the agent in that evolution of names and forms is the *g*îva (the living, i.e. the individual Self or soul) or the highest Lord.—The pûrvapakshin maintains the former alternative, on account of the qualification contained in the words 'with this living Self.' The use of ordinary language does, in such phrases as 'Having entered the army of the enemy by means of a spy I count it,' attribute the counting of the army in which the spy is the real agent to the Self of the king who is the causal agent; which attribution is effected by means of the use of the first person, 'I count.' So here the sacred text attributes the evolving of names and forms—in which the *g*îva is the real agent—to the Self of the divinity which is the causal agent; the attribution being effected by means

[1] Literally, with this living Self having entered let me evolve, &c.

of the use of the first person, 'let me evolve.'—Moreover we see in the case of names such as *D*ittha, *D*avittha, &c., and in the case of forms such as jars, dishes and the like that the individual soul only is the evolving agent [1]. Hence the evolution of names and forms is the work of the *g*îva.

To this the Sûtra replies: 'But the fashioning of names and forms belongs to him who renders tripartite.' The particle 'but' discards the pûrvapaksha. Fashioning means evolving. The term 'he who renders tripartite' denotes the highest Lord, his agency being designated as beyond contradiction in the case of the rendering tripartite (of fire, &c.). The entire evolution of names and forms which is seen, e.g. in fire, sun, moon, lightning, or in different plants such as ku*s*a-grass, kâ*s*a-grass, palâ*s*a-trees, or in various living beings such as cattle, deer, men, all this manifold evolution according to species and individuals can surely be the work of the highest Lord only, who fashioned fire, water, and earth.—Why?—On account of the teaching of the sacred text.—For the text says at first 'that divinity,' &c., and then goes on in the first person 'let me evolve;' which implies the statement that the highest Brahman only is the evolving agent.—But we ascertain from the qualification contained in the words 'with this living Self,' that the agent in the evolution is the living Self!—No, we reply. The words 'with this living Self' are connected with the words 'having entered,' in proximity to which they stand; not with the clause 'let me evolve.' If they were connected with the former words, we should have to assume that the first person, which refers to the divinity—viz. 'let me evolve'—is used in a metaphorical sense. And with regard to all the manifold names and forms such as mountains, rivers, oceans, &c., no soul, apart from the Lord, possesses the power of evolution; and if any have such power, it is dependent on the highest Lord. Nor is the so-called 'living Self' absolutely different from the highest Lord, as the spy is from the king; as we see from its being qualified

[1] Names being given and vessels being shaped by a class of *g*îvas, viz. men.

as the living Self, and as its being the *g*îva (i.e. an individual soul apparently differing from the universal Self) is due to the limiting adjuncts only. Hence the evolution of names and forms which is effected by it is in reality effected by the highest Lord. And that the highest Lord is he who evolves the names and forms is a principle acknowledged by all the Upanishads; as we see from such passages as 'He who is called ether is the evolver of all forms and names' (*Kh*. Up. VIII, 14). The evolution of names and forms, therefore, is exclusively the work of the highest Lord, who is also the author of the tripartite arrangement.—The meaning of the text is that the evolution of names and forms was preceded by the tripartition, the evolution of each particular name and form being already explained by the account of the origin of fire, water, and earth. The act of tripartition is expressly described by *S*ruti in the cases of fire, sun, moon, and lightning, 'The red colour of burning fire is the colour of fire, the white colour of fire is the colour of water, the black colour of fire the colour of earth,' &c. In this way there is evolved the distinctive form of fire, and in connexion therewith the distinctive name 'fire,' the name depending on the thing. The same remarks apply to the cases of the sun, the moon, and lightning. The instance (given by the text) of the tripartition of fire implies the statement that the three substances, viz. earth, water, fire, were rendered tripartite in the same manner; as the beginning as well as the concluding clause of the passage equally refers to all three. For the beginning clause says, 'These three beings became each of them tripartite;' and the concluding clause says, 'Whatever they thought looked red they knew was the colour of fire,' &c. &c., up to 'Whatever they thought was altogether unknown they knew was some combination of these three beings.' Having thus described the external tripartition of the three elements the text goes on to describe another tripartition with reference to man, 'those three beings when they reach man become each of them tripartite.' This tripartition in man the teacher sets forth (in the following Sûtra) according to scripture, with a view to the refutation of some foreseen objection.

21. The flesh, &c., originates from earth, according to the scriptural statement; and (so also) in the case of the two other (elements).

From tripartite earth when assimilated by man there are produced as its effects flesh, &c., according to scripture. For the text says, 'Food (earth) when eaten becomes threefold; its grossest portion becomes feces, its middle portion flesh, its subtlest portion mind.' The meaning is that the tripartite earth is eaten in the shape of food such as rice, barley, &c.; that its grossest parts are discharged in the form of feces, that its middle parts nourish the flesh of the body, and its subtlest parts feed the mind. Analogously we have to learn from the text the effects of the two other elements, viz. fire and water; viz. that urine, blood, and breath are the effects of water; bone, marrow, and speech those of fire.—Here now an objection is raised. If all material things are tripartite (i.e. contain parts of the three elements alike)—according to the indifferent statement, 'He made each of these tripartite'—for what reason then has there been made the distinction of names, 'this is fire, this is water, this is earth?' And again, why is it said that among the elements of the human body, flesh, &c., is the effect of the eaten earth only; blood, &c., the effect of the water drunk; bone, &c., the effect of the fire eaten?—To this objection the next Sûtra replies.

22. But on account of their distinctive nature there is a (distinctive) designation of them.

The word 'but' repels the objection raised. By 'distinctive nature' we have to understand preponderance. Although all things are tripartite, yet we observe in different places a preponderance of different elements: heat preponderates in fire, water in all that is liquid, food in earth. This special tripartition aims at rendering possible the distinctions and terms of ordinary life. For if the tripartition resulted in sameness, comparable to that of the three strands of a tripartite rope, we could not distinguish—and speak of as distinguished—the three elements.—Hence, although there is a tripartition, we are enabled 'on account of distinctive nature' to give special designations to the three elements, viz. fire, water, and earth and their products.—The repetition (of 'designation of them') indicates the termination of the adhyâya.

THIRD ADHYÂYA.

FIRST PÂDA.

REVERENCE TO THE HIGHEST SELF!

1. In obtaining a different (body) (the soul) goes enveloped (by subtle parts of the elements), (as appears from) question and explanation.

In the second adhyâya we have refuted the objections raised against the Vedântic view of Brahman on the ground of Smriti and reasoning; we have shown that all other opinions are devoid of foundation, and that the alleged mutual contradictions of Vedic texts do not exist. Further we have demonstrated that the entities different from—but subordinate to—the individual soul (such as prâna, &c.) spring from Brahman.—Now in the third adhyâya we shall discuss the following subjects: the manner in which the soul together with its subordinate adjuncts passes through the samsâra (III, 1); the different states of the soul and the nature of Brahman (III, 2); the separateness or non-separateness of the vidyâs and the question whether the qualities (of Brahman) have to be cumulated or not (III, 3); the accomplishment of man's highest end by means of perfect knowledge (samyagdarsana), the different injunctions as to the means of perfect knowledge and the absence of certain rules as to release which is the fruit (of perfect knowledge[1]) (III, 4). As occasion leads some other matters also will be explained.—The first pâda explains, on the ground of the so-called vidyâ of the five fires (*Kh.* Up. V, 3–10), the different modes of the soul's passing through the samsâra; the reason of that doctrine being (the inculcation of) absence

[1] I.e. the absence of a rule laying down that release consequent on knowledge takes place in the same existence in which the means of reaching perfect knowledge are employed.

of all desire (vairâgya), in accordance with the scriptural remark at the end (of the vidyâ), 'hence let a man take care to himself.'—The soul accompanied by the chief vital air, the sense-organs and the mind, and taking with itself nescience (avidyâ), moral good or ill-desert (karman), and the impressions left by its previous existences[1], leaves its former body and obtains a new body; this is known from the scriptural passage extending from B*ri*. Up. IV, 4, 1 ('Then those prâ*n*as gather around him') up to IV, 4, 4 ('It makes to itself another newer and more beautiful shape'); which passage forms part of a chapter treating of the sa*m*sâra-state. And it moreover follows from the possibility (thus resulting) of the soul enjoying the fruits of good and evil actions.—Here the question arises whether the soul when going to the new body is enveloped or not by subtle parts of the elements constituting the seeds of the body.—It is not so enveloped, the pûrvapakshin says.—Why?—Because scripture, while stating that the soul takes the organs with itself, does not state the same with regard to the elements. For the expression 'those parts of light' (te*g*omâtrâ*h*) which occurs in the passage 'He taking with him those parts of light,' &c., intimates that the organs only are taken (and not the elements), since in the complementary portion of the passage the eye, &c., are spoken of, and not the subtle parts of the elements. The subtle parts of the elements can moreover easily be procured anywhere; for wherever a new body is to be originated they are present, and the soul's taking them with itself would, therefore, be useless. Hence we conclude that the soul when going is not enveloped by them.

To this the teacher replies, 'in obtaining another it goes enveloped.' That means: we must understand that the soul when passing from one body to another is enveloped by the subtle parts of the elements which are the seeds of the new

[1] I read avidyâ with the commentators (Go. Ân., however, mentions the reading 'vidyâ' also); although vidyâ appears preferable. Cp. Max Müller's note 2, p. 175, Upan. II; Deussen, p. 405.—Pûrvapra*gñ*â *g*anmântarîya-sa*m*skâra*h*. Ân. Gi.

body.—How do we know this?—'From the question and the explanation.' The question is, 'Do you know why in the fifth libation water is called man? (V, 3, 3.) The explanation, i.e. answer, is given in the entire passage which, after having explained how the five libations in the form of sraddhâ, Soma, rain, food, seed are offered in the five fires, viz. the heavenly world, Parganya, the earth, man and woman, concludes, 'For this reason is water in the fifth oblation called man.' Hence we understand that the soul goes enveloped by water.—But—an objection will be raised—another scriptural passage declares that like a caterpillar the soul does not abandon the old body before it makes an approach to another body[1]. (Bri. Up. IV, 4, 3, 'And as a caterpillar.')—We reply that what there is compared to the (action of the) caterpillar is (not the non-abandonment of the old body but) merely the lengthening out of the creative effort whose object is the new body to be obtained, which (new body) is presented by the karman of the soul[2]. Hence there is no contradiction.—As the mode of obtaining a new body is thus declared by Sruti, all hypotheses which owe their origin to the mind of man only are to be set aside because they are contradicted by scripture. So e.g. the opinion (of the Sâṅkhyas) that the Self and the organs are both all-pervading[3], and when obtaining a new body only begin to function in it in consequence of the karman; or the opinion (of the Bauddhas) that the Self alone

[1] Evam hi sûkshmadehaparishvakto ramhet yady asya sthûlam sarîram ramhato na bhavet, asti tv asya vartamânasthûlasarîrayogah âdehântaraprâptes trinagalâyukânidarsanena, tasmân nidarsanasrutivirodhân na sûkshmadehaparishvakto ramhatîti. Bhâ.

[2] Pratipattavyah prâptavyo yo dehas tadvishayâyâ bhâvanâyâ utpâdanâyâ dîrghîbhâvamâtram galûkayopamîyate. Bhâ.—Ân. Gi. explains: prâptavyo yo dehas tadvishayabhâvanâyâ devo-ham ityâdikâyâ dîrghîbhâvo vyavahitârthâlambanatvam tâvanmâtram ityâdi.

[3] Karanânâm âhamkârikatvât tasya vyâpitvât teshâm api tadâtmakânâm vyâpitvam. Go. Ân.—The organs are, according to the Sâṅkhya, the immediate effects of the ahamkâra, but why all-pervading on that account?

(without the organs) begins to function in a new body, and that as the body itself, so new sense-organs also are produced in the new abode of fruition[1]; or the opinion (of the Vaiseshikas) that the mind only proceeds to the new abode of fruition[2]; or the opinion (of the Digambara Gainas) that the individual soul only flying away from the old body alights in the new one as a parrot flies from one tree to another.—But—an objection will be raised—from the quoted question and answer it follows that the soul goes enveloped by water only, according to the meaning of the word made use of by scripture, viz. water. How then can the general statement be maintained that the soul goes enveloped by subtle parts of all elements?—To this doubt the next Sûtra replies.

2. But on account of (water) consisting of three (elements) (the soul is enveloped not by water merely; the latter alone is, however, mentioned) on account of preponderance.

The word 'but' disposes of the objection raised.—Water consists of three elements, as we know from the scriptural statement regarding tripartition. If, therefore, water is admitted to originate (the new body) the other two elements also have necessarily to be admitted (as taking part in the origination). The body moreover consists of three elements, as the effects of the three, i.e. fire, water, and earth, are observed in it, and further as it contains three materials, viz. wind bile, and phlegm[3]. Being such it cannot originate from mere water, the other elements being left aside. Hence the term water made use of in the scriptural question and answer refers to the fact of water preponderating,

---

[1] Âtmâ khalv âlayagñânasamtânas tasya vrittayah sabdâdigñânâni tallâbhah sarîrântare bhavati, kevalasabdas tu karanasâhityam âtmano vârayati. Go. Ân.

[2] Kevalam karanair âtmanâ ka rahitam iti yâvat, karanâni nûtanany eva tatrârabhyante âtmâ tu vibhutvâd akriyo*pi tatra vrittimâtram âpnoti. Ân. Gi.

[3] The last of which only is of prevailingly watery character.

not to its being the only element. As a matter of fact we see that in all animated bodies liquid substances such as juices, blood, and the like preponderate.—But we likewise observe in bodies a large amount of earthy matter!—True, but the amount of water is larger than that of any other matter. Moreover, liquid matter prevails in that which is the seed of the body. Further, we know that works (karman) constitute the efficient cause for the origination of a new body, and (sacrificial) works such as the agnihotra, &c., consist in the offering of liquid substances such as Soma, butter, milk and the like. Thereby also the preponderance of water is established. And on account of that preponderance the word 'water' implies the subtle parts of all the elements which constitute the seed of the body.

3. And on account of the going of the prâ*n*as.

Scripture states that, when a new body is obtained, the prâ*n*as also go (from the old body to the new one). Cp. 'When he thus departs the (chief) prâ*n*a departs after him, and when the prâ*n*a thus departs all the other prâ*n*as depart after it' (B*ri*. Up. IV, 4, 2), and similar passages. Now this going of the prâ*n*as is not possible without a base; hence we infer that water also—mixed with parts of the other elements—goes (from the old body to the new one), serving the purpose of supplying a base for the moving prâ*n*as. For the prâ*n*as cannot, without such a base, either move or abide anywhere; as we observe in living beings.

4. If it be said (that the prâ*n*as do not go) on account of the scriptural statement as to entering into Agni, &c., we deny this on account of the metaphorical nature (of those statements).

Well, the pûrvapakshin resumes, we deny that at the time when a new body is obtained the prâ*n*as go with the soul, because scripture speaks of their going to Agni, &c. For that at the time of death speech and the other prâ*n*as go to Agni and the other gods the following passage expressly declares: 'When the speech of the dead person enters into the fire, breath into the air,' &c. (B*ri*. Up. III, 2, 13).—To this we reply that the objection is of no force on account of the metaphorical character of those statements. The entering of speech, &c., into Agni is metaphorical, because we observe no such entering in the case of the hairs of the head and body. For although the text says that 'the hairs of the body enter into the shrubs and the hairs of the head into the trees;' still we cannot understand this to mean that the hairs actually fly away from the body and enter into trees and shrubs. On the other hand, the soul could not go at all if we denied to it the limiting adjunct formed by the prâ*n*as, and without the latter it could not, in the new body, enter into the state of fruition. Besides, other passages distinctly declare that the prâ*n*as go with the soul.—From all this we conclude that the passage about speech, &c. entering into Agni, metaphorically expresses that Agni and the other divinities who act as guides of the prâ*n*as and co-operate with them stop their co-operation at the time of death.

5. If an objection be raised on the ground of (water) not being mentioned in the first fire, we refute it by remarking that just it (viz. water) (is meant), on the ground of fitness.

Well, the pûrvapakshin resumes, but how can it be ascertained that 'in the fifth oblation water is called man,' considering that water is not mentioned by scripture with reference to the first fire (altar)? For the text enumerates five fires—the first of which is the heavenly world—as the abodes of the five oblations. With reference to the first of those fires—introduced by the words 'The fire is that world, O Gautama,' it is stated that *s*raddhâ (faith) is the material constituting the oblation ('on that altar the devas offer *s*raddhâ'); while nothing is said about water being the offered material. If, with reference to the four following fires, viz. Par*g*anya, &c., water is assumed to constitute the offering, we have no objection because in the substances stated there as forming the oblations, viz. Soma, and so on, water may preponderate. But to set aside, in the case of the first fire, *s*raddhâ (i.e. faith) which is directly mentioned in the text, and to substitute in its place the assumption of water, about which the text says nothing, is an arbitrary proceeding. In reality *s*raddhâ must be explained, in conformity with its ordinary meaning, as a kind of mental state, viz. faith. Hence it is objectionable to maintain that water, in the fifth oblation, becomes man.

To this view of the pûrvapakshin we demur, because, in the case of the first fire, the word *s*raddhâ is to be taken in the sense of 'water.'—On what ground?—On the ground of fitness. For on that explanation only beginning, middle, and end of the passage harmonise so that the syntactical unity of the whole remains undisturbed. On the other explanation (i.e. *s*raddhâ being taken in the sense of 'faith'), if the question were asked how water, in the fifth oblation, can be called man, and if, in way of reply, the text could point only to faith, i.e. something which is not water, as constituting the material of the oblation; then question and answer would not agree, and so the unity of the whole passage would be destroyed. The text, moreover, by concluding 'For this reason is water in the fifth oblation called man,' indicates the same interpretation[1].—Further, the text points out, as effects of *s*raddhâ, substances in which water in its gross form preponderates, viz. Soma, rain, &c. And this again furnishes a reason for interpreting *s*raddhâ as water, because the effect generally is cognate in nature to the cause. Nor again can the mental conception called faith be taken out from the mind or soul, whose attribute it is, and be employed as an offering, as the heart can be cut out of the sacrificial animal. For this reason also the word *s*raddhâ must be taken to mean 'water.' Water can, moreover, be fitly called by that name, on the ground of Vedic usage, cp. '*s*raddhâ indeed is water' (Taitt. Sa*m*h. I, 6, 8, 1). Moreover, water when forming the seed of the body enters into the state of thinness, subtilty, and herein again resembles faith, so that its being called *s*raddhâ

[1] Upasa*m*hârâlo*k*anâyâm api *s*raddhâ*s*abdatvam apâm evety âha tv iti. Ân. Gi.

is analogous to the case of a man who is as valiant as a lion being himself called a lion.—Again, the word *s*raddhâ may fitly be applied to water, because water is intimately connected with religious works (sacrifices, &c.) which depend on faith; just as the word 'platform' is applied to men (standing on the platform). And finally the waters may fitly be called *s*raddhâ, on account of their being the cause of faith, according to the scriptural passage, 'Water indeed produces faith in him for holy works[1].'

6. (Should it be said that the souls are not enveloped by water) on account of this not being stated by scripture, we refute the objection on the ground of those who perform ish*t*is, &c., being understood.

Well, let it be granted that, on account of question and answer, water, passing through the forms of *s*raddhâ, &c., may in the fifth oblation obtain the shape of man. But still we cannot allow that the souls when moving from one body into another are enveloped by water. For this is not directly stated by scripture, there being in the whole passage no word referring to the souls, while there are words referring to water. Hence the assertion that the soul goes enveloped by water is unfounded.—This objection is invalid, we reply, 'on account of those who perform ish*t*is, &c., being understood.' For in the passage beginning 'But they who living in a village practise sacrifices, works of public utility and alms, they go to the smoke' (V, 3, 10), it is said that those who perform ish*t*is reach, on the road of the fathers leading through smoke, &c., the moon, 'From ether they go to the moon; that is Soma, the king.' Now these same persons are meant in the passage about the five fires also, as we conclude from the equality of scriptural statement in the passage, 'In that fire the devas offer

[1] Âpo heti, asmai pu*m*se*s*dhikâri*n*e sa*m*namante *g*anayanti dar*s*anamâtre*n*a snânâdipu*n*yakarmasiddhyartha*m* *s*raddhâm ity artha*h*. Ân. Gi.

*s*raddhâ. From that oblation rises Soma the king[1].' To those[2] (persons who have performed ish*t*is, &c.) water is supplied in the shape of the materials employed to perform the agnihotra, the dar*s*apûr*n*amâsa and other sacrifices, viz. sour milk, milk, &c., which substances, as consisting mostly of water, may directly be considered as water. Of these, when offered in the âhavanîya, the subtle parts assume the form of an apûrva resulting from the oblation[3], and attach themselves to the performer of the sacrifice. Then (when the sacrificer dies) the priests offer his body, with the funeral ceremonies[4], into the crematory fire, with the mantra, '(may) he (go) to the heavenly world, svâhâ.' Then the water forming the oblation—which was connected with deeds resulting from faith[5]—having assumed the form of an apûrva envelops the souls of those who had performed the sacrifices, and leads them up to the heavenly world to receive their reward.—In accordance with the preceding interpretation scripture says in the agnihotra chapter also—in the complementary passage constituting the reply to the six questions—that the two agnihotra-oblations go up to the other world in order to originate the fruit (of the work of the sacrificer), 'Those two oblations when offered go up, &c.' (*S*at. Br. XI, 6, 2, 6).—Hence we conclude that the

[1] Both passages speak of something reaching, i.e. becoming the moon. Now, as that something is, in the passage about the road of the fathers, the *g*îvas of those who have performed ish*t*is, &c., we conclude that by the *s*raddhâ also, from which in the other passage the moon is said to rise, those *g*îvas are meant, or, properly speaking, the subtle body of water which envelops those *g*îvas.—Dhûmâdivâkye pa*ñk*âgnivâkye *k*a somarâ*g*atvaprâptis*r*ava*n*âvi*s*eshâd ish*t*âdikâri*n*a*h* *s*raddhâ*s*abditâdbhir vesh*t*/*h*itâ dyuloka*m* yântîti bhâtîty artha*h*. Ân. Gi.

[2] Ân. Gi. introduces this clause by: nanu mahad iha *s*rutyor vailakshanyam, *s*raddhâ*s*abditânâm apâ*m* kva*k*id dyuloke homa*h* *s*ruta*h* kva*k*id ish*t*âdikâri*n*âm dhûmâdikrame*n*âkâ*s*aprâptir na *k*a teshâm âpa*h* santi yena tadvesh*t*/*h*itânâ*m* gatis tatrâha*'* veshâ*m* *k*eti.

[3] I read, with a MS. of Ân. Gi., âhutyapûrvarûpâ*h*.

[4] The so-called antyesh*t*i.

[5] And is on that account properly called *s*raddhâ.

souls, when going to the enjoyment of the fruits of their works, are enveloped by the water of which the oblations consist[1].

But how can it be maintained that those who perform sacrifices, &c., go to the enjoyment of the fruit of their works, considering that scripture declares them when having reached the moon—by the path leading through smoke, &c.—to become food, 'That is Soma the king; that is the food of the gods; the gods do eat it' (*Kh*. Up. V, 10, 4); and the corresponding passage, 'Having reached the moon they become food, and then the Devas feed on them there as sacrificers feed on Soma as it increases and decreases' (B*ri*. Up. VI, 2, 16)? If, in accordance with these passages, they are eaten by the gods as by tigers, &c., it is not possible that they should enjoy the fruit of their deeds.—To this the following Sûtra replies.

7. Or (the souls' being the food of the gods is) metaphorical, on account of their not knowing the Self. For thus (scripture) declares.

The word 'or' is meant to set aside the started objection. The souls' being food has to be understood in a metaphorical, not a literal, sense, as otherwise all scriptural statements of claims (adhikâra)—such as 'He who is desirous of the heavenly world is to sacrifice'—would be contradicted. If

[1] *S*aṅkara's attempts to render plausible the interpretation of *s*raddhâ by 'water,' and to base thereon the doctrine of the souls when going to a new body being enveloped by a subtle involucrum of water (and the other elements contained therein) are, of course, altogether artificial. I do not, however, see that he can be taxed with inconsistency (as he is by Deussen, p. 408). *S*raddhâ is to him in the first place the gross water which constitutes the chief material employed in the sacrifices; in the second place the apûrva which results from the sacrifice, and which is imagined to consist of the subtle parts of the water whose gross parts have been consumed by the sacrificial fire. These subtle parts attach themselves to the soul, accompany it as an involucrum when it goes to another world, and form the base of any new body which the soul may have to assume in accordance with its previous deeds.

the performers of sacrifices, &c., did not, in the sphere of the moon, enjoy the fruits of their works, why should they undertake works such as sacrifices, which are to him who performs them the cause of great trouble? We see, moreover, that the word 'food,' as denoting in general whatever is the cause of enjoyment, is metaphorically used of that also which is not food (in the narrower sense), as, for instance, in such phrases as 'the Vai*s*yas are the food of kings, the animals are the food of the Vai*s*yas.' Hence what is meant there by the term 'eating' is the rejoicing of the gods with the performers of sacrifices, &c., who stand in a subordinate (instrumental) relation to that rejoicing—a rejoicing analogous to that of an ordinary man with beloved persons such as wife, children, friends, and so on—not actual eating like the chewing and swallowing of sweetmeats. For that the gods eat in the ordinary way a scriptural passage expressly denies (*Kh*. Up. III, 6, 1), 'The gods do not eat or drink; by seeing the nectar they are satisfied.' At the same time the performers of sacrifices, although standing in a subordinate relation to the gods, may themselves be in a state of enjoyment, like servants who (although subordinate to the king) themselves live on the king.—That the performers of sacrifices are objects of enjoyment for the gods follows, moreover, from their quality of not knowing the Self. For that those who do not know the Self are objects of enjoyment for the gods the following scriptural passage shows, 'Now, if a man worships another deity, thinking the deity is one and he is another, he does not know. He is like a beast for the Devas' (B*ri*. Up. I, 4, 10). That means: he, in this life, propitiating the gods by means of oblations and other works, serves them like a beast, and does so in the other world also, depending on them like a beast and enjoying the fruits of his works as assigned by them.—The latter part of the Sûtra can be explained in another manner also[1]. Those who do not know the Self are those who perform works only, such as sacrifices, &c.,

---

[1] Anâtma*s*abda*s*ruter mukhyârthatvânurodhena sûtrâ*ms*asyârtham uktvâ prakara*n*ânurodhenârthântaram âha. Ân. Gi.

and do not join knowledge to works. We then take the expression, 'the knowledge of the Self,' as indirectly denoting the knowledge of the five fires; an explanation which rests on the general subject-matter. And on account of the performers of sacrifices being destitute of the knowledge of the five fires the circumstance of their serving as food is brought forward as a mere gu*n*avâda[1] for the purpose of glorifying the knowledge of the five fires. For the latter is what the text aims at enjoining, as we infer from the general purport of the passage.—'For thus' another scriptural passage 'declares,' viz. that enjoyment (on the part of the *g*îva) takes place in the sphere of the moon, 'Having enjoyed greatness in the Soma world he returns again' (Pr. Up. V, 4). Another scriptural passage also declares that the performers of sacrifices dwelling together with the gods obtain enjoyment, 'A hundred blessings of the fathers who have conquered this world make one blessing of the work-gods, who obtain their godhead by work' (B*ri*. Up. IV, 3, 33).—As thus the statement about the performers of sacrifices becoming food is metaphorical only, we understand that it is their souls which go, and hence there is no longer any objection to the doctrine that they go enveloped by water.

8. On the passing away of the works (the soul redescends) with a remainder, according to scripture and Sm*ri*ti, as it went (i.e. passing through the same stations) and not thus (i.e. in the inverse order).

Scripture states that the souls of those who perform sacrifices, and the like, rise on the road leading through smoke, and so on, to the sphere of the moon, and when they have done with the enjoyment (of the fruits of their works) again descend, 'Having dwelt there, yâvatsampâtam[2], they return again that way as they came,' &c., up to 'Those whose conduct has been good obtain some good birth, the

---

[1] See part i, p. 221.

[2] About which term see further on.

birth of a Brâhma*n*a, &c.—Those whose conduct has been evil obtain the birth of a dog, &c.' (*Kh*. Up. V, 10, 5-7). Here it must be considered whether the souls, after having enjoyed the fruits of all their works, descend without a remainder (anu*s*aya, of their works), or with such a remainder (of unrequited works).—The pûrvapakshin says: without such a remainder.—Why? On account of the specification 'yâvat sampâtam.' The word sampâta here denotes the aggregate of works (karmâ*s*aya)[1], which is so called because by it the souls pass from this world to that world for the purpose of enjoying the fruits of the works. So that the entire clause 'Having dwelt there as far as the aggregate of the works extends' indicates their works being completely requited there. The same thing is indicated by another scriptural passage, 'But when in their case that (i.e. the effect of their works) ceases' (B*ri*. Up. VI, 2, 16).—Well, but why should we not assume that these passages (do not mean that all works are requited there but) only indicate that the soul enjoys in the other world so long as there are works to be enjoyed there?—It is impossible to assume this, because elsewhere a reference is made to the totality of works. For the passage, B*ri*. Up. IV, 4, 6, 'Having obtained the end of whatever deed he does here on earth, he again returns from that world to this world to action,' intimates, by means of the comprehensive term 'whatever,' that all works done here are exhausted there.—Moreover, death has the power of manifesting those works whose fruit has not yet begun[2]; the manifestation of those works not being possible previously to death because then they are obstructed by those works whose fruits have already begun. Now death must manifest alike all works whose fruits had not begun previously, because the cause being the same the effects cannot be different. Analogously a lamp which is placed at the same distance from a jar and a piece of cloth

[1] The Comm. on *Kh*. Up. V, 10, 5, explains it by 'sampatanti yeneti sampâta*h* karma*n*a*h* kshaya*h*, yâvat sampâtam yâvat karma*n*a*h* kshaya*h*.'

[2] Abhivyaktis *k*a karma*n*âm phaladânâyonmukhatvam. Ân. Gi.

illuminates the latter as well as the former.—Hence it follows that the souls descend without a remainder of unrequited works.

To this we reply as follows: 'On the passing away of the works with a remainder.' That means: when the aggregate of works with which the souls had risen to the moon for the purpose of the enjoyment of their fruits is, by such enjoyment, exhausted, then the body, consisting of water, which had originated in the moon for the purpose of such enjoyment, is dissolved by contact with the fire of the grief springing from the observation that the enjoyment comes to an end; just as snow and hail are melted by contact with the rays of the sun, or the hardness of ghee by contact with the heat of fire. Then, at the passing away of the works, i.e. when the works performed, such as sacrifices, &c., are, by the enjoyment of their fruits, exhausted, the souls descend with a remainder yet left.—But on what grounds is that remainder assumed?—On the ground of what is seen (*S*ruti) and Sm*ri*ti. For scripture declares manifestly that the souls descend joined with such a remainder, 'Those whose conduct (*k*ara*n*a) has been good will quickly attain some good birth, the birth of a Brâhma*n*a, or a Kshattriya, or a Vai*s*ya. But those whose conduct has been evil will quickly attain an evil birth, the birth of a dog, or a hog, or a *K*â*nd*âla.' That the word *k*ara*n*a here means the remainder (of the works) will be shown later on. Moreover, the different degrees of enjoyment which are implied in the difference of birth on the part of the living beings point, as they cannot be accidental, to the existence of such a remainder of works. For we know from scripture that good fortune as well as misfortune is caused by good and evil works. Sm*ri*ti also teaches that the members of the different castes and â*s*ramas do, in accordance with their works, at first enjoy the fruit of their works and then enter into new existences, in which they are distinguished from each other by locality, caste, family, shape, length of life, knowledge, conduct, property, pleasure, and intelligence, which doctrine implies that they descend with a remainder of their works.—Of what kind then is that so-called remainder?—Some say that thereby we have to understand a remainder of the works which had been performed (in the previous existence) for the sake of the heavenly world, and whose fruits have (for the greater part) been enjoyed. That remainder might then be compared to the remainder of oil which sticks to the inside of a vessel previously filled with oil even after it has been emptied.—But you have no right to assume a remainder in the case of works, the fruits of which have been enjoyed already, since the ad*ri*sh*t*a (which springs from works) is opposed to the works (so as to destroy them completely [1]).—This objection, we reply, is not valid, as we do not maintain that the works are completely requited (previously to the new existence).—But the souls do ascend to the sphere of the moon for the express purpose of finding there a complete requital of their works! —True; but when only a little of the effects of their works is left, they can no longer stay there. For as some courtier who has joined the king's court with all the requisites which the king's service demands is unable to remain at court any longer, when in consequence of his long stay most of his things are worn out, so that he is perhaps left with a pair of shoes and an umbrella only; so the soul, when possessing only a small particle of the effects of its works, can no longer remain in the sphere of the moon.—But all this reasoning is in fact altogether unfounded [2]. For it has already been stated that, on account of (the ad*ri*sh*t*a) being opposed to the work, the continued existence of a remainder cannot be admitted in the case of works which had been performed with a view to the heavenly world, and which have been requited in the moon.—But has it not also been said above that not all the work whose fruit the heavenly world is meets with requital there?—Yes, but that statement is not defensible. For works which are performed for

[1] Bhâ*nd*ânusâri*nah* snehasyâvirodhâd yukta*h s*esha*h*, karma tu phalodayavirodhitvât phala*m k*eg *g*âta*m* nash*t*am eveti na tasya *s*eshasiddhir iti *s*ankate nanv iti. Ân. Gi.

[2] Ivakâro madhuroktyâ prayukto vastutas tv evakâro vivakshita*h*. Ân. Gi.

the purpose of obtaining the heavenly world produce their entire heavenly fruit for the soul only as long as it stays in heaven, and if we take our stand on scripture we have no right to assume that they produce even a particle of fruit for the souls after those have again descended from heaven. That some part of the oil continues to remain in the vessel is unobjectionable because we see it, and we likewise see that some part of the courtier's equipment continues to remain with him; but that some part of those works which led the soul to heaven continues to exist, that we neither see nor are able to surmise, because it would contradict the texts declaring that the heavenly world (alone) is the fruit of the works.—That of works whose fruit is heaven, such as sacrifices and the like, no remainder continues to exist, we must necessarily acknowledge for the following reason also. If some part of those good works, such as sacrifices, &c., on account of which the agents enjoyed the heavenly world, were surmised to continue in existence as a remainder, that remainder would in all cases be itself a good one, would never be of a contrary nature. But then our supposition would be in conflict with the scriptural passage which distinguishes remainders of a different kind, viz. 'Those whose conduct has been good;—those whose conduct has been evil,' &c. Hence after the fruits of that set of works which is requited in the other world have been (completely) enjoyed, the remaining other set of works whose fruits are to be enjoyed in this world constitutes the so-called anu*s*aya with which the souls re-descend.—It was said above that we must assume the souls to descend without any such remainder, after having reached, by the enjoyment of the fruits, the end of all the works done here below, on account of the comprehensive statement implied in the expression 'whatever.' But that assertion cannot be upheld as the existence of such a remainder has been proved. Hence we have to understand that the souls re-descend after having exhausted, by the enjoyment of its fruits, only that entire part of the works done here below whose fruit belongs to the other world and is begun to be enjoyed there.—The proof given by us of the existence of the remainder refutes at the same time the other assertion made above, viz. that death manifests equally all works the enjoyment of whose fruits was not begun here below, and that on that account we are not entitled to draw a line between works whose fruits begin in the other world and works whose fruits begin in this world only (i.e. in a new existence on earth).—We, moreover, have to ask for what reason it is maintained that death manifests (i.e. lays open and makes ready for requital) those works whose fruits have not begun here below. The answer will be that in this life the operation of certain works cannot begin because it is obstructed by other works whose fruits already begin here below, that, however, that operation does begin as soon as, at the moment of death, the obstruction ceases. Well, then, if previously to death those actions whose fruits have already begun prevent other actions from beginning their operation, at the time of death also certain works of less force will be obstructed in their operation by other works of greater force, it being impossible that the fruits of works of opposite tendency should begin at the same time. For it is impossible to maintain that different deeds whose fruits must be experienced in different existences should, merely because they have this in common that their fruits have not begun (previously to death), become manifest on the occasion of one and the same death, and originate one new existence only; against this militates the fact of the definite fruits (attached to each particular work) being of contrary natures[1]. Nor, on the other hand, can we maintain that at the time of death some works manifest themselves while others are altogether extinguished; for that would contradict the fact that absolutely all works have their fruits. No work in fact can be extinguished except by means of expiatory actions, &c.[2] Sm*ri*ti also declares that works whose operation is ob-

[1] On which account they cannot be experienced in one and the same existence.

[2] Works are extinguished either by expiatory ceremonies or by the knowledge of Brahman or by the full fruition of their consequences.

structed by other works leading to fruits of a contrary nature last for a long time, 'Sometimes a good deed persists immovable as it were, the doer meanwhile remaining immerged in the sa*m*sâra, until at last he is released from pain.'

Moreover, if all unrequited works becoming manifest on the occasion of one and the same death were to begin one new existence only, the consequence would be that those who are born again in the heavenly world, or in hell, or as animals, could, as not entitled thereto, perform no religious works, and being thus excluded from all chance of acquiring religious merit and demerit could not enter on any new forms of existence, as all reason for the latter would be absent[1]. And that would further contradict Sm*ri*ti, which declares that some single actions, such as the murder of a Brâhma*n*a, are the causes of more than one new existence. Nor can we assume, for the knowledge of the particular results springing from religious merit and demerit, any other cause than the sacred texts[2]. Nor, again, does death manifest (bring about the requital of) those works whose fruit is observed to be enjoyed already here below, as, for instance, the kârîresh*t*i, &c.[3] How then can we allow the assumption that death manifests all actions? The instance of the lamp (made use of by the pûrvapakshin) is already refuted by our having shown the relative strength of actions[4]. Or else we may look on the matter as analogous to the manifestation (by a lamp) of bigger and smaller objects. For as a lamp, although equally distant from a big and a very small thing, may manifest the former only

[1] And in consequence of this they could never obtain final release.

[2] We have the sacred texts only to teach us what the effects of particular good or evil actions may be.

[3] The kârîresh*t*i is a sacrifice offered by those who are desirous of rain.

[4] I.e. by our having shown that death does not equally manifest all works, but that, after death has taken place, the stronger works bring about their requital while the operation of the weaker ones is retarded thereby.

and not the latter, so death provokes the operation of the stronger works only, not of the weaker ones, although an equal opportunity presents itself for both sets of works as hitherto unrequited.—Hence the doctrine that all works are manifested by death cannot be maintained, as it is contradicted by *S*ruti, Sm*ri*ti, and reason alike. That the existence of a remainder of works should stand in the way of final release is a misplaced fear, as we know from *S*ruti that all works whatever are destroyed by perfect knowledge. It therefore is a settled conclusion that the souls re-descend with a remainder of works. They descend 'as they came' (mounted up); 'not thus,' i.e. in inverted order. We conclude that they descend 'as they came' from the fact of ether and smoke, which the text includes in the road of the fathers, being mentioned in the description of the descent also, and from the expression 'as they came.' That they follow the inverted order we conclude from night, &c., not being mentioned, and from the cloud, &c., being added.

9. Should it be objected that on account of conduct (the assumption of a remainder is not needed), we deny this because (the scriptural expression 'conduct') is meant to connote (the remainder); so Kârsh*n*â*g*ini thinks.

But—an objection may be raised—the scriptural passage, which has been quoted for the purpose of proving that the existence of a remainder of works ('those whose conduct has been good,' &c.), declares that the quality of the new birth depends on *k*ara*n*a, not on anu*s*aya. Now *k*ara*n*a and anu*s*aya are different things; for *k*ara*n*a is the same as *k*aritra, â*k*âra, *s*îla, all of which mean conduct[1], while anu*s*aya denotes work remaining from requited work. Scripture also speaks of actions and conduct as different things, 'According as he acts and according as he conducts himself so will he be' (B*ri*. Up. IV, 4, 5); and 'Whatever

[1] *S*îla also means here 'conduct' only, as we see from its being co-ordinated with *k*ara*n*a, *k*aritra, &c.; not character.

works are blameless those should be regarded, not others; whatever our good conduct was that should be observed by thee' (Taitt. Up. I, 11, 2). From the passage which proclaims the dependence of the quality of birth on conduct the existence of an unrequited remainder of works cannot therefore be proved.—This objection is without force, we reply, because the scriptural term 'conduct' is meant to connote the remainder of the works. This is the opinion of the teacher Kârsh*n*â*g*ini.

10. If it be said that purposelessness (of conduct would result therefrom), we deny this on account of the dependence (of work) on that (conduct).

That may be; but for what reason should we abandon that meaning which the term '*k*ara*n*a' directly conveys, viz. the meaning 'conduct,' and accept the merely connotative meaning 'remainder of the works?' Conduct, which the text directly mentions, may be supposed to have for its fruit either a good or an evil birth, according as it is enjoined or prohibited, good or evil. Some fruit will have to be allowed to it in any case; for otherwise it would follow that it is purposeless.—This objection is without force 'on account of the dependence on it.' Such works as sacrifices, and the like, depend on conduct in so far as somebody whose conduct is not good is not entitled to perform them. This we know from Sm*ri*ti-passages, such as the following, 'Him who is devoid of good conduct the Vedas do not purify.'—And also if conduct is considered as subservient to man [1] it will not be purposeless. For when the aggregate of works such as sacrifices, &c., begins to originate its fruit, the conduct which has reference to the sacrifice will originate there (i.e. in the fruit) some addition.

[1] I.e. as something which produces in man a sa*m*skâra analogous to that produced by other preparatory or purificatory rites such as bathing, &c.—In the preceding sentences conduct had been spoken of not as purushârtha but as karmâṅga. In that case it produces no separate result; while if considered as purushârtha it has a special result of its own.

And it is known from *S*ruti as well as Sm*ri*ti that work effects everything[1]. It is, therefore, the opinion of Kârsh*nâg*ini that the remainder of works only—which is connoted by the term 'conduct'—is the cause of the souls entering on new births. For as work may be the cause of new births, it is not proper to assume that conduct is the cause. If a man is able to run away by means of his feet he will surely not creep on his knees.

11. But (*k*ara*n*a means) nothing but good and evil works; thus Bâdari opines.

The teacher Bâdari, however, thinks that the word '*k*ara*n*a' denotes nothing else but good works and evil works. It means the same as anush*th*âna (performance) or karman (work). For we see that the root *k*ar (to walk, to conduct oneself) is used in the general sense of acting. Of a man who performs holy works such as sacrifices, &c., people say in ordinary language, 'that excellent man walks in righteousness.' The word â*k*âra also denotes only a kind of religious duty. That works and *k*ara*n*a (conduct) are sometimes spoken of as different things is analogous to the distinction sometimes made between Brâhma*n*as and Parivrâ*g*akas[2]. We, therefore, decide that by men of good *k*ara*n*a are meant those whose works are worthy of praise, by men of evil *k*ara*n*a those whose works are worthy of blame.

12. Of those also who do not perform sacrifices (the ascent to the moon) is stated by scripture.

It has been said that those who perform sacrifices, &c., go to the moon. The question now arises whether those also who do not perform sacrifices go to the moon or not.—The pûrvapakshin maintains that it cannot be asserted that men belonging to the former class only go to the moon,

[1] A clause added to guard against the assumption—which might be based on the preceding remarks—that conduct is, after all, the cause of the quality of the new birth.

[2] Although the latter are a mere sub-class of the former.

because scripture speaks of the moon as being resorted to by those also who have not performed sacrifices. For the Kâushîtakins make the following general statement, 'All who depart from this world go to the moon' (Kau. Up. I, 2). Moreover, the origination of a new body in the case of those who are born again is not possible without their having (previously) reached the moon, on account of the precise definition of number contained in the statement, 'In the fifth oblation' (*Kh.* Up. V, 9, 1)[1]. Hence all men must be supposed to resort to the moon. If it be objected that it does not appear proper that those who perform sacrifices and those who do not should go to the same place, we reply that there is no real objection, because those who do not perform sacrifices do not enjoy anything in the moon.

13. But of the others, after having enjoyed the fruits of their actions in Sa*m*yamana, ascent and descent take place; as such a course is declared (by scripture).

'But' discards the pûrvapaksha. It is not true that all men go to the moon. For the ascent to the moon is for the purpose of enjoyment only; it is neither without a special purpose nor for the mere purpose of subsequent re-descent. Just as a man climbs on a tree for the purpose of breaking fruit or blossoms, not either without any aim or for the mere purpose of coming down again. Now it has been admitted already that for those who do not offer sacrifices there is not any enjoyment in the moon; hence those only who perform sacrifices rise to the moon, not any other persons. The latter descend to Sa*m*yamana, the abode of Yama, suffer there the torments of Yama corresponding to their evil deeds, and then again re-ascend to this world. Such is their ascent and descent; as we maintain on the ground of such a course being declared by scripture. For a scriptural passage embodying Yama's own words declares that those who die without having offered sacrifices fall into Yama's

[1] Which statement presupposes four other oblations, the first of which is the one from which 'Soma the king rises.'

power. 'The other world never rises before the eyes of the careless child deluded by the delusion of wealth. This is the world, he thinks, there is no other; thus he falls again and again under my sway' (Ka. Up. I, 2, 6). Scripture contains many other passages likewise leading us to infer that men fall into Yama's power; cp. e.g. 'Yama, the gathering-place of men' (*Ri*. Sa*m*h. X, 14, 1).

14. The Sm*ri*tis also declare this.

Moreover, authorities like Manu, Vyâsa, &c., declare that in the city Sa*m*yamana evil works are requited under Yama's rule; cp. the legend of Nâ*k*iketa and others.

15. Moreover there are seven (hells).

Moreover, the purâ*n*a-writers record that there are seven hells, Raurava, &c., by name, which serve as abodes of enjoyment of the fruits of evil deeds. As those who do not sacrifice, &c. go there, how should they reach the moon?—But, an objection is raised, the assertion that evil doers suffer punishments allotted by Yama is contradicted by the circumstance that Sm*ri*ti mentions different other beings, such as *K*itragupta, &c., who act as superintendents in Raurava and the other hells.—This objection the next Sûtra refutes.

16. On account of his activity there also no contradiction exists.

There is no contradiction, as the same Yama is admitted to act as chief ruler in those seven hells. Of *K*itragupta and others Sm*ri*ti merely speaks as superintendents employed by Yama.

17. But on (the two roads) of knowledge and works, those two being under discussion.

In that place of the knowledge of the five fires, where the answer is expected to the question, 'Do you know why that world never becomes full?' the text runs as follows: 'On neither of these two ways are those small creatures continually returning, of whom it may be said, Live and die. Theirs is a third place. Therefore that world never becomes full.'

By the two ways mentioned in this passage we have to understand knowledge and works.—Why?—On account of their being the subjects under discussion. That means: knowledge and works are under discussion as the means for entering on the road of the gods and the road of the fathers. The clause, 'those who know this,' proclaims knowledge to be the means whereby to obtain the road of the gods; the clause, 'sacrifices, works of public utility, and alms,' proclaims works to be that by which we obtain the road of the fathers. Under the heading of these two paths there stands the subsequent passage, 'on neither of these two ways, &c.' To explain. Those who are neither entitled, through knowledge, to follow the road of the gods, nor, by works, to follow the road of the fathers, for those there is a third path on which they repeatedly return to the existence of small animals. For this reason also those who do not perform sacrifices, &c. do not reach the moon.—But why should they not first mount to the sphere of the moon and thence descending enter on the existence of small animals? —No, that would imply entire purposelessness of their mounting.—Moreover, if all men when dying would reach the sphere of the moon, that world would be filled by the departed, and from that would result an answer contrary to the question (viz. 'why does not that world become full?'). For an answer is expected showing that that world does not become full.—Nor can we admit the explanation that the other world possibly does not become full because re-descent is admitted; since this is not stated by scripture. For it is true, indeed, that the not becoming full might be explained from their re-descending; but scripture actually explains it from the existence of a third place, 'Theirs is a third place; therefore that world never becomes full.' Hence the fact of the other world not becoming full must be explained from their not-ascending only. For, otherwise, the descent equally taking place in the case of those who do perform sacrifices, &c., it would follow that the statement of a third place is devoid of purpose.—The word 'but' (in the Sûtra) is meant to preclude the idea—arising from the passage of another *s*âkhâ (i.e. the Kaush. Up.)

—that all departed go to the moon. Under the circumstances the word 'all' which occurs in that passage has to be taken as referring only to those qualified, so that the sense is 'all those who depart from this world properly qualified go to the moon.'—The next Sûtra is directed against the averment that all must go to the moon for the purpose of obtaining a new body, in accordance with the definite statement of number ('in the fifth oblation &c.').

18. Not in (the case of) the third place, as it is thus perceived.

With regard to the third place, the rule of the oblations being five in number need not be attended to for the purpose of obtaining a new body.—Why?—On account of it being perceived thus. That means: because it is seen that the third place is reached in the manner described without any reference to the oblations being limited to the number five, 'Live and die. That is the third place.'—Moreover, in the passage, 'In the fifth oblation water is called man,' the number of the oblations is stated to be the cause of the water becoming the body of a man, not of an insect or moth, &c.; the word 'man' applying to the human species only.—And, further, the text merely teaches that in the fifth oblation the waters are called man, and does not at the same time deny that, where there is no fifth oblation, they are not called man; for if it did the latter, the sentence would have the imperfection of having a double sense. We therefore have to understand that the body of those men who are capable of ascending and descending originates in connexion with the fifth oblation, that in the case of other men, however, a body forms itself from water mixed with the other elements even without a settled number of oblations.

19. It is, moreover, recorded in the (ordinary) world.

There are, moreover, traditions, apart from the Veda, that certain persons like Dro*n*a, Dh*ri*sh*t*adyumna, Sîtâ, Draupadî, &c., were not born in the ordinary way from mothers. In the case of Dro*n*a and others there was absent the oblation which is made into the woman; while in the case of Dh*ri*sh*t*adyumna and others, even two of the oblations, viz. the one offered into woman and the one offered into man, were absent. Hence in other cases also birth may be supposed to take place independently of the number of oblations.—It is, moreover, commonly known that the female crane conceives without a male.

20. And on account of observation.

It is, moreover, observed that out of the four classes of organic beings—viviparous animals, oviparous animals, animals springing from heat, and beings springing from germs (plants)—the two latter classes are produced without sexual intercourse, so that in their case no regard is had to the number of oblations. The same may therefore take place in other cases also.—But, an objection may here be raised, scripture speaks of those beings as belonging to three classes only, because there are three modes of origin only; 'That which springs from an egg, that which springs from a living being, that which springs from a germ' (*Kh.* Up. VI, 3, 1). How then can it be maintained that there are four classes?—To this objection the next Sûtra replies.

21. The third term comprises that which springs from heat.

The third term in the scriptural passage quoted, i.e. 'that which springs from a germ,' must be understood as implying those beings also which spring from heat; the two classes having in common that they spring from earth or water, i.e. from something stable. Different from their origin is the origin of those beings which spring from moving things (viz. animals).—In other places the beings springing from heat and those springing from germs are spoken of as constituting separate classes.—Hence there is no contradiction.

22. (On the part of the soul's descending from the

moon) there is entering into similarity of being (with ether and so on); as this (only) is possible.

It has been explained that the souls of those who perform sacrifices, &c., after having reached the moon dwell there as long as their works last and then re-descend with a remainder of their works. We now have to inquire into the mode of that descent. On this point scripture makes the following statement: 'They return again the way they came, to the ether, from the ether to the air. Then the sacrificer having become air becomes smoke, having become smoke he becomes mist, having become mist he becomes a cloud, having become a cloud he rains down.'—Here a doubt arises whether the descending souls pass over into a state of identity with ether, &c., or into a state of similarity.—The pûrvapakshin maintains that the state is one of identity, because this is directly stated by the text. Otherwise there would take place so-called indication (lakshanâ). Now whenever the doubt lies between a directly expressed and a merely indicated meaning the former is to be preferred. Thus the following words also, 'Having become air he becomes smoke,' &c., are appropriate only if the soul be understood to identify itself with them.—Hence it follows that the souls become identical with ether, &c.—To this we reply that they only pass into a state of similarity to ether, &c. When the body, consisting of water which the soul had assumed in the sphere of the moon for the purpose of enjoyment, dissolves at the time when that enjoyment comes to an end, then it becomes subtle like ether, passes thereupon into the power of the air, and then gets mixed with smoke, &c. This is the meaning of the clauses, 'They return as they came to the ether, from the ether to the air, &c.'—How is this known to be the meaning?—Because thus only it is possible. For it is not possible that one thing should become another in the literal sense of the word. If, moreover, the souls became identified with ether they could no longer descend through air, &c. And as connexion with the ether is, on account of its all-pervadingness, eternal, no other connexion (of the souls) with it can here be meant but their entering into a state of similarity to it[1]. And in cases where it is impossible to accept the literal meaning of the text it is quite proper to assume the meaning which is merely indicated.—For these reasons the souls' becoming ether, &c., has to be taken in the secondary sense of their passing into a state of similarity to ether, and so on.

23. (The soul passes through the stages of its descent) in a not very long time; on account of the special statement.

A doubt arises with reference to the period beginning with the soul's becoming ether and extending up to its entering into rice, &c., viz. whether the soul remains a long time in the state of similarity to each of the stages of its way before it enters into similarity to the next one, or only a short time.—The pûrvapakshin maintains that, on account of the absence of a definite text, no binding rule exists.—To this we reply that the souls remain in the state of similarity to ether, &c., for a short period only before they fall to the earth in raindrops. We infer this from the circumstance of the text making a special statement. For after having said that the souls enter into rice, &c., it adds, 'From thence the escape is beset with more pain;' a statement implying that the escape from the previous states was comparatively easy and pleasant. Now this difference in point of pleasantness must be based on the comparative shortness or length of the escape; for as, at that time, the body is not yet formed, enjoyment (in the ordinary sense) is not possible. Hence we conclude that, up to the moment when the souls enter into rice, &c., their descent is accomplished in a short time.

---

[1] It might be said that the relation to ether, &c., into which the souls enter, is the relation of conjunction (sa*m*yoga), not the relation of similarity. But as nothing can enter into the relation of sa*m*yoga with ether (everything being in eternal sa*m*yoga with it) we must assume that 'becoming ether' means 'becoming like ether,' and by parity of reasoning, that 'becoming air, &c.,' means 'becoming like air.'

24. (The descending souls enter) into (plants) animated by other (souls), as in the previous cases, on account of scriptural declaration.

In the description of the souls' descent we read, after their coming down in raindrops has been mentioned, 'Then they are born as rice and corn, herbs and trees, sesamum and beans.'—Here a doubt arises whether, at this stage of their descent, the souls to which a remainder of their works continues to cling really pass over into the different species of those immoveable things (plants) and enjoy their pleasures and pains, or if they enter merely into a state of conjunction with the bodies of those plants which are animated by different souls.—The pûrvapakshin maintains that they pass over into those species and enjoy their pleasures and pains, on account of the remainder of works still attaching to them; firstly, because that enables us to take the verb 'to be born' in its literal sense; secondly, because we know from *S*ruti and Sm*ri*ti that the condition of a plant may be a place of enjoyment (of the fruits of actions); and thirdly, because sacrifices and similar actions, being connected with harm done to animals, &c., may lead to unpleasant results. We therefore take the 'being born as rice,' &c., of those to whom a remainder of their works attaches, in its literal sense, and consider the case to be analogous to that of a man who is born either as a dog or a hog or a *K*â*nd*âla, where we have to understand that the man really becomes a dog, and so on, and experiences the pleasures and pains connected with that condition.

To this reasoning we reply as follows:—The souls to which a remainder attaches enter merely into conjunction with rice plants, &c., which are already animated by other souls; and do not enjoy their pleasures and pains; 'as in the previous cases.' As the souls' becoming air, smoke, &c., was decided to mean only that they become connected with them [1], so here too their becoming rice, &c. merely means that they

[1] This does not agree well with what had been said above about the souls becoming similar to ether, air, &c.

become connected with those plants.—How is this known? —From the fact of the statement here also being of the same nature.—Of what nature?—Here, also, as in the case of the souls becoming ether, &c., down to rain, the text does not refer to any operation of the works; hence we conclude that the souls do not enjoy pleasure and pain. Where, on the other hand, the text wants to intimate that the souls undergo pleasure and pain, there it refers to the operation of the former works; so, e.g. in the passage which treats of men of good or evil conduct. Moreover, if we should take the souls' being born as rice, &c., in its literal sense, it would follow that when the rice plants are reaped, unhusked, split, cooked and eaten, the souls which have descended into them and are animating them would have to leave them; it being generally known that when a body is destroyed the soul animating it abandons it. And then (if the souls left the plants) the text could not state (as it does state, V, 10, 6) that the souls which had entered into the plants are transmitted by animal generation (on the part of those who eat the plants). Hence it follows that the souls which have descended are merely outwardly connected with the plants animated by other souls. This suffices to refute the assertions that 'to be born' must be taken in its literal sense; and that the state of vegetable existence affords a place for enjoyment. We do not entirely deny that vegetable existence may afford a place for enjoyment; it may do so in the case of other beings which, in consequence of their unholy deeds, have become plants. We only maintain that those souls which descend from the moon with an unrequited remainder of works do not experience the enjoyment connected with plant life.

25. Should it be said that (sacrificial work is) unholy; we deny this on the ground of scripture.

We proceed to refute the remark made by the pûrvapakshin that sacrificial works are unholy because involving harm done to animals, &c., that they may therefore lead to unpleasant results, and that hence the statement as to the souls being born as plants, &c., may be taken in its literal sense; in consequence of which it would be uncalled-for to assume a derived sense.—This reasoning is not valid, because our knowledge of what is duty and the contrary of duty depends entirely on scripture. The knowledge of one action being right and another wrong is based on scripture only; for it lies out of the cognizance of the senses, and there moreover is, in the case of right and wrong, an entire want of binding rules as to place, time, and occasion. What in one place, at one time, on one occasion is performed as a right action, is a wrong action in another place, at another time, on another occasion; none therefore can know, without scripture, what is either right or wrong. Now from scripture we derive the certain knowledge that the *g*yotish*t*oma sacrifice, which involves harm done to animals (i.e. the animal sacrifice), &c., is an act of duty; how then can it be called unholy?—But does not the scriptural precept, 'Do not harm any creature,' intimate that to do harm to any being is an act contrary to duty?—True, but that is a general rule, while the precept, 'Let him offer an animal to Agnîshomau,' embodies an exception; and general rule and exception have different spheres of application. The work (i.e. sacrifice) enjoined by the Veda is therefore holy, being performed by authoritative men and considered blameless; and to be born as a plant cannot be its fruit. Nor can to be born as rice and other plants be considered analogous to being born as dogs, &c. For the latter birth scripture teaches with reference to men of evil conduct only; while no such specific qualification is stated in the case of vegetable existence. Hence we conclude that when scripture states that the souls descending from the moon become plants, it only means that they become enclosed in plants.

26. After that (there takes place) conjunction (of the soul) with him who performs the act of generation.

The conclusion arrived at under the preceding Sûtra is confirmed also by scripture stating that the souls, after having entered into plants, 'become' beings performing the act of generation, 'for whoever eats the food, whoever performs the act of generation, that again he (the soul) becomes.' Here again the soul's 'becoming' he who performs the act of generation cannot be taken in its literal sense; for a person becomes capable of generation a long time after his birth only, viz. when he reaches puberty. How then should the soul contained in the food eaten enter into that condition in its true sense? Hence we must interpret the passage to mean only that the soul enters into conjunction with one who performs the act of generation; and from this we again infer that the soul's becoming a plant merely means its entering into conjunction with a plant.

27. From the yoni a (new) body (springs).

Then, subsequently to the soul having been in conjunction with a person of generative power, generation takes place, and a body is produced in which the soul can enjoy the fruits of that remainder of works which still attaches to it. This scripture declares in the passage, 'Those whose conduct has been good,' &c. From this, also, it appears that the souls to which a remainder clings, when descending and becoming rice plants, and so on, do not enter into the state of forming the body of those plants with its attendant pleasure and pain, but are 'born as plants' in so far only as they enter into conjunction with them.

SECOND PÂDA.

Reverence to the highest Self!

1. In the intermediate place there is (a real) creation; for (scripture) says (that).

In the preceding pâda we have set forth, with reference to the knowledge of the five fires, the various stages of the soul's passing through the samsâra. We shall now set forth the soul's different states (waking, dreaming, &c.)—Scripture says (Bri. Up. IV, 3, 9; 10), 'When he falls asleep —; there are no chariots in that state, no horses, no roads, but he himself creates chariots, horses, and roads,' &c.—Here a doubt arises whether the creation thus taking place in dreams is a real one (pâramârthika) like the creation seen in the waking state, or whether it consists of illusion (mâyâ).—The pûrvapakshin maintains that 'in the intermediate place (or state) there is (a real) creation.' By intermediate place we have to understand the place of dreams, in which latter sense the word is used in the Veda, 'There is a third intermediate state, the state of dreams' (Bri. Up. IV, 3, 9). That place is called the intermediate place because it lies there where the two worlds, or else the place of waking and the place of bliss (deep sleep), join. In that intermediate place the creation must be real; because scripture, which is authoritative, declares it to be so, 'He creates chariots, horses, roads,' &c. We, moreover, infer this from the concluding clause, 'He indeed is the maker' (Bri. Up. IV, 3, 10).

2. And some (state the Self to be) the shaper (creator); sons and so on (being the lovely things which he shapes).

Moreover the members of one sâkhâ state that the Self is, in that intermediate state, the shaper of lovely things, 'He, the person who is awake in us while we are asleep, shaping one lovely thing after another' (Ka. Up. II, 5, 8).

Kâma (lovely things) in this passage means sons, &c., that are so called because they are beloved.—But may not the term 'kâmâ*h*' denote desires merely?—No, we reply; the word kâma is here used with reference to sons, &c.; for those form the general subject of discussion, as we see from some preceding passages, 'Choose sons and grandsons,' &c., and 'I make thee the enjoyer of all kâmas' (Ka. Up. I, 1, 23; 24).—And that that shaper is the highest Self (prâ*gñ*a) we infer from the general subject-matter and from the complementary sentence. That the highest Self is the general subject-matter appears from II, 14, 'That which thou seest as neither this nor that.' And to that highest Self there also refers the complementary sentence II, 5, 8, 'That indeed is the Bright, that is Brahman, that alone is called the Immortal. All worlds are contained in it, and no one goes beyond.'—Now it is admitted that the world (creation) of our waking state of which the highest Self (prâ*gñ*a) is the maker is real; hence the world of our dreaming state must likewise be real. That the same reasoning applies to the waking and the sleeping state a scriptural passage also declares, 'Here they say: No, this is the same as the place of waking, for what he sees while awake the same he sees while asleep' (B*ri*. Up. IV, 3, 14).—Hence the world of dreams is real.—To this we reply as follows.

3. But it (viz. the dream world) is mere illusion (mâyâ), on account of its nature not manifesting itself with the totality (of the attributes of reality).

The word 'but' discards the pûrvapaksha. It is not true that the world of dreams is real; it is mere illusion and there is not a particle of reality in it.—Why?—'On account of its nature not manifesting itself with the totality,' i.e. because the nature of the dream world does not manifest itself with the totality of the attributes of real things.—What then do you mean by the 'totality'?—The fulfilment of the conditions of place, time, and cause, and the circumstance of non-refutation. All these have their sphere in real things, but cannot be applied to dreams. In the first place there is, in a dream, no space for chariots and the like; for those cannot possibly find room in the limited confines of the body.—Well, but why should not the dreaming person see the objects of his dream outside of his body? He does as a matter of fact perceive things as separated from himself by space; and *S*ruti, moreover, declares that the dream is outside the body, 'Away from the nest the Immortal moves; that immortal one goes wherever he likes' (B*ri*. Up. IV, 3, 12). And this distinction of the conceptions of staying and going would have no good sense if the being (the soul) did not really go out.—What you maintain is inadmissible, we reply. A sleeping being cannot possibly possess the power to go and return in a moment the distance of a hundred yo*g*anas. Sometimes, moreover, a person recounts a dream in which he went to some place without returning from it, 'Lying on my bed in the land of the Kurus I was overcome by sleep and went in my dream to the country of the Pa*ñk*âlas, and being there I awoke.' If, now, that person had really gone out of his country, he would on waking find himself in the country of the Pa*ñk*âlas to which he had gone in his dream; but as a matter of fact he awakes in the country of the Kurus.—Moreover, while a man imagines himself in his dream going, in his body, to another place, the bystanders see that very same body lying on the couch. Further, a dreaming person does not see, in his dream, other places such as they really are. But if he in seeing them did actually go about, they would appear to him like the things he sees in his waking state. *S*ruti, moreover, declares that the dream is within the body, cp. the passage beginning 'But when he moves about in dream,' and terminating 'He moves about, according to his pleasure, within his own body' (B*ri*. Up. II, 1, 18). Hence the passage about the dreamer moving away from his nest must be taken in a metaphorical sense, as otherwise we should contradict scripture as well as reason; he who while remaining within his own body does not use it for any purpose may be said to be outside the body as it were. The difference of the ideas of staying within the body and going outside must, therefore, be viewed as a mere deception.—In the second place we see that dreams are in conflict with the conditions of time. One person lying asleep at night dreams that it is day in the Bhârata Varsha; another lives, during a dream which lasts one muhûrta only, through many crowds of years.—In the third place there do not exist in the state of dreaming the requisite efficient causes for either thought or action; for as, in sleep, the organs are drawn inward, the dreaming person has no eyes, &c. for perceiving chariots and other things; and whence should he, in the space of the twinkling of an eye, have the power of—or procure the material for—making chariots and the like?—In the fourth place the chariots, horses, &c., which the dream creates, are refuted, i.e. shown not to exist by the waking state. And apart from this, the dream itself refutes what it creates, as its end often contradicts its beginning; what at first was considered to be a chariot turns, in a moment, into a man, and what was conceived to be a man has all at once become a tree.—Scripture itself, moreover, clearly declares the chariots, &c., of a dream to have no real existence, 'There are no chariots in that state, no horses, no roads, &c.'—Hence the visions of a dream are mere illusion.

4. (Not altogether) for it (the dream) is indicative (of the future), according to *S*ruti; the experts also declare this.

Well then, as dreams are mere illusion, they do not contain a particle of reality?—Not so, we reply; for dreams are prophetic of future good and bad fortune. For scripture teaches as follows, 'When a man engaged in some work undertaken for a special wish sees in his dreams a woman, he may infer success from that dream-vision.' Other scriptural passages declare that certain dreams indicate speedy death, so, e.g. 'If he sees a black man with black teeth, that man will kill him.'—Those also who understand the science of dreams hold the opinion that to dream of riding on an elephant and the like is lucky; while it is unlucky to dream of riding on a donkey, &c.; and that certain other dreams also caused by special mantras or devatâs or substances contain a particle of truth.—In all these cases the thing indicated may be real; the indicating dream, however, remains unreal as it is refuted by the waking state. The doctrine that the dream itself is mere illusion thus remains uncontradicted.—On this account the Vedic passage to which the first Sûtra of this pâda refers is to be explained metaphorically. When we say 'the plough bears, i.e. supports the bullocks,' we say so because the plough is the indirect cause of the bullocks being kept[1], not because we mean that the plough directly supports the bullocks. Analogously scripture says that the dreaming person creates chariots, &c., and is their maker, not because he creates them directly but because he is the cause of their creation. By his being their cause we have to understand that he is that one who performs the good and evil deeds which are the cause of the delight and fear produced by the apparition, in his dream, of chariots and other things[2].—Moreover, as in the waking state, owing to the contact of the senses and their objects and the resulting interference of the light of the sun, &c., the self-luminousness of the Self is, for the beholder, difficult to discriminate, scripture gives the description of the dreaming state for the purpose of that discrimination. If then the statements about the creation of chariots, &c., were taken as they stand (i.e. literally) we could not ascertain that the Self is self-luminous[3]. Hence we have to explain the passage relative to the creation of chariots, &c., in a metaphorical sense, so as to make it agree with the statement about the non-existence of chariots, &c. This explains also the scriptural passage about the shaping (III, 2, 2). The statement made above that in the Kâ*th*aka the highest Self is spoken of as the shaper

[1] Bullocks have to be kept because the fields must be tilled.

[2] The dreams have the purpose of either cheering or saddening and frightening the sleeper; so as to requite him for his good and evil works. His ad*r*ish*t*a thus furnishes the efficient cause of the dreams.

[3] Because then there would be no difference between the dreaming and the waking state.

of dreams is untrue; for another scriptural passage ascribes that activity to the individual soul, 'He himself destroying, he himself shaping dreams with his own splendour, with his own light' (B*ri*. Up. IV, 3, 9)[1]. And in the Kâ*th*aka Upanishad itself also we infer from the form of the sentence, 'That one who wakes in us while we are asleep,'—which is an anuvâda, i.e. an additional statement about something well known—that he who is there proclaimed as the shaper of lovely things is nobody else than the (well-known) individual soul. The other passage which forms the complementary continuation of the one just quoted ('That indeed is the Bright, that is Brahman') discards the notion of the separate existence of the individual soul and teaches that it is nothing but Brahman, analogously to the passage 'That art thou.' And this interpretation does not conflict with Brahman being the general subject-matter.—Nor do we thereby deny altogether that the highest (prâ*gñ*a) Self is active in dreams; for as being the Lord of all it may be considered as the guide and ruler of the soul in all its states. We only maintain that the world connected with the intermediate state (i.e. the world of dreams) is not real in the same sense as the world consisting of ether and so on is real. On the other hand we must remember that also the so-called real creation with its ether, air, &c., is not absolutely real; for as we have proved before (II, 1, 14) the entire expanse of things is mere illusion. The world consisting of ether, &c., remains fixed and distinct up to the moment when the soul cognizes that Brahman is the Self of all; the world of dreams on the other hand is daily sublated by the waking state. That the latter is mere illusion has, therefore, to be understood with a distinction.

5. But by the meditation on the highest that which is hidden (viz. the equality of the Lord and

[1] Svaya*m* vihatya pûrvadeha*m* nis*k*esh*t*a*m* k*ri*tvâ svaya*m* nirmâyâpûrva*m* vâsanâmaya*m* deha*m* sampâdya svena bhâsâ svakîyabuddhiv*ri*ttyâ svena *g*yotishâ svarûpa*k*aitanyenety artha*h*. Ân. Gi.

the soul, becomes manifest); for from him (the Lord) are its (the soul's) bondage and release.

Well, but the individual soul is a part of the highest Self as the spark is a part of the fire. And as fire and spark have in common the powers of burning and giving light, so the individual soul and the Lord have in common the powers of knowledge and rulership; hence the individual soul may, by means of its lordship, effect in the dreaming state a creation of chariots and the like, springing from its wishes (sa*m*kalpa).—To this we reply that although the Lord and the individual soul stand to each other in the relation of whole and part, yet it is manifest to perception that the attributes of the two are of a different nature.—Do you then mean to say that the individual soul has no common attributes with the Lord?—We do not maintain that; but we say that the equality of attributes, although existing, is hidden by the veil of Nescience. In the case of some persons indeed who strenuously meditate on the Lord and who, their ignorance being dispelled at last, obtain through the favour of the Lord extraordinary powers and insight, that hidden equality becomes manifest—just as through the action of strong medicines the power of sight of a blind man becomes manifest; but it does not on its own account reveal itself to all men.—Why not?—Because 'from him,' i.e. from the Lord there are bondage and release of it, viz. the individual soul. That means: bondage is due to the absence of knowledge of the Lord's true nature; release is due to the presence of such knowledge. Thus *S*ruti declares, 'When that god is known all fetters fall off; sufferings are destroyed and birth and death cease. From meditating on him there arises, on the dissolution of the body, a third state, that of universal Lordship; he who is alone is satisfied' (*S*vet. Up. I, 11), and similar passages.

6. Or that (viz. the concealment of the soul's powers springs) from its connexion with the body.

But if the soul is a part of the highest Self, why should its knowledge and lordship be hidden? We should rather expect them to be as manifest as the light and the heat of the spark.—True, we reply; but the state of concealment of the soul's knowledge and lordship is due to its being joined to a body, i.e. to a body, sense-organs, mind, buddhi, sense-objects, sensations, &c. And to this state of things there applies the simile: As the heat and light of the fire are hidden as long as the fire is still hidden in the wood from which it will be produced by friction, or as long as it is covered by ashes; so, in consequence of the soul being connected with limiting adjuncts in the form of a body, &c., founded on name and form as presented by Nescience, its knowledge and lordship remain hidden as long as it is possessed by the erroneous notion of not being distinct from those adjuncts.—The word 'or' in the Sûtra is meant to discard the suspicion that the Lord and the soul might be separate entities.—But why should not the soul be separate from the Lord, considering the state of concealment of its knowledge and power? If we allow the two to be fundamentally separate, we need not assume that their separateness is due to the soul's connexion with the body.—It is impossible, we reply, to assume the soul to be separate from the Lord. For in the scriptural passage beginning with 'That divinity thought' &c. (*Kh.* Up. VI, 3, 2) we meet with the clause, 'It entered into those beings with this living Self (*g*îva âtman); where the individual soul is referred to as the Self. And then we have the other passage, 'It is the True; it is the Self; that art thou, O *S*vetaketu,' which again teaches that the Lord is the Self of the soul. Hence the soul is non-different from the Lord, but its knowledge and power are obscured by its connexion with the body. From this it follows that the dreaming soul is not able to create, from its mere wishes, chariots and other things. If the soul possessed that power, nobody would ever have an unpleasant dream; for nobody ever wishes for something unpleasant to himself.—We finally deny that the scriptural passage about the waking state ('dream is the same as the place of waking' &c.) indicates the reality of dreams. The statement made there about the equality of the two states is not meant to indicate that dreams are real, for that would conflict with the soul's self-luminousness (referred to above), and scripture, moreover, expressly declares that the chariots, &c., of a dream have no real existence; it merely means that dreams, because due to mental impressions (vâsanâ) received in the waking state, are equal to the latter in appearance.—From all this it follows that dreams are mere illusion.

7. The absence of that (i.e. of dreams, i.e. dreamless sleep) takes place in the nâ*d*îs and in the Self; according to scriptural statement.

The state of dream has been discussed; we are now going to enquire into the state of deep sleep. A number of scriptural passages refer to that state. In one place we read, 'When a man is asleep, reposing and at perfect rest so that he sees no dream, then he has entered into those nâ*d*îs' (*Kh.* Up. VIII, 6, 3). In another place it is said with reference to the nâ*d*îs, 'Through them he moves forth and rests in the surrounding body' (B*ri.* Up. II, 1, 19). So also in another place, 'In these the person is when sleeping he sees no dream. Then he becomes one with the prâ*n*a alone' (Kau. Up. IV, 20). Again in another place, 'That ether which is within the heart in that he reposes' (B*ri.* Up. IV, 4, 22). Again, 'Then he becomes united with that which is; he is gone to his Self' (*Kh.* Up. VI, 8, 1). And, 'Embraced by the highest Self (prâ*gñ*a) he knows nothing that is without, nothing that is within' (B*ri.* Up. IV, 3, 21). Here the doubt arises whether the nâ*d*îs, &c., mentioned in the above passages are independent from each other and constitute various places for the soul in the state of deep sleep, or if they stand in mutual relation so as to constitute one such place only. The pûrvapakshin takes the former view on account of the various places mentioned serving one and the same purpose. Things serving the same purpose, as, e.g. rice and barley [1], are never seen to be dependent

[1] Either of which may be employed for making the sacrificial cake.

on each other. That the nâ*d*ìs, &c., actually serve the same purpose appears from the circumstance of their being all of them exhibited equally in the locative case, 'he has entered into the nâ*d*ìs,' 'he rests in the pericardium,' &c.[1]—But in some of the passages quoted the locative case is not employed, so, e.g. in 'He becomes united with that which is' (satâ, instrumental case)!—That makes no difference, we reply, because there also the locative case is meant. For in the complementary passage the text states that the soul desirous of rest enters into the Self, 'Finding no rest elsewhere it settles down on breath' (*Kh*. Up. VI, 8, 2); a passage in which the word 'breath' refers to that which is (the sat). A place of rest of course implies the idea of the locative case. The latter case is, moreover, actually exhibited in a further complementary passage, 'When they have become merged in that which is (sati), they know not that they are merged in it.'—In all these passages one and the same state is referred to, viz. the state of deep sleep which is characterised by the suspension of all special cognition. Hence we conclude that in the state of deep sleep the soul optionally goes to any one of those places, either the nâ*d*ìs, or that which is, &c.

To this we make the following reply—'The absence of that,' i.e. the absence of dreams—which absence constitutes the essence of deep sleep—takes place 'in the nâ*d*ìs and in the Self;' i.e. in deep sleep the soul goes into both together, not optionally into either.—How is this known?—'From scripture.'—Scripture says of all those things, the nâ*d*ìs, &c., that they are the place of deep sleep; and those statements we must combine into one, as the hypothesis of option would involve partial refutation[2]. The assertion

---

[1] The argument of the pûrvapakshin is that the different places in which the soul is said to abide in the state of deep sleep are all exhibited by the text in the same case and are on that account co-ordinate. Mutual relation implying subordination would require them to be exhibited in different cases enabling us to infer the exact manner and degree of relation.

[2] By allowing option between two Vedic statements we lessen the

made above that we are compelled to allow option because the nâdîs, &c., serve one and the same purpose, is without foundation; for from the mere fact of two things being exhibited in the same case it does not follow by any means that they serve the same purpose, and that for that reason we have to choose between them. We on the contrary see that one and the same case is employed even where things serve different purposes and have to be combined; we say, e.g. 'he sleeps in the palace, he sleeps on the couch[1].' So in the present case also the different statements can be combined into one, 'He sleeps in the nâdîs, in the surrounding body, in Brahman.' Moreover, the scriptural passage, 'In these the person is when sleeping he sees no dream; then he becomes one with the prâna alone,' declares, by mentioning them together in one sentence, that the nâdîs and the prâna are to be combined in the state of deep sleep. That by prâna Brahman is meant we have already shown (I, 1, 28). Although in another text the nâdîs are spoken of as an independent place of deep sleep as it were ('then he has entered into those nâdîs'), yet, in order not to contradict other passages in which Brahman is spoken of as the place of deep sleep, we must explain that text to mean that the soul abides in Brahman through the nâdîs. Nor is this interpretation opposed to the employment of the locative case ('into—or in—those nâdîs'); for if the soul enters into Brahman by means of the nâdîs it is at the same time in the nâdîs; just as a man who descends to the sea by means of the river Gangâ is at the same time on the Gangâ.—Moreover that passage about the nâdîs, because its purpose is to describe the road, consisting of the rays and nâdîs, to the Brahma world, mentions the entering of the soul into the nâdîs in order to glorify the latter (not in order to describe the state of deep sleep); for the clause following upon the one which refers to the enter-

authority of the Veda; for the adoption of either alternative sublates, for the time, the other alternative.

[1] Where the two locatives are to be combined into one statement, 'he sleeps on the couch in the palace.'

ing praises the nâ*d*is, 'There no evil touches him.' The text, moreover, adds a reason for the absence of all evil, in the words, 'For then he has become united with the light.' That means that on account of the light contained in the nâ*d*is (which is called bile) having overpowered the organs the person no longer sees the sense-objects. Or else Brahman may be meant by the 'light;' which term is applied to Brahman in another passage also, 'It is Brahman only, light only' (B*ri*. Up. IV, 4, 7). The passage would then mean that the soul becomes, by means of the nâ*d*is, united with Brahman, and that hence no evil touches it. That the union with Brahman is the reason for the absence of all contact with evil, is known from other scriptural passages, such as, 'All evils turn back from it; for the world of Brahman is free from all evil' (*Kh*. Up. VIII, 4, 1). On that account we have to combine the nâ*d*is with Brahman, which from other passages is known to be the place of deep sleep.—Analogously we conclude that the pericardium also, because it is mentioned in a passage treating of Brahman, is a place of deep sleep only in subordination to Brahman. For the ether within the heart is at first spoken of as the place of sleep ('He lies in the ether which is in the heart,' B*ri*. Up. II, 1, 17), and with reference thereto it is said later on, 'He rests in the pericardium' (II, 1, 19). Pericardium (purîtat) is a name of that which envelops the heart; hence that which rests within the ether of the heart —which is contained in the pericardium—can itself be said to rest within the pericardium; just as a man living in a town surrounded by walls is said to live within the walls. That the ether within the heart is Brahman has already been shown (I, 3, 14).—That again the nâ*d*is and the pericardium have to be combined as places of deep sleep appears from their being mentioned together in one sentence ('Through them he moves forth and rests in the purîtat). That that which is (sat) and the intelligent Self (prâ*gñ*a) are only names of Brahman is well known; hence scripture mentions only three places of deep sleep, viz. the nâ*d*is, the pericardium, and Brahman. Among these three again Brahman alone is the lasting place of deep sleep; the nâ*d*îs and the pericardium are mere roads leading to it. Moreover (to explain further the difference of the manner in which the soul, in deep sleep, enters into the nâ*d*îs, the pericardium and Brahman respectively), the nâ*d*îs and the pericardium are (in deep sleep) merely the abode of the limiting adjuncts of the soul; in them the soul's organs abide[1]. For apart from its connexion with the limiting adjuncts it is impossible for the soul in itself to abide anywhere, because being non-different from Brahman it rests in its own glory. And if we say that, in deep sleep, it abides in Brahman we do not mean thereby that there is a difference between the abode and that which abides, but that there is absolute identity of the two. For the text says, 'With that which is he becomes united, he is gone to his Self;' which means that the sleeping person has entered into his true nature.—It cannot, moreover, be said that the soul is at any time not united with Brahman—for its true nature can never pass away—; but considering that in the state of waking and that of dreaming it passes, owing to the contact with its limiting adjuncts, into something else, as it were, it may be said that when those adjuncts cease in deep sleep it passes back into its true nature. Hence it would be entirely wrong to assume that, in deep sleep, it sometimes becomes united with Brahman and sometimes not[2]. Moreover, even if we admit that there are different places for the soul in deep sleep, still there does not result, from that difference of place, any difference in the quality of deep sleep which is in all cases characterised by the cessation of special cognition; it is, therefore, more appropriate to say that the soul does (in deep sleep) not cognize on account of its oneness, having become united with Brahman; according to the *S*ruti, 'How should he know another?' (B*ri*. Up. IV, 5, 15).—If, further, the sleeping soul did rest in the nâ*d*îs and the purîtat, it would be impossible

[1] Ân. Gi. explains kara*n*âni by karmâ*n*i: nâ*d*îshu purîtati *k*a *g*îvasyopâdhyantarbhûtani kara*n*âni karmâ*n*i tish*th*antîty upâdhyâdhâratvam, *g*îvasya tv âdhâro brahmaiva.

[2] But with the nâ*d*îs or the pericardium only.

to assign any reason for its not cognizing, because in that case it would continue to have diversity for its object; according to the *S*ruti, 'When there is, as it were, duality, then one sees the other,' &c.—But in the case of him also who has diversity for his object, great distance and the like may be reasons for absence of cognition!—What you say might indeed apply to our case if the soul were acknowledged to be limited in itself; then its case would be analogous to that of Vish*n*umitra, who, when staying in a foreign land, cannot see his home. But, apart from its adjuncts, the soul knows no limitation.—Well, then, great distance, &c., residing in the adjuncts may be the reason of non-cognition!—Yes, but that leads us to the conclusion already arrived at, viz. that the soul does not cognize when, the limiting adjuncts having ceased, it has become one with Brahman.

Nor do we finally maintain that the nâ*d*îs, the pericardium, and Brahman are to be added to each other as being equally places of deep sleep. For by the knowledge that the nâ*d*îs and the pericardium are places of sleep, nothing is gained, as scripture teaches neither that some special fruit is connected with that knowledge nor that it is the subordinate member of some work, &c., connected with certain results. We, on the other hand, do want to prove that that Brahman is the lasting abode of the soul in the state of deep sleep; that is a knowledge which has its own uses, viz. the ascertainment of Brahman being the Self of the soul, and the ascertainment of the soul being essentially non-connected with the worlds that appear in the waking and in the dreaming state. Hence the Self alone is the place of deep sleep.

8. Hence the awaking from that (viz. Brahman).

And because the Self only is the place of deep sleep, on that account the scriptural chapters treating of sleep invariably teach that the awaking takes place from that Self. In the B*ri*. Up. when the time comes for the answer to the question, 'Whence did he come back?' (II, 1, 16), the text says, 'As small sparks come forth from fire, thus all prâ*n*as come forth from that Self' (II, 1, 20). And *Kh*. Up. VI, 10, 2, we read: 'When they have come back from the True they do not know that they have come back from the True.' If there were optional places to which the soul might resort in deep sleep, scripture would teach us that it awakes sometimes from the nâ*d*îs, sometimes from the pericardium, sometimes from the Self.—For that reason also the Self is the place of deep sleep.

9. But the same (soul returns from Brahman); on account of work, remembrance, text, and precept.

Here we have to enquire whether the soul when awaking from the union with Brahman is the same which entered into union with Brahman, or another one.—The pûrvapakshin maintains that there is no fixed rule on that point. For just as a drop of water, when poured into a large quantity of water, becomes one with the latter, so that when we again take out a drop it would be hard to manage that it should be the very same drop; thus the sleeping soul, when it has become united with Brahman, is merged in bliss and not able again to rise from it the same. Hence what actually awakes is either the Lord or some other soul.—To this we reply that the same soul which in the state of sleep entered into bliss again arises from it, not any other. We assert this on the ground of work, remembrance, sacred text, and precept; which four reasons we will treat separately. In the first place the person who wakes from sleep must be the same, because it is seen to finish work left unfinished before. Men finish in the morning what they had left incomplete on the day before. Now it is not possible that one man should proceed to complete work half done by another man, because this would imply too much[1].

[1] There would follow from it, e.g. that in the case of sacrifices occupying more than one day, there would be several sacrificers, and that consequently it would be doubtful to whom the fruit of the sacrifice, as promised by the Veda, belongs. And this would imply a stultification of the sacred text.

Hence we conclude that it is one and the same man who finishes on the latter day the work begun on the former.—In the second place the person rising from sleep is the same who went to sleep, for the reason that otherwise he could not remember what he had seen, &c., on the day before; for what one man sees another cannot remember. And if another Self rose from sleep, the consciousness of personal identity (âtmânusmara*n*a) expressed in the words, 'I am the same I was before,' would not be possible.—In the third place we understand from Vedic texts that the same person rises again, 'He hastens back again as he came, to the place from which he started, to be awake' (B*ri*. Up. IV, 3, 16); 'All these creatures go day after day into the Brahma-world and yet do not discover it' (*Kh*. Up. VIII, 3, 2); 'Whatever these creatures are here, whether a lion, or a wolf, or a boar, or a worm, or a midge, or a gnat, or a musquito, that they become again and again' (*Kh*. Up. VI, 10, 2). These and similar passages met with in the chapters treating of sleeping and waking have a proper sense only if the same soul rises again.—In the fourth place we arrive at the same conclusion on the ground of the injunctions of works and knowledge, which, on a different theory, would be meaningless. For if another person did rise, it would follow that a person might obtain final release by sleep merely, and what then, we ask, would be the use of all those works which bear fruit at a later period, and of knowledge?—Moreover on the hypothesis of another person rising from sleep, that other person would either be a soul which had up to that time carried on its phenomenal life in another body; in that case it would follow that the practical existence carried on by means of that body would be cut short. If it be said that the soul which went to sleep may, in its turn, rise in that other body (so that B would rise in A's body and A in B's body), we reply that that would be an altogether useless hypothesis; for what advantage do we derive from assuming that each soul rises from sleep not in the same body in which it had gone to sleep, but that it goes to sleep in one body and rises in another?—Or else the soul rising (in A's body) would be one which had obtained final release, and that would imply that final release can have an end. But it is impossible that a soul which has once freed itself from Nescience should again rise (enter into phenomenal life). Hereby it is also shown that the soul which rises cannot be the Lord, who is everlastingly free from Nescience.—Further, on the hypothesis of another soul rising, it would be difficult to escape the conclusion that souls reap the fruits of deeds not their own, and, on the other hand, are not requited for what they have done.—From all this it follows that the person rising from sleep is the same that went to sleep.—Nor is it difficult to refute the analogical reasoning that the soul, if once united with Brahman, can no more emerge from it than a drop of water can again be taken out from the mass of water into which it had been poured. We admit the impossibility of taking out the same drop of water, because there is no means of distinguishing it from all the other drops. In the case of the soul, however, there are reasons of distinction, viz. the work and the knowledge (of each individual soul). Hence the two cases are not analogous.—Further, we point out that the flamingo, e.g. is able to distinguish and separate milk and water when mixed, things which we men are altogether incapable of distinguishing.—Moreover, what is called individual soul is not really different from the highest Self, so that it might be distinguished from the latter in the same way as a drop of water from the mass of water; but, as we have explained repeatedly, Brahman itself is on account of its connexion with limiting adjuncts metaphorically called individual soul. Hence the phenomenal existence of one soul lasts as long as it continues to be bound by one set of adjuncts, and the phenomenal existence of another soul again lasts as long as it continues to be bound by another set of adjuncts. Each set of adjuncts continues through the states of sleep as well as of waking; in the former it is like a seed, in the latter like the fully developed plant. Hence the proper inference is that the same soul awakes from sleep.

10. In him who is senseless (in a swoon, &c.)

there is half-union; on account of this remaining (as the only possible hypothesis).

There now arises the question of what kind that state is which ordinarily is called a swoon or being stunned. Here the pûrvapakshin maintains that we know only of three states of the soul as long as it abides in a body, viz. the waking state, dreaming, and deep dreamless sleep; to which may be added, as a fourth state, the soul's passing out of the body. A fifth state is known neither from *S*ruti nor Sm*ri*ti; hence what is called fainting must be one of the four states mentioned.—To this we make the following reply. In the first place a man lying in a swoon cannot be said to be awake; for he does not perceive external objects by means of his senses.—But, it might be objected, may not his case be analogous to that of the arrow-maker? Just as the man working at an arrow, although awake, is so intent on his arrow that he sees nothing else; so the man also who is stunned, e.g. by a blow, may be awake, but as his mind is concentrated on the sensation of pain caused by the blow of the club, he may not at the time perceive anything else.—No, we reply, the case is different, on account of the absence of consciousness. The arrow-maker says, 'For such a length of time I was aware of nothing but the arrow;' the man, on the other hand, who returns to consciousness from a swoon, says, 'For such a length of time I was shut up in blind darkness; I was conscious of nothing.'—A waking man, moreover, however much his mind may be concentrated on one object, keeps his body upright; while the body of a swooning person falls prostrate on the ground. Hence a man in a swoon is not awake.—Nor, in the second place, is he dreaming; because he is altogether unconscious.—Nor, in the third place, is he dead; for he continues to breathe and to be warm. When a man has become senseless and people are in doubt whether he be alive or dead, they touch the region of his heart, in order to ascertain whether warmth continues in his body or not, and put their hands to his nostrils to ascertain whether breathing goes on or not. If, then, they perceive neither warmth nor breath, they conclude that he is dead, and carry off his body into the forest in order to burn it; if, on the other hand, they do perceive warmth and breath, they decide that he is not dead, and begin to sprinkle him with cold water so that he may recover consciousness.—That a man who has swooned away is not dead follows, moreover, from the fact of his rising again (to conscious life); for from Yama's realm none ever return.—Let us then say that a man who has swooned lies in deep sleep, as he is unconscious, and, at the same time, not dead!—No, we reply; this also is impossible, on account of the different characteristics of the two states. A man who has become senseless does sometimes not breathe for a long time; his body trembles; his face has a frightful expression; his eyes are staring wide open. The countenance of a sleeping person, on the other hand, is peaceful, he draws his breath at regular intervals; his eyes are closed, his body does not tremble. A sleeping person again may be waked by a gentle stroking with the hand; a person lying in a swoon not even by a blow with a club. Moreover, senselessness and sleep have different causes; the former is produced by a blow on the head with a club or the like, the latter by weariness. Nor, finally, is it the common opinion that stunned or swooning people are asleep.—It thus remains for us to assume that the state of senselessness (in swooning, &c.) is a half-union (or half-coincidence)[1], as it coincides in so far as it is an unconscious state and does not coincide in so far as it has different characteristics.—But how can absence of consciousness in a swoon, &c., be called half-coincidence (with deep sleep)? With regard to deep sleep scripture says, 'He becomes united with the True' (*Kh.* Up. VI, 8, 1); 'Then a thief is not a thief' (B*ri.* Up. IV, 3, 22); 'Day and night do not pass that bank, nor old age, death, and grief, neither good nor evil deeds' (*Kh.* Up. VIII, 4, 1). For the good and evil deeds reach the soul in that way that there arise in it the ideas of being affected by pleasure or pain. Those ideas are absent in deep sleep, but

[1] Viz. with deep sleep, as will be explained below.

they are likewise absent in the case of a person lying in a swoon; hence we must maintain that, on account of the cessation of the limiting adjuncts, in the case of a senseless person as well as of one asleep, complete union takes place, not only half-union.—To this we make the following reply.—We do not mean to say that in the case of a man who lies in a swoon the soul becomes half united with Brahman; but rather that senselessness belongs with one half to the side of deep sleep, with the other half to the side of the other state (i.e. death). In how far it is equal and not equal to sleep has already been shown. It belongs to death in so far as it is the door of death. If there remains (unrequited) work of the soul, speech and mind return (to the senseless person); if no work remains, breath and warmth depart from him. Therefore those who know Brahman declare a swoon and the like to be a half-union.—The objection that no fifth state is commonly acknowledged, is without much weight; for as that state occurs occasionally only it may not be generally known. All the same it is known from ordinary experience as well as from the âyurveda (medicine). That it is not considered a separate fifth state is due to its being avowedly compounded of other states.

11. Not on account of (difference of) place also twofold characteristics can belong to the highest; for everywhere (scripture teaches it to be without any difference).

We now attempt to ascertain, on the ground of *S*ruti, the nature of that Brahman with which the individual soul becomes united in the state of deep sleep and so on, in consequence of the cessation of the limiting adjuncts.—The scriptural passages which refer to Brahman are of a double character; some indicate that Brahman is affected by difference, so, e.g. 'He to whom belong all works, all desires, all sweet odours and tastes' (*Kh.* Up. III, 14, 2); others, that it is without difference, so, e.g. 'It is neither coarse nor fine, neither short nor long,' &c. (B*ri.* Up. III, 8, 8). Have we, on the ground of these passages, to assume that Brahman has a double nature, or either nature, and, if either, that it is affected with difference, or without difference? This is the point to be discussed.

The pûrvapakshin maintains that, in conformity with the scriptural passages which indicate a double nature, a double nature is to be ascribed to Brahman.

To this we reply as follows.—At any rate the highest Brahman cannot, by itself, possess double characteristics; for on account of the contradiction implied therein, it is impossible to admit that one and the same thing should by itself possess certain qualities, such as colour, &c., and should not possess them.—Nor is it possible that Brahman should possess double characteristics 'on account of place,' i.e. on account of its conjunction with its limiting adjuncts, such as earth, &c. For the connexion with limiting adjuncts is unavailing to impart to a thing of a certain nature an altogether different nature. The crystal, e.g. which is in itself clear, does not become dim through its conjunction with a limiting adjunct in the form of red colour; for that it is pervaded by the quality of dimness is an altogether erroneous notion. In the case of Brahman the limiting adjuncts are, moreover, presented by Nescience merely[1]. Hence (as the upâdhis are the product of Nescience) if we embrace either of the two alternatives, we must decide in favour of that according to which Brahma is absolutely devoid of all difference, not in favour of the opposite one. For all passages whose aim it is to represent the nature of Brahman (such as, 'It is without sound, without touch, without form, without decay,' Ka. Up. I, 3, 15) teach that it is free from all difference.

12. If it be objected that it is not so, on account of the difference (taught by the Veda); we reply that it is not so on account of the declaration of (Brahman)

[1] The limiting adjunct of the crystal, i.e. the red colour of a thing, e.g. a flower with which the crystal is in contact, is as real as the crystal itself; only the effect is an illusion.—But the limiting adjuncts of Brahman are in themselves illusion.

being not such, with reference to each (declaration of difference).

Let this be, but nevertheless it cannot be maintained that Brahman is devoid of difference and attributes, and does not possess double attributes either in itself or on account of difference of station.—Why not?—'On account of difference.' The various vidyâs teach different forms of Brahman; it is said to have four feet (*Kh*. Up. III, 18, 1); to consist of sixteen parts (Pr. Up. VI, 1); to be characterised by dwarfishness (Ka. Up. V, 3); to have the three worlds for its body (B*ri*. Up. I, 3, 22); to be named Vai*s*vanara (*Kh*. Up. V, 11, 2), &c. Hence we must admit that Brahman is qualified by differences also.—But above it has been shown that Brahman cannot possess twofold characteristics!—That also does not contradict our doctrine; for the difference of Brahman's forms is due to its limiting adjuncts. Otherwise all those scriptural passages which refer to those differences would be objectless.

All this reasoning, we say, is without force 'on account of the declaration of its being not such, with reference to each,' i.e. because scripture declares, with reference to all the differences produced by the limiting adjuncts, that there is no difference in Brahman. Cp. such passages as the following: 'This bright immortal person in this earth, and that bright immortal person incorporated in the body; he indeed is the same as that Self' (B*ri*. Up. II, 5, 1). It, therefore, cannot be maintained that the connexion of Brahman with various forms is taught by the Veda.

13. Some also (teach) thus.

The members of one *s*âkhâ also make a statement about the cognition of non-difference which is preceded by a censure of the perception of difference, 'By the mind alone it is to be perceived, there is in it no diversity. He who perceives therein any diversity goes from death to death' (B*ri*. Up. IV, 4, 19). Others also ('By knowing the enjoyer, the enjoyed, and the ruler, everything has been declared to be threefold, and this is Brahman,' *S*vet. Up. I, 12) record in their text that the entire world, characterised by enjoyers, things to be enjoyed, and a ruler, has Brahman for its true nature.—But as among the scriptural passages referring to Brahman, there are some which represent it as having a form, and others teaching that it is devoid of form, how can it be asserted that Brahman is devoid of form, and not also the contrary?—To this question the next Sûtra replies.

14. For (Brahman) is merely devoid of form, on account of this being the main purport of scripture.

Brahman, we must definitively assert, is devoid of all form, colour, and so on, and does not in any way possess form, and so on.—Why?—'On account of this being the main purport (of scripture).'—'It is neither coarse nor fine, neither short nor long' (B*ri*. Up. III, 8, 8); 'That which is without sound, without touch, without form, without decay' (Ka. Up. I, 3, 15); 'He who is called ether is the revealer of all forms and names. That within which forms and names are, that is Brahman' (*Kh*. Up. VIII, 14, 1); 'That heavenly person is without body, he is both without and within, not produced' (Mu. Up. II, 1, 2); 'That Brahman is without cause and without effect, without anything inside or outside, this Self is Brahman, omnipresent and omniscient' (B*ri*. Up. II, 5, 19). These and similar passages have for their purport the true nature of Brahman as non-connected with any world, and have not any other purport, as we have proved under I, 1, 4. On the ground of such passages we therefore must definitively conclude that Brahman is devoid of form. Those other passages, on the other hand, which refer to a Brahman qualified by form do not aim at setting forth the nature of Brahman, but rather at enjoining the worship of Brahman. As long as those latter texts do not contradict those of the former class, they are to be accepted as they stand; where, however, contradictions occur, the passages whose main subject is Brahman must be viewed as having greater force than those of the other kind.—This is the reason for our deciding that although there are two different classes of scriptural texts, Brahman must be held to be altogether without form, not at the same time of an opposite nature.—But what then is the position of those passages which refer to Brahman as possessing form?—To this question the next Sûtra replies.

15. And as light (assumes forms as it were by its contact with things possessing form, so does Brahman;) since (the texts ascribing form to Brahman) are not devoid of meaning.

Just as the light of the sun or the moon after having passed through space enters into contact with a finger or some other limiting adjunct, and, according as the latter is straight or bent, itself becomes straight or bent as it were; so Brahman also assumes, as it were, the form of the earth and the other limiting adjuncts with which it enters into connexion. Hence there is no reason why certain texts should not teach, with a view to meditative worship, that Brahman has that and that form. We thus escape the conclusion that those Vedic passages which ascribe form to Brahman are devoid of sense; a conclusion altogether unacceptable since all parts of the Veda are equally authoritative, and hence must all be assumed to have a meaning. —But does this not imply a contradiction of the tenet maintained above, viz. that Brahman does not possess double characteristics although it is connected with limiting adjuncts?—By no means, we reply. What is merely due to a limiting adjunct cannot constitute an attribute of a substance, and the limiting adjuncts are, moreover, presented by Nescience only. That the primeval natural Nescience leaves room for all practical life and activity—whether ordinary or based on the Veda—we have explained more than once.

16. And (scripture) declares (Brahman) to consist of that (i.e. intelligence).

And scripture declares that Brahman consists of intelligence, is devoid of any other characteristics, and is altogether without difference; 'As a mass of salt has neither inside nor outside, but is altogether a mass of taste, thus, indeed, has that Self neither inside nor outside, but is altogether a mass of knowledge' (B*ri*. Up. IV, 5, 13). That means: That Self has neither inside nor outside any characteristic form but intelligence; simple non-differentiated intelligence constitutes its nature; just as a lump of salt has inside as well as outside one and the same saltish taste, not any other taste.

17. (This scripture) also shows, and it is likewise stated in Sm*ri*ti.

That Brahman is without any difference is proved by those scriptural passages also which expressly deny that it possesses any other characteristics; so, e.g. 'Next follows the teaching by No, no' (B*ri*. Up. II, 3, 6); 'It is different from the known, it is also above the unknown' (Ke. Up. I, 4); 'From whence all speech, with the mind, turns away unable to reach it' (Taitt. Up. II, 9). Of a similar purport is that scriptural passage which relates how Bâhva, being questioned about Brahman by Vâshkalin, explained it to him by silence, 'He said to him, "Learn Brahman, O friend," and became silent. Then, on a second and third question, he replied, "I am teaching you indeed, but you do not understand. Silent is that Self."' The same teaching is conveyed by those Sm*ri*ti-texts which deny of Brahman all other characteristics; so, e.g. 'I will proclaim that which is the object of knowledge, knowing which one reaches immortality; the highest Brahman without either beginning or end, which cannot be said either to be or not to be' (Bha. Gîtâ XIII, 12). Of a similar purport is another Sm*ri*ti-passage, according to which the omniform Nârâya*n*a instructed Nârada, 'The cause, O Nârada, of your seeing me endowed with the qualities of all beings is the Mâyâ emitted by me; do not cognize me as being such (in reality).'

18. For this very reason (there are applied to Brahman) comparisons such as that of the images of the sun and the like.

Because that Self is of the nature of intelligence, devoid of all difference, transcending speech and mind, to be described only by denying of it all other characteristics, therefore the Moksha *S*âstras compare it to the images of the sun reflected in the water and the like, meaning thereby that all difference in Brahman is unreal, only due to its limiting conditions. Compare, e.g. out of many, the two following passages: 'As the one luminous sun when entering into relation to many different waters is himself rendered multiform by his limiting adjuncts; so also the one divine unborn Self;' and 'The one Self of all beings separately abides in all the individual beings; hence it appears one and many at the same time, just as the one moon is multiplied by its reflections in the water.'

The next Sûtra raises an objection.

19. But there is no parallelism (of the two things compared), since (in the case of Brahman) there is not apprehended (any separate substance) comparable to the water.

Since no substance comparable to the water is apprehended in the case of Brahman, a parallelism between Brahman and the reflected images of the sun cannot be established. In the case of the sun and other material luminous bodies, there exists a separate material substance occupying a different place, viz. water; hence the light of the sun, &c., may be reflected. The Self, on the other hand, is not a material thing, and, as it is present everywhere and all is identical with it, there are no limiting adjuncts different from it and occupying a different place.—Therefore the instances are not parallel.

The next Sûtra disposes of this objection.

20. Since (the highest Brahman) is inside (of the limiting adjuncts), it participates in their increase and decrease; owing to the appropriateness (thus resulting) of the two (things compared) it is thus (i.e. the comparison holds good).

The parallel instance (of the sun's reflection in the water) is unobjectionable, since a common feature—with reference to which alone the comparison is instituted—does exist.

Whenever two things are compared, they are so only with reference to some particular point they have in common. Entire equality of the two can never be demonstrated; indeed if it could be demonstrated there would be an end of that particular relation which gives rise to the comparison. Nor does the sûtrakâra institute the comparison objected to on his own account; he merely sets forth the purport of a comparison actually met with in scripture.—Now, the special feature on which the comparison rests is 'the participation in increase and decrease.' The reflected image of the sun dilates when the surface of the water expands; it contracts when the water shrinks; it trembles when the water is agitated; it divides itself when the water is divided. It thus participates in all the attributes and conditions of the water; while the real sun remains all the time the same. —Similarly Brahman, although in reality uniform and never changing, participates as it were in the attributes and states of the body and the other limiting adjuncts within which it abides; it grows with them as it were, decreases with them as it were, and so on. As thus the two things compared possess certain common features no objection can be made to the comparison.

21. And on account of the declaration (of scripture).

Scripture moreover declares that the highest Brahman enters into the body and the other limiting adjuncts, 'He made bodies with two feet, he made bodies with four feet. Having first become a bird he entered the bodies as purusha' (B*ri*. Up. II, 5, 18); and 'Having entered into them with this living (individual) Self' (*Kh*. Up. VI, 3, 2). —For all these reasons the comparison set forth in Sûtra 18 is unobjectionable.

Some teachers assume that the preceding discussion (beginning from Sûtra 11) comprises two adhikara*n*as, of which the former discusses the question whether Brahman is an absolutely uniform being in which all the plurality of the apparent world vanishes, or a being multiform as the apparent world is; while the latter tries to determine whether Brahman—whose absolute uniformity was established in the former adhikara*n*a—is to be defined as that which is (sat), or as thought (intelligence; bodha), or as both.—Against this we remark that in no case there is a valid reason for beginning a second adhikara*n*a. For what should be the subject of a special second adhikara*n*a? Sûtra 15 and foll. cannot be meant to disprove that Brahman possesses a plurality of characteristics; for that hypothesis is already sufficiently disposed of in Sûtras 11–14. Nor can they be meant to show that Brahman is to be defined only as 'that which is,' not also as 'thought;' for that would imply that the scriptural passage, 'consisting of nothing but knowledge' (B*ri*. Up. II, 4, 12), is devoid of meaning. How moreover could Brahman, if devoid of intelligence, be said to be the Self of the intelligent individual soul? Nor again can the hypothetical second adhikara*n*a be assumed to prove that Brahman must be defined as 'thought' only, not at the same time as 'that which is;' for if it were so, certain scriptural passages—as e.g. Ka. Up. II, 6, 13, 'He is to be conceived by the words, He is'—would lose their meaning. And how, moreover, could we admit thought apart from existence?—Nor can it be said that Brahman has both those characteristics, since that would contradict something already admitted. For he who would maintain that Brahman is characterised by thought different from existence, and at the same time by existence different from thought, would virtually maintain that there is a plurality in Brahman, and that view has already been disproved in the preceding adhikara*n*a.—But as scripture teaches both (viz. that Brahman is one only and that it possesses more than one characteristic) there can be no objection to such a doctrine!—There is, we reply, for one being cannot possibly possess more than one nature.—And if it finally should be said that existence is thought and thought existence and that the two do not exclude each other; we remark that in that case there is no reason for the doubt[1] whether Brahman is that which is, or intelligence,

[1] And hence no reason for a separate adhikara*n*a.

or both.—On the other hand we have shown that the Sûtras can be explained as constituting one adhikara*n*a only. Moreover, as the scriptural texts concerning Brahman disagree in so far as representing Brahman as qualified by form and again as devoid of form we, when embracing the alternative of a Brahman devoid of form, must necessarily explain the position of the other texts, and if taken in that sense the Sûtras (15–21) acquire a more appropriate meaning. And if it is maintained that those scriptural passages also which speak of Brahman as qualified by form have no separate meaning of their own, but likewise teach that Brahman is devoid of all form, viz. by intimating that the plurality referred to has to be annihilated; we reply that this opinion also appears objectionable. In those cases, indeed, where elements of plurality are referred to in chapters treating of the highest knowledge, we may assume them to be mentioned merely to be abstracted from; so e.g. in the passage, B*ri*. Up. II, 5, 19, 'His horses are yoked hundreds and ten. This is the horses, this is the ten and the thousands, many and endless,' which passage is immediately followed by the words, 'This is the Brahman without cause and without effect, without anything inside or outside.' But where elements of plurality are referred to in chapters treating of devout meditation, we have no right to assume that they are mentioned only to be set aside. This is the case e.g. in the passage, 'He who consists of mind, whose body is prâ*n*a, whose form is light' (*Kh*. Up. III, 14, 2), which is connected with an injunction of devout meditation contained in the preceding passage, 'Let him have this will and belief.' In passages of the latter kind, where the determinations attributed to Brahman may be taken as they stand and viewed as subserving the purposes of devout meditation, we have no right to assume that they are mentioned with the indirect purpose of being discarded. Moreover, if all texts concerning Brahman equally aimed at discarding all thought of plurality, there would be no opportunity for stating the determinative reason (why Brahman is to be viewed as devoid of all form) as was done in Sûtra 14. And further scripture informs us that devout meditations on Brahman as characterised by form have results of their own, viz. either the warding off of calamities, or the gaining of power, or else release by successive steps. All these reasons determine us to view the passages concerning devout meditation on the one hand and the passages concerning Brahman on the other hand as constituting separate classes, not as forming one whole. In what way moreover, we ask, could the two classes of texts be looked upon as constituting one whole? —Our opponent will perhaps reply, 'Because we apprehend them to form parts of one injunction, just as we do in the case of the dar*s*apûr*n*amâsa-sacrifice and the oblations called prayâ*g*as.'—But this reply we are unable to admit, since the texts about Brahman, as shown at length under I, 1, 4, merely determine an existing substance (viz. Brahman), and do not enjoin any performances. What kind of activity, we moreover ask, are those texts, according to our opponent's view, meant to enjoin? For whenever an injunction is laid upon a person, it has reference to some kind of work to be undertaken by him.—Our opponent will perhaps make the following reply. The object of the injunction is, in the present case, the annihilation of the appearance of duality. As long as the latter is not destroyed, the true nature of Brahman is not known; hence the appearance of duality which stands in the way of true knowledge must be dissolved. Just as the Veda prescribes the performance of certain sacrifices to him who is desirous of the heavenly world, so it prescribes the dissolution of the apparent world to him who is desirous of final release. Whoever wants to know the true nature of Brahman must first annihilate the appearance of plurality that obstructs true knowledge, just as a man wishing to ascertain the true nature of some jar or similar object placed in a dark room must at first remove the darkness. For the apparent world has Brahman for its true nature, not vice versa; therefore the cognition of Brahman is effected through the previous annihilation of the apparent world of names and forms.

This argumentation we meet by asking our opponent

of what nature that so-called annihilation of the apparent world is. Is it analogous to the annihilation of hardness in butter which is effected by bringing it into contact with fire? or is the apparent world of names and forms which is superimposed upon Brahman by Nescience to be dissolved by knowledge, just as the phenomenon of a double moon which is due to a disease of the eyes is removed by the application of medicine[1]? If the former, the Vedic injunctions bid us to do something impossible; for no man can actually annihilate this whole existing world with all its animated bodies and all its elementary substances such as earth and so on. And if it actually could be done, the first released person would have done it once for all, so that at present the whole world would be empty, earth and all other substances having been finally annihilated.—If the latter, i.e. if our opponent maintains that the phenomenal world is superimposed upon Brahman by Nescience and annihilated by knowledge, we point out that the only thing needed is that the knowledge of Brahman should be conveyed by Vedic passages sublating the apparent plurality superimposed upon Brahman by Nescience, such as 'Brahman is one, without a second;' 'That is the true, it is the Self and thou art it.' (*Kh.* Up. VI, 2, 1; 8, 7.) As soon as Brahman is indicated in this way, knowledge arising of itself discards Nescience, and this whole world of names and forms, which had been hiding Brahman from us, melts away like the imagery of a dream. As long, on the other hand, as Brahman is not so indicated, you may say a hundred times, 'Cognize Brahman! Dissolve this world!' and yet we shall be unable to do either the one or the other.

But, our opponent may object, even after Brahman has been indicated by means of the passages quoted, there is room for injunctions bidding us either to cognize Brahman or to dissolve the world.—Not so, we reply; for both these

[1] I.e. does the injunction bidding us to annihilate the phenomenal world look on it as real or as fictitious, due to Nescience only?

things are already effected by the indication of the true nature of Brahman as devoid of all plurality; just as the pointing out of the true nature of the rope has for its immediate result the cognition of the true nature of the rope, and the dissolution of the appearance of a snake or the like. And what is done once need not be done again[1].—We moreover ask the following question: Does the individual soul on which the injunction is laid belong to the unreal element of the phenomenal world or to the real element, i.e. Brahman, which underlies the phenomenal world? If the former, the soul itself is dissolved just as earth and the other elements are, as soon as the knowledge of Brahman's true nature has arisen, and on whom then should the dissolution of the world be enjoined, or who should, by acting on that injunction, obtain release?—If the latter, we are led to the same result. For as soon as there arises the knowledge that Brahman, which never can become the subject of an injunction, is the true being of the soul while the soul as such is due to Nescience, there remains no being on which injunctions could be laid, and hence there is no room for injunctions at all.

What then, it may be asked, is the meaning of those Vedic passages which speak of the highest Brahman as something to be seen, to be heard, and so on?—They aim, we reply, not at enjoining the knowledge of truth, but merely at directing our attention to it. Similarly in ordinary life imperative phrases such as 'Listen to this!' 'Look at this!' are frequently meant to express not that we are immediately to cognize this or that, but only that we are to direct our attention to it. Even when a person is face to face with some object of knowledge, knowledge may either arise or not; all that another person wishing to inform him about the object can do is to point it out to him; knowledge will thereupon spring up in his mind of itself, according to the object of knowledge and according

[1] I.e. after the true nature of Brahman has been once known, there is no longer room for a special injunction to annihilate this apparent world.

to the means of knowledge employed.—Nor must it be said that an injunction may have the purpose of modifying the knowledge of a thing which was originally obtained by some other means of knowledge [1]. For the modified knowledge due to such injunctions is not knowledge in the true sense of the word, but merely a mental energy (i.e. the product, not of an object of knowledge presented to us through one of the means of true knowledge, but of an arbitrary mental activity), and if such modification of knowledge springs up in the mind of itself (i.e. without a deliberate mental act) it is mere error. True knowledge on the other hand, which is produced by the means of true knowledge and is conformable to its object, can neither be brought about by hundreds of injunctions nor be checked by hundreds of prohibitions. For it does not depend on the will of man, but merely on what really and unalterably exists.—For this reason also injunctions of the knowledge of Brahman cannot be admitted.

A further point has to be considered here. If we admitted that injunctions constitute the sole end and aim of the entire Veda, there would remain no authority for the, after all, generally acknowledged truth that Brahman—which is not subject to any injunction—is the Self of all. —Nor would it be of avail to maintain that the Veda may both proclaim the truth stated just now and enjoin on man the cognition of that truth; for that would involve the conclusion that the one Brahma-*s*âstra has two—and moreover conflicting—meanings.—The theory combated by us gives moreover rise to a number of other objections which nobody can refute; it compels us to set aside the text as it stands and to make assumptions not guaranteed by the text; it implies the doctrine that final release is, like the results of sacrificial works, (not the direct result of true knowledge but) the mediate result of the so-called unseen

[1] The pûrvapakshin might refer e.g. to the Vedic injunction, 'he is to meditate upon woman as fire,' and maintain that the object of this injunction is to modify our knowledge of woman derived from perception &c., according to which a woman is not fire.

principle (ad*r*ish*t*a), and non-permanent &c. &c.—We therefore again assert that the texts concerning Brahman aim at cognition, not at injunction, and that hence the pretended reason of 'their being apprehended as parts of one injunction' cannot induce us to look upon the entire Veda as one whole.

And finally, even if we admitted that the texts concerning Brahman are of an injunctive character, we should be unable to prove that the texts denying plurality, and the texts setting forth plurality enjoin one and the same thing; for this latter conclusion cannot be accepted in the face of the several means of proof such as difference of terms[1], and so on, which intimate that there is a plurality of injunctions. The passages respectively enjoining the dar*s*apûr*n*amâsa-sacrifice and the offerings termed prayâ*g*as may indeed be considered to form one whole, as the qualification on the part of the sacrificer furnishes an element common to the two[2]. But the statements about the Brahman devoid of qualities and those about the qualified Brahman have not any element in common; for qualities such as 'having light for one's body' contribute in no way towards the dissolution of the world, nor again does the latter help in any way the former. For the dissolution of the entire phenomenal world on the one hand, and regard for a part of that world on the other hand do not allow themselves to be combined in one and the same subject.—The preferable theory, therefore, is to distinguish with us two classes of texts, according as Brahman is represented as possessing form or as devoid of it.

22. For (the clause 'Not so, not so') denies (of Brahman) the suchness which forms the topic of

[1] 'Difference of terms' (*s*abdântaram) is according to the Pûrva Mîmâ*m*sâ the first of the six means of proof showing karmabheda or niyogabheda. Cp. *S*abara bhâshya on II, 1, 1.

[2] For the sacrifice as well as its subordinate part—the offering of the prayâ*g*as—has to be performed by a sacrificer acting for one end, viz. the obtainment of the heavenly world.

discussion; and (the text) enounces something more than that.

We read, B*ri*. Up. II, 3, 'Two forms of Brahman there are indeed, the material and the immaterial, the mortal and the immortal, the solid and the fluid, sat and tya.' The text thereupon divides the five elements into two classes, predicates of the essence of that which is immaterial—which it calls purusha—saffron-colour, and so on, and then goes on to say, 'Now then the teaching by Not so, not so! For there is nothing else higher than this (if one says): It is not so.' Here we have to enquire what the object of the negative statement is. We do not observe any definite thing indicated by words such as 'this' or 'that;' we merely have the word 'so' in 'Not so, not so!' to which the word 'not' refers, and which on that account indicates something meant to be denied. Now we know that the word 'so' (iti) is used with reference to approximate things, in the same way as the particle 'evam' is used; compare, e.g. the sentence 'so (iti) indeed the teacher said' (where the 'so' refers to his immediately preceding speech). And, in our passage, the context points out what has to be considered as proximate, viz. the two cosmic forms of Brahman, and that Brahman itself to which the two forms belong. Hence there arises a doubt whether the phrase, 'Not so, not so!' negatives both Brahman and its two forms, or only either; and if the latter, whether it negatives Brahman and leaves its two forms, or if it negatives the two forms and leaves Brahman.—We suppose, the pûrvapakshin says, that the negative statement negatives Brahman as well as its two forms; both being suggested by the context. As the word 'not' is repeated twice, there are really two negative statements, of which the one negatives the cosmic form of Brahman, the other that which has form, i.e. Brahman itself. Or else we may suppose that Brahman alone is negatived. For as Brahman transcends all speech and thought, its existence is doubtful, and admits of being negatived; the plurality of cosmic forms on the other hand falls within the sphere of perception and the other means of right knowledge, and can, therefore, not be negatived.—On this latter interpretation the repetition of 'not' must be considered as due to emphasis only.

To this we make the following reply. It is impossible that the phrase, 'Not so, not so!' should negative both, since that would imply the doctrine of a general Void. Whenever we deny something unreal, we do so with reference to something real; the unreal snake, e.g. is negatived with reference to the real rope. But this (denial of something unreal with reference to something real) is possible only if some entity is left. If everything is denied, no entity is left, and if no entity is left, the denial of some other entity which we may wish to undertake, becomes impossible, i.e. that latter entity becomes real and as such cannot be negatived. —Nor, in the second place, can Brahman be denied; for that would contradict the introductory phrase of the chapter, 'Shall I tell you Brahman? (B*ri*. Up. II, 1, 1); would show disregard of the threat conveyed in Taitt. Up. II, 6, 'He who knows the Brahman as non-existing becomes himself non-existing;' would be opposed to definitive assertions such as 'By the words "He is" is he to be apprehended' (Ka. Up. II, 6, 13); and would involve a stultification of the entire Vedânta.—The phrase that Brahman transcends all speech and thought does certainly not mean to say that Brahman does not exist; for after the Vedânta-part of scripture has established at length the existence of Brahman —in such passages as 'He who knows Brahman obtains the highest;' 'Truth, knowledge, infinite is Brahman'—it cannot be supposed all at once to teach its non-existence. For, as the common saying is, 'Better than bathing it is not to touch dirt at all.' The passage, 'from whence all speech with the mind turns away unable to reach it' (Taitt. Up. II, 4), must, therefore, rather be viewed as intimating Brahman.

The passage of the B*ri*. Up. under discussion has, therefore, to be understood as follows. Brahman is that whose nature is permanent purity, intelligence, and freedom; it transcends speech and mind, does not fall within the category of 'object,' and constitutes the inward Self of all. Of this Brahman our text denies all plurality of forms; but

Brahman itself it leaves untouched. This the Sûtra expresses in the words, 'for it denies the suchness which forms the topic of discussion.' That means: The passage 'Not so,' &c., denies of Brahman the limited form, material as well as immaterial, which in the preceding part of the chapter is described at length with reference to the gods as well as the body, and also the second form which is produced by the first, is characterised by mental impressions, forms the essence of that which is immaterial, is denoted by the term purusha, rests on the subtle Self (liṅgâtman) and is described by means of comparisons with saffron-colour, &c., since the purusha, which is the essence of what is immaterial, does not itself possess colour perceivable by the eye. Now these forms of Brahman are by means of the word 'so' (iti), which always refers to something approximate brought into connexion with the negative particle 'not.' Brahman itself, on the other hand (apart from its forms), is, in the previous part of the chapter, mentioned not as in itself constituting the chief topic, but only in so far as it is qualified by its forms; this appears from the circumstance of Brahman being exhibited in the genitive case only ('These are two forms *of Brahman*'). Now, after the two forms have been set forth, there arises the desire of knowing that to which the two forms belong, and hence the text continues, 'Now then the teaching by means of "Not so, not so."' This passage, we conclude, conveys information regarding the nature of Brahman by denying the reality of the forms fictitiously attributed to it; for the phrase, 'Not so, not so!' negatives the whole aggregate of effects superimposed on Brahman. Effects we know to have no real existence, and they can therefore be negatived; not so, however, Brahman, which constitutes the necessary basis for all fictitious superimposition.—Nor must the question be asked here, how the sacred text, after having itself set forth the two forms of Brahman, can negative them in the end, contrary to the principle that not to touch dirt is better than bathing after having done so. For the text does not set forth the two forms of Brahman as something the truth of which is to be established, but merely mentions those two forms, which in the sphere of ordinary thought are fictitiously attributed to Brahman, in order finally to negative them and establish thereby the true nature of the formless Brahman.

The double repetition of the negation may either serve the purpose of furnishing a special denial of the material as well as the immaterial form of Brahman; or the first 'Not so' may negative the aggregate of material elements, while the second denies the aggregate of mental impressions. Or else the repetition may be an emphatic one, intimating that whatever can be thought is not Brahman. This is, perhaps, the better explanation. For if a limited number of things are denied each individually, there still remains the desire to know whether something else may not be Brahman; an emphatic repetition of the denial on the other hand shows that the entire aggregate of objects is denied and that Brahman is the inward Self; whereby all further enquiry is checked.—The final conclusion, therefore, is, that the text negatives only the cosmic plurality fictitiously superimposed on Brahman, but leaves Brahman itself untouched.

The Sûtra gives another argument establishing the same conclusion, 'and the text enounces something more than that,' i.e. more than the preceding negation. The words of the text meant are '(not) is there anything beyond.'—If the negation, 'Not so, not so!' were meant to negative all things whatever, and this terminated in absolute non-existence, the text could not even allude to 'anything beyond.'—The words of the text are to be connected as follows. After the clause, 'Not so, not so!' has given information about Brahman, the clause next following illustrates this teaching by saying: There is nothing beyond or separate from this Brahman; therefore Brahman is expressed by 'Not so, not so!' which latter words do not mean that Brahman itself does not exist. The implied meaning rather is that different from everything else there exists the 'non-negatived' Brahman.—The words of the text admit, however, of another interpretation also; for they may mean that there is no teaching of Brahman higher than that teaching which is implied in the negation of plurality expressed by 'Not so, not so!' On this latter interpretation the words of the Sûtra, 'and the text enounces something more than that,' must be taken to refer to the name mentioned in the text, 'Then comes the name, the True of the True; the senses being the True and he the True of them.'—This again has a sense only if the previous negative clause denies everything but Brahman, not everything but absolute non-existence. For, if the latter were the case, what then could be called the True of the True?—We therefore decide that the clause, 'Not so, not so!' negatives not absolutely everything, but only everything but Brahman.

23. That (Brahman) is unevolved; for (thus scripture) says.

If that highest Brahman which is different from the world that is negatived in the passage discussed above really exists, why then is it not apprehended?—Because, the Sûtrakâra replies, it is unevolved, not to be apprehended by the senses; for it is the witness of whatever is apprehended (i.e. the subject in all apprehension). Thus *S*ruti says, 'He is not apprehended by the eye, nor by speech, nor by the other senses, not by penance or good works' (Mu. Up. III, 1, 8); 'That Self is to be described by No, no! He is incomprehensible, for he cannot be comprehended' (B*ri*. Up. III, 9, 26); 'That which cannot be seen nor apprehended' (Mu. Up. I, 1, 6); 'When in that which is invisible, incorporeal, undefined, unsupported' &c. (Taitt. Up. II, 7). Similar statements are made in Sm*ri*ti-passages; so e.g. 'He is called unevolved, not to be fathomed by thought, unchangeable.'

24. And in the state of perfect conciliation also (the Yogins apprehend the highest Brahman), according to *S*ruti and Sm*ri*ti.

At the time of perfect conciliation the Yogins see the unevolved Self free from all plurality. By 'perfect conciliation' we understand the presentation before the mind (of the highest Self), which is effected through meditation and devotion.—This is vouched for by *S*ruti as well as

Sm*ri*ti. So, e.g. Ka. Up. IV, 1, 'The Self-existent pierced the openings of the senses so that they turn outward; therefore man looks without, not within himself. Some wise man, however, with his eyes closed and wishing for immortality, saw the Self within.' And Mu. Up. III, 1, 8, 'When a man's mind has become purified by the serene light of knowledge then he sees him, meditating on him as without parts.' Sm*ri*ti-passages of the same tendency are the following ones, 'He who is seen as light by the Yogins meditating on him sleepless, with suspended breath, with contented minds, with subdued senses; reverence be to him[1]!' and 'The Yogins see him, the august, eternal one.'

But if in the state of perfect conciliation there is a being to be conciliated and a being conciliating, does not this involve the distinction of a higher and a lower Self?—No, the next Sûtra replies.

25. And as in the case of (physical) light and the like, there is non-distinction (of the two Selfs), the light (i.e. the intelligent Self) (being divided) by its activity; according to the repeated declarations of scripture.

As light, ether, the sun and so on appear differentiated as it were through their objects such as fingers, vessels, water and so on which constitute limiting adjuncts[2], while in reality they preserve their essential non-differentiatedness; so the distinction of different Selfs is due to limiting adjuncts only, while the unity of all Selfs is natural and original. For on the doctrine of the non-difference of the individual soul and the highest Self the Vedânta-texts insist again and again[3].

---

[1] Whose Self is Yoga.

[2] Light is differentiated as it were by the various objects on which it shines; the all-pervading ether is divided into parts as it were by hollow bodies; the sun is multiplied as it were by its reflections in the water.

[3] It certainly looks here as if the Bhâshyakâra did not know what to do with the words of the Sûtra. The 'karma*n*i,' which is

26. Hence (the soul enters into unity) with the infinite (i.e. the highest Self); for this scripture indicates.

Hence i.e. because the non-difference of all Selfs is essential and their difference due to Nescience only, the individual soul after having dispelled Nescience by true knowledge passes over into unity with the highest Self. For this is indicated by scripture, cp. e.g. Mu. Up. III, 2, 9, 'He who knows that highest Brahman becomes even Brahman;' B*ri*. Up. IV, 4, 6, 'Being Brahman he goes to Brahman.'

27. But on account of twofold designation, (the relation of the highest Self to the individual soul has to be viewed) like that of the snake to its coils.

In order to justify his own view as to the relation of the conciliating individual soul and the conciliated highest Self, the Sûtrakâra mentions a different view of the same matter. —Some scriptural passages refer to the highest Self and the individual soul as distinct entities, cp. e.g. Mu. Up. III, 1, 8, 'Then he sees him meditating on him as without parts,' where the highest Self appears as the object of the soul's vision and meditation; Mu. Up. III, 2, 8, 'He goes to the divine Person who is greater than the great;' and B*ri*. Up. III, 7, 15, 'Who rules all beings within;' in which passages the highest Self is represented as the object of approach and as the ruler of the individual soul. In other places again the two are spoken of as non-different, so e.g. *Kh*. Up. VI, 8, 7, 'Thou art that;' B*ri*. Up. I, 4, 10, 'I am Brahman;' B*ri*. Up. III, 4, 1, 'This is thy Self who is within all;' B*ri*. Up. III, 7, 15, 'He is thy Self, the ruler within, the immortal.'—As thus difference and non-difference are equally vouched for by scripture, the acceptation of absolute non-difference would render futile all those

as good as passed over by him, is explained by Go. Ân. as 'dhyânâdikarma*n*y upâdhau.' Ân. Gi. says, 'âtmâprakâ*s*a*s*abdito*g*ñânatatkârye karma*n*y upâdhau savi*s*eshas' &c.

texts which speak of difference. We therefore look on the relation of the highest Self and the soul as analogous to that of the snake and its coils. Viewed as a whole the snake is one, non-different, while an element of difference appears if we view it with regard to its coils, hood, erect posture and so on.

28. Or else like that of light to its substratum, both being fire.

Or else the relation of the two may be viewed as follows. Just as the light of the sun and its substratum, i.e. the sun himself, are not absolutely different—for they both consist of fire—and yet are spoken of as different, so also the soul and the highest Self.

29. Or else (the relation of the two is to be conceived) in the manner stated above.

Or else the relation of the two has to be conceived in the manner suggested by Sûtra 25. For if the bondage of the soul is due to Nescience only, final release is possible. But if the soul is really and truly bound—whether the soul be considered as a certain condition or state of the highest Self as suggested in Sûtra 27, or as a part of the highest Self as suggested in Sûtra 28—its real bondage cannot be done away with, and thus the scriptural doctrine of final release becomes absurd.—Nor, finally, can it be said that *S*ruti equally teaches difference and non-difference. For non-difference only is what it aims at establishing; while, when engaged in setting forth something else, it merely refers to difference as something known from other sources of knowledge (viz perception, &c.).—Hence the conclusion stands that the soul is not different from the highest Self, as explained in Sûtra 25.

30. And on account of the denial.

The conclusion arrived at above is confirmed by the fact of scripture expressly denying that there exists any intelligent being apart from the highest Self. Cp. 'There is no other seer but he' (B*ri*. Up. III, 7, 23). And the same conclusion follows from those passages which deny the existence of a world apart from Brahman and thus leave Brahman alone remaining, viz. 'Now then the teaching, Not so, not so!' (*Bri.* Up. II, 3, 6); 'That Brahman is without cause and without effect, without anything inside or outside' (*Bri.* Up. II, 5, 19).

31. Beyond (Brahman, there is something) further, on account of the designations of bank, measure, connexion, separation.

With reference to this Brahman which we have ascertained to be free from all plurality there now arises the doubt—due to the conflicting nature of various scriptural statements—whether something exists beyond it or not. We therefore enter on the task of explaining the true meaning of those scriptural passages which s e e m to indicate that there is some entity beyond, i.e. apart from Brahman.

The pûrvapakshin maintains that some entity must be admitted apart from Brahman, because Brahman is spoken of as being a bank; as having size; as being connected; as being separated.—As a bank it is spoken of in the passage, *Kh.* Up. VIII, 4, 1, 'That Self is a bank, a boundary.' The word 'bank' (setu) ordinarily denotes a structure of earth, wood and the like, serving the purpose of checking the flow of water. Here, being applied to the Self, it intimates that there exists something apart from the Self, just as there exists something different from an ordinary bank. The same conclusion is confirmed by the words, 'Having passed the bank' (VIII, 4, 2). For as in ordinary life a man after having crossed a bank reaches some place which is not a bank, let us say a forest; so, we must understand, a man after having crossed, i.e. passed beyond the Self reaches something which is not the Self.—As having size Brahman is spoken of in the following passages, 'This Brahman has four feet (quarters), eight hoofs, sixteen parts.' Now it is well known from ordinary experience that wherever an object, a coin, e.g. has a definite limited size, there exists something different from that object; we therefore must assume that there also exists something different from Brahman.—Brahman is declared to be connected in the following passages, 'Then he is united with the True' (*Kh.* Up. VI, 8, 1), and 'The embodied Self is embraced by the highest Self' (B*ri*. Up. IV, 3, 21). Now we observe that non-measured things are connected with things measured, men, e.g. with a town. And scripture declares that the individual souls are, in the state of deep sleep, connected with Brahman. Hence we conclude that beyond Brahman there is something unmeasured.—The same conclusion is finally confirmed by those texts which proclaim difference, so e.g. the passage, I, 6, 6 ff. ('Now that golden person who is seen within the sun' &c.), which at first refers to a Lord residing in the sun and then mentions a Lord residing in the eye, distinct from the former ('Now the person who is seen within the eye'). The text distinctly transfers to the latter the form &c. of the former [1] ('The form of that person is the same as the form of the other' &c.), and moreover declares that the lordly power of both is limited, 'He obtains through the one the worlds beyond that and the wishes of the devas' &c.; which is very much as if one should say, 'This is the reign of the king of Magadha and that the reign of the king of Videha.'

From all this it follows that there exists something different from Brahman.

32. But (Brahman is called a bank &c.) on account of (a certain) equality.

The word 'but' is meant to set aside the previously established conclusion.—There can exist nothing different from Brahman, since we are unable to observe a proof for such existence. That all existences which have a beginning spring from, subsist through, and return into Brahman we have already ascertained, and have shown that the effect is non-different from the cause.—Nor can there exist, apart from Brahman, something which has no beginning, since scripture affirms that 'Being only this was

[1] Which would be unnecessary if the two were not distinct.

in the beginning, one, without a second.' The promise moreover that through the cognition of one thing everything will be known, renders it impossible that there should exist anything different from Brahman.—But does not the fact that the Self is called a bank, &c. indicate that there exists something beyond the Self?—No, we reply; the passages quoted by the pûrvapakshin have no power to prove his conclusion. For the text only says that the Self is a bank, not that there is something beyond it. Nor are we entitled to assume the existence of some such thing, merely to the end of accounting for the Self being called a bank; for the simple assumption of something unknown is a mere piece of arbitrariness. If, moreover, the mere fact of the Self being called a bank implied the existence of something beyond it, as in the case of an ordinary bank, we should also be compelled to conclude that the Self is made of earth and stones; which would run counter to the scriptural doctrine that the Self is not something produced.—The proper explanation is that the Self is called a bank because it resembles a bank in a certain respect; as a bank dams back the water and marks the boundary of contiguous fields, so the Self supports the world and its boundaries. The Self is thus glorified by the name of bank because it resembles one.—In the clause quoted above, 'having passed that bank,' the verb 'to pass' cannot be taken in the sense of 'going beyond,' but must rather mean 'to reach fully.' In the same way we say of a student, 'he has passed the science of grammar,' meaning thereby that he has fully mastered it.

33. (The statement as to Brahman having size) subserves the purpose of the mind; in the manner of the four feet (quarters).

In reply to the pûrvapakshin's contention that the statements as to Brahman's size, prove that there exists something different from Brahman, we remark that those statements merely serve the purposes of the mind, i.e. of devout meditation.—But how can the cognition of something consisting of four, or eight, or sixteen parts be referred to Brahman?—Through its modifications (effects), we reply, Brahman is assumed to be subject to measure. For as some men are of inferior, others of middling, others again of superior intelligence, not all are capable of fixing their mind on the infinite Brahman, devoid of all effects. 'In the manner of the four feet,' i.e. in the same way as (*Kh.* Up. III, 18), for the purpose of pious meditation, speech and three other feet are ascribed to mind viewed as the personal manifestation of Brahman, and fire and three other feet to the ether viewed as the cosmic manifestation of Brahman.—Or else the phrase, 'in the manner of the four quarters,' may be explained as follows. In the same way as to facilitate commerce, a kârshâpa*n*a is assumed to be divided into four parts—for there being no fixed rule as to the value of bargains, people cannot always carry on their transactions with whole kârshâpa*n*as only—, (so, in order to facilitate pious meditation on the part of less intelligent people, four feet, &c., are ascribed to Brahman).

34. (The statements concerning connexion and difference) are due to difference of place; in the manner of light and so on.

The present Sûtra refutes the allegation that something different from Brahman exists, firstly, because things are said to be connected with Brahman, and secondly, because things are said to be separate from it. The fact is, that all those statements regarding connexion and difference are made with a view to difference of place. When the cognition of difference which is produced by the Self's connexion with different places, i.e. with the buddhi and the other limiting adjuncts, ceases on account of the cessation of those limiting adjuncts themselves, connexion with the highest Self is metaphorically said to take place; but that is done with a view to the limiting adjuncts only, not with a view to any limitation on the part of the Self.—In the same way, all statements regarding difference have reference to the difference of Brahman's limiting adjuncts only, not to any difference affecting Brahman's own nature.—All this is analogous to the case of light and the like. For the light of the sun or the moon also is differentiated by its connexion with limiting adjuncts, and is, on account of these adjuncts, spoken of as divided, and, when the adjuncts are removed, it is said to enter into connexion (union). Other instances of the effect of limiting adjuncts are furnished by the ether entering into connexion with the eyes of needles and the like.

35. And because (only such a connexion) is possible.

Moreover, only such a connexion as described above is possible. For scriptural passages, such as 'He is gone to his Self' (*Kh.* Up. VI, 8, 1), declare that the connexion of the soul with the highest Self is one of essential nature. But as the essential nature of a thing is imperishable, the connexion cannot be analogous to that of the inhabitants with the town, but can only be explained with reference to an obscuration, owing to Nescience, of the soul's true nature.—Similarly the difference spoken of by scripture cannot be real, but only such as is due to Nescience; for many texts declare that there exists only one Lord. Analogously, scripture teaches that the one ether is made manifold as it were by its connexion with different places 'The ether which is outside man is the ether which is inside man, and the ether within the heart' (*Kh.* Up. III, 12, 7 ff.).

36. (The same thing follows) from the express denial of other (existences).

Having thus refuted the arguments of the pûrvapakshin, the Sûtrakâra in conclusion strengthens his view by a further reason. A great number of Vedic passages—which, considering the context in which they stand, cannot be explained otherwise—distinctly deny that there exists anything apart from Brahman; 'He indeed is below; I am below; the Self is below' (*Kh.* Up. VII, 25, 1; 2); 'Whosoever looks for anything elsewhere than in the Self was abandoned by everything' (B*ri*. Up. II, 4, 6); 'Brahman alone is all this' (Mu. Up. II, 2, 11); 'The Self is all this' (*Kh*. Up. VII, 25, 2): 'In it there is no diversity' (B*ri*. Up. IV, 4, 19); 'He to whom there is nothing superior, from whom there is nothing different' (*S*vet. Up. III, 9); 'This is the Brahman without cause and without effect, without anything inside or outside' (B*ri*. Up. II, 5, 19).—And that there is no other Self within the highest Self, follows from that scriptural passage which teaches Brahman to be within everything (B*ri*. Up. II, 5, 19).

37. Thereby the omnipresence (of Brahman is established), in accordance with the statements about (Brahman's) extent.

The preceding demonstration that the texts calling B ahman a bank, and so on, are not to be taken literally, and that, on the other hand, the texts denying all plurality must be accepted as they stand, moreover, serves to prove that the Self is omnipresent. If the former texts were taken literally, banks and the like would have to be looked upon as belonging to the Self, and thence it would follow that the Self is limited. And if the texts of the latter class were not accepted as valid, there would be substances exclusive of each other, and thus the Self would again be limited.—That the Self is omnipresent follows from the texts proclaiming its extent, &c., cp. *Kh*. Up. VIII, 1, 3, 'As large as this ether is, so large is that ether within the heart;' 'Like the ether, he is omnipresent and eternal;' 'He is greater than the sky, greater than the ether' (*S*at. Br. X, 6, 3, 2); 'He is eternal, omnipresent, firm, immoveable' (Bha. Gitâ II, 24); and other similar passages from *S*ruti and Sm*ri*ti.

38. From him (i.e. the Lord, there comes) the fruit (of works); for (that only) is possible.

We now turn to another characteristic belonging to Brahman, in so far as it is connected with the every-day world in which we distinguish a ruler and the objects of his rule.—There arises the question whether the threefold fruits of action which are enjoyed by the creatures in their sa*m*sâra-state—viz. pain, pleasure, and a mixture of the two—spring from the actions themselves or come from the Lord.—The Sûtrakâra embraces the latter alternative, on the ground that it is the only possible one. The ruler of all who by turns provides for the creation, the subsistence and the reabsorption of the world, and who knows all the differences of place and time, he alone is capable of effecting all those modes of requital which are in accordance with the merit of the agents; actions, on the other hand, which pass away as soon as done, have no power of bringing about results at some future time, since nothing can spring from nothing. Nor can the latter difficulty be overcome by the assumption that an action passes away only after having produced some result according to its nature, and that the agent will at some future time enjoy that fruit of his action. For the fruit of an action is such only through being enjoyed by the agent; only at the moment when some pleasure or some pain—the result of some deed—is enjoyed by the doer of the deed people understand it to be a 'fruit.'—Nor, in the second place, have we the right to assume that the fruit will, at some future time, spring from the so-called supersensuous principle (apûrva), which itself is supposed to be a direct result of the deed; for that so-called supersensuous principle is something of non-intelligent nature, comparable to a piece of wood or metal, and as such cannot act unless moved by some intelligent being. And moreover there is no proof whatever for the existence of such an apûrva.—But is it not proved by the fact that deeds are actually requited?—By no means, we reply; for the fact of requital may be accounted for by the action of the Lord.

39. And because it is declared by scripture.

We assume the Lord to bring about the fruits of actions, not only because no other assumption appears plausible, but also because we have direct scriptural statement on our side. Cp. e.g. the passage, 'This indeed is the great, unborn Self, the giver of food, the giver of wealth' (B*ri*. Up. IV, 4, 24).

40. *G*aimini (thinks) for the same reasons that religious merit (is what brings about the fruits of actions).

*G*aimini bases a contrary opinion on the reasons specified in the last two Sûtras. Scripture, he argues, proclaims injunctions such as the following one, 'He who is desirous of the heavenly world is to sacrifice.' Now as it is admitted that such scriptural injunctions must have an object, we conclude that the sacrifice itself brings about the result, i. e. the obtainment of the heavenly world; for if this were not so, nobody would perform sacrifices and thereby scriptural injunctions would be rendered purposeless.—But has not this view of the matter already been abandoned, on the ground that an action which passes away as soon as done can have no fruit?—We must, the reply is, follow the authority of scripture and assume such a connexion of action and fruit as agrees with scriptural statement. Now it is clear that a deed cannot effect a result at some future time, unless, before passing away, it gives birth to some unseen result; we therefore assume that there exists some result which we call apûrva, and which may be viewed either as an imperceptible after-state of the deed or as an imperceptible antecedent state of the result. This hypothesis removes all difficulties, while on the other hand it is impossible that the Lord should effect the results of actions. For in the first place, one uniform cause cannot be made to account for a great variety of effects; in the second place, the Lord would have to be taxed with partiality and cruelty; and in the third place, if the deed itself did not bring about its own fruit, it would be useless to perform it at all.—For all these reasons the result springs from the deed only, whether meritorious or non-meritorious.

41. Bâdâraya*n*a, however, thinks the former (i. e. the Lord, to be the cause of the fruits of action), since he is designated as the cause (of the actions themselves).

The teacher Bâdârayana thinks that the previously-mentioned Lord is the cause of the fruits of action. The word 'however' sets aside the view of the fruit being produced either by the mere deed or the mere apûrva.—The final conclusion then is that the fruits come from the Lord acting with a view to the deeds done by the souls, or, if it be so preferred, with a view to the apûrva springing from the deeds. This view is proved by the circumstance of scripture representing the Lord not only as the giver of fruits but also as the causal agent with reference to all actions whether good or evil. Compare the passage, Kau. Up. III, 8, 'He makes him whom he wishes to lead up from these worlds do a good deed; and the same makes him whom he wishes to lead down from these worlds do a bad deed.' The same is said in the Bhagavadgîtâ (VII, 21), 'Whichever divine form a devotee wishes to worship with faith, to that form I render his faith steady. Holding that faith he strives to propitiate the deity and obtains from it the benefits he desires, as ordained by me.'

All Vedânta-texts moreover declare that the Lord is the only cause of all creation. And his creating all creatures in forms and conditions corresponding to—and retributive of—their former deeds, is just what entitles us to call the Lord the cause of all fruits of actions. And as the Lord has regard to the merit and demerit of the souls, the objections raised above—as to one uniform cause being inadequate to the production of various effects, &c.—are without any foundation.

THIRD PÂDA.

Reverence to the highest Self!

1. (The cognitions) intimated by all the Vedânta-texts (are identical), on account of the non-difference of injunction and so on.

In the preceding part of this work we have explained the nature of the object of cognition, i.e. Brahman. We now enter on the discussion of the question whether the cognitions of Brahman, which form the subject of the different Vedânta-texts, are separate cognitions or not.

But, an objection may here be raised, so far we have determined that Brahman is free from all distinctions whatever, one, of absolutely uniform nature like a lump of salt; hence there appears to be no reason for even raising the question whether the cognitions of Brahman are separate cognitions or constitute only one cognition. For as Brahman is one and of uniform nature, it certainly cannot be maintained that the Vedânta-texts aim at establishing a plurality in Brahman comparable to the plurality of works (inculcated by the karmakâ*nd*a of the Veda). Nor can it be said that although Brahman is uniform, yet it may be the object of divers cognitions; for any difference in nature between the cognition and the object known points to a mistake committed. If, on the other hand, it should be assumed that the different Vedânta-texts aim at teaching different cognitions of Brahman, it would follow that only one cognition can be the right one while all others are mistaken, and that would lead to a general distrust of all Vedânta.—Hence the question whether each individual Vedânta-text teaches a separate cognition of Brahman or not cannot even be raised.—Nor, supposing that question were raised after all, can the non-difference of the cognition of Brahman be demonstrated (as the Sûtra attempts) on the ground that all Vedânta-texts are equally injunctions, since the cognition of Brahman is not of the nature of an injunction. For the teacher has proved at length (I, 1, 4) that the knowledge of Brahman is produced by passages which treat of Brahman as an existing accomplished thing and thus do not aim at enjoining anything.—Why then begin at all this discussion about the difference or non-difference of the cognitions of Brahman?

To all this we reply that no objection can be raised against a discussion of that kind, since the latter has for its object only the qualified Brahman and prâ*n*a and the like. For devout meditations on the qualified Brahman may, like acts, be either identical or different. Scripture moreover teaches that, like acts, they have various results; some of them have visible results, others unseen results, and others again—as conducive to the springing up of perfect knowledge—have for their result release by successive steps. With a view to those meditations, therefore, we may raise the question whether the individual Vedânta-texts teach different cognitions of Brahman or not.

The arguments which may here be set forth by the pûrvapakshin are as follows. In the first place it is known that difference may be proved by names, as e.g. in the case of the sacrificial performance called 'light' (*g*yotis)[1]. And the cognitions of Brahman which are enjoined in the different Vedânta-texts are connected with different names such as the Taittirîyaka, the Vâ*g*asaneyaka, the Kauthumaka, the Kaushîtaka, the *S*â*t*yâyanaka, &c.—In the second place the separateness of actions is proved by the difference of form (characteristics; rûpa). So e.g. with reference to the passage, 'the milk is for the Vi*s*vedevas, the water for the vâ*g*ins[2].'

---

[1] See the sa*mg*ñâkr*i*takarmabhedâdhikara*n*a, Pû. Mî. Sû. II, 2, 22, where the decision is that the word *g*yotis (in 'athaisha *g*yotir' &c.) denotes not the *g*yotish*t*oma but a separate sacrificial performance.

[2] See Pû. Mî. Sû. II, 2, 23. The offering of water made to the divinities called vâ*g*in is separate from the offering of milk to the Vi*s*vedevas; for the material offered as well as the divinity to which the offering is made (i.e. the two rûpa of the sacrifice) differs in the two cases.

Now similar differences of form are met with in the Vedânta-texts; the followers of one *S*âkhâ, e.g. mention, in the chapter called 'the knowledge of the five fires,' a sixth fire, while other *S*âkhâs mention five only; and in the colloquy of the prâ*n*as some texts mention a lesser, others a greater number of organs and powers of the body. —In the third place differences in qualifying particulars (dharma) are supposed to prove difference of acts, and such differences also are met with in the Vedânta-texts; only in the Mu*nd*aka-Upanishad, e.g. it is said that the science of Brahman must be imparted to those only who have performed the rite of carrying fire on the head (Mu. Up. III, 2, 10).—In the same way the other reasons which are admitted to prove the separateness of actions, such as repetition and so on, are to be applied in a suitable manner to the different Vedânta-texts also.—We therefore maintain that each separate Vedânta-text teaches a different cognition of Brahman.

To this argumentation of the pûrvapakshin we make the following reply.—The cognitions enjoined by all the Vedânta-texts are the same, owing to the non-difference of injunction and so on. The 'and so on' refers to the other reasons proving non-difference of acts which are enumerated in the Siddhânta-sûtra of the adhikara*n*a treating of the different *S*âkhâs (Pû. Mî. II, 4, 9, '(the act) is one on account of the non-difference of connexion of form, of injunction, and of name'). Thus, as the agnihotra though described in different *S*âkhâs is yet one, the same kind of human activity being enjoined in all by means of the words, 'He is to offer;' so the injunction met with in the text of the Vâ*g*asaneyins (B*ri*. Up. VI, 1, 1), 'He who knows the oldest and the best,' &c., is the same as that which occurs in the text of the *Kh*andogas, 'He who knows the first and the best' (*Kh*. Up. V, 1, 1). The connexion of the meditation enjoined with its aim is likewise the same in both texts, 'He becomes the first and best among his people.' In both texts again the cognition enjoined has the same form. For in both the object of knowledge is the true nature of the prâ*n*a which is characterised by certain qualities such as being the first and best, and just as the material and the divinity constitute the form of the sacrifice, so the object known constitutes the form of the cognition. And finally both cognitions have the same name, viz. the knowledge of the prâ*n*a.—For these reasons we declare that the different Vedânta-texts enjoin identical cognitions.—A similar line of reasoning applies to other cognitions which are met with in more than one Vedânta-text, so e.g. to the knowledge of the five fires, the knowledge of Vais*v*ânara, the knowledge of *S*â*nd*ilya and so on.—Of the apparent reasons on the ground of which the pûrvapakshin above tried to show that the meditations are not identical but separate a refutation is to be found in the Pûrvâ Mîmâ*m*sâ-sûtras II, 4, 10 ff.

The next Sûtra disposes of a doubt which may remain even after the preceding discussion.

2. (If it be said that the vidyâs are separate) on account of the difference (of secondary matters), we deny that, since even in one and the same vidyâ (different secondary matters may find place).

In spite of the preceding argumentation we cannot admit that the different cognitions of Brahman are equally intimated by all Vedânta-texts, because we meet with differences in secondary matters (gu*n*a). Thus the Vâ*g*asaneyins mention in their text of the knowledge of the five fires a sixth fire ('And then the fire is indeed fire,' B*ri*. Up. VI, 2, 14), while the *Kh*andogas mention no sixth fire but conclude their text of the pa*ñk*âgnividyâ with the express mention of five fires ('But he who thus knows the five fires,' *Kh*. Up. V, 10, 10).

Now it is impossible to admit that the cognition of those who admit that particular qualification (i.e. the sixth fire) and of those who do not should be one and the same. Nor may we attempt to evade the difficulty by saying that the sixth fire may be tacitly included in the vidyâ of the *Kh*andogas; for that would contradict the number 'five' expressly stated by them.—In the colloquy of the prâ*n*as again the *Kh*andogas mention, in addition to the most important prâ*n*a, four other prânas, viz. speech, the eye, the ear, and the mind; while the Vâ*g*asaneyins mention a fifth one also, 'Seed indeed is generation. He who knows that becomes rich in offspring and cattle' (B*ri*. Up. VI, 1, 6).—Now a difference of procedure in the point of addition and omission effects a difference in the object known, and the latter again effects a difference in the vidyâ, just as a difference in the point of material and divinity distinguishes one sacrifice from another.

To this we make the following reply.—Your objection is without force, since such differences of qualification as are met with in the above instances are possible even in one and the same vidyâ. In the *Kh*ândogya-text a sixth fire is indeed not included; yet, as five fires, beginning with the heavenly world, are recognised as the same in both texts the mentioned difference cannot effect a split of the vidyâ; not any more than the atirâtra-sacrifice is differentiated by the sho*d*a*s*in-rite being either used or not-used. Moreover, the *Kh*ândogya-text also actually mentions a sixth fire, viz. in the passage, V, 9, 2, 'When he has departed, his friends carry him, as appointed, to the fire.'—The Vâ*g*asaneyins, on the other hand, mention their sixth fire ('and then the fire is indeed fire, the fuel fuel,' &c.) for the purpose of cutting short the fanciful assumption regarding fuel, smoke, and so on, which runs through the description of the five fires with which the heavenly world and so on are imaginatively identified. Their statement regarding the sixth fire (has therefore not the purpose of enjoining it as an object of meditation but) is merely a remark about something already established (known)[1]. And even if we assume that the statement about the sixth fire has the purpose of representing that fire as an object of devout meditation, yet the fire may be inserted in the vidyâ of the *Kh*andogas without any fear of its being in conflict with the number five mentioned there;

[1] Viz. the real fire in which the dead body is burned and which is known from perception.

for that number is not an essential part of the injunction[1], but merely makes an additional statement regarding something known already from the text, viz. the five fires with which the heavenly world and so on are identified[2]. Similarly nothing stands in the way of some additional qualification being included in the vidyâ concerning the colloquy of the prâ*n*as and so on. The addition or omission of some particular qualification is unable to introduce difference into the object of knowledge and thereby into the knowledge itself; for although the objects of knowledge may differ partly, yet their greater part and at the same time the knowing person are understood to be the same. Hence the vidyâ also remains the same.

3. (The rite of carrying fire on the head is an attribute) of the study of the Veda (of the Âtharva*n*ikas); because in the Samâ*k*âra (it is mentioned) as being such. (This also follows) from the general subject-matter, and the limitation (of the rite to the Âtharva*n*ikas) is analogous to that of the libations.

With reference to the pûrvapakshin's averment that the rite of carrying fire on the head is connected with the vidyâ of the followers of the Atharva-veda only, not with any other vidyâ, and that thereby the vidyâ of the Âtharva*n*ikas is separated from all other vidyâs, the following remarks have to be made.—The rite of carrying fire on the head is an attribute not of the vidyâ, but merely of the study of the Veda on the part of the Âtharva*n*ikas. This we infer from the circumstance that the Âtharva*n*ikas, in the book called 'Samâ*k*âra' which treats of Vedic observances, record the above rite also as being of such a nature, i.e. as constituting an attribute of the study of the Veda. At the close of the Upanishad moreover we have the following sentence, 'A

[1] I.e. the *Kh*ândogya-text contains no injunction that five fires only are to be meditated upon.

[2] So that there stands nothing in the way of our amplifying our meditation by the addition of a sixth fire.

man who has not performed the rites does not read this;' here we conclude from the word 'this' which refers to the subject previously treated, and from the fact of 'reading' being mentioned, that the rite is an attribute of the study of the Upanishad of the Âtharva*n*ikas (but has nothing to do with the Upanishad itself).—But what about the immediately preceding passage, 'Let a man tell this science of Brahman to those only by whom the rite of carrying fire on the head has been performed according to rule?' Here the rite in question is connected with the science of Brahman, and as all science of Brahman is one only, it follows that the rite has to be connected with all science of Brahman!—Not so, we reply; for in the above passage also the word 'this' refers back to what forms the subject of the antecedent part of the Upanishad, and that subject is constituted by the science of Brahman only in so far as depending on a particular book (viz. the Mu*nd*aka-Upanishad); hence the rite also is connected with that particular book only.—The Sûtra adds another illustrative instance in the words 'and as in the case of the libations there is limitation of that.' As the seven libations—from the saurya libation up to the *s*ataudana libation—since they are not connected with the triad of fires taught in the other Vedas, but only with the one fire which is taught in the Atharvan, are thereby enjoined exclusively on the followers of the Atharvan; so the rite of carrying fire on the head also is limited to the study of that particular Veda with which scriptural statements connect it.—The doctrine of the unity of the vidyâs thus remains unshaken.

4. (Scripture) also declares this.

The Veda also declares the identity of the vidyâs; for all Vedânta-texts represent the object of knowledge as one; cp. e.g. Kâ. Up. I, 2, 15, 'That word which all the Vedas record;' Ait. Âr. III, 2, 3, 12, 'Him only the Bahv*rik*as consider in the great hymn, the Adhvaryus in the sacrificial fire, the *Kh*andogas in the Mahâvrata ceremony.'—To quote some other instances proving the unity of the vidyâs: Kâ. Up. I, 6, 2, mentions as one of the Lord's qualities that he causes fear; now this very same quality is referred to in the Taitt. Up. II, 7, in order to intimate disapprobation of those who are opposed to the absolute unity of that which is, 'For if he makes but the smallest distinction in it (the Self), there is fear for him. But that fear is only for him who knows (a difference) and does not know (the oneness).' —Similarly the Vais*v*ânara, who in the Vâ*g*asaneyaka is imaginatively represented as a span long, is referred to in the *Kh*ândogya as something well known, 'But he who worships that Vais*v*ânara Self which is a span long,' &c. (*Kh*. Up. V, 18, 1).

And as, on the ground of all Vedânta-texts intimating the same matters, hymns and the like which are enjoined in one place are employed in other places (where they are not expressly enjoined) for the purposes of devout meditation, it follows that all Vedânta-texts intimate also (identical) devout meditations.

5. In the case of (a devout meditation) common (to several *S*âkhâs) (the particulars mentioned in each *S*âkhâ) have to be combined, since there is no difference of essential matter; just as in the case of what is complementary to injunctions.

[This Sûtra states the practical outcome of the discussion carried on in the first four Sûtras.] It having been determined that the cognitions of Brahman are equally intimated by all Vedânta-texts, it follows that as long as the cognition is one and the same its specific determinations mentioned in one text are to be introduced into other texts also where they are not mentioned. For if the matter of these determinations subserves some particular cognition in one place, it subserves it in another place also, since in both places we have to do with one and the same cognition. The case is analogous to that of the things subordinate to some sacrificial performance, as, e.g. the agnihotra. The agnihotra also is one performance, and therefore its subordinate members, although they may be mentioned in different texts, have to be combined into one whole.—If the cognitions were separate, the particulars mentioned in different texts could not be combined; for they would be confined each to its own cognition and would not stand to each other in that relation in which the typical form of a sacrifice stands to its modifications[1]. But as the cognitions are one, things lie differently.—The above Sûtra will be explained and applied at length further on, in Sûtra 10 ff.

6. If it be said that (the udgîtha vidyâ of the B*ri*. Up. and that of the *Kh*ând. Up.) are separate on account (of the difference) of the texts; we deny this on the ground of their (essential) non-difference.

We read in the Vâ*g*asaneyaka I, 3, 1, 'The Devas said, well, let us overcome the Asuras at the sacrifices by means of the Udgîtha. They said to speech: Do thou sing out for us.—Yes, said speech,' &c. The text thereupon relates how speech and the other prâ*n*as were pierced by the Asuras with evil, and therefore unable to effect what was expected from them, and how in the end recourse was had to the chief vital air, 'Then they said to the breath in the mouth: Do thou sing for us.—Yes, said the breath, and sang.'—A similar story is met with in the *Kh*ândogya I, 2. There we read at first that 'the devas took the udgîtha, thinking they would vanquish the Asuras with it;' the text then relates how the other prâ*n*as were pierced with evil and thus foiled by the Asuras, and how the Devas in the end had recourse to the chief vital air, 'Then comes this chief vital air; on that they meditated as udgîtha.'—As both these passages glorify the chief vital air, it follows that they both are injunctions of a meditation on the vital air. A doubt, however, arises whether the two vidyâs are separate vidyâs or one vidyâ only.

Here the pûrvapakshin maintains that for the reasons specified in the first adhikara*n*a of the present pâda the two

[1] The Pûrvâ Mîmâ*m*sâ teaches that all subordinate things which the Veda prescribes for some typical sacrifice are eo ipso prescribed for the modified forms of the sacrifice also.

vidyâs have to be considered as one.—But, an objection is raised, there is a difference of procedure which contradicts the assumption of unity. The Vâ*g*asaneyins represent the chief vital air as the producer of the udgîtha ('Do thou sing out for us'), while the *Kh*andogas speak of it as itself being the udgîtha ('on that they meditated as udgîtha'). How can this divergence be reconciled with the assumption of the unity of the vidyâs?—The difference pointed out, the pûrvapakshin replies, is not important enough to bring about a separation of the two vidyâs, since we observe that the two both agree in a plurality of points. Both texts relate that the Devas and the Asuras were fighting; both at first glorify speech and the other prâ*n*as in their relation to the udgîtha, and thereupon, finding fault with them, pass on to the chief vital air; both tell how through the strength of the latter the Asuras were scattered as a ball of earth is scattered when hitting a solid stone. And, moreover, the text of the Vâ*g*asaneyaka also co-ordinates the chief vital air and the udgîtha in the clause, 'He is udgîtha' (B*ri*. Up. I, 3, 23). We therefore have to assume that in the *Kh*ândogya also the chief prâ*n*a has secondarily to be looked upon as the producer of the udgîtha. —The two texts thus constitute one vidyâ only.

7. Or rather there is no (unity of the vidyâs), owing to the difference of subject-matter.

Setting aside the view maintained by the pûrvapakshin, we have rather to say that, owing to the difference of subject-matter, the two vidyâs are separate.—In the *Kh*ândogya the introductory sentence (I, 1, 1), 'Let a man meditate on the syllable Om (as) the udgîtha,' represents as the object of meditation the syllable Om which is a part of the udgîtha; thereupon proceeds to give an account of its qualities such as being the inmost essence of all ('The full account, however, of Om is this,' &c.); and later on tells, with reference to the same syllable Om which is a part of the udgîtha, a story about the Gods and Asuras in which there occurs the statement, 'They meditated on the udgîtha as that breath[1].' If now we should assume[2] that the term 'udgîtha' denotes here the whole act of worship (not only the syllable Om which is a part of the udgîtha), and that (in the passage, 'they meditated on the udgîtha as that breath') the performer of that worship, i.e. the Udgât*ri*-priest, is said to be meditated upon as breath; our interpretation would be open to two objections: in the first place it would be opposed to the introductory sentence (which directly declares the syllable Om to be the object of devotion); and in the second place it would oblige us to take the word udgîtha (in 'they meditated on the udgîtha'), not in its direct sense, but as denoting by implication the udgât*ri*. But the rule is that in one and the same connected passage the interpretation of later passages has to adapt itself to the earlier passages. We therefore conclude the passage last quoted to teach that the syllable Om which is a part of the udgîtha is to be meditated upon as prâ*n*a.—In the Vâ*g*asaneyaka on the other hand there is no reason for taking the word udgîtha to denote a part of the udgîtha only, and we therefore must interpret it to denote the whole; and in the passage, 'Do thou sing out for us,' the performer of the worship, i.e. the Udgât*ri*-priest, is described as prâ*n*a. In reply to the pûrvapakshin's remark that in the Vâ*g*asaneyaka also the udgîtha and the prâ*n*a occur in co-ordination (in the passage, 'He is udgîtha'), we point out that that statement merely aims at showing that the Self of all is that prâ*n*a which the text wishes to represent as udgât*ri*. The statement, therefore, does not imply the unity of the two vidyâs. Moreover, there also the term udgîtha denotes the whole act of worship (while in the *Kh*ândogya it denotes the omkâra only). Nor must it be said that the prâ*n*a can

---

[1] From which it appears that the *Kh*ândogya enjoins throughout a meditation on the syllable Om which is only a part of the udgîtha; while the object of meditation enjoined in the B*ri*had-âra*n*yaka is the whole udgîtha.

[2] Viz. for the purpose of making out that the object of meditation is the same in the *Kh*ândogya and the B*ri*had-âra*n*yaka.

impossibly be an udgât*ri*, and that on that account our interpretation of the B*ri*had-âra*n*yaka passage is erroneous; for with a view to pious meditation scripture may represent the prâ*n*a as udgât*ri* as well as udgîtha. And, moreover, the Udgât*ri* actually performs his work by the strength of his breath; hence the prâ*n*a may be called udgât*ri*. In accordance with this the text says (I, 3, 24), 'He sang it indeed as speech and breath.'—And if we understand that the text clearly intends to convey a difference of matter we have no right to conclude from merely apparent similarities of expression that only one matter is intended to be expressed. To quote an analogous instance from the karmakâ*nd*a: In the section relative to the unexpected rising of the moon during the dar*s*a-sacrifice, as well as in the section about the offering to be made by him who is desirous of cattle, we meet with identical injunctions such as the following one, 'He is to divide the grains into three portions, and to make those of medium size into a cake offered on eight potsherds to Agni the Giver,' &c.; nevertheless it follows from the difference of the introductory passages of the two sections that the offerings to be made on account of the moon's rising are indeed not connected with the divinities of the dar*s*a-sacrifice (but do not constitute a new sacrifice separate from the dar*s*a), while the section about him who is desirous of cattle enjoins a separate sacrificial performance[1].—Analogously a difference in the nature of the introductory clauses effects a difference of the vidyâs, 'As in the case of that which is greater than great.' That means: Just as the meditation on the udgîtha enjoined in the passage, 'Ether is greater than these, ether is their rest; he is indeed the udgîtha, greater than great, he is without end' (*Kh*. Up. I, 9, 1), and the other meditation on the udgîtha as possessing the qualities of abiding within the eye and the sun, &c. (*Kh*. Up. I, 6), are separate meditations, although in both the udgîtha is identified with the highest Self; so it is with vidyâs in general. The special features of different vidyâs are not to be combined even when the

[1] Cp. Taitt. Sa*m*h. II, 5, 5, 2; Pû. Mî. Sû. VI, 5, 1.

vidyâs belong to one and the same *S*âkhâ; much less then when they belong to different *S*âkhâs.

8. If it be said (that the vidyâs are one) on account of (the identity of) name; (we reply that) that is explained (already); moreover that (identity of name) is (found in the case of admittedly separate vidyâs).

Here it might be said that after all the unity of the two vidyâs discussed must be admitted, since they are called by one and the same name, viz. 'the science of the udgîtha.'—But this argument is of no avail against what has been said under the preceding Sûtra. The decision there advocated has the advantage of following the letter of the revealed text; the name 'udgîtha-vidyâ' on the other hand is not a part of the revealed text, but given to the vidyâs for convenience sake by ordinary men for the reason that the word 'udgîtha' is met with in the text.—Moreover, we observe that admittedly separate meditations such as the two mentioned under the last Sûtra have one and the same name. Similarly altogether separate sacrificial performances, such as the agnihotra, the dar*s*apûr*n*amâsa, and so on, are all comprised under the one name Kâ*th*aka, merely because they are recorded in the one book called Kâ*th*aka.—Where, on the other hand, there is no special reason for assuming the difference of vidyâs, their unity may be declared on the ground of identity of name; as, e.g. in the case of the Sa*m*vargavidyâs.

9. And on account of the (omkâra) extending over the whole (Veda), (the view that the term udgîtha expresses a specialisation) is appropriate.

In the passage, 'Let a man meditate on the syllable Om (as) the udgîtha,' the two words 'omkâra' and 'udgîtha' are placed in co-ordination[1]. The question then arises

[1] Sâmânâdhikara*n*ya, i.e. literally, 'the relation of abiding in a common substratum.'—The two words are shown to stand in that relation by their being exhibited in the same case.

whether the relation in which the ideas conveyed by these two words stand to each other is the relation of superimposition (adhyâsa) or sublation (apavâda) or unity (ekatva) or specification (visesha*n*a); for primâ facie each of these relations may present itself to the mind.—Adhyâsa takes place when the idea of one of two things not being dismissed from the mind, the idea of the second thing is superimposed on that of the first thing; so that together with the superimposed idea the former idea remains attached to the thing on which the second idea is superimposed. When e.g. the idea of (the entity) Brahman superimposes itself upon the idea of the name, the latter idea continues in the mind and is not driven out by the former. A similar instance is furnished by the superimposition of the idea of the god Vish*n*u on a statue of Vish*n*u. So, in the case under discussion also, the idea of the udgîtha may be superimposed on the omkâra or the idea of the omkâra on the udgîtha.—We, in the second place, have apavâda when an idea previously attached to some object is recognised as false and driven out by the true idea springing up after the false one. So e.g. when the false idea of the body, the senses, and so on being the Self is driven out by the true idea springing up later—and expressed by judgments such as 'Thou art that'—that the idea of the Self is to be attached to the Self only. Or, to quote another example, when a previous mistaken notion as to the direction of the points of the compass is replaced by the true notion. So here also the idea of the udgîtha may drive out the idea of the omkâra or vice versâ.—The relation would, in the third place, be that of 'unity' if the terms 'omkâra' and 'udgîtha' were co-extensive in meaning; just as the terms, 'the Best of the Twice-born,' 'the Brâhma*n*a,' 'the god among men,' all denote an individual of the noblest caste.—The relation will, finally, be that of specification if, there being a possibility of our understanding the omkâra in so far as co-extensive with all the Vedas, the term 'udgîtha' calls up the idea of the sphere of action of the udgât*ri*. The passage would then mean, 'Let a man meditate on that omkâra which is the udgîtha,' and would be analogous to an injunction such as 'Let him bring that lotus-flower which is blue.'

All these alterations present themselves to the mind, and as there is no reason for deciding in favour of any one, the question must remain an unsettled one.

To this pûrvapaksha-view the Sûtra replies, 'And on account of extending over the whole, it is appropriate.'

The word 'and' stands here in place of 'but,' and is meant to discard the three other alternatives. Three out of the four alternatives are to be set aside as objectionable; the fourth, against which nothing can be urged, is to be adopted.—The objections lying against the first three alternatives are as follows. In the case of adhyâsa we should have to admit that the word which expresses the idea superimposed is not to be taken in its direct sense, but in an implied sense[1]; and we should moreover have to imagine some fruit for a meditation of that kind[2]. Nor can it be said that we need not imagine such a fruit, as scripture itself mentions it in the passage, 'He becomes indeed a fulfiller of desires' (I, 1, 7); for this passage indicates the fruit, not of the ideal superimposition of the udgîtha on the omkâra, but of the meditation in which the omkâra is viewed as the fulfilment of desires.—Against the hypothesis of an apavâda there likewise lies the objection that no fruit is to be seen. The cessation of wrong knowledge can certainly not be alleged as such; for we see no reason why the cessation of the idea that the omkâra is udgîtha and not omkâra or vice versâ should be beneficial to man. Sublation of the one idea by the other is moreover not even possible in our case; for to the omkâra the idea of the omkâra remains always attached, and so to the udgîtha the idea of the udgîtha. The passage, moreover, does not aim at teaching the true

[1] I.e. in the present case we should have to assume that the word udgîtha means, by implication, the omkâra.—Recourse may be had to implied meanings only when the direct meaning is clearly impossible.

[2] For a special adhyâsa-meditation must be attended with a special result.

nature of something, but at enjoining a meditation of a certain kind.—The hypothesis of unity again is precluded by the consideration that as in that case one term would suffice to convey the intended meaning, the employment of two terms would be purposeless. And moreover the term 'udgîtha' is never used to denote the omkâra in its connexion with the *Ri*g-veda and Ya*g*ur-veda; nor is the word 'omkâra' used to denote that entire second subdivision of a sâman which is denoted by the word 'udgîtha.' Hence it cannot be said that we have to do with different words only denoting one and the same thing.—There thus remains the fourth alternative, 'On account of its comprising all the Vedas.' That means: In order that the omkâra may not be understood here as that one which comprises all the Vedas, it is specified by means of the word 'udgîtha,' in order that that omkâra which constitutes a part of the udgîtha may be apprehended.—But does not this interpretation also involve the admission of implication, as according to it the word 'udgîtha' denotes not the whole udgîtha but only a part of it, viz. the omkâra?—True, but we have to distinguish those cases in which the implied meaning is not far remote from the direct meaning and those in which it is remote. If, in the present case, we embrace the alternative of adhyâsa, we have to assume an altogether remote implication, the idea of one matter being superimposed on the idea of an altogether different matter. If, on the other hand, we adopt the alternative of specification, the implication connected therewith is an easy one, the word which in its direct sense denotes the whole being understood to denote the part. And that words denoting the whole do duty for words denoting the part is a matter of common occurrence; the words 'cloth,' 'village,' and many others are used in this fashion [1].—For all these reasons we declare that the appropriate view of the *Kh*ândogya-passage is to take the word 'udgîtha' as specialising the term 'omkâra [2].'

[1] We say, e.g. 'the cloth is burned,' even if only a part of the cloth is burned.

[2] We therefore, according to *S*aṅkara, have to render the passage

10. Those (qualities which are attributed to the subject of a vidyâ in one *S*âkhâ only) (are to be inserted) in other places (also), since (the vidyâs) are non-different on the whole.

In the colloquy of the prâ*n*as recorded by the Vâ*g*asaneyins and the *Kh*andogas the prâ*n*a, endowed with various qualities such as being the best and so on, is represented as the object of meditation, and various qualities such as being the richest and the like are ascribed to speech and the other organs. And these latter qualities are in the end attributed to the prâ*n*a also, 'If I am the richest thou art the richest,' &c. Now in other *S*âkhâs also, as e.g. that of the Kaushîtakins, the former set of qualities such as being the best and so on is ascribed to the prâ*n*a (cp. Kau. Up. II, 14, 'Now follows the Ni*hs*reyasâdâna,' &c.), but at the same time the latter set of attributes, viz. being the richest and so on, is not mentioned.—The question then is whether those qualities which are mentioned in some places only are, for the purposes of meditation, to be inserted there also where nothing is said about them.

They are not so to be inserted, the pûrvapakshin maintains, on account of the employment of the word 'thus.' In the Kaushîtakin-text we meet with the clause, 'He who knows thus, having recognised the pre-eminence in prâ*n*a.' Now the word 'thus' which here indicates the object of knowledge always refers to something mentioned not far off, and cannot therefore denote a set of qualities mentioned in other *S*âkhâs only. We therefore maintain that each of the colloquies of the prâ*n*as must be considered complete with the qualities stated in itself.

To this we make the following reply. The qualities mentioned in one text are to be inserted in the other corresponding texts also, 'Since on the whole they are non-different,' i.e. because the prâna-vidyâs are recognised to be the same in all essential points. And if they are the same,

under discussion as follows, 'Let a man meditate on the syllable Om which is (i.e. which is a part of) the udgîtha.'

why should the qualities stated in one not be inserted in the others also?—But how about the objection founded by the pûrvapakshin on the employment of the word 'thus?'—Although it is true, we reply, that the word 'thus' in the Kaushîtakin-brâhma*n*a does not denote the set of qualities mentioned in the Vâ*g*asaneyin-brâhma*n*a, yet that set of qualities is denoted by the 'thus' met with in the Vâ*g*asaneyin-brâhma*n*a, while the vidyâ is, as proved by us, one and the same; hence no difference has to be made between qualities mentioned in one's own *S*âkhâ and qualities mentioned in another *S*âkhâ, as long as the vidyâ is one and the same. Nor does this by any means imply a disregard of the text of scripture, and the assumption of things not warranted by the text. The qualities declared in one *S*âkhâ are valid for all scripture as long as the thing to which the qualities belong is the same. Devadatta, who in his own country is known to possess valour and certain other qualities, does not lose those qualities by going to a foreign land, although the inhabitants of that land may know nothing about them. And through better acquaintance his qualities will become manifest to the people of the foreign country also. Similarly the qualities stated in one *S*âkhâ may, through special application, be inserted in another *S*âkhâ.—Hence the attributes belonging to one and the same subject have to be combined wherever that subject is referred to, although they may be expressly stated in one place only.

11. Bliss and other (qualities) as belonging to the subject of the qualities (have to be attributed to Brahman everywhere).

Those scriptural texts which aim at intimating the characteristics of Brahman separately ascribe to it various qualities, such as having bliss for its nature, being one mass of knowledge, being omnipresent, being the Self of all and so on. Now the doubt here presents itself whether in each place where Brahman is spoken of we have to understand only those qualities which actually are mentioned there, or whether we have to combine all qualities of Brahman mentioned anywhere.

The pûrvapakshin maintains that only the attributes actually stated are to be understood as referred to in each particular scriptural text.—But this view the Sûtrakâra discards by declaring that delight and all the other qualities which belong to the subject, i.e. Brahman, are all of them to be understood in each place. The reason for this conclusion is the one given in Sûtra 10. In all the passages treating of Brahman the subject to which the qualities belong is one, non-different; hence, as explained at length under the preceding Sûtra, the qualities attributed to Brahman in any one place have to be combined wherever Brahman is spoken of.

But in that case also such qualities as having joy for its head, &c., would have to be ascribed to Brahman everywhere; for we read in the Taittirîyaka with reference to the Self consisting of Bliss, 'Joy is its head, satisfaction is its right arm, great satisfaction its left arm, bliss is its trunk, Brahman is its tail, its support' (II, 5).

To this objection the next Sûtra replies.

12. (Such qualities as) joy being its head and so on have no force (for other passages); for increase and decrease belong to plurality (only).

Attributes such as having joy for its head and so on, which are recorded in the Taittirîyaka, are not to be viewed as having force with regard to other passages treating of Brahman, because the successive terms, 'Joy,' 'Satisfaction,' 'Great Satisfaction,' 'Bliss,' indicate qualities possessing lower and higher degrees with regard to each other and to other enjoyers. Now for higher and lower degrees there is room only where there is plurality; and Brahman is without all plurality, as we know from many scriptural passages ('One only, without a Second').—Moreover, we have already demonstrated under I, 1, 12, that having joy for one's head and so on are qualities not of Brahman, but of the so-called involucrum of delight. And further, those qualities are attributed to the highest Brahman merely as means of fixing one's mind on it, not as themselves being objects of contemplation, and from this also it follows that they are not valid everywhere[1].—That the Â*k*ârya refers to them, in the Sûtra, as attributes of Brahman (while in reality they are attributes of the ânandamaya ko*s*a) is merely done for the purpose of establishing a general principle to be extended to all attributes of Brahman—also the undoubted ones—which are stated with a view to a special form of meditation only; such as the quality of being that towards which all blessings go (*Kh.* Up. IV, 15, 2), or he whose desires are true (*Kh.* Up. VIII, 7, 1). For those passages may all indeed have to do with the one Brahman as the object of meditation, but as owing to the different nature of the opening sentences the meditations are different ones, the attributes mentioned in any one are not valid for the others. The case is analogous to that of two wives ministering to one king, one with a fly-flap, the other with an umbrella; there also the object of their ministrations is one, but the acts of ministration themselves are distinct and have each their own particular attributes. So in the case under discussion also. Qualities in which lower and higher degrees can be distinguished belong to the qualified Brahman only in which plurality is admitted, not to the highest Brahman raised above all qualification. Such attributes therefore as having true desires and the like which are mentioned in some particular place only have no validity for other meditations on Brahman.

13. But other (attributes are valid for all passages relative to Brahman), the purport being the same.

Other attributes, however, such as bliss and so on which scripture sets forth for the purpose of teaching the true nature of Brahman are to be viewed as valid for all passages referring to Brahman; for their purport, i.e. the Brahman

---

[1] For if they are not real attributes of Brahman there is all the less reason to maintain them to be universally valid. The mere means of fixing the mind, moreover, are special to each separate upâsana.

whose nature is to be taught, is one. Those attributes are mentioned with a view to knowledge only, not to meditation.

14. (The passage, Kâ*th*aka I, 3, 10, gives information about the person) for the purpose of pious meditation, as there is no use (of the knowledge of the objects being higher than the senses and so on).

We read in the Kâ*th*aka (I, 3, 10), 'Higher than the senses are the objects, higher than the objects there is the mind, &c. &c.; higher than the person there is nothing—this is the goal, the highest road.'—Here the doubt arises whether the purport of the passage is to intimate that each of the things successively enumerated is higher than the preceding one, or only that the person is higher than all of them.

The pûrvapakshin maintains the former alternative, for the reason that the text expressly declares the objects to be higher than the senses, the mind higher than the objects and so on.

The objection that the assumption of the passage intending to represent many things as successively superior to their antecedents would involve a so-called split of the sentence, he meets by the remark that the passage may be viewed as containing a plurality of sentences. Many sentences may represent many things as superior to their antecedents, and hence each clause of the passage must be viewed as containing a separate statement of the superiority of something to other things.

To this we reply as follows.

We must assume that the whole passage aims at intimating only that the person is higher than everything. Any information as to the relative superiority of the preceding members of the series would be devoid of all purpose; for of the knowledge derived from such observation a use is neither to be seen nor declared by scripture. Of the knowledge, on the other hand, of the person being higher than the senses and everything else, raised above all evil, we do see a purpose, viz. the accomplishment of final release. And so scripture also says, 'He who has perceived that is freed from the jaws of death' (I, 3, 15). Moreover, the text by declaring that nothing is higher than the person and that he is the highest goal intimates reverence for the person, and thereby shows that the whole series of objects is enumerated only to the end of giving information about the person.—'For the purpose of pious meditation,' i.e. for the purpose of perfect knowledge which has pious meditation for its antecedent. For the passage under consideration does not teach pious meditation by itself.

15. And on account of the word 'Self.'

The above conclusion is confirmed by the circumstance that the person under discussion is called the Self in I, 3, 12, 'That Self is hidden in all beings and does not shine forth, but it is seen by subtle seers through their sharp and subtle intellect.' From this we conclude that the text wishes to represent the other beings enumerated as the Non-Self. The passage quoted, moreover, indicates that the person is hard to know, and to be reached by sharp minds only.—Again, the passage (I, 3, 13), 'A wise man should keep down speech and mind,' enjoins pious meditation as a means of the knowledge of the highest person, as we have explained under I, 4, 1.—It thus follows that scripture indicates various excellences in the case of the purusha only, and not in that of the other beings enumerated.—The passage, moreover, 'He reaches the end of his journey and that is the highest place of Vishnu,' suggests the question as to who is the end of the journey and so on, and we therefore conclude that the enumeration of the senses, objects, &c., has merely the purpose of teaching the highest place of Vishnu (not of teaching anything about the relation of the senses, objects, and so on).

16. The (highest) Self has to be understood (in Ait. Âr. II, 4, 1), as in other places; on account of the subsequent (qualification).

We read in the Aitareyaka (II, 4, 1), 'Verily, in the beginning all this was Self, one only; there was nothing else blinking whatsoever. He thought, shall I send forth worlds? He sent forth these worlds, the (heavenly) waters, the rays, the mortal (earth), and water.'—Here the doubt presents itself whether the term 'Self' denotes the highest Self or some other being.

The pûrvapakshin maintains the latter view, which is borne out, he says, by an examination of the connected sense of the whole passage.—But, an objection is raised, an examination of that kind rather leads to the conclusion that the highest Self is meant; for the passage says that before the creation the Self only existed and that the creation was preceded by thought.—No such conclusion is possible, the pûrvapakshin replies, since the passage relates the creation of the worlds. If it aimed at representing the highest Self as the creator, it would speak of the creation of the elements, of which the worlds are only certain combinations. That the worlds are meant by the terms 'water,' &c., appears from the subsequent clause (4), 'That water is above the heaven,' &c.—Now *S*ruti and Sm*ri*ti teach that the creation of the worlds is accomplished by some inferior Lord different from—and superintended by—the highest Self; cp. e.g. B*ri*. Up. I, 4, 1, 'In the beginning this was Self alone, in the shape of a person,' and the Sm*ri*ti-passage, 'He is the first embodied soul, he is called the person; he the prime creator of the beings was in the beginning evolved from Brahman.' And the Aitareyins themselves record in a previous prakara*n*a (II, 1, 3, 1, 'Next follows the origin of seed. The seed of Pra*g*âpati are the Devas') that this manifold creation was accomplished by Pra*g*âpati. That to the latter being the word 'Self' is sometimes applied appears from the passage quoted above from the B*ri*. Up. And Pra*g*âpati also may be spoken of as being before the creation one only, if we consider that then his products did not yet exist; and thought also may be ascribed to him as he, of course, is of an intelligent nature. Moreover, the passages, 'He led a cow towards them; he led a horse towards them; he led man towards them; then they said,' &c. (II, 4, 2, 2), which are in agreement with what is known about the various activities of particular qualified Selfs belonging to the apparent world, show that in the Aitareyaka also some such qualified Self is meant.

To this we reply that the highest Self is meant in the Aitareyaka 'as in other places.' As in other accounts of the creation ('From that Self ether was produced,' Taitt. Up. II, 1, &c.) the highest Self has to be understood, and, as in other cases where the term 'Self' is applied to particular Selfs, the 'Self within' (i.e. the highest Self) has to be understood in the first place; so it is here also.—In those passages, on the other hand, where the Self is qualified by some other attribute, such as 'having the shape of a person,' we must understand that some particular Self is meant.—In the Aitareyaka, however, we meet with a qualification, subsequent to the first reference to the Self, which agrees only with the highest Self; we mean the one implied in the passage, 'He thought, shall I send forth worlds? He sent forth these worlds.'—Hence we maintain that the highest Self is meant.

17. Should it be said that on account of the connected meaning (of the whole passage) (the highest Self cannot be meant); (we reply that) it is so, on account of the assertion.

We now have to refute the objection, made above by the pûrvapakshin, that the highest Self cannot be meant 'on account of the connected meaning of the passage.'—The Sûtrakâra remarks, 'It is so, on account of the assertion.' That means: It is appropriate to understand the passage as referring to the highest Self, because thus the assertion that the Self, previously to the creation, was one only, gives a fully satisfactory sense, while on the other interpretation it would be far from doing so. The creation of the worlds recorded in the Aitareyaka we connect with the creation of the elements recorded in other Vedic texts, in that way that we understand the worlds to have been created subsequently to the elements; just as we showed above (II, 4, 1) that the passage, 'It sent forth fire,' must be understood to say that the creation of fire followed on the creation of ether and air as known from other texts. For, as proved by us before, particulars mentioned in one scriptural text have to be combined with particulars mentioned in other texts, if only the chief subject of the passages is the same.—The details about the activity of the Self referred to by the pûrvapakshin have likewise to be understood in such a way as to agree with the general matter about which the text desires to make assertions. For we must by no means assume that the text is interested in setting forth all the details of the story on their own account; the knowledge of them would be in no way beneficial to man. The only thing the text really means to teach is the truth that Brahman is the Self of everything. Hence it first relates how the different worlds and the guardians of the worlds, viz. Agni and so on, were created; explains thereupon the origination of the organs and the body, their abode; and shows how the creator having thought, 'How can all this be without me?' (II, 4, 3, 4), entered into this body, 'Opening the suture of the skull he got in by that door' (7). Then again the text relates how the Self after having considered the activities of all the organs ('if speech names,' &c.; 6) asked himself the question, 'What am I?' and thereupon 'saw this person as the widely spread Brahman' (10). The aim of all which is to declare that Brahman is the universal Self. The same truth is inculcated in a subsequent passage also, viz. II, 6, 1, 5; 6, where the text at first enumerates the whole aggregate of individual existences together with the elements, and then continues, 'All this is led by knowledge (i.e. the highest Self); it rests on knowledge. The world is led by knowledge, knowledge is its rest, knowledge is Brahman.'—For all these reasons the view that the highest Brahman is meant in the Aitareyaka is not open to any objections.

The two preceding Sûtras may also be explained with reference to some other Vedic passages. We read in the Vâ*g*asaneyaka (B*ri*. Up. IV, 3, 7), 'Who is that Self?—He who is within the heart, surrounded by the prâ*n*as, consisting of knowledge, the person of light.' Of the Self here first mentioned the text goes on to show that it is free from all contact and thus proves it to have Brahman for its Self, the concluding statement being, 'This great unborn Self undecaying, undying, immortal, fearless is indeed Brahman' (IV, 4, 25).—In the *Kh*ândogya again we have a chapter in which the introductory statement does not use the term 'Self' ('Being only this was in the beginning, one, without a second'), while at the conclusion the term 'Self' is used in the declaration of identity ('That is the Self. Thou art that').—A doubt here arises whether these two scriptural texts treat of the same matter or not.

They do not, the pûrvapakshin maintains, since they are not equal. Since the determination of the sense depends on the letter of the text, we have no right to maintain equality of sense where the texts differ. In the Vâ*g*asaneyaka the initial statement about the Self shows that the whole passage conveys instruction about the true nature of the Self. In the *Kh*ândogya, on the other hand, the initial clause is of a different kind, and we therefore must assume that the whole passage imparts instruction differing in nature from that of the Vâ*g*asaneyaka.—But has it not been said that the *Kh*ândogya-passage also teaches in the end the doctrine of universal identity with the Self?—That has been said indeed (but wrongly); for as the concluding passage must be made to agree with the initial passage (which latter does not say anything about the identity of the Self and Brahman), we assume that the concluding passage merely enjoins an imaginative combination (sampatti) of the Self and Brahman.

To this we reply that also the passage, 'Being only this was in the beginning,' has to be understood as referring to the Self; 'as other places,' i.e. in the same way as the passage quoted from the Vâ*g*asaneyaka. For what reason?—'On account of the subsequent (statement),' viz. the statement as to identity. And if it be said that 'on account of the connected meaning' of the initial passage in which no mention is made of the Self, the chapter cannot be understood to refer to the Self; we reply 'that it may be so understood on account of the assertion' made in the passage about that 'by which we hear what is not heard, perceive what is not perceived, know what is not known.' For this passage asserts that through the knowledge of one thing all things become known, and to make good this assertion the text later on declares that 'Being only this was,' &c. Now this knowledge of all things through one thing is possible only if we understand the passage last quoted to refer to the Self; for if the principal Self were not known, how could all things be known? Moreover the assertion that, before creation, there existed one thing only, and the reference to the individual soul by means of the word 'Self,' and the statement that in deep sleep the soul becomes united with the True, and the repeated inquiries on the part of *S*vetaketu, and the repeated assertions, 'Thou art that,'—all this is appropriate only if the aim of the whole section is not to enjoin an imaginative meditation on all things as identical with the Self, but to teach that the Self really is everything.—Nor must it be said that, in the section under discussion, the concluding passage must be interpreted so as to agree with the introductory clause (and cannot on that account teach anything about the Self); for the introductory passage declares neither that the Self is everything, nor that the Non-self is everything (but merely makes a statement regarding what is in general), and such an altogether general statement cannot be in conflict with any particular statement made in a supplementary passage, but rather is in want of some such particular statement whereby to define itself[1].—And moreover (to view the matter from a different point of view), the word 'Being' if looked into closely can denote nothing else but the principal Self, since we have proved, under II, 1, 14, the unreality of the whole aggregate of being different from the Self.—Nor, finally, does a difference of expression necessarily imply a difference of sense; not any more than in ordinary language the two phrases, 'Bring that vessel

[1] I.e. the definite statement about the Self in the concluding passage may be used for defining the sense of the indefinite initial statement about that which is. 'That which is' comprises the Self as well as the Not-Self.

over there,' and, 'That vessel over there, bring it,' have different meanings.—It therefore remains a settled conclusion that in texts such as discussed above, the matter of instruction is the same, however much the mode may vary in which the instruction is conveyed.

18. As (scripture where speaking of the rinsing of the mouth with water) makes a reference to an act (established by Sm*ri*ti), (that act is not enjoined by *S*ruti, but rather) the new (act of meditation on the water viewed as the dress of prâ*n*a).

The *Kh*andogas as well as the Vâ*g*asaneyins record, in the colloquy of the prâ*n*as, that the food of Breath comprizes everything even unto dogs and birds, and that water is its dress. To this the *Kh*andogas add, 'Therefore when going to eat food they surround it before and after with water' (*Kh*. Up. V, 2, 2). And the Vâ*g*asaneyins add (B*ri*. Up. VI, 1, 14), '*S*rotriyas who know this rinse the mouth with water when they are going to eat and rinse the mouth with water after they have eaten, thinking that thereby they make the breath dressed. Therefore a man knowing this is to rinse the mouth with water when going to eat and after having eaten; he thereby makes that breath dressed.'—These texts intimate two things, rinsing of the mouth and meditation on the breath as dressed. The doubt then arises whether the texts enjoin both these matters, or only the rinsing of the mouth, or only the meditation on breath as dressed.

The pûrvapakshin maintains that the text enjoins both, since the one as well as the other is intimated by the text, and since both matters not being settled by any other means of knowledge are worthy of being enjoined by the Veda.—Or else, he says, the rinsing of the mouth only is enjoined, since with reference to the latter only the text exhibits the particular injunctive verbal form ('he is to rinse'). In this latter case the mention made in the text of the meditation on breath as dressed has merely the purpose of glorifying the act of rinsing.

To this we make the following reply.—The rinsing of the mouth cannot possibly be enjoined by the quoted passages 'since they merely contain references to an act,' i.e. since they merely contain remarks concerning the purificatory act of rinsing the mouth which is known from and settled by Smr*i*ti.—But are not the very *S*ruti-passages under discussion to be looked upon as the fundamental texts on which the Smr*i*ti-injunctions regarding the rinsing of the mouth are based?—This is not possible, we reply, since the *S*ruti and Smr*i*ti-passages refer to different matters. All the Smr*i*ti-passages enjoin the act of rinsing the mouth only in so far as it purifies man; while the quoted *S*ruti texts which occur in prâ*n*a-vidyâs, if enjoining the rinsing of the mouth at all, enjoin it with reference to the knowledge of prâ*n*a. And a *S*ruti-passage cannot constitute the basis of a Smr*i*ti-passage referring to an altogether different matter. Nor can it be maintained that the *S*ruti-passage enjoins some altogether new rinsing of the mouth connected with the prâ*n*a-vidyâ, as we recognise the rinsing mentioned in *S*ruti as the ordinary rinsing performed by men for the sake of purification.—The preceding argumentation already precludes the alternative of two matters being enjoined, which would moreover lead to a so-called split of the sentence.—We therefore conclude that the text—with reference to the rinsing of the mouth before and after eating which is enjoined by Smr*i*ti—enjoins (by means of the passage, 'thinking that thereby they make the breath dressed') a new mental resolve with regard to the water used for rinsing purposes, viz. that that water should act as a means for clothing the prâ*n*a. The statement about the clothing of the prâ*n*a cannot (as suggested by the pûrvapakshin) be taken as a glorification of the act of rinsing the mouth; for in the first place the act of rinsing is not enjoined in the Vedic passage[1], and in the second place we apprehend that the passage itself conveys an injunction, viz. of the mental

[1] A glorifying arthavâda-passage would be in its place only if it were preceded by some injunction; for the glorification of certain acts is meant to induce men to comply with the injunctions concerning those acts.

resolve to provide clothing for the prâna. Nor must the objection be raised that in that case two purposes are admitted for the one act of rinsing the mouth, viz. the purpose of purification and the purpose of providing the prâna with clothing. For we have actually to do not with one action, but with two separate actions. For one action is the rinsing of the mouth which serves the purpose of purifying man, and another action is the mental resolve that that water should serve the purpose of clothing the prâna. Similarly the preceding passage, 'Whatever there is, even unto dogs, &c., that is thy food,' does not enjoin the promiscuous use of food of all kinds—for that would be contrary to scripture and impossible in itself—but merely enjoins the meditation on all food as food of the prâna. We therefore conclude that also the passage, 'Water is thy dress,' which forms the immediate continuation of the passage last quoted does not enjoin the act of rinsing the mouth but merely the act of meditating on the rinsing-water as constituting the dress of the prâna.

Moreover the mere present-form, 'they rinse the mouth with water,' has no enjoining force.—But also in the passage, 'They think that thereby they make the breath dressed,' we have a mere present-form without injunctive power (and yet you maintain that that passage conveys an injunction)!—True; but as necessarily one of the two must be enjoined[1], we assume, on the ground of what the text says about the making of a dress, that what is enjoined is the meditation on water being the dress of prâna; for this is something 'new,' i.e. not established by other means of knowledge[2]. The rinsing of the mouth with water, on the other hand, is already established by other means (i.e. Smriti), and therefore need not be enjoined again.—The argument founded

[1] Because otherwise we should have only arthavâdas. But arthavâdas have a meaning only in so far as connected with an injunction.

[2] The above argumentation avails itself of the Sûtra, putting a new construction on it.—Tarhi dvayor avidheyatvam ity âsankyânuvâdamâtrasyâ-kiñkitkaratvâd anyataravidher âvasyakatve samkalpanam eva vidheyam iti vidhântarena sûtram yogayati. Ân. Gi.

by the pûrvapakshin on the circumstance that, in the B*ri*. Up., the verb 'to rinse' is found in the injunctive form ('therefore a man, &c., is to rinse'), is already refuted by our showing that the act of rinsing the mouth is not a new one (and therefore requires no Vedic injunction).

For the very reason that the text does not aim at enjoining the rinsing of the mouth, the Kâ*n*vas (in their recension of the B*ri*. Up.) conclude the chapter with the clause, 'They think,' &c., and do not add the concluding clause of the Mâdhyandinas, 'Therefore a man,' &c. From this we have to conclude that what is enjoined in the text of the Mâdhyandinas also is 'the knowledge of that,' i.e. the knowledge of the water being the dress of the previously mentioned prâ*n*a.—Nor finally can it be maintained that in one place (i.e. the Mâdhyandina-*s*âkhâ) the rinsing of the mouth is enjoined, and in other places the knowledge of water as the dress of prâ*n*a; for the introductory passage, 'Water is the dress,' is the same everywhere.—We are therefore entitled to conclude that what is enjoined in all *S*âkhâs is the cognition of water being the dress of the prâ*n*a.

19. In the same (*S*âkhâ also) it is thus (i.e. there is unity of vidyâ), on account of the non-difference (of the object of meditation).

In the Agnirahasya forming part of the Vâ*g*asaneyi-*s*âkhâ there is a vidyâ called the *S*â*nd*ilya-vidyâ, in which we meet with the following statement of particulars, 'Let him meditate on the Self which consists of mind, which has the prâ*n*a for its body and light for its form,' &c.—In the B*ri*had-âra*n*yaka again, which belongs to the same *S*âkhâ, we read (V, 10, 6), 'That person consisting of mind, whose being is light, is within the heart, small like a grain of rice or barley. He is the ruler of all, the Lord of all—he rules all this whatsoever exists.'—A doubt here presents itself whether these two passages are to be taken as one vidyâ in which the particulars mentioned in either text are to be combined or not.

The pûrvapakshin maintains that we have to do with two separate vidyâs whose particulars cannot be combined. For otherwise, he argues, the text could not be cleared from the reproach of useless repetition. As long as we have to do with texts belonging to different *S*âkhâs we can rebut the charge of useless repetition by pointing to the fact that the texts are read and known by separate classes of men; we can then ascertain the unity of the vidyâs and combine the particulars mentioned in one text only with those mentioned in the others; so e.g. in the colloquy of the prâ*n*as. On the other hand, texts belonging to one and the same *S*âkhâ cannot be freed from the reproach of tautology as the same persons study and know them, and passages occurring in different places cannot therefore be combined into one vidyâ. Nor can we make out a separate position for each of the texts of the latter kind by saying that it is the task of one text to enjoin the vidyâ and that of the other to enjoin the particulars of the vidyâ. For in that case each of the two passages would mention only such particulars as are not mentioned in the other one; while as a matter of fact particulars common to both as well as not common to both are mentioned in each. Hence the particulars of the one passage are not to be combined with those of the other.

To this we make the following reply. Just as passages met with in different *S*âkhâs form one vidyâ in which the different particulars are to be combined, so the two passages under discussion also, although belonging to one and the same *S*âkhâ, constitute one vidyâ only, since the object of meditation is the same in both. For as such we recognise Brahman possessing certain qualities such as consisting of mind and so on. Now we know that the object constitutes the character of a meditation; as long as there is no difference of character we cannot determine difference of vidyâ; and if there is no difference of vidyâ the particulars mentioned in different places cannot be held apart.—But has it not been demonstrated above that the vidyâs have to be held apart, as otherwise tautology would arise?—Tautology does not result, we reply, because the two passages may be understood to have each its particular meaning, one of them enjoining the vidyâ, and the other the particulars of the vidyâ.—But in that case the B*ri*had-âra*n*yaka ought to mention only those points which are not mentioned in the Agnirahasya, as e.g. 'he is the Lord of all;' while it ought not to mention what is already mentioned in the Agnirahasya, as e.g. the Self's consisting of mind!—Not so, we reply. Only the repetition, in one passage, of what is already mentioned in the other passage enables us to recognise the vidyâ. The B*ri*had-âra*n*yaka-passage, by mentioning some common qualities, first enables us to recognise the *S*â*nd*ilya-vidyâ, and then teaches certain particulars with reference to the latter; how otherwise should we know that the B*ri*.-passage is meant to enjoin particulars for the *S*â*nd*ilya-vidyâ? Moreover, as in a passage which has a purpose of its own in so far as it teaches something not yet established, a reference to something already established is justified on the ground of its being a (so-called) nityânuvâda, we cannot overlook the recognition (of the identity of the passage with another one) which is rendered possible through that anuvâda. Hence, although the two passages belong to one and the same *S*âkhâ, they yet constitute one vidyâ only, and their particulars have to be combined into one whole.

20. Thus in other cases also, on account of the connexion (of particulars with one and the same vidyâ).

We read in the B*ri*had-âra*n*yaka (V, 5), 'The true is Brahman,' and, further on, 'Now what is the true, that is the Âditya, the person that dwells in yonder orb, and the person in the right eye.' Having thus declared the different abodes of that true Brahman with reference to the gods and with reference to the body, and having, in what follows, identified its body with the sacred syllables (bhû*h*, &c.), the text teaches its two secret names (upanishad), 'Its secret name is ahar' with reference to the gods; and 'its secret name is aham' with reference to the body.—A doubt here arises whether these two secret names are both to be applied to the deva-abode of Brahman as well as to its bodily abode, or only one name to each.

The above Sûtra maintains the pûrvapaksha view. Just as certain particulars though recorded elsewhere are yet to be combined with the *Sând*ilya-vidyâ, so we have to proceed in other cases also, as e.g. the one under discussion, because the particulars mentioned are all connected with one vidyâ. The vidyâ of the True with its double reference to the Devas and to the body is one only, as we infer from the fact of its having one exordium only ('The true is Brahman'), and from the way in which the text interconnects Âditya and the person in the eye. Why then should an attribute belonging to one of the latter not belong to the other also? For, to quote an analogous case, certain rules of life which are prescribed for a teacher —as e.g. having a following of pupils—remain equally valid whether the teacher be in a village or in a wood. For these reasons both secret names equally belong to the Âditya as well as to the person within the eye. This view the next Sûtra refutes.

21. Or this is not so, on account of the difference (of place).

The two secret names do not apply quite equally to the two persons mentioned, because they are connected with different places in the vidyâ. For the clause, 'Its secret name is ahar,' the text exhibits in connexion with the person in the solar orb, while the clause, 'Its secret name is aham,' occurs in connexion with the person in the eye. Now the pronoun 'its' always refers to something mentioned close by; we therefore conclude that the text teaches each secret name as belonging to one special abode of Brahman only. How then can both names be valid for both?—But, an objection is raised, the person within the orb of the sun and the person within the eye are one only; for the text teaches them both to be abodes of the one true Brahman!—True, we reply; but as each secret name is taught only with reference to the one Brahman as conditioned by a particular state, the name applies to Brahman only in so far as it is in that state. We on our part also illustrate the case by a comparison. The teacher always remains the teacher; yet those kinds of services which the pupil has to do to the teacher when sitting have not to be done when he stands; and vice versâ.—The comparison, on the other hand, instituted by the pûrvapakshin is ill chosen, since the duties of the disciple towards his teacher depend on the latter's character as teacher, and that is not changed by his being either in the village or the forest.—Hence the two secret names have to be held apart.

22. (Scripture) also declares that.

Scripture moreover contains a distinct intimation that the attributes under discussion are to be held apart. We read, *Kh*. Up. I, 8, 5, 'The form of that person is the same as the form of the other person, the joints of the one are the joints of the other, the name of the one is the name of the other.'—But how does this passage convey the desired intimation?—By expressly transferring the attributes of the person within the sun to the person within the eye; for this express transfer shows that the text looks upon the attributes of the two as separated by the difference of abode and therefore not to be combined (unless specially enjoined to be so combined).—The conclusion therefore is that the two secret names are to be held apart.

23. And for the same reason the holding together and the pervading the sky (attributed to Brahman in the Râ*n*âyanîya-khila) (are not to be inserted in other vidyâs).

In the khilas (supplementary writings) of the Râ*n*âyanîyas we meet with a passage, 'Held together are the powers among which Brahman is the best; the best Brahman in the beginning stretched out the sky[1],' which mentions certain energies of Brahman, such as holding together its powers, entering into the sky, &c. And in the

[1] Vîryâ vîryâ*n*i parâkramabhedâ*h*, anye hi purushâ*h* sahâyân apekshya vikramân bibhrati tena tatparâkramâ*n*âm na ta eva niyatapûrvatvarûpakâra*n*atvena *g*yesh*th*â bhavanti ki*m* tu tatsahakâri*n*o *s*pi, brahmavîryâ*n*â*m* tu brahmaiva *g*yesh*th*a*m* brahma *g*yesh*th*a*m* yeshâ*m* tâni tathâ brahma khalv ananyâpeksha*m* *g*aga*gg*anmâdi karoti. Ki*m* *k*ânyeshâ*m* parâkramâ*n*âm balavadbhir madhye bha*n*ga*h* sambhavati tena te svavîryâ*n*i na bibhrati, brahmavîryâ*n*i tu brahma*n*â sambh*ri*tâni avighnena sambh*ri*tâny ity artha*h*. Ân. Gi.

Upanishad of the same (i.e. the Râ*n*âyanîyas) we meet with vidyâs of Brahman among which the *S*â*nd*ilya-vidyâ is the first.—The question then arises whether the energies of Brahman just mentioned are to be inserted in those Brahma-vidyâs or not. To the pûrvapaksha view that they are to be so inserted because they are connected with Brahman, the Sûtrakâra replies that the holding together and pervading the sky are not to be inserted in the *S*â*nd*ilya-vidyâ and other vidyâs, for the same reason, i.e. on account of their being connected with different abodes. In the *S*â*nd*ilya-vidyâ, Brahman is said to have its abode in the heart, 'He is the Self within the heart' (*Kh*. Up. III, 14, 3); the same statement is made in the dahara-vidyâ, 'There is the palace, the small lotus (of the heart), and in it that small ether' (VIII, 1, 1). In the Upako*s*ala-vidyâ again, Brahman is said to reside within the eye, 'That person that is seen in the eye' (IV, 15, 1). In all these vidyâs Brahman is described as residing within the body; it is therefore impossible to insert into them the energies of Brahman which the khila of the Râ*n*âyanîyas mentions, and which are connected with the Devas (i.e. external nature).—But the vidyâs of the *Kh*ândogya likewise mention such powers of Brahman as are connected with the Devas; cp. e.g. III, 14, 3, 'He is greater than the heaven, greater than these worlds;' IV, 15, 4, 'He is also Bhâmanî, for he shines in all worlds;' VIII, 1, 3, 'As large as this ether is, so large is that ether within the heart. Both heaven and earth are contained within it.' And again there are other vidyâs of Brahman, such as the one which represents Brahman as comprising sixteen parts, in which not any special abode is mentioned.—True; but there is a special reason why the attributes stated in the Râ*n*âyanîya-khila cannot be introduced into the other vidyâs. Particulars mentioned in one place can indeed be inserted in vidyâs met with in another place if the latter are suggested to the mind by containing some reference to agreeing particulars; the qualities of holding together, however, on one side and those mentioned in the *S*â*nd*ilya-vidyâ, &c., on the other side are of such a nature as to exclude each other, and therefore do not mutually suggest each other. The mere circumstance of all the particulars being connected with Brahman does not suffice to suggest vidyâs occurring in other places; for even in vidyâs which are avowedly separate, all the particulars may be connected with Brahman. And it is an established fact that Brahman, although one only, is, owing to the plurality of its powers, meditated upon in more than one way, as shown under Sûtra 7.—The conclusion therefore is that the attributes of holding together its powers and so on are not to be inserted in the *S*â*nd*ilya and similar vidyâs.

24. And as the record of others (viz. the Taittirîyaka) is not such as in the purusha-vidyâ (of the *Kh*ândogya), (the two purusha-vidyâs are not to be combined).

In the Rahasya-brâhma*n*a of the Tâ*nd*ins and the Paiṅgins (the *Kh*ândogya) there is a vidyâ treating of man, in which man is fancifully identified with the sacrifice, the three periods of his life with the three libations, his hunger and so on, with the dîkshâ, &c. And other particulars also are mentioned there, such as formulas of prayer, use of mantras and so on.—A similar fanciful assimilation of the sacrifice and man the Taittirîyakas exhibit, 'For him who knows thus the Self of the sacrifice is the sacrificer, Faith is the wife of the sacrificer,' and so on (Taitt. Âr. X, 64).—The doubt here arises whether the particulars of the man-sacrifice given in the *Kh*ândogya are to be inserted in the Taittirîyaka or not.

Against the view of the pûrvapakshin that they are so to be inserted because in both places we have a purusha-ya*gñ*a, we maintain that they are not to be inserted because the characteristics of the purusha-ya*gñ*a of the *Kh*andogas are not recognised in the Taittirîya-text. This the Sûtrakâra expresses by saying, 'As (the record of the followers of some *S*âkhâs, viz. the Tâ*nd*ins and Paiṅgins, is) in the purusha-vidyâ, not such is the record of others,' viz. the Taittirîyakas. For the latter exhibit an identification of man with the sacrifice, in which the wife, the sacrificer, the

Veda, the vedi, the sacrificial grass, the post, the butter, the sacrificial animal, the priest, &c., are mentioned in succession; none of which particulars are mentioned in the *Kh*ândogya. The use also to which the Taittirîyaka turns the three libations is different from the *Kh*ândogya. And the few points in which the two texts agree, such as the identification of the Avab*ri*tha-ceremony with death, lose their significance side by side with the greater number of dissimilarities, and are therefore not able to effect the recognition of the vidyâ.—Moreover the Taittirîyaka does not represent man as the sacrifice (as the *Kh*ândogya does); for the two genitives ('of him who thus knows' and 'of the sacrifice') are not co-ordinate, and the passage therefore cannot be construed to mean, 'The knowing one who is the sacrifice, of him the Self is,' &c. For it cannot be said that man is the sacrifice, in the literal sense of the word [1]. The two genitives are rather to be taken in that way, that one qualifies the other, 'The sacrifice of him who thus knows, of that sacrifice,' &c. For the connexion of the sacrifice with man (which is expressed by the genitive, 'the sacrifice of him') is really and literally true; and to take a passage in its literal meaning, if possible at all, is always preferable to having recourse to a secondary metaphorical meaning [2]. Moreover the words next following in the Taittirîyaka-passage, 'the Self is the sacrificer,' declare that man (man's Self) is the sacrificer, and this again shows that man's relation to the sacrifice is not that of co-ordination [3]. Moreover as the section beginning with 'Of him who thus knows' forms an anuvâda of something previously established (and as such forms one vâkya to which one sense only must be ascribed), we must not bring about 'a split of the sentence' by interpreting it as

[1] And therefore we are not warranted in taking the two genitives as co-ordinate, as otherwise they might be taken.

[2] Which latter would be the case if we should take the two genitives as co-ordinate and therefore expressing an imaginative identification of the man and the sacrifice.

[3] If man is the sacrificer he cannot be identified with the sacrifice; he is rather the Lord of the sacrifice.

teaching in the first place that man is the sacrifice, and in the second place that the Self and the other beings enumerated are the sacrificer and so on. And as we see that the passage, 'Of him who thus knows,' &c., follows upon some instruction about the knowledge of the Self coupled with sa*m*nyâsa, we apprehend that the Taittirîyaka-chapter is not an independent vidyâ but merely supplementary to the instruction previously given. In agreement with this conclusion we observe that the Taittirîyaka promises only one result for both chapters, viz. the one stated in the passage, 'He obtains the greatness of Brahman.'—On the other hand the text embodying the purusha-vidyâ in the *Kh*ândogya is an independent text; for we see that an independent result is attached to it, viz. an increase of length of life, 'He who knows this lives on to a hundred and sixteen years.'—Hence the particulars mentioned in the purusha-vidyâ of another *S*âkhâ, such as formulas of prayer, mantras and so on, are not to be combined with the Taittirîya-text of the vidyâ.

25. Because the matter (of certain mantras) such as piercing and so on is different (from the matter of the approximate vidyâs) (the former have not to be combined with the latter).

At the beginning of an Upanishad of the Âtharva*n*ikas the following mantra is recorded, 'Pierce him (the enemy) whole, pierce his heart: crush his veins, crush his head; thrice crushed,' &c. At the beginning of the Upanishad of the Tâ*nd*ins we have the mantra, 'O God Savitar, produce the sacrifice.' At the beginning of that of the *S*â*t*yâyanins, 'Thou hast a white horse and art green as grass,' &c.; at the beginning of that of the Ka*th*as and the Taittirîyakas, 'May Mitra be propitious to us and Varu*n*a,' &c. At the beginning of the Upanishad of the Vâ*g*asaneyins we have a Brâhma*n*a-passage about the pravargya-ceremony, 'The gods indeed sat down to a sattra;' and at the beginning of that of the Kaushîtakins there is a Brâhma*n*a-passage about the agnish*t*oma, 'Brahman indeed is the Agnish*t*oma, Brahman is that day; through Brahman they pass into

Brahman, immortality those reach who observe that day.'—The point to be inquired into with reference to all these mantras and the sacrifices referred to in the Brâhma*n*a-passages is whether they are to be combined with the vidyâs (contained in the Upanishads) or not.

The pûrvapakshin maintains that they are so to be combined, because the text exhibits them in proximity to the Upanishad-portions of the Brâhma*n*as whose chief contents are formed by the vidyâs.—But we do not observe those mantras and sacrifices to be actually enjoined as subordinate members of the vidyâs!—True, but in spite of this we, on the ground of proximity, infer them to be connected with the vidyâs. For we have no right to set aside the fact of proximity as irrelevant as long as an inference can be established on it.—But we are unable to see that the mantras have anything to do with the vidyâs, and how can it be assumed that ceremonies, such as the pravargya which scripture enjoins with reference to other occasions, sacrifices, and so on, stand in any relation to the vidyâs!—Never mind, the pûrvapakshin replies. In the case of mantras we can always imagine some meaning which connects them with the vidyâs; the first mantra quoted, e.g. may be viewed as glorifying the heart. For the heart and other parts of the body are often represented, in the vidyâs, as abodes of meditation, and hence mantras glorifying the heart, &c., may appropriately form subordinate members of those vidyâs. Some mantras, moreover, we clearly see to be enjoined with reference to vidyâs, so, e.g. the mantra, 'I turn to Bhû*h* with such and such' (*Kh*. Up. III, 15, 3). Sacrificial acts again may indeed be enjoined in connexion with other occasions; yet there is no reason why they should not also be applied to the vidyâs, just as the offering called B*ri*haspatisava is a subordinate part of the Vâ*g*apeya-sacrifice[1].

To this we make the following reply. The mantras and

[1] The B*ri*haspatisava, although enjoined with special reference to him who is desirous of Brahmavar*k*as, is yet at the same time a subordinate part of the Vâ*g*apeya-sacrifice. Cp. Pû. Mî. Sû. IV, 3, 29.

ceremonies mentioned cannot be drawn into connexion with the vidyâs, 'because their matter, such as piercing the heart, &c., is different (from the matter of the vidyâs),' and therefore cannot be connected with the latter.—But has it not been said above that the mantras may be connected with the meditations enjoined in the vidyâs, on the ground of their coming of use in meditations on the heart, &c.?—The mantras, we reply, might be so employed, if their entire contents were glorification of the heart, and the like; but this is by no means the case. The mantra first quoted, e.g. clearly expresses hostility to somebody, and is therefore to be connected, not with the vidyâs of the Upanishads, but with some ceremony meant to hurt an enemy. The mantra of the Tâ*nd*ins again, 'O God Savitar, produce the sacrifice,' indicates by its very words that it is connected with some sacrifice; with what particular sacrifice it is connected has to be established by other means of proof. Similarly other mantras also—which, either by 'indication' (liṅga), or 'syntactical connexion' (vâkya), or some other means of proof, are shown to be subordinate to certain sacrificial actions—cannot, because they occur in the Upanishads also, be connected with the vidyâs on the ground of mere proximity. For that 'proximity,' as a means of proof regarding the connexion of subordinate matters with principal matters, is weaker than direct enunciation (*S*ruti), and so on, is demonstrated in the former science (i.e. in the Pûrva Mîmâ*m*sâ) under III, 3, 14. Of sacrificial works also, such as the pravargya, which are primarily enjoined with reference to other occasions, it cannot be demonstrated that they are supplementary to vidyâs with which they have nothing in common. The case of the B*ri*haspatisava, quoted by the pûrvapakshin, is of an altogether different kind, as there we have an injunction clearly showing that that oblation is a subordinate member of the Vâ*g*apeya, viz. 'Having offered the Vâ*g*apeya he offers the B*ri*haspatisava.' And, moreover, if the one pravargya-ceremony has once been enjoined for a definite purpose by a means of proof of superior strength, we must not, on the strength of an inferior means of proof, assume it to be enjoined for some different purpose. A proceeding of that kind would be possible only if the difference of the means of proof were not apprehended; but in our case this latter possibility is excluded since the relative strength and weakness of the various means of proof is fully apprehended (on the ground of the conclusions arrived at in the Pûrva Mîmâ*m*sâ).—For these reasons the mentioned mantras and acts are not, on the ground of mere textual collocation, to be viewed as supplementary to the vidyâs of the Upanishads. To account for the fact of their textual collocation with the latter we must keep in view that the mantras, &c. as well as the vidyâs have to be studied, &c. in the woods.

26. Where the getting rid (of good and evil) is mentioned (the obtaining of this good and evil by others has to be added) because the statement about the obtaining is supplementary (to the statement about the getting rid of), as in the case of the ku*s*âs, the metres, the praise and the singing. This (i.e. the reason for this) has been stated (in the Pûrva Mîmâ*m*sâ).

In the text of the Tâ*nd*ins we meet with the following passage: 'Shaking off all evil as a horse shakes his hair, and shaking off the body as the moon frees herself from the mouth of Râhu, I obtain self made and satisfied the uncreated world of Brahman' (*Kh*. Up. VIII, 13). Again, in the text of the Âtharva*n*ikas, we read, 'Then knowing, shaking off good and evil he reaches the highest oneness, free from passion' (Mu. Up. III. 1, 3). The *S*â*t*yâyanins read, 'His sons obtain his inheritance, his friends the good, his enemies the evil he has done.' And the Kaushîtakins, 'He shakes off his good and his evil deeds. His beloved relatives obtain the good, his unbeloved relatives the evil he has done' (Kau. Up. I, 4).—Of these texts two state that the man who has reached true knowledge rids himself of his good and evil deeds; one, that his friends and enemies obtain his good and evil deeds respectively; and one finally declares that both things take place.

This latter text calls for no remark; nor again that one which refers only to his friends and enemies obtaining his good and evil deeds; for in order that they may obtain those he must necessarily first have got rid of them, and the act of getting rid of them has therefore to be supplied in the text. Those passages, however, which merely mention a man's shaking off his deeds, give rise to a discussion whether those deeds, when shaken off, are obtained by his friends and enemies, or not. Here the pûrvapakshin maintains that the latter circumstance is not to be supplied in the two passages mentioned—firstly because the text does not state it; secondly because what other *S*âkhâs say about it falls within the sphere of a different vidyâ; and thirdly because the getting rid of the evil and good deeds is something done by the man himself, while the obtaining of them is the work of others. As thus there is no necessary connexion between the two, we have no right to supply the latter on the basis of the former.

To this we make the following reply. Although the text mentions only the getting rid of the deeds, yet the obtaining of them by others must necessarily be added, because the statement concerning the latter is merely supplementary to the statement about the former, as appears from the text of the Kaushîtakins.—In reply to the arguments brought forward by the pûrvapakshin we offer the following remarks.

The separation of the different passages would indeed have to be insisted upon, if anybody intended to introduce an injunction about something to be done, which is contained in one text only, into some other text also. But in the passages under discussion the act of getting rid of—and the act of obtaining—the good and evil deeds are not mentioned as something to be performed, but merely as implying a glorification of knowledge; the intended sense being, 'Glorious indeed is that knowledge through whose power the good and evil deeds, the causes of the sa*m*sâra, are shaken off by him who knows, and are transferred to his friends and enemies.' The passage thus being glorificatory only, the teacher is of opinion that, to the end of strengthening the glorification, the obtaining of the good and evil deeds by the friends and enemies—which in some passages is represented as the consequence of their being shaken off by the man who knows—must be supplied in those passages also which mention only the shaking off. That one arthavâda-passage often depends on another arthavâda-passage is a well-known fact; the following passage, e.g. 'The twenty-first indeed from this world is that sun,' would be unintelligible if no regard were paid to the other passage, 'Twelve are the months, five the seasons, three these worlds; that sun is the twenty-first.' Similarly the passage, 'The two Trish*t*ubh verses are for strengthening,' necessarily requires to be taken in connexion with the other passage, 'Strength of the senses indeed is Trish*t*ubh.' And as the statement about the obtaining of the good and evil deeds has only the purpose of glorifying knowledge (and is not made on its own account), we need not insist too much on the question how the results of actions done by one man can be obtained by others. That the obtaining of the deeds by others is connected with their being got rid of by the man who knows, merely for the purpose of glorifying knowledge, the Sûtrakâra moreover indicates by making use of the expression, 'because the statement about obtaining is supplementary to,' &c.; for if he wished to intimate that the actual circumstance of other persons obtaining a man's good and evil deeds is to be inserted in those vidyâs where it is not mentioned he would say, 'because the fact of obtaining,' &c. The Sûtra therefore, availing itself of the opportunity offered by the discussion of the combination of particular qualities, shows how mere glorificatory passages have to be inserted in texts where they are wanting.

The remaining part of the Sûtra, 'Like the ku*s*âs, the metres, the praise and the singing,' introduces some analogous instances.—The case under discussion is analogous to the case of the ku*s*âs[1]. Those, a mantra of the Bhâl-

[1] I.e. according to the commentators, small wooden rods used by the Udgât*ri*s in counting the stotras.

lavins ('You kusâs are the children of the tree, do you protect me!') represents as coming from trees in general, without any specification. The corresponding mantra of the *S*â*t*yâyanins on the other hand is, 'You ku*s*âs are the children of the Udumbara-tree; a particularizing statement which must be considered as valid for the ku*s*âs in general.—Another analogous case is that of the metres. In some places no special statement is made about their order of succession; but the text of the Paiṅgins, 'The metres of the Devas come first,' determines the general priority of the metres of the Devas to those of the Asuras[1].—Similarly the time of the stotra accompanying the performance of the Sho*d*a*s*in-rite which in some texts is left undefined is settled by the text of the *R*ig-vedins (âr*k*â*h*), 'when the Sun has half risen.'—And similarly a particularizing text of the Bhâllavins defines what priests have to join in the singing; a point left unsettled in other *S*rutis[2].—As in these parallel cases, so we have to proceed in the case under discussion also. For if we refused to define a general text by another more particular one, we should be driven to assume optional procedure (vikalpa), and that the latter is if possible to be avoided is a well-known principle. This is stated in the Pûrva Mîmâ*m*sâ-sûtras X, 8, 15.

The passages about the shaking (off) can be viewed as giving rise to a different discussion also, and the Sûtra can accordingly be explained in a different manner. The question can be raised whether the 'shaking' means the getting rid of one's good and evil deeds or something else.—The pûrvapaksha will in that case have to be established in the following manner. Shaking (dhû) here does not mean 'getting rid of,' since the root 'dhû' according to grammar means shaking in an intransitive sense or trembling; of flags streaming in the wind we say, for

[1] Metres of less than ten syllables belong to the Asuras, those of ten and more to the Devas.

[2] The general text is, according to the commentators, 'The priests join in the singing;' the defining text of the Bhâllavins, 'The adhvaryu does not join in the singing.'

instance, 'the flags are shaking' (dodhûyante). We therefore take the word in the same sense in the passages under discussion and understand by the 'trembling' of the good and evil deeds the fact of their not meeting, for a certain time, with their results.

To this pûrvapaksha we make the following reply. The word 'shaking' has to be taken in the sense of 'getting rid of,' because it is supplemented by the statement of others obtaining the good and evil deeds. For those deeds cannot be obtained by others unless they are got rid of by their former owner. Hence although it is not easily imaginable that the deeds got rid of by one man should be obtained by others, we yet, on the ground of its being mentioned, may determine accordingly that 'shaking' means 'getting rid of.' And although only in some passages the statement about the obtaining is actually found in proximity to the statement about the shaking, it yet has, on the ground of the latter, to be supplied everywhere and thus becomes a general reason of decision (viz. that 'shaking' means 'getting rid of'). Against the pûrvapakshin's view we further remark that good and evil deeds cannot be said to 'tremble' in the literal sense of the word, like flags in the wind, since they are not of substantial nature.—(Nor must it be said that of the horse which exemplifies the shaking, the text only says that it shakes its hair, not that it casts anything off, for) the horse when shaking itself shakes off dust and also old hairs. And with that shaking (which at the same time is a shaking off) the text expressly compares the shaking (off) of evil.—Nor do we when assigning different meanings to one and the same root enter thereby into conflict with Sm*ri*ti (grammar). The clause 'this has been stated' we have already explained.

27. At the (moment of) departing (he frees himself from his works), there being nothing to be reached (by him, on the way to Brahman, through those works); for thus others (declare, in their sacred texts).

The Kaushîtakins record in the paryaṅka-vidyâ how the man (who possesses true knowledge) when approaching Brahman seated on the couch frees himself on the way from his good and evil deeds, 'He having reached the path of the gods comes to the world of Agni,' &c. (Kau. Up. I, 3), and later on (I, 4), 'He comes to the river Vi*g*arâ and crosses it by the mind alone and there shakes off his good and evil deeds.'—The question here arises whether in strict agreement with the text we have to understand that the deceased man frees himself from his good and evil deeds on the way to Brahman, or rather that he does so at the outset when he departs from his body.

The letter of the text favouring the former alternative, the Sûtrakâra rebuts it by declaring 'at the going,' i.e. at the time of departing from the body the man frees himself, through the strength of his knowledge, from his good and evil deeds. The reason for this averment is assigned in the words, 'On account of the absence of anything to be reached.' For when the man possessing true knowledge has departed from the body and is, through his knowledge, about to reach Brahman, there exists nothing to be reached by him on the way through his good and evil works, and we therefore have no reason to assume the latter to remain uneffaced during a certain number of moments. We rather have to conclude that as the results of his good and evil works are contrary to the result of knowledge, they are destroyed by the power of the latter; and that hence the moment of their destruction is that moment in which he sets out toward the fruit of his knowledge (i.e. the world of Brahman).—The conclusion thus is that the deliverance of the man from his works takes place early, and is only mentioned later on in the text of the Kaushîtakins.—Thus other *S*âkhâs also, as that of the Tâ*nd*ins and *S*â*t*yâyanins, declare that he frees himself from his deeds at an earlier stage; cp. the passages, 'Shaking off all evil as a horse shakes his hair,' and 'His sons obtain his inheritance, his friends the good, his enemies the evil he has done.'

28. And because (on the above interpretation)

there is no contradiction to both (i.e. man's making an effort to free himself from his deeds and actually freeing himself) according to his liking.

Moreover if we assumed that the man frees himself from his good and evil deeds on the way—after having departed from the body and having entered on the path of the gods—we should implicate ourselves in impossibilities; for after the body has been left behind, man can no longer accomplish, according to his liking, that effort which consists in self-restraint and pursuit of knowledge. and which is the cause of the obliteration of all his good and evil deeds, and consequently that obliteration also cannot take place. We therefore must assume that the requisite effort is made—and its result takes place—at an earlier moment, viz. in the state in which man is able to effect it, and that in consequence thereof man rids himself of his good and evil deeds. Nothing then stands in the way of the conditioning and the conditioned events taking place, and the assumption moreover agrees with the statements of the Tâ*nd*ins and *S*â*t*yâyanins.

29. A purpose has to be attributed to the going (on the path of the gods) in a twofold manner; otherwise there would be contradiction of scripture.

In some scriptural texts the (dead man's) going on the path of the gods is mentioned in connexion with his freeing himself from good and evil; in other texts it is not mentioned. The doubt then arises whether the two things go together in all cases or only in certain cases.—The pûrvapakshin maintains that the two are to be connected in all cases, just as the man's freeing himself from his good and evil deeds is always followed by their passing over to his friends and enemies.

To this we make the following reply. That a man's going on the path of the gods has a purpose is to be admitted in a twofold manner, i.e. with a distinction only. His going on that path has a sense in certain cases, in others not. For otherwise, i.e. if we admitted that men, in all cases, proceed on that path, we should have to assume that even the passage, Mu. Up. III, 1, 3, 'Shaking off good and evil, free from passions, he reaches the highest unity,' refers to actual going through which another place is reached, and that would clearly be contrary to reason. For a person free from all desire and therefore non-moving does not go to another place, and the highest unity is not to be reached by a man transporting himself to another locality.

30. (The twofold view taken above) is justified because we observe a purpose characterised thereby (i.e. a purpose of the going); as in ordinary life.

Our view of the matter, viz. that a man's proceeding on the path of the gods has a meaning in certain cases but not in others, is justified by the following consideration. In meditations on the qualified Brahman such as the paryaṅka-vidyâ we see a reason for the man's proceeding on the path of the gods; for the text mentions certain results which can be reached only by the man going to different places, such as his mounting a couch, his holding a colloquy with Brahman seated on the couch, his perceiving various odours and so on. On the other hand we do not see that going on the path of the gods has anything to do with perfect knowledge. For those who have risen to the intuition of the Self's unity, whose every wish is fulfilled, in whom the potentiality of all suffering is already destroyed here below, have nothing further to look for but the dissolution of the abode of activity and enjoyment of former deeds, i.e. the body; in their case therefore to proceed on the road of the gods would be purposeless.—The distinction is analogous to what is observed in ordinary life. If we want to reach some village we have to proceed on a path leading there; but no moving on a path is required when we wish to attain freedom from sickness.—The distinction made here will be established more carefully in the fourth adhyâya.

31. There is no restriction (as to the going on the path of the gods) for any vidyâ; nor any contra-

diction (of the general subject-matter), according to scripture and inference (i.e. Smriti).

We have shown that the going on the path of the gods is valid only for the vidyâs of the qualified Brahman, not for the knowledge of the highest Brahman which is destitute of all qualities.—Now we observe that the going on the path of the gods is mentioned only in some of the qualified vidyâs, such as the paryaṅka-vidyâ, the pañkâgni-vidyâ, the upakosala-vidyâ, the dahara-vidyâ; while it is not mentioned in others, such as the madhu-vidyâ, the sândilya-vidyâ, the shodasakala-vidyâ, the vaisvânara-vidyâ.—The doubt then arises whether the going on the path of the gods is to be connected with those vidyâs only in which it is actually mentioned or generally with all vidyâs of that kind.

The pûrvapakshin maintains the former view; for, he says, the limitative force of the general subject-matter of each particular section compels us to connect the going on the path of the gods with those vidyâs only which actually mention it. If we transferred it to other vidyâs also, the authoritativeness of scripture would suffer; for then anything might be the sense of anything. Moreover, the details about the path of the gods beginning with light and so on are given equally in the upakosala-vidyâ and the pañkâgni-vidyâ, which would be a useless repetition if as a matter of course the going on the path of the gods were connected with all vidyâs.

To this we make the following reply. The going on the path of the gods is not to be restricted but to be connected equally with all those qualified vidyâs which have exaltation (abhyudaya) for their result. The objection above raised by the pûrvapakshin that thereby we contradict the general subject-matter, we refute by appealing to scripture and Smriti. Scripture in the first place declares that not only those 'who know this,' i.e. the pañkâgni-vidyâ (*Kh.* Up. V, 10, 1), proceed on the path of the gods, but also those who understand other vidyâs, 'and also those who in the forest follow faith and austerities.'—But how do we know that the latter passage refers to those who are conversant with other vidyâs? The text certainly speaks of those only who are intent on faith and austerities!—Not by faith and austerities alone, we reply, unaided by knowledge, can that path be attained; for another scriptural passage says, 'Through knowledge they mount to that place from which all wishes have passed away; those who are skilled in works only do not go there, nor penitents devoid of knowledge' (*S*at. Brâ. X, 5, 4, 16). We therefore conclude that faith and austerities denote at the same time other vidyâs.—The Vâ*g*asaneyins again read in the Pa*ñk*âgni-vidyâ, 'Those who thus know this and those who in the forest worship faith and the True.' The latter part of this passage we must explain to mean, 'Those who in the forest with faith worship the True, i.e. Brahman;' the term 'the True' being often employed to denote Brahman. And as those who know the pa*ñk*âgni-vidyâ are in the above passage referred to as 'those who thus know this,' we must understand the clause, 'and those who in the forest,' &c., as referring to men in the possession of other vidyâs. And, moreover, also the passage, 'Those, however, who know neither of these two paths become worms, birds, and creeping things' (VI, 2, 16), which teaches that those who miss the two paths have to go downwards, intimates that those who possess other vidyâs have to proceed either on the path of the gods or that of the fathers, and as their vidyâs are as such not different from the pa*ñk*âgni-vidyâ, we conclude that they proceed on the path of the gods (not on that of the fathers)[1].

In the second place Sm*ri*ti also confirms the same doctrine, 'These two, the white and the black path, are known as the eternal paths of the world; on the one man goes not to return, on the other he again returns' (Bha. Gî. VIII, 26).

With regard, finally, to the circumstance that the details about the path of the gods are given in the Upako*s*ala-

[1] Ita*s* *k*a vidyântara*s*îlinâ*m* gatir iti liṅgadar*s*ana*m* samu*kh*inoti atheti, etân iti vidyântaraparâ *gri*hyante, tathâpi katha*m* devayânayogas teshâm ity â*s*aṅkya yogyatayety âha tatrâpîti. Ân. Gi.

vidyâ as well as the Pañkâgni-vidyâ, we remark that the repetition is meant to assist reflection.

For all these reasons the going on the path of the gods is not limited to those vidyâs in which it is actually mentioned.

32. Of those who have a certain office there is subsistence (of the body) as long as the office lasts.

The question here is whether for him who has reached true knowledge a new body originates after he has parted with the old one or not.—But, an objection is here raised at the outset there is really no occasion for inquiring whether knowledge when reaching its perfection brings about its due effect, viz. complete isolation of the Self from all bodies or not; not any more than there is room for an inquiry whether there is cooked rice or not, after the process of cooking has reached its due termination; or, for an inquiry whether a man is satisfied by eating or not.—Not so, we reply. There is indeed room for the inquiry proposed, as we know from itihâsa and purâna that some persons although knowing Brahman yet obtained new bodies. Tradition informs us, e.g. that Apântaratamas, an ancient rishi and teacher of the Vedas, was, by the order of Vishnu, born on this earth as Krishna Dvaipâyana at the time when the Dvâparayuga was succeeded by the Kaliyuga. Similarly Vasishtha, the son of Brahman's mind, having parted from his former body in consequence of the curse of Nimi, was, on the order of Brahman, again procreated by Mitra and Varuna. Smriti further relates that Bhrigu and other sons of Brahman's mind were again born at the sacrifice of Varuna. Sanatkumâra also, who likewise was a son of Brahman's mind, was, in consequence of a boon being granted to Rudra, born again as Skanda. And there are similar tales about Daksha, Nârada, and others having, for various reasons, assumed new bodies. Stories of the same kind are met with in the mantras and arthavâdas of Sruti. Of some of the persons mentioned it is said that they assumed a new body after the old body had perished; of others that they assumed, through their supernatural powers, various new bodies, while the old body remained intact all the while. And all of them are known to have completely mastered the contents of the Vedas.

On the ground of all this the pûrvapakshin maintains that the knowledge of Brahman may, indifferently, either be or not be the cause of final release.

This we deny, for the reason that the continuance of the bodily existence of Aparântamas and others—who are entrusted with offices conducive to the subsistence of the worlds, such as the promulgation of the Vedas and the like—depends on those their offices. As Savitar (the sun), who after having for thousands of yugas performed the office of watching over these worlds, at the end of that period enjoys the condition of release in which he neither rises nor sets, according to *Kh.* Up. III, 11, 1, 'When from thence he has risen upwards, he neither rises nor sets. He is alone, standing in the centre;' and as the present knowers of Brahman reach the state of isolation after the enjoyment of those results of action, which have begun to operate, has come to an end, according to *Kh.* Up. VI, 14, 2, 'For him there is only delay so long as he is not delivered from the body;' so Aparântamas and other Lords to whom the highest Lord has entrusted certain offices, last—although they possess complete knowledge, the cause of release—as long as their office lasts, their works not yet being exhausted, and obtain release only when their office comes to an end. For gradually exhausting the aggregate of works the consequences of which have once begun, so as to enable them to discharge their offices; passing according to their free will from one body into another, as if from one house into another, in order to accomplish the duties of their offices; preserving all the time the memory of their identity; they create for themselves through their power over the material of the body and the sense organs new bodies, and occupy them either all at once or in succession. Nor can it be said that when passing into new bodies they remember only the fact of their former existence (not their individuality); for it is known that they preserve the sense of their individuality[1]. Smriti tells us, e.g. that Sulabhâ, a woman conversant with Brahman, wishing to dispute with Ganaka, left her own body, entered into that of Ganaka, carried on a discussion with him, and again returned into her own body. If in addition to the works the consequences of which are already in operation, other works manifested themselves, constituting the cause of further embodiments, the result would be that in the same way further works also, whose potentiality would in that case not be destroyed, would take place, and then it might be suspected that the knowledge of Brahman may, indifferently, either be or not be the cause of final release. But such a suspicion is inadmissible since it is known from Sruti and Smriti that knowledge completely destroys the potentiality of action. For Sruti says, 'The fetter of the heart is broken, all doubts are solved, all his works perish when He has been beheld who is high and low' (Mu. Up. II, 2, 8); and, 'When the memory remains firm, then all the ties are loosened' (*Kh.* Up. VII, 26, 2). And Smriti similarly says, 'As a fire well kindled, O Arguna, reduces fuel to ashes, so the fire of knowledge reduces all actions to ashes;' and, 'As seeds burned by fire do not sprout again, so the Self is not again touched by the afflictions which knowledge has burned.' Nor is it possible that when the afflictions such as ignorance and the like are burned, the aggregate of works which is the seed of affliction should be partly burned, but partly keep the power of again springing up; not any more than the seed of the Sâli, when burned, preserves the power of sprouting again with some part. The aggregate of works, however, whose fruits have once begun to develop themselves comes to rest through effecting a delay which terminates with the death of the body, just as an arrow discharged stops in the end owing to the gradual cessation of its impetus; this in agreement with *Kh.* Up. VI, 14, 2, 'For him there is only delay,' &c. We have thus shown that persons to whom an office is

[1] Utpadyamânânâm aparimushitasmaratve*pi gâtismaratvam eva na vasishthâdinânatvam ity âsankyâha na keti. Ân. Gi.

entrusted last as long as their office lasts, and that nevertheless there is absolutely only one result of true knowledge.—In accordance with this, scripture declares that the result of knowledge on the part of all beings is equally final release, cp. 'So whatever Deva was awakened he indeed became that, and the same with *Ri*shis and men' (B*ri*. Up. I, 4, 10). Moreover[1] it may be the case that (some) great *ri*shis had attached their minds to other cognitions whose result is lordly power and the like, and that later on only when they became aware of the transitory nature of those results they turned from them and fixed their minds on the highest Self, whereby they obtained final release. As Sm*ri*ti says, 'When the mahâpralaya has arrived and the highest (i. e. Hira*n*yagarbha) himself comes to an end, then they all, with well-prepared minds, reach together with Brahman the highest place.'—Another reason precluding the suspicion that true knowledge may be destitute of its result is that that result is the object of immediate intuition. In the case of such results of action as the heavenly world and the like which are not present to intuitional knowledge, there may be a doubt; but not so in the case of the fruit of true knowledge, with regard to which scripture says, 'The Brahman which is present to intuition, not hidden' (B*ri*. Up. III, 4, 1), and which in the passage, 'That art thou,' is referred to as something already accomplished. This latter passage cannot be interpreted to mean, 'Thou wilt be that after thou hast died;' for another Vedic passage declares that the fruit of complete knowledge, viz. union with the universal Self, springs up at the moment when complete knowledge is attained, 'The *Ri*shi Vâmadeva saw and understood it, singing, "I was Manu, I was the sun."'

For all these reasons we maintain that those who possess true knowledge reach in all cases final release.

33. But the (denials of) conceptions concerning the

[1] Api *k*a nâdhikâravatâ*m* sarveshâm *ri*shî*n*âm âtmatattvag*ñ*âna*m* tenâvyâpako*x*py ayam pûrvapaksha ity âha g*ñ*ânântareshu *k*eti. Bhâ.

akshara are to be comprehended (in all meditations on the akshara), on account of the equality and of the object being the same, as in the case of the upasad; this has been explained (in the Pûrva Mîmâ*m*sâ).

We read in the Vâ*g*asaneyaka, 'O Gârgî, the Brâhma*n*as call this the Akshara. It is neither coarse, nor fine, nor short, nor long,' &c. (B*ri*. Up. III, 8, 8). Similarly the Âtharva*n*a says, 'The higher knowledge is that by which the Indestructible is apprehended. That which cannot be seen nor seized, which has no family and no caste,' &c. (Mu. Up. I, 1, 5; 6). In other places also the highest Brahman, under the name of Akshara, is described as that of which all qualities are to be denied. Now in some places qualities are denied of Brahman which are not denied in other places, and hence a doubt arises whether the mental conception of these particular denials is to form part of all those passages or not.

To the assertion of the pûrvapakshin that each denial is valid only for that passage in which the text actually exhibits it, we make the following reply.—The conceptions of the akshara, i.e. the conceptions of the particular denials concerning the akshara, are to be included in all those passages, 'on account of the equality and on account of the same object being referred to.' The equality consists therein that all the texts alluded to convey an idea of Brahman in the same way, viz. by denying of it all attributes; and we recognise in all of them the same object of instruction, viz. the one undivided Brahman. Why then should the conceptions stated in one passage not be valid for all others also? To the present case the same argumentation applies which had been made use of under III, 3, 11. There positive attributes were discussed; here we are concerned with negative ones. The division of the discussion into two (instead of disposing of positive and negative attributes in one adhikara*n*a) is due to the wish of explaining the differences in detail.—The clause, 'as in the case of the upasads,' introduces a parallel case. For the *G*âmadagnya-ahîna-sacrifice[1] the text enjoins that the upasad offerings are to consist of puro*d*â*s*as. Now although the mantras accompanying the offering of the puro*d*â*s*as are originally enjoined in the Veda of the Udgât*ri*s (Tâ*nd*ya Brâ. XXI, 10, 11, 'Agni, promote the hotra,' &c.), yet they are to be enounced by the adhvaryu; for the offering of the puro*d*â*s*as is the work of the adhvaryu, and subordinate matters (i.e. here, the mantras) are governed by the principal matter (i.e. the offering of the puro*d*â*s*a). Similarly, in the case under discussion, the attributes of the akshara have, because they are subordinate to the akshara itself, to be connected with the latter everywhere, in whatever places the text may originally state them.—The principle of decision employed is explained in the Pûrva Mîmâ*m*sâ-sûtras III, 3, 9.

34. On account of (the same) number being recorded.

The Âtharva*n*ikas exhibit, with reference to the Self, the following mantra, 'Two birds, inseparable friends, cling to the same tree. One of them eats the sweet fruit, the other looks on without eating' (Mu. Up. III, 1, 1). The same mantra is found in the text of the *S*vetâ*s*vataras (IV, 6). The Ka*th*as again read, 'There are the two drinking their reward in the world of their own works, entered into the cave, dwelling on the highest summit. Those who know Brahman call them shade and light, likewise those householders who perform the Tri*n*â*k*iketa-sacrifice.'—The doubt here arises whether the two sections introduced by these mantras constitute one vidyâ or two vidyâs. Here the pûrvapakshin maintains that we have to do with two separate vidyâs, because the texts exhibit certain differences. For the mantra of the Mu*nd*aka and *S*vetâ*s*vatara Upanishads represents one bird as enjoying and the other as not enjoying; while in the mantra of the Ka*th*as

[1] I.e. a sacrifice lasting four days, called *G*âmadagnya, because first offered by *G*amadagni. Cp. Taitt. Sa*m*h. VII, 1, 9.

both are said to enjoy.—As thus the objects of knowledge differ in character, the vidyâs themselves must be looked upon as separate.

To this we make the following reply. The vidyâ is one only because both mantras exhibit the character of the objects of knowledge as one and the same, viz. as defined by the number two.—But has not the pûrvapakshin shown that there exists a certain difference of character?—By no means, we reply. Both texts intimate one and the same matter, viz. the Lord together with the individual soul. In the Mu*nd*aka-text the clause, 'The other looks on without eating,' intimates the highest Self which is raised above all desire; the same highest Self forms also the subject of the complementary passage, 'But when he sees the other Lord contented.' And the Ka*th*a-text intimates the same highest Self which is raised above all desire; only, as it is mentioned together with the enjoying individual soul, it is itself metaphorically spoken of as enjoying; just as we speak of the 'men with the umbrella,' although only one out of several carries an umbrella. For that in the Ka*th*a-text also the highest Self forms the general subje t-matter we have to conclude from the preceding passag., 'That which thou seest as neither this nor that' (I, 2, 14), and from the complementary passage ref.rring to the same Self, 'Which is a bridge for sacrificers, which is the highest imperishable Brahman' (I, 3, 2). All this has been explained at length under I, 2, 11. As therefore there is one object of knowledge only, the vidyâ also is one.—Moreover, if we carefully examine the context of the three mantras quoted, we observe that they are concerned merely with the knowledge of the highest Self, and that they mention the individual soul not as a new object of instruction but merely to show its identity with the highest Self. And that, as far as the knowledge of the highest Self is concerned, the question as to the oneness or separateness of vidyâs cannot be even raised, we have already shown above. The present Sûtra therefore merely aims at a fuller discussion of the matter, the practical outcome of which is that any particulars stated in one of the texts only have to be supplied in the others also.

35. As the Self is within all, as in the case of the aggregate of the elements, (there is oneness of vidyâ).

The Vâ*g*asaneyins record, in the questions asked by Ushasta and by Kahola, the same passage twice in succession, 'Tell me the Brahman which is present to intuition, not hidden; the Self who is within all' (B*ri*. Up. III, 4, 1; 5, 1).—The question here presents itself whether the two sections introduced by the questions constitute one vidyâ only or two separate vidyâs.

Two separate vidyâs, the pûrvapakshin maintains; owing to the force of repetition. For if the second passage added nothing to—or took nothing away from—the contents of the first, the repetition would be altogether meaningless. We therefore conclude that the repetition intimates the separateness of the two vidyâs, just as in the Pûrva Mîmâ*m*sâ repetition shows two sacrificial actions to be separate.

To this we make the following reply. As both texts equally declare the Self to be within all, they must be taken as constituting one vidyâ only. In both passages question and answer equally refer to a Self which is within everything. For in one body there cannot be two Selfs, each of which is inside everything else. One Self indeed may without difficulty be within everything, but of a second one this could not be predicated, not any more than of the aggregate of the elements; i.e. the case of that second Self is analogous to that of the aggregate of the five elements, i.e. the body. In the body the element of water is indeed within the element of earth, and the element of fire within the element of water; but each of these elements is 'within all' in a relative sense only, not in the literal sense of the phrase.—Or else the 'like the aggregate of the elements (or beings)' of the Sûtra has to be taken as pointing to another scriptural passage, viz. *S*ve. Up. VI, 11, 'He is the one god, hidden in all beings, all-pervading, the Self within all beings.' As this mantra records that one Self lives within the aggregate of all beings, the same holds good with regard to the two Brâhma*n*a-passages. And the object of knowledge being one, the vidyâ also is one only.

36. If it be said that otherwise the separation (of the statements) cannot be accounted for; we reply that it is (here) as in the case of other instructions.

We yet have to refute the remark made by the pûrvapakshin that, unless the separateness of the two vidyâs be admitted, the separation of the two statements cannot be accounted for. We do this by pointing to analogous cases. In the sixth prapâ*th*aka of the upanishad of the Tâ*nd*ins the instruction conveyed in the words, 'That is the Self, thou art that, O *S*vetaketu,' is repeated nine times, and yet the one vidyâ is not thereby split into many. Similarly in our case.—But how do you know that the vidyâ remains one and the same in spite of the ninefold repetition?—Because, we reply, the introductory and concluding clauses show that all those passages have the same sense. For the repeated request on the part of *S*vetaketu, 'Please, Sir, inform me still more,' shows that one and the same matter is again and again proposed for further discussion, and further instruction regarding it is repeatedly given by means of new doubts being removed. Similarly, in the case under discussion, the sameness of form of the two introductory questions and the equality of the concluding clauses, 'Everything else is of evil,' show that both sections refer to one and the same matter.—Moreover, in the second question the text adds the word 'just' (eva), 'Tell me just that Brahman,' &c., which shows that the second question refers to the same matter as the first one. That the matter of the two sections is really the same, we establish by pointing out that the former section declares the existence of the highest Self which is neither cause nor effect, while the latter qualifies it as that which transcends all the attributes of the Sa*m*sâra state, such as hunger, thirst, and so on.—The two sections, therefore, form one vidyâ only.

37. There is exchange (of meditation), for the texts distinguish (two meditations); as in other cases.

The Aitareyins declare with reference to the person in the sun, 'What I am, that is he; what he is, that am I' (Ait. Âr. II, 2, 4, 6). And the *G*âbâlas say, 'I am thou indeed, O reverend divinity, and thou art I indeed.'—The doubt here arises whether the reflection founded upon this text is to be a double one 'by means of exchange' (i.e. whether the soul is to be meditated upon as âditya and âditya as the soul), or a simple one (the soul only being meditated upon as âditya).

The pûrvapakshin maintains the latter view; for, he says, the text cannot possibly propose as matter of meditation anything but the oneness of the individual soul with the Lord. For if we assumed that two different forms of meditation are intended, viz. firstly the soul's being the Self of the Lord, and, secondly, the Lord's being the Self of the soul, the soul indeed would be exalted by the former meditation, but the Lord, at the same time, be lowered by the latter one. We therefore conclude that the meditation is to be of one kind only, and that the double form, in which the text exhibits it, merely aims at confirming the oneness of the Self.

To this we make the following reply. 'Exchange' is expressly recorded in the text for the purposes of meditation, just as other qualities (of the Self), such as its being the Self of all, &c., are recorded for the same purpose. For both texts make the distinctive double enunciation, 'I am thou,' and 'Thou art I.' Now this double enunciation has a sense only if a twofold meditation is to be based upon it; otherwise it would be devoid of meaning, since one statement would be all that is required.—But has not the pûrvapakshin urged above that this your explanation involves a lowering of the Lord, who is thereby represented as having the transmigrating soul for his Self?—Never mind, we reply; even in that way only the unity of the Self is meditated upon.—But does your explanation then not come to that of the pûrvapakshin, viz. that the double statement is merely meant to confirm the oneness of the Self?—We do not, our reply is, deny that the text confirms the oneness of the Self; we only want to prove that, on the ground of the text as it stands, a twofold meditation has to be admitted, not a simple one. That this virtually confirms the unity of the Self we admit; just as the instruction about (the Lord's) possessing such qualities as having only true wishes, and so on—which instruction is given for the purpose of meditation—at the same time proves the existence of a Lord endowed with such qualities. —Hence the double relation enounced in the text has to be meditated upon, and is to be transferred to other vidyâs also which treat of the same subject.

38. For the True and so on are one and the same (vidyâ).

The text of the Vâ*g*asaneyaka, after having enjoined the knowledge of the True, together with a meditation on the syllables of its name ('Whosoever knows this great glorious first-born as the true Brahman,' &c., B*ri*. Up. V, 4, 1), continues, 'Now what is the True, that is the Âditya, the person that dwells in yonder orb, and the person in the right eye' (V, 5, 2).—The doubt here arises whether the text enjoins two vidyâs of the True or one only.

Two, the pûrvapakshin maintains. For the text declares two different results, one in the earlier passage, 'He conquers these worlds' (V, 4, 1); the other one later on, 'He destroys evil and leaves it' (V, 5, 3). And what our opponent may call a reference to the subject-matter under discussion[1], is merely due to the circumstance of the object of meditation being the same (in the two vidyâs).

To this we make the following reply.—There is only one vidyâ of the True, because the clause, 'That which is the True,' &c., refers back to that True which is treated

[1] Viz. the clause in V, 5, 2, 'That which is the true,' which apparently—or really—connects the vidyâ of V, 5 with that of V, 4.

of in V, 4.—But has not the pûrvapakshin shown that the clause alluded to can be accounted for even on the supposition of there being two vidyâs?—The reasoning of the pûrvapakshin, we reply, would be admissible only if the separateness of the two vidyâs were established by some other clear and undoubted reason; in our case, however, there is a general possibility of both (viz. of the vidyâs being separate or not), and the very circumstance that the mentioned clause contains a back reference to the True spoken of in V, 4, determines us to conclude that there is only one vidyâ of the True.—To the remark that there must be two vidyâs because the text states two different results, we reply that the statement of a second result merely has the purpose of glorifying the new instruction given about the True, viz. that its secret names are ahar and aham. Moreover, as in the case under discussion, the fruit of the vidyâ has really to be supplied from its arthavâda part[1], and as there is unity of vidyâ, all those fruits which the text states in connexion with the single parts of the vidyâ are to be combined and put in connexion with the vidyâ taken as a whole.—The conclusion therefore is that the text records only one vidyâ of the True, distinguished by such and such details, and that hence all the qualities mentioned, such as Truth and so on, are to be comprehended in one act of meditation.

Some commentators are of opinion that the above Sûtra refers (not to the question whether B*ri*. Up. V, 4 and V, 5 constitute one vidyâ but) to the question whether the Vâ*g*asaneyaka-passage about the persons in the sun and in the eye, and the similar *Kh*ândogya-passage (I, 6, 6, 'Now that golden person who is seen within the sun,' &c.) form one vidyâ or not. They conclude that they do so, and that hence truth and the other qualities mentioned in

[1] For the vidyâ contains no explicit statement that a man desirous of such and such a fruit is to meditate on the True in such and such a way.—That in cases where the fruit is not stated in a vidhi-passage it must be supplied from the arthavâda-passages, is taught in the Pû. Mî. Sû. IV, 3, eighth adhikara*n*a.

the Vâgasaneyaka are to be combined with the *Kh*ândogya-text also.—But this interpretation of the Sûtra appears objectionable. For the *Kh*ândogya-vidyâ refers to the udgîtha and is thus connected with sacrificial acts, marks of which connexion are exhibited in the beginning, the middle, and the end of the vidyâ. Thus we read at the beginning, 'The *Rik* is the earth, the Sâman is fire;' in the middle, '*Rik* and Sâman are his joints and therefore he is udgîtha;' and in the end, 'He who knowing this sings a Sâman' (*Kh*. Up. I, 6, 1; 8; I, 7, 7). In the Vâgasaneyaka, on the other hand, there is nothing to connect the vidyâ with sacrificial acts. As therefore the subject-matter is different, the vidyâs are separate and the details of the two are to be held apart.

39. (Having true) wishes and other (qualities) (have to be combined) there and here, on account of the abode and so on.

In the chapter of the *Kh*ândogya which begins with the passage, 'There is this city of Brahman and in it the palace, the small lotus, and in it that small ether' (VIII, 1, 1), we read, 'That is the Self free from sin, free from old age, from death and grief, from hunger and thirst, whose desires are true, whose imaginations are true.' A similar passage is found in the text of the Vâgasaneyins, 'He is that great unborn Self who consists of knowledge, is surrounded by the Prâ*n*as, the ether within the heart. In it there reposes the ruler of all' (B*ri*. Up. IV, 4, 22).

A doubt here arises whether these two passages constitute one vidyâ, and whether the particulars stated in one text are to be comprehended within the other text also.

There is oneness of vidyâ[1].—Here (the Sûtrakâra) says, 'Wishes and so on,' i. e. 'The quality of having true wishes and so on' (the word kâma standing for satyakâma, just

[1] This clause must apparently be taken as stating the siddhânta-view, although later on it is said that the two vidyâs are distinct (that, however, in spite of their distinctness, their details have to be combined).

as people occasionally say Datta for Devadatta and Bhâmâ for Satyabhâmâ). This quality and the other qualities, which the *Kh*ândogya attributes to the ether within the heart, have to be combined with the Vâ*g*asaneyaka-passage, and vice versâ the qualities stated in the Vâ*g*asaneyaka, such as being the ruler of all, have also to be ascribed to the Self free from sin, proclaimed in the *Kh*ândogya. The reason for this is that the two passages display a number of common features. Common to both is the heart viewed as abode, common again is the Lord as object of knowledge, common also is the Lord being viewed as a bank preventing these worlds from being confounded; and several other points.—But, an objection is raised, there are also differences. In the *Kh*ândogya the qualities are attributed to the ether within the heart, while in the Vâ*g*asaneyaka they are ascribed to Brahman abiding in that ether.—This objection, we reply, is unfounded, for we have shown under I, 3, 14 that the term 'ether' in the *Kh*ândogya designates Brahman.

There is, however, the following difference between the two passages. The *Kh*ândogya-vidyâ has for its object the qualified Brahman, as we see from the passage VIII, 1, 6, 'But those who depart from hence after having discovered the Self and those true desires,' in which certain desires are represented as objects of knowledge equally as the Self. In the Vâ*g*asaneyaka, on the other hand, the highest Brahman devoid of all qualities forms the object of instruction, as we conclude from the consideration of the request made by *G*anaka, 'Speak on for the sake of emancipation,' and the reply given by Yâ*gñ*avalkya, 'For that person is not attached to anything' (B*ri*. Up. IV, 3, 14; 15). That the text ascribes to the Self such qualities as being the Lord of all and the like is (not for the purpose of teaching that the Self really possesses those qualities, but is) merely meant to glorify the Self. Later on also (IV, 5, 15) the chapter winds up with a passage clearly referring to the Self devoid of all qualities, 'That Self is to be described by No, no!' But as the qualified Brahman is (fundamentally) one (with the unqualified Brahman), we must conclude that the Sûtra teaches the combination of the qualities to the end of setting forth the glory of Brahman, not for the purpose of devout meditation.

40. On account of (the passage showing) respect, there is non-omission (of the prâ*n*âgnihotra) (even when the eating of food is omitted).

We read in the *Kh*ândogya under the heading of the Vais*v*ânara-vidyâ, 'Therefore the first food which comes is in the place of Homa. And he who offers that first oblation should offer it to Prâ*n*a, saying Svâhâ' (*Kh.* Up. V, 19, 1). The text thereupon enjoins five oblations, and later on applies to them the term 'Agnihotra;' 'He who thus knowing this offers the agnihotra,' and 'As hungry children here on earth sit round their mother, so do all beings sit round the agnihotra' (V, 24, 2; 4).

Here the doubt arises whether the agnihotra offered to the prâ*n*as is to be omitted when the eating itself is omitted or not.—As, according to the clause, 'The first food which comes,' &c., the oblation is connected with the coming of food, and as the coming of food subserves the eating, the agnihotra offered to the prâ*n*as is omitted when the eating is omitted.—Against this conclusion the Sûtra (embodying the pûrvapaksha) declares, 'It is not omitted.'—Why?—'On account of the respect.' This means: In their version of the Vais*v*ânara-vidyâ the *G*âbâlas read as follows: 'He (i.e. the host) is to eat before his guests; for (if he would make them eat first) it would be as if he without having himself offered the agnihotra offered that of another person.' This passage, which objects to the priority of the eating on the part of the guests and establishes priority on the part of the host, thereby intimates respect for the agnihotra offered to the prâ*n*as. For as it does not allow the omission of priority it will allow all the less the omission of that which is characterised by priority, viz. the agnihotra offered to the prâ*n*as.—But (as mentioned above) the connexion—established by the *Kh*ândogya-passage—of the oblation with the coming of food—which subserves the eating—establishes the omission of the oblation in the case of the eating being omitted!—Not so, the pûrvapakshin replies. The purpose of that passage is to enjoin some particular material (to be offered). For the fundamental agnihotra certain materials, such as milk and so on, are exclusively prescribed. Now, as through the term 'agnihotra' (which the text applies to the offering to the prâ*n*as) all the particulars belonging to the fundamental agnihotra are already established for the secondary agnihotra also (viz. the oblation made to the prâ*n*as), just as in the case of the ayana of the Ku*nd*apâyins[1]; the clause, 'the first food which comes,' &c., is meant to enjoin, for the prâ*n*âgnihotra, some particular secondary matter, viz. the circumstance of food constituting the material of the oblation[2]. Hence, considering the Mîmâ*m*sâ principle that the omission of a secondary matter does not involve the omission of the principal matter, we conclude that even in the case of the omission of eating, the agnihotra offered to the prâ*n*as has to be performed by means of water or some other not altogether unsuitable material, according to the Mîmâ*m*sâ principle that in the absence of the prescribed material some other suitable material may be substituted.

To this pûrvapaksha the next Sûtra replies.

41. When (eating) is taking place, (the prâ*n*âgnihotra has to be performed) from that (i.e. the food first eaten); on the ground of the passage declaring this.

When eating is actually taking place, 'from that,' i.e. with that material of food which first presents itself, the agnihotra offered to the prâ*n*as is to be effected.—On what

[1] For one of the great sacrifices lasting a whole year—called the ayana of the Ku*nd*apâyins—the texts enjoin the offering of the 'agnihotra' during a full month (cp. e.g. Tâ*nd*ya Mahâbrâhma*n*a XXV, 4). Now from the term 'agnihotra' we conclude that all the details of the ordinary agnihotra are valid for the agnihotra of the ayana also.

[2] Whereby the materials offered in the ordinary agnihotra are superseded.

ground?—'On the ground of the passage declaring this.' For the clause, 'The first food which a man may take is in the place of a homa,' enjoins the circumstance of the oblations to the prâ*n*as being effected by means of a material (primarily) subserving another purpose (viz. eating), as appears from its referring to the presentation of food as something accomplished (i. e. accomplished independently of the oblations; not tending to accomplish the oblations). How then should these oblations—which are characterised as not having any motive power with regard to the employment of the food—be capable of causing us to substitute, in the absence of eating, some other material (than food)?—Nor is it true that there are already established, for the prâ*n*âgnihotra, all the details belonging to the fundamental agnihotra. In the case of the ayana of the Ku*nd*apâyins, the term 'agnihotra' forms part of the injunctive passage, 'They offer the agnihotra during a month,' and therefore may have the force of enjoining a general character of the sacrifice identical with that of the fundamental agnihotra; and it is therefore appropriate to consider the details of the latter as valid for the agnihotra of the Ku*nd*apâyins also. In the case of the so-called prâ*n*âgnihotra, on the other hand, the term 'agnihotra' occurs in an arthavâda-passage only, and does not therefore possess an analogous injunctive force. If, again, we admitted that the details of the fundamental agnihotra are valid for the prâ*n*âgnihotra also, such details as the transference of the fire (from the gârhapatya fire to the two other fires) would be likewise valid. But this is impossible, as the transference of the fire is made for the purpose of establishing a fire-place in which the oblations are made; in our case, on the other hand, the oblations are not made in the fire at all—because that would interfere with their being used as food, and because they are connected with a material procured for the purpose of eating,—but are made in the mouth (of the eater). Thus the text of the *G*âbâlas also, 'He is to eat before the guests,' shows that the accomplishment of the oblation has the mouth for its abode. For the same reason (i. e. because the details of the fundamental agnihotra are not valid for the prâ*n*âgnihotra) the text declares the subordinate members of the agnihotra to be present here (i.e. in the prâ*n*âgnihotra) in the way of fanciful combination only, 'the chest is the vedi, the hairs the sacrificial grass, the heart the Garhapatya fire, the mind the Anvâhâryapa*k*ana fire, the mouth the Âhavanîya fire.' By the vedi mentioned in this passage we have to understand a levelled spot, as in the fundamental agnihotra there is no vedi, and as the intention of the passage is to effect a fanciful combination of the members of the fundamental agnihotra (with members of the prâ*n*âgnihotra).—And as the prâ*n*âgnihotra is connected with eating which has its definite times, it is also not possible that it should be restricted to the time enjoined for the fundamental agnihotra. In the same way other particulars also of the fundamental agnihotra, such as the so-called upasthâna, cannot be reconciled with the requirements of the prâ*n*âgnihotra. From all this it follows that the five oblations, as connected with their respective mantras, materials, and divinities, have to be performed only in the case of food being eaten.—With reference to the passage showing 'respect,' we remark that it is meant to intimate priority (of the host), in the case of food being actually eaten. But the passage has no power to declare that the offering of the prâ*n*âgnihotra is of permanent obligation.—It therefore is a settled conclusion that the prâ*n*âgnihotra is omitted when the eating of food is omitted.

42. There is non-restriction of the assertions concerning them (i.e. the assertions made concerning certain sacrificial acts are not permanently connected with those acts), because this is seen (in scripture); for a separate fruit, viz. non-obstruction (of the success of the sacrifice), (belongs to them).

We meet in the Vedânta-texts with certain vidyâs which are founded on matters subordinate to sacrificial acts. To this class belongs, e.g. the first vidyâ of the *Kh*ândogya Upanishad, 'Let a man meditate on the syllable Om as udgîtha.'—We now enter on an inquiry whether those vidyâs are permanently connected with the acts in the same way as the circumstance of being made of par*n*a-wood is permanently connected with all sacrifices in which the *g*uhû (the sacrificial ladle) is used; or if they are non-permanent like the vessel called godohana[1]. The pûrvapakshin maintains that the meditations are permanently connected with the sacrificial acts, because they also are comprised within the scriptural enouncements concerning performances. For they also do not stand under some special heading[2], and as they are connected with the sacrifice through the udgîtha and so on, they combine themselves, like other subordinate members, with the scriptural statements as to the performance of the sacrifice.

If against the doctrine of the meditations forming permanent parts of the sacrificial performances it should be urged, that in the chapters containing them special results are mentioned (which seem to constitute the meditations into independent acts), as e.g. in the passage, 'he indeed becomes a fulfiller of desires' (*Kh*. Up. I, 1, 7); we reply that those statements of results being given in the text in the present form only (not in an injunctional form), are mere

---

[1] The question is raised whether the meditations, enjoined in the Upanishads, on certain parts or elements of sacrificial acts, are permanently connected with the latter, i.e. are to be undertaken whenever the sacrificial act is performed, or not.—In the former case they would stand to the sacrifice in the same relation as the par*n*amayîtva, i.e. the quality of being made of par*n*a-wood, does. Just as the latter is connected with the sacrifice by means of the *g*uhû—the sacrificial ladle,—so the meditation on the syllable Om, e.g. would be connected with the sacrifice by means of that syllable.—In the latter case, i.e. in the case of being connected with the sacrifice on certain occasions only, the upâsana is analogous to the godohana-vessel which is used in the dar*s*apûr*n*amâsa-sacrifice instead of the usual *k*amasa, only if the sacrificer specially wishes for cattle.—See Pû. Mî. Sû. III, 6, 1; IV, 1, 2.

[2] Like the statement about the par*n*amayîtva of the *g*uhû which the sacred text does not exhibit under some particular prakara*n*a, but ex abrupto as it were; on which account it is to be connected with the sacrifice in general.

arthavâda-passages—like the statement about him whose *g*uhû is made of par*n*a-wood hearing no evil sound—and thus do not aim at enjoining certain results.—Hence, just as the statement about being made of par*n*a-wood—which does not occur under a definite prakara*n*a—connects itself, by means of the sacrificial ladle, with the sacrifice, and thus forms a permanent element of the latter no less than if it were actually made under the heading of the sacrifice; so the meditations on the udgîtha, &c., also form permanent parts of the sacrifices.

To this we make the following reply. 'There is non-restriction of the assertions concerning them.' That means: the assertions which the text makes concerning the nature of certain subordinate members of sacrificial acts such as the udgîtha and so on—as e.g. that the udgîtha is the best of all essences (*Kh.* Up. I, 1, 3), the fulfiller of desires (I, 1, 7), a gratifier of desires (I, 1, 8), the chief prâ*n*a (I, 2, 7), Âditya (I, 3, 1)—cannot be permanently connected with the sacrificial acts in the same way as other permanent members are, 'because that is seen,' i.e. because scripture shows that they are not so permanently connected. For scripture allows also such as are not acquainted with the details mentioned above to perform the sacrificial actions (cp. the passage I, 1, 10, 'Therefore both he who knows this, and he who does not, perform the sacrifice'), and declares that even those priests, Prastot*ri* and so on, who are devoid of the knowledge of the divinities of the prastâva and the like, do perform the sacrifices Prastot*ri*, if you without knowing the deity which belongs to the prastâva are going to sing it,' &c. (I, 10, 9 and ff.).—The sacred text moreover declares that the vidyâs founded on certain elements of sacrificial acts have results of their own, apart from those acts, viz. 'non-obstruction' in the accomplishment of the fruit of the sacrifice, i.e. a certain additional success of the sacrifice, cp. the passage I, 1, 10, 'Therefore he who knows this and he who does not perform the sacrifice. But knowledge and ignorance are separate. The sacrifice which a man performs with knowledge, faith, and the Upanishad is more powerful.' The declaration made in this passage that the performances of him who knows and of him who does not know are separate, and the employment of the comparative form ('more powerful') show that even the sacrifice destitute of the vidyâ is powerful. But how would that be possible if the vidyâ formed a permanent necessary part of the sacrifice? In the latter case a sacrifice devoid of that vidyâ could never be admitted to be powerful; for it is an established principle that only those sacrifices are effective which comprise all subordinate members. Thus the text also teaches definite results for each meditation, in the section treating of the meditation on the Sâman as the worlds and others: 'The worlds in an ascending and in a descending line belong to him,' &c. (*Kh*. Up. II, 2, 3).—Nor must we understand those declarations of results to be mere arthavâdas; for in that case they would have to be taken as stating a secondary matter only, while if understood to teach certain results they may be taken in their principal (i. e. direct, literal) sense[1]. The case of the results which scripture declares to be connected with the prayâ*g*as e. g. is of a different nature. For the prayâ*g*as are enjoined with reference to a sacrifice (viz. the dar*s*apûr*n*amâsa) which requires certain definite modes of procedure (such as the offering of the prayâ*g*as and the like), and hence subserve that sacrifice; so that the passage stating a fruit for the prayâ*g*as has to be considered as a mere arthavâda-passage[2]. In the case again of the quality of consisting of par*n*a-wood—which quality is stated ex abrupto, not under a definite heading—no special result can be assumed; for as a quality is not an act it cannot be connected with any result unless it be joined to something to abide in. The use of the godohana indeed may have its own injunction of

[1] The statement as to the result of an action is a 'statement of a principal matter' if it is really meant to inform us that a certain result will attend a certain action. It is a statement of a 'secondary matter' if it is only meant to glorify the action.

[2] Not as a passage enjoining a special result for the prayâ*g*as; for the latter merely help to bring about the general result of the dar*s*apûr*n*amâsa and have no special result of their own.

result, for it does possess such an abode—viz. the act of water being carried (in it)—with reference to which it is enjoined. So again a special fruit may be enjoined for the case of the sacrificial post being made of bilva-wood; for this latter quality likewise has an abode, viz. the sacrificial post with reference to which it is enjoined. But in the case of the quality of consisting of par*n*a-wood there is no such established abode under the heading of which that quality is enjoined; and if we assumed that the sentence ('He whose *g*uhû is made of par*n*a-wood hears no evil sound') after intimating that the quality of consisting of par*n*a-wood resides in the *g*uhû is also meant to enjoin the fruit thereof, we should impute to the text the imperfection called 'split of the sentence.'—The meditations on the other hand are themselves acts, and as such capable of a special injunction; hence there is no reason why a special result should not be enjoined for those meditations which are based on sacrificial acts. The conclusion therefore is that the meditations on the udgîtha, &c., although based on sacrifices, are yet not necessary members of the latter, because they have results of their own like the use of the godohana-vessel. For this reason the authors of the Kalpa-sûtras have not represented such meditations as belonging to the sacrificial performances.

43. As in the case of the offerings, (Vâyu and Prâ*n*a must be held apart). This has been explained (in the Pûrva Mîmâ*m*sâ-sûtra).

The section of the Vâ*g*asaneyaka which begins, 'Voice held, I shall speak' (B*ri*. Up. I, 5, 21), determines Prâ*n*a to be the best among the organs of the body, viz. speech and so on, and Vâyu to be the best among the Devas, viz. Agni and so on.—Similarly in the *Kh*ândogya, Vâyu is affirmed to be the general absorber of the Devas, 'Vâyu indeed is the absorber' (IV, 3, 1), while Prâ*n*a is said to be the general absorber of the organs of the body, 'Breath indeed is the absorber' (IV, 3, 3).—The doubt here arises whether Vâyu and Prâ*n*a are to be conceived as separate or not.

As non-separate, the pûrvapakshin maintains; because in

their true nature they do not differ. And as their true nature does not differ they must not be meditated upon separately. Another scriptural passage also declares that the organs of the body and the divinities are non-different in their true nature, 'Agni having become speech entered the mouth,' &c. (Ait. Âr. II, 4, 2, 4). Moreover, the passage B*ri*. Up. I, 5, 13, 'These are all alike, all endless,' declares that the powers of the Devas constitute the Self of the organs of the body. And various other passages also testify to the fundamental non-difference of the two. In some places we have even a direct identification of the two, 'What Prâ*n*a is, that is Vâyu.' And in the *s*loka concluding the Vâ*g*asaneyaka-chapter to which the passage under discussion belongs, the text refers to prâ*n*a only ('He verily rises from the breath and sets in the breath'), and thus shows the breath to be one with the previously mentioned Vâyu. This conclusion is moreover confirmed by the fact that the observance enjoined in the end refers to prâ*n*a only, 'Therefore let a man perform one observance only, let him breathe up and let him breathe down' (B*ri*. Up. I, 5, 23). Similarly, the *Kh*ândogya-passage, IV, 3, 6, 'One god swallowed the four great ones,' intimates that there is one absorber only, and does not say that one god is the absorber of the one set of four, and another the absorber of the other set of four.—From all this it follows that Vâyu and Prâ*n*a are to be conceived as one.

To this we make the following reply. Vâyu and Prâ*n*a are to be conceived separately, because the text teaches them in separation. The separate instruction given by the text with reference to the organs and the Devas for the purposes of meditation would be meaningless if the meditations were not held apart.—But the pûrvapakshin maintains that owing to the essential non-difference of Vâyu and Prâ*n*a the meditations are not to be separated!—Although, we reply, there may be non-difference of true nature, yet there may be difference of condition giving rise to difference of instruction, and, through the latter, to difference of meditation. And although the introduction of the concluding *s*loka may be accounted for on the ground of its showing the fundamental non-difference of the two, it yet has no power to sublate the previously declared difference of the objects of meditation. Moreover, the text institutes a comparison between Vâyu and Prâ*n*a, which again shows that the two are different, 'And as it was with the central breath among the breaths, so it was with Vâyu, the wind among those deities' (B*ri*. Up. I, 5, 22).—This explains also the mention made of the observance (I, 5, 23). The word 'only' (in 'Let a man perform one observance only') has the purpose of establishing the observance with regard to Prâ*n*a, by sublating the observances with regard to speech and so on, regarding which the text had remarked previously that they were disturbed by Death ('Death having become weariness took them'), and does not by any means aim at sublating the observance with regard to Vâyu; for the section beginning 'Next follows the consideration of the observances' distinctly asserts that the observances of Vâyu and Prâ*n*a were equally unbroken.—Moreover, the text, after having said, 'Let a man perform one observance only,' declares in the end that the fruit of that observance is the obtaining of (union with) Vâyu ('Then he obtains through it union and oneness with that deity'), and thus shows that the observance with regard to Vâyu is not to be considered as sublated. That by that 'deity' we have to understand Vâyu, we conclude from the circumstance that what the worshipper wishes to obtain is non-limitation of his Self[1], and that previously the term 'deity' had been applied to Vâyu, 'Vâyu is the deity that never sets.'—Analogously in the *Kh*ândogya-passage the text represents Vâyu and Prâ*n*a as different, 'These are the two absorbers, Vâyu among the Devas, Prâ*n*a among the prâ*n*as,' and in the concluding paragraph also (IV, 3, 8) refers to them as distinct, 'These five and the other five make ten, and that is the K*ri*ta.'—For these reasons Vâyu and Prâ*n*a are to be conceived as different.

The Sûtra compares the case under discussion to a

[1] Agnyâdîn apekshyânava*kkh*ino devo vâyus te tu tenaivâva*kkh*innâ iti sa*m*vargagu*n*o vâyur anava*kkh*innâ devatâ. Ân. Gi.

parallel one from the karmakâ*nd*a, by means of the clause, 'as in the case of the offerings.' With regard to the ish*t*i comprising three sacrificial cakes, which is enjoined in the passage, Taitt. Sa*m*h. II, 3, 6, 'A puro*d*â*s*a on eleven potsherds to Indra the ruler, to Indra the over-ruler, to Indra the self-ruler,' it might be supposed that the three cakes are to be offered together because they are offered to one and the same Indra, and because the concluding sentence says, 'conveying to all (gods) he cuts off to preclude purposelessness.' But as the attributes (viz. 'ruler' and so on) differ, and as scripture enjoins that the yâ*g*yâ and anuvâkyâmantras are to exchange places with regard to the different cakes[1], the divinity is each time a different one according to the address, and from this it follows that the three offerings also are separate.—Thus, in the case under discussion, Vâyu and Prâ*n*a, although fundamentally non-different, are to be held apart as objects of meditation, and we have therefore to do with two separate meditations.—This is explained in the Saṅkarsha-kâ*nd*a, 'The divinities are separate on account of their being cognized thus.'

But while in the case of the three puro*d*â*s*as the difference of material and divinity involves a difference on the part of the oblations, we have in the case under discussion to do with one vidyâ only; for that the text enjoins one vidyâ only we conclude from the introductory and concluding statements. There is contained, however, in this one vidyâ a double meditative activity with regard to the bodily organs and the divinities, just as the agnihotra which is offered in the morning as well as in the evening requires a double activity. In this sense the Sûtra says, 'as in the case of the offerings.'

44. On account of the majority of indicatory marks (the fire-altars built of mind, &c. do not form elements of any act); for this (i.e. the indicatory

[1] The yâ*g*yâ-mantra of the first offering being used as anuvâkyâ in the second one and so on.

mark) is stronger (than the general subject-matter); this also (has been explained in the Pû. Mî. Sûtras).

In the Agnirahasya of the Vâ*g*asaneyins, in the Brâhma*n*a beginning 'for in the beginning indeed this was not existent,' we read with reference to mind (manas), 'It saw thirty-six thousand shining fire-altars, belonging to itself, made of mind, built of mind.' And, further on, the text makes similar statements about other fanciful fire-altars built of speech, built of breath, built of sight, built of hearing, built of work, built of fire.—A doubt here arises whether these fire-altars built of mind and so on are connected with the act (i. e. the construction of the fire-altar made of bricks), and supplementary to it, or whether they are independent, constituting a mere vidyâ.

Against the primâ facie view that those agnis are connected with the sacrificial act under whose heading the text records them, the Sûtra maintains their independence, 'on account of the majority of indicatory marks.' For we meet in that Brâhma*n*a with a number of indicatory marks confirming that those agnis constitute a mere vidyâ; cp. e. g. the following passages: 'Whatever these beings conceive in their minds, that is a means for those fire-altars,' and 'All beings always pile up those fire-altars for him who thus knows, even when he sleeps,' and so on[1].—And that indicatory marks (liṅga) are of greater force than the leading subject-matter (prakara*n*a) has been explained in the Pûrva Mîmâ*m*sâ (III, 3, 14).

45. (The agni built of mind, &c.) is a particular form of the preceding one (i.e. the agni built of bricks), on account of the leading subject-matter; it is (part of) the act; as in the case of the mânasa cup.

Your supposition, the pûrvapakshin objects, as to those fire-altars being not supplementary to the sacrificial act,

[1] For something which forms part of an act cannot be brought about by something so indefinite as 'whatever these beings conceive in their minds,' nor can it be accomplished indifferently at any time by any beings.

but altogether independent of it, is untenable. The influence of the leading subject-matter rather compels us to conclude that the instruction given by the text about the agni made of mind and so on, enjoins some particular mode of the same agni which the preceding sections describe as the outcome of a real act[1].—But are not indicatory marks stronger than the leading subject-matter?—True in general; but indicatory marks such as those contained in the passages quoted above are by no means stronger than the general subject-matter. For as those passages are of the nature of glorifications of the fanciful fire-altars, the liṅgas (have no proving power in themselves but) merely illustrate some other matter (viz. the injunction to which those passages are arthavâdas); and as they are of that nature they may, there being no other proof, be taken as mere gu*n*avâdas, and as such are not able to sublate the influence of the prakara*n*a. On the ground of the latter, therefore, all those fanciful agnis must be viewed as forming parts of the sacrificial action.

The case is analogous to that of the 'mental' (cup). On the tenth day of the Soma sacrifices occupying twelve days —which day is termed avivâkya—a soma cup is offered mentally, the earth being viewed as the cup, the sea as the Soma and Pra*g*âpati as the divinity to which the offering is made. All rites connected with that cup, viz. taking it up, putting it down in its place, offering the liquid in it, taking up the remaining liquid, the priests inviting one another to drink the remainder, and the drinking, all these rites the text declares to be mental only, i.e. to be done in thought only[2]. Yet this mental quasi-cup, as standing under the heading of a sacrificial act, forms part of that act.—The same then holds good with regard to the quasi-agnis made of mind and so on.

46. And on account of the transfer (of particulars).

That those agnis enter into the sacrificial action follows

[1] I.e. of the agni made of bricks which is the outcome of the agni*k*ayana.—Ân. Gi. explains vikalpavi*s*esha by prakârabheda.

[2] Cp. Tâ*n*dya Brâh. IV, 9; Taitt. Sa*m*h. VII, 3, 1.

moreover from the fact that the text extends to them (the injunctions given about the agni made of bricks). Compare the passage, 'Thirty-six thousand shining Agnis; each one of them is as large as the previously mentioned Agni.' Such extension of injunctions is possible only where there is general equality. The text therefore by extending the determinations relative to the previous agni, i.e. the agni built of bricks, which forms a constituent element of the sacrificial action, to the fanciful agnis, intimates thereby that they also form part of the sacrificial performance.

47. But (the agnis rather constitute) a vidyâ, on account of the assertion (made by the text).

The word 'but' sets aside the pûrvapaksha.—The agnis built of mind and so on are to be viewed not as complementary to a sacrificial action, but as independent and constituting a vidyâ of their own. For the text expressly asserts that 'they are built of knowledge (vidyâ) only,' and that 'by knowledge they are built for him who thus knows.'

48. And because (indicatory marks of that) are seen (in the text).

And that there are to be observed indicatory marks leading to the same conclusion, has already been declared in Sûtra 44.—But, under Sûtra 45, it was shown that indicatory marks unaided by other reasons cannot be admitted as proving anything, and it was consequently determined that, owing to the influence of the leading subject-matter, the Agnis form part of the sacrificial action!—To this objection the next Sûtra replies.

49. (The view that the agnis constitute an independent vidyâ) cannot be refuted, owing to the greater force of direct enunciation and so on.

Our opponent has no right to determine, on the ground of prakara*n*a, that the agnis are subordinate to the sacrificial action, and so to set aside our view according to which they are independent. For we know from the Pûrvâ Mîmâ*m*sâ that direct enunciation (*S*ruti), indicatory mark (liṅga), and syntactical connexion (vâkya) are of greater force than leading subject-matter (prakara*n*a), and all those three means of proof are seen to confirm our view of the agnis being independent. In the first place we have the direct enunciation, 'These agnis are indeed knowledge-piled only.' In the second place we have the indicatory mark supplied by the passage, 'All beings ever pile for him sleeping,' &c. And in the third place we have the sentence, 'By knowledge indeed those (agnis) are piled for him who thus knows.'

In the first of these passages the emphatical expression, 'built by knowledge only,' would be contradicted if we admitted that the agnis form part of the sacrificial action.—But may this emphatical phrase not merely have the purpose of indicating that those agnis are not to be accomplished by external means?—No, we reply, for if that were intended, it would be sufficient to glorify the fact of knowledge constituting the character of the agnis by means of the word 'knowledge-piled,' and the emphatical assertion (implied in the addition of the word 'only') would be useless. For it is the nature of such agnis to be accomplished without any external means. But, although the agnis are clearly to be accomplished without external means, yet it might be supposed that, like the mental cup, they form part of the sacrificial action, and the object of the emphatical assertion implied in 'only' is to discard that suspicion.—So likewise (to pass over to liṅga) the continuity of action implied in the passage, 'For him who thus knows whether sleeping or waking all beings always pile these agnis,' is possible only on the supposition of those agnis being independent. The case is analogous to that of the imaginary agnihotra consisting of speech and breath, with reference to which the text says at first, 'He offers his breath in his speech, he offers his speech in his breath,' and then adds, 'These two endless and immortal oblations he offers always whether waking or sleeping' (Kau. Up. II, 6).—If, on the other hand, the imaginary agnis were parts of the sacrificial action it would be impossible for them to be accomplished continually, since the accomplishment of the sacrificial action itself occupies only a short time.—Nor may we suppose the passage (which contains the liṅga) to be a mere arthavâda-passage (in which case, as the pûrvapakshin avers, the liṅga would be unable to refute prakaraṇa). For in those cases where we meet with an unmistakeable injunctory passage—marked out as such by the use of the optative or imperative form—there indeed we may assume a glorificatory passage (met with in connexion with that injunctory passage) to be an arthavâda. In the present case, however, we observe no clear injunctory passage, and should therefore be obliged to construct one enjoining the knowledge of the various fanciful agnis, merely on the basis of the arthavâda-passage. But in that case the injunction can be framed only in accordance with the arthavâda, and as the arthavâda speaks of the continual building of the agnis, the latter item would have to appear in the injunction also. But, if so, it follows (as shown above) that the mental construction of those agnis constitutes an independent vidyâ (and does not form part of the actual agni*k*ayana).—The same argumentation applies to the second liṅga-passage quoted above, 'Whatever those beings conceive in their minds,' &c.—And the sentence finally shows, by means of the clause, 'For him who thus knows,' that those agnis are connected with a special class of men (viz. those who thus know), and are therefore not to be connected with the sacrificial action.—For all these reasons the view of those agnis constituting an independent vidyâ is preferable.

50. On account of the connexion and so on (the agnis built of mind, &c. are independent); in the same way as other cognitions are separate. And there is seen (another case of something having to be withdrawn from the leading subject-matter); this has been explained (in the Pûrva Mîmâ*m*sâ-sûtras).

Independence has, against the general subject-matter, to be assumed for the fire-altars built of mind and so on, for that reason also that the text connects the constituent members of the sacrificial action with activities of the mind, &c.; viz. in the passage, 'With mind only they are established, with mind only they are piled, with mind only the cups were taken, with mind the udgâtr*i*s praised, with mind the hotr*i*s recited; whatever work is done at the sacrifice, whatever sacrificial work, was done as consisting of mind, by mind only, at those fire-altars made of mind, piled by mind,' &c. For that connexion has for its result an imaginative combination (of certain mental energies with the parts of the sacrifice), and the obtainment of the parts of the sacrifice which are objects of actual perception cannot be made dependent on such imaginative combination[1]. Nor must it be supposed that, because here also, as in the case of the meditation on the udgîtha, the vidyâ is connected with members of the sacrificial action, it enters into that action as a constituent part; for the statements of the text differ in the two cases. For in our case scripture does not say that we are to take some member of a sacrificial action and then to superimpose upon it such and such a name; but rather takes six and thirty thousand different energies of the mind and identifies them with the fire-altars, the cups, and so on, just as in some other place it teaches a meditation on man viewed as the sacrifice. The number given by the text is originally observed as belonging to the days of a man's life, and is then transferred to the mental energies connected therewith.—From the connexion (referred to in the Sûtra) it therefore follows that the agnis piled of mind, &c. are independent.—The clause 'and so on' (met with in the Sûtra) must be explained as comprehending 'transference' and the like as far as possible. For if the text says, 'Each of those Agnis is as great as that prior one,' it transfers the glory of the fire-altar consisting of the work (i.e. the real altar piled of bricks) to the altars consisting of knowledge and so on, and thereby

[1] Kimartham idam anubandhakara*n*a*m* tad âha, sampad iti, upâstyartho hy anubandhas tathâpi mana*sk*idâdînâm akriyâṅgatve kim âyâta*m* tad âha, na *k*eti, teshâ*m* kriyâṅgatve sâkshâd evâdhânâdiprasiddher anarthikâ sampad ity artha*h*. Ân. Gi.

expresses want of regard for the work. Nor can it be said that if there is connexion (of all the agnis) with the sacrificial action, the later ones (i.e. those made of mind) may optionally be used instead of the original agnis made of bricks (as was asserted by the pûrvapakshin in Sûtra 45). For the later agnis are incapable of assisting the sacrificial action by means of those energies with which the original agni assists it, viz. by bearing the âhavanîya fire and so on.—The assertion, again, made by the pûrvapakshin (Sûtra 46) that 'transference' strengthens his view in so far as transference is possible only where there is equality, is already refuted by the remark that also on our view transference is possible, since the fanciful fire-altars are equal to the real fire-altar in so far as both are fire-altars.—And that direct enunciation and so on favour our conclusion has been shown.—From connexion and so on it therefore follows that the agnis piled of mind, &c. are independent.—'As in the case of the separateness of other cognitions.' As other cognitions, such as e.g. the *S*â*nd*ilya-vidyâ, which have each their own particular connexion, separate themselves from works and other cognitions and are independent; so it is in our case also.—Moreover 'there is seen' an analogous case of independence from the leading subject-matter. The offering called avesh*t*i which is mentioned in the sacred texts under the heading of the râ*g*asûya-sacrifice, is to be taken out from that heading because it is connected with the three higher castes, while the râ*g*asûya can be offered by a member of the warrior caste only. This has been explained in the first section (i.e. in the Pûrva Mîmâ*m*sâ-sûtras).

51. Not also on account of its resembling (the mânasa cup) (can the fires constitute parts of an action); for it is observed (on the ground of *S*ruti, &c., that they are independent); as in the case of death; for the world does not become (a fire) (because it resembles a fire in some points).

Against the allegation made by the pûrvapakshin that the present case is analogous to that of the mânasa cup, we remark that the fire-altars made of mind and so on cannot be assumed to supplement a sacrificial action although they may resemble the mânasa cup, since on the ground of direct enunciation &c. they are seen to subserve the purpose of man only (not the purpose of some sacrificial action). Anything indeed may resemble anything in some point or other; but in spite of that there remains the individual dissimilarity of each thing from all other things. The case is analogous to that of death. In the passages, 'The man in that orb is death indeed' (*S*at. Brâ. X, 5, 2, 3), and 'Agni indeed is death' (Taitt. Sa*m*h. V, 1, 10, 3), the term 'death' is applied equally to Agni and the man in the sun; all the same the two are by no means absolutely equal. And if the text says in another place, 'This world is a fire indeed, O Gotama; the sun is its fuel,' &c. (*Kh.* Up. V, 4, 1), it does not follow from the similarity of fuel and so on that the world really is a fire. Thus also in our case.

52. And from the subsequent (Brâhma*n*a) it follows that being of that kind (i.e. injunction of a mere vidyâ) (is the aim) of the text. The connexion (of the fanciful agnis with the real one) is due to the plurality (of details of the real agni which are imaginatively connected with the vidyâ).

With regard to a subsequent Brâhma*n*a also, viz. the one beginning, 'That piled agni is this world indeed,' we apprehend that what is the purpose of the text is 'being of that kind,' i.e. injunction of a mere vidyâ, not injunction of the member of a mere action. For we meet there with the following *s*loka, 'By knowledge they ascend there where all wishes are attained. Those skilled in works do not go there, nor those who destitute of knowledge do penance.' This verse blames mere works and praises knowledge. A former Brâhma*n*a also, viz. the one beginning, 'What that orb leads' (*S*at. Brâ. X, 5, 2, 23), concludes with a statement of the fruit of knowledge ('Immortal becomes he whose Self is death'), and thereby indicates that works are not the chief thing.—The text connects the vidyâ (of the agnis built of mind) with the real agni built of bricks, not because those agnis are members of the act of building the real agni, but because many of the elements of the real agni are imaginatively combined with the vidyâ.

All this establishes the conclusion that the fire-altars built of mind and so on constitute a mere vidyâ.

53. Some (maintain the non-existence) of a (separate) Self, on account of the existence (of the Self) where a body is (only).

At present we will prove the existence of a Self different from the body in order to establish thereby the qualification (of the Self) for bondage and release. For if there were no Self different from the body, there would be no room for injunctions that have the other world for their result; nor could it be taught of anybody that Brahman is his Self.—But, an objection is raised, already in the first pâda which stands at the head of this *S*âstra (i. e. the first pâda of the Pûrva Mîmâ*m*sâ-sûtras) there has been declared the existence of a Self which is different from the body and hence capable of enjoying the fruits taught by the *S*âstra.—True, this has been declared there by the author of the bhâshya, but there is in that place no Sûtra about the existence of the Self. Here, on the other hand, the Sûtrakâra himself establishes the existence of the Self after having disposed of a preliminary objection. And from hence the teacher *S*abara Svâmin has taken the matter for his discussion of the point in the chapter treating of the means of right knowledge. For the same reason the reverend Upavarsha remarks in the first tantra—where an opportunity offers itself for the discussion of the existence of the Self—'We will discuss this in the *S*ârîraka,' and allows the matter to rest there. Here, where we are engaged in an inquiry into the pious meditations which are matter of injunction, a discussion of the existence of the Self is introduced in order to show that the whole *S*âstra depends thereon.

Moreover, in the preceding adhikara*n*a we have shown that passages may be exempted from the influence of the leading subject-matter, and that for that reason the fire-altars built of mind and so on subserve the purpose of man (not of the sacrifice). In consequence thereof there naturally arises the question who that man is whose purposes the different fire-altars subserve, and in reply to it the existence of a Self which is separate from the body is affirmed.—The first Sûtra embodies an objection against that doctrine; according to the principle that a final refutation of objections stated in the beginning effects a stronger conviction of the truth of the doctrine whose establishment is aimed at.

Here now some materialists (lokâyatika), who see the Self in the body only, are of opinion that a Self separate from the body does not exist; assume that consciousness (*k*aitanya), although not observed in earth and the other external elements—either single or combined—may yet appear in them when transformed into the shape of a body, so that consciousness springs from them; and thus maintain that knowledge is analogous to intoxicating quality (which arises when certain materials are mixed in certain proportions), and that man is only a body qualified by consciousness. There is thus, according to them, no Self separate from the body and capable of going to the heavenly world or obtaining release, through which consciousness is in the body; but the body alone is what is conscious, is the Self. For this assertion they allege the reason stated in the Sûtra, 'On account of its existence where a body is.' For wherever something exists if some other thing exists, and does not exist if that other thing does not exist, we determine the former thing to be a mere quality of the latter; light and heat, e. g. we determine to be qualities of fire. And as life, movement, consciousness, remembrance and so on—which by the upholders of an independent Self are considered qualities of that Self—are observed only within bodies and not outside bodies, and as an abode of those qualities, different from the body, cannot be proved, it follows that they must be qualities of the body only. The Self therefore is not different from the body.—To this conclusion the next Sûtra replies.

54. There is separation (of the Self from the

body) because its existence does not depend on the existence of that (viz. the body), but there is not (non-separation); as in the case of perceptive consciousness.

The assertion that the Self is not separate from the body cannot be maintained. The Self rather must be something separate from the body, 'because the existence (of the Self) does not depend on the existence of that (i.e. the body).' For if from the circumstance that they are where the body is you conclude that the qualities of the Self are qualities of the body, you also must conclude from the fact that they are not where the body is that they are not qualities of the body, because thereby they show themselves to be different in character from the qualities of the body. Now the (real) qualities of the body, such as form and so on, may be viewed as existing as long as the body exists; life, movement, &c., on the other hand, do not exist even when the body exists, viz. in the state of death. The qualities of the body, again, such as form and so on, are perceived by others; not so the qualities of the Self, such as consciousness, remembrance, and so on. Moreover, we can indeed ascertain the presence of those latter qualities as long as the body exists in the state of life, but we cannot ascertain their non-existence when the body does not exist; for it is possible that even after this body has died the qualities of the Self should continue to exist by passing over into another body. The opposite opinion is thus precluded also for the reason of its being a mere hypothesis.—We further must question our opponent as to the nature of that consciousness which he assumes to spring from the elements; for the materialists do not admit the existence of anything but the four elements. Should he say that consciousness is the perception of the elements and what springs from the elements, we remark that in that case the elements and their products are objects of consciousness and that hence the latter cannot be a quality of them, as it is contradictory that anything should act on itself. Fire is hot indeed but does not burn itself, and the acrobat, well trained as he may be, cannot mount on his own shoulders. As little could consciousness, if it were a mere quality of the elements and their products, render them objects of itself. For form and other (undoubted) qualities do not make their own colour or the colour of something else their objects; the elements and their products, on the other hand, whether external or belonging to the Self (the organism) are rendered objects by consciousness. Hence in the same way as we admit the existence of that perceptive consciousness which has the material elements and their products for its objects, we also must admit the separateness of that consciousness from the elements. And as consciousness constitutes the character of our Self, the Self must be distinct from the body. That consciousness is permanent, follows from the uniformity of its character (and we therefore may conclude that the conscious Self is permanent also; as also follows) from the fact that the Self, although connected with a different state, recognises itself as the conscious agent—a recognition expressed in judgments such as 'I saw this,'—and from the fact of remembrance and so on being possible[1].

The argumentation that consciousness is an attribute of the body because it is where a body is, is already refuted by the reasons stated above. Moreover, perceptive consciousness takes place where there are certain auxiliaries such as lamps and the like, and does not take place where those are absent, without its following therefrom that perception is an attribute of the lamp or the like. Analogously

---

[1] The 'nityatva*m* *k*a' of the text might perhaps be connected directly with 'âtmano.' Ânanda Giri on the entire passage: Bhavatu tarhi bhûtebhyo*tiriktâ svâtantryopalabdhis tathâpi katham âtmasiddhis tatrâha upalabdhîti, ksha*n*ikatvât tasyâ nityâtmarûpatvam ayuktam ity â*s*ankyâ*g*ânatas tadbhedâbhâvâd vishayoparâgât tadbhânâd asâv eva nityopalabdhir ity âha nityatva*m* *k*eti, ki*m* *k*a sthûladehâbhimânahînasya svapne pratyabhi*gñ*ânâd atiriktâtmasiddhir ity âha aham iti, svapne sthûladehântarasyaivopalabdh*ri*tvam ity â*s*ankyâha sm*ri*tyâdîti, upalabdh*ri*smartror bhede saty anyopalabdhe*nyasya sm*ri*tir i*kkh*âdaya*s* *k*a neti na tayor anyatety artha*h*.

the fact that perception takes place where there is a body, and does not take place where there is none, does not imply that it is an attribute of the body; for like lamps and so on the body may be used (by the Self) as a mere auxiliary. Nor is it even true that the body is absolutely required as an auxiliary of perception; for in the state of dream we have manifold perceptions while the body lies motionless.—The view of the Self being something separate from the body is therefore free from all objections.

55. But the (meditations) connected with members (of sacrificial acts are) not (restricted) to (particular) *S*âkhâs, according to the Veda (to which they belong).

The above occasional discussion being terminated, we return to the discussion of the matter in hand.—We meet in the different *S*âkhâs of each Veda with injunctions of vidyâs connected with certain members of sacrificial acts, such as the udgîtha and the like. Cp. e.g. 'Let a man meditate on the syllable Om (as) the udgîtha' (*Kh.* Up. I, 1, 1); 'Let a man meditate on the fivefold Sâman as the five worlds' (*Kh.* Up. II, 2, 1); 'People say: "Hymns, hymns!" the hymn is truly this earth' (Ait. Âr. II, 1, 2, 1); 'The piled up fire-altar truly is this world' (*S*at. Brâ. X, 5, 4. 1). A doubt here arises whether the vidyâs are enjoined with reference to the udgîtha and so on as belonging to a certain *S*âkhâ only or as belonging to all *S*âkhâs. The doubt is raised on the supposition that the udgîtha and so on differ in the different *S*âkhâs because the accents, &c. differ.

Here the pûrvapakshin maintains that the vidyâs are enjoined only with reference to the udgîtha and so on which belong to the particular *S*âkhâ (to which the vidyâ belongs).—Why?—On account of proximity. For as such general injunctions as 'Let a man meditate on the udgîtha' are in need of a specification, and as this need is satisfied by the specifications given in the same *S*âkhâ which stand in immediate proximity, there is no reason for passing over that *S*âkhâ and having recourse to specifications enjoined in other *S*âkhâs. Hence the vidyâs are to be held apart, according to the *S*âkhâs to which they belong.

To this the Sûtra replies 'but those connected with members,' &c.—The word 'but' discards the primâ facie view. The meditations are not restricted to their own *S*âkhâs according to the Veda to which they belong, but are valid for all *S*âkhâs.—Why?—Because the direct statements of the texts about the udgîtha and so on enounce no specification. For to such general injunctions as 'Let a man meditate on the udgîtha'—which say nothing about specifications—violence would be done, if on the ground of proximity we restricted them to something special belonging to its own *S*âkhâ, and that would be objectionable because direct statement has greater weight than proximity. There is, on the other hand, no reason why the vidyâ should not be of general reference. We therefore conclude that, although the *S*âkhâs differ as to accents and the like, the vidyâs mentioned refer to the udgîtha and so on belonging to all *S*âkhâs, because the text speaks only of the udgîtha and so on in general.

56. Or else there is no contradiction (implied in our opinion); as in the case of mantras and the like.

Or else we may put the matter as follows. There is no reason whatever to suspect a contradiction if we declare certain vidyâs enjoined in one *S*âkhâ to be valid for the udgîtha and so on belonging to other *S*âkhâs also; for there is no more room for contradiction than in the case of mantras. We observe that mantras, acts, and qualities of acts which are enjoined in one *S*âkhâ are taken over by other *S*âkhâs also. So e.g. the members of certain Ya*g*ur-veda *S*âkhâs do not exhibit in their text the mantra, 'Thou art the ku*t*aru[1],' which accompanies the taking of the stone (with which the rice-grains are ground); all the same we meet in their text with the following injunction of application, 'Thou art the cock, with this mantra he takes the stone; or else with the mantra, Thou art the ku*t*aru.'

[1] Maitrâya*n*îya Sa*m*hitâ I, 1, 6.

Again, the text of some *S*âkhâ does not contain a direct injunction of the five offerings called prayâ*g*as which are made to the fuel and so on, but it contains the injunction of secondary matters connected with the prayâ*g*as, viz. in the passage, 'the seasons indeed are the prayâ*g*as; they are to be offered in one and the same spot[1].'—Again, the text of some *S*âkhâ does not contain an injunction as to the species of the animal to be sacrificed to Agnîshomau—such as would be 'a he-goat is sacrificed to Agnîshomau[2];'—but in the same *S*âkhâ we meet with a mantra which contains the required specification, 'Hot*ri*, recite the anuvâkyâ, for the fat of the omentum of the he-goat[3].' Similarly mantras enjoined in one Veda only, such as 'O Agni, promote the hautra, promote the sacrifice,' are seen to be taken over into other Vedas also. Another example (of the transference of mantras) is supplied by the hymn, 'He who as soon as born showed himself intelligent,' &c. (*Rik*. Sa*m*h. II, 12), which although read in the text of the Bahv*rik*as is employed in the Taittirîya Veda also, according to Taitt. Sa*m*h. VII, 5, 5, 2, 'The Sa*g*anîya hymn is to be recited.'—Just as, therefore, the members of sacrificial actions on which certain vidyâs rest are valid everywhere, so the vidyâs themselves also which rest on those members are valid for all *S*âkhâs and Vedas.

57. There is pre eminence of the (meditation on) plenitude (i.e. Agni Vai*s*vânara in his aggregate form), as in the case of sacrifices; for thus scripture shows.

In the legend beginning 'Prâ*k*ina*s*âla Aupamanyava,' the text speaks of meditations on Vai*s*vânara in his dis-

[1] As this passage states the number of the prayâ*g*as (viz. five, which is the number of the seasons) and other secondary points, we conclude that the injunction of the offering of the prayâ*g*as, which is given in other *S*âkhâs, is valid also for the *S*âkhâ referred to in the text (the Maitrâya*n*îyas, according to the commentators).

[2] But only says 'they offer an animal to Agnîshomau.'

[3] Wherefrom we infer that not any animal may be offered to Agnîshomau, but only a he-goat.

tributed as well as his aggregate condition. References to him in his distributed state are made in the passage, 'Aupamanyava, whom do you meditate on as the Self? He replied: Heaven only, venerable king. He said: The Self which you meditate on is the Vais*v*ânara Self called Sute*g*as;' and in the following passages (*Kh*. Up. V, 12–17). A meditation on him in his aggregate state, on the other hand, is referred to in the passage (V, 18), 'Of that Vais*v*ânara Self the head is Sute*g*as, the eye Vis*v*arûpa, the breath P*ri*thagvartman, the trunk Bahula, the bladder Rayi, the feet the earth,' &c.—A doubt here arises whether the text intimates a meditation on Vais*v*ânara in both his forms or only in his aggregate form.

The pûrvapakshin maintains that we have to do with meditations on Vais*v*ânara in his distributed form, firstly because the text exhibits a special verb, viz. 'you meditate on,' with reference to each of the limbs, Sute*g*as and so on; and secondly because the text states special fruits (connected with each special meditation) in the passage, 'Therefore every kind of Soma libation is seen in your house,' and the later similar passages.

To this we make the following reply. We must suppose that the entire section aims at intimating 'the preeminence,' i.e. at intimating as its pre-eminent subject, a meditation on 'plenitude,' i.e. on Vais*v*ânara in his aggregate state, who comprises within himself a plurality of things; not a number of special meditations on the limbs of Vais*v*ânara. 'As in the case of sacrifices.' In the same way as the Vedic texts referring to sacrifices such as the dars*a*pûr*n*amâsa aim at enjoining the performance of the entire sacrifice only, i.e. of the chief sacrificial action together with its members—and not in addition the performance of single subordinate members such as the prayâ*g*as, nor again the performance of the chief action together with some of its subordinate members; so it is here also.—But whence do you know that 'plenitude' is the preeminent topic of the passage?—It is shown by scripture, we reply, since we apprehend that the entire section forms a connected whole. For on examining the connexion of the parts we find that the entire section has for its subject the knowledge of Vais*v*ânara. The text at first informs us that six *Ri*shis—Prâ*k*înas*â*la, &c., up to Uddâlaka—being unable to reach a firm foundation in the knowledge of Vais*v*ânara, went to the king A*s*vapati Kaikeya; goes on to mention the object of each *Ri*shi's meditation, viz. the sky and so on; determines that the sky and so on are only the head and so on of Vai*s*vânara—in the passage 'he said: that is but the head of the Self,' and the later similar passages;—and thereupon rejects all meditations on Vai*s*vânara in his distributed form, in the passage, 'Your head would have fallen if you had not come to me,' and so on. Finally having discarded all distributed meditation it turns to the meditation on the aggregate Vai*s*vânara and declares that all results rest on him only, 'he eats food in all worlds, in all beings, in all Selfs.'—That the text mentions special fruits for the special meditations on Sute*g*as and so on we have, in accordance with our view, to explain as meaning that the results of the subordinate meditations are to be connected in their aggregate with the principal meditation. And that the text exhibits a special verb—'you do meditate'—in connexion with each member is not meant to enjoin special meditations on those members, but merely to make additional remarks about something which has another purpose (i. e. about the meditation on the aggregate Vai*s*vânara).—For all these reasons the view according to which the text enjoins a meditation on the aggregate Vai*s*vânara only is preferable.

Some commentators here establish the conclusion that the meditation on the aggregate Vai*s*vânara is the preferable alternative, but assume, on the ground of the Sûtra employing the term 'pre-eminence' only, that the Sûtrakâra allows also the alternative of distributed meditation. But this is inadmissible, since it is improper to assume a 'split of the sentence' (i.e. to ascribe to a passage a double meaning), as long as the passage may be understood as having one meaning only. Their interpretation, moreover, contradicts those passages which expressly blame distributed meditations; such as 'Thy head would have fallen.' And as the conclusion of the section clearly intimates a meditation on the aggregate Vais*v*ânara, the negation of such meditation could not be maintained as pûrvapaksha [1]. The term 'pre-eminence' which the Sûtra employs may moreover be explained as meaning (not mere preferability, but exclusive) authoritativeness.

58. (The vidyâs are) separate, on account of the difference of words and the like.

In the preceding adhikara*n*a we have arrived at the conclusion that a meditation on Vais*v*ânara as a whole is the pre-eminent meaning of the text, although special results are stated for meditations on Sute*g*as and so on. On the ground of this it may be presumed that other meditations also which are enjoined by separate scriptural texts have to be combined into more general meditations. Moreover, we cannot acknowledge a separation of vidyâs (acts of cognition; meditations) as long as the object of cognition is the same; for the object constitutes the character of a cognition in the same way as the material offered and the divinity to which the offering is made constitute the character of a sacrifice. Now we understand that the Lord forms the only object of cognition in a number of scriptural passages, although the latter are separate in enunciation; cp. e.g. 'He consisting of mind, whose body is prâ*n*a' (*Kh.* Up. III, 14, 2); 'Brahman is Ka, Brahman is Kha' (*Kh.* Up. IV, 10, 5); 'He whose wishes are true, whose purposes are true' (*Kh.* Up. VIII, 7, 3). Analogously one and the same Prâ*n*a is referred to in different texts; cp. 'Prâ*n*a indeed is the end of all' (*Kh.* Up. IV, 3, 3); 'Prâ*n*a indeed is the oldest and the best' (*Kh.* Up. V, 1, 1); 'Prâ*n*a is father, Prâ*n*a is mother' (*Kh.* Up. VII, 15, 1). And from the unity of the object of cognition there follows unity of cognition. Nor

[1] Yadobhayatropâstisiddhântas tadâ vyastopâstir evâtra samastopâstir eva vâ pûrvapaksha*h* syân nâdya ity âha, spash*t*e *k*eti, dvitîyas *k*a tatrâyukto vâkyopakramasthavyastopâstidhîvirodhât. Ân. Gi.

can it be said that, on this view, the separateness of the different scriptural statements would be purposeless, since each text serves to set forth other qualities (of the one pradhâna which is their common subject). Hence the different qualities which are enjoined in one's own and in other *S*âkhâs, and which all belong to one object of knowledge, must be combined so that a totality of cognition may be effected.

To this conclusion we reply, 'Separate,' &c. Although the object of cognition is one, such cognitions must be considered as separate 'on account of the difference of words and the like.'—For the text exhibits a difference of words such as 'he knows,' 'let him meditate,' 'let him form the idea' (cp. *Kh*. Up. III, 14, 1). And difference of terms is acknowledged as a reason of difference of acts, according to Pûrva Mîmâ*m*sâ-sûtras II, 2, 1.—The clause 'and the like' in the Sûtra intimates that also qualities and so on may be employed, according to circumstances, as reasons for the separateness of acts.—But, an objection is raised, from passages such as 'he knows' and so on we indeed apprehend a difference of words, but not a difference of sense such as we apprehend when meeting with such clauses as 'he sacrifices' and the like (ya*g*ate, *g*uhoti, dadâti). For all these words (viz. veda, upâsîta, &c.) denote one thing only, viz. a certain activity of the mind, and another meaning is not possible in their case[1]. How then does difference of vidyâ follow from difference of words?—This objection is without force, we reply; for although all those words equally denote a certain activity of the mind only, yet a difference of vidyâ may result from a difference of connexion. The Lord indeed is the only object of meditation in the passages quoted, but according to its general purport each passage teaches different qualities of the Lord; and similarly, although one and the same Prâ*n*a is the object of meditation in the other series

[1] Vedopâsîtetyâdi*s*abdânâ*m* kva*k*ig *gñ*âna*m* kva*k*id dhyânam ity arthabhedam â*s*ankya *gñ*ânasyâvidheyatvâd vidhîyamânam upâsanam evety âha arthântareti. Ân. Gi.

of passages, yet one of his qualities has to be meditated upon in one place and another in another place. From difference of connexion there thus follows difference of injunction, and from the latter we apprehend the separateness of the vidyâs. Nor can it be maintained (as the pûrvapakshin did) that one of those injunctions is the injunction of the vidyâ itself, while the others enjoin mere qualities; for there is no determining reason (as to which is the vidyâvidhi and which the gu*n*avidhis), and as in each passage more than one quality are mentioned it is impossible that those passages should enjoin qualities with reference to a vidyâ established elsewhere[1]. Nor should, in the case of the pûrvapakshin's view being the true one, the qualities which are common to several passages, such as 'having true wishes,' be repeated more than once. Nor can the different sections be combined into one syntactical whole, because in each one a certain kind of meditation is enjoined on those who have a certain wish, whence we understand that the passage is complete in itself[2]. Nor is there in the present case an additional injunction of a meditation on something whole—such as there is in the case of the cognition of the Vai*s*vânara—owing to the force of which the meditations on the single parts which are contained in each section would combine themselves into a whole. And if on the ground of the object of cognition being one we should admit unity of vidyâ without any restriction, we should thereby admit an altogether impossible combination of all qualities (mentioned anywhere in the Upanishads). The Sûtra therefore rightly declares the separateness of the vidyâs.—The present adhikara*n*a being thus settled, the first Sûtra of the pâda has now to be considered[3].

---

[1] For to enjoin in one passage several qualities—none of which is established already—would involve an objectionable vâkyabheda.

[2] A sentence is to be combined with another one into a larger whole only if the sentences are not complete in themselves but evince an âkaṅkshâ, a desire of complementation.

[3] I.e. the present adhikara*n*a ought in reality to head the entire pâda.

59. There is (restriction to) option (between the vidyâs), on account of their having non-differing results.

The difference of the vidyâs having been determined, we now enter on an inquiry whether, according to one's liking, there should be cumulation of the different vidyâs or option between them; or else restriction to an optional proceeding (to the exclusion of cumulation). For restriction to cumulation (which might be mentioned as a third alternative) there is no reason, because the separation of the vidyâs has been established.—But we observe that in the case of the sacrifices, agnihotra, dar*s*apûr*n*amâsa and so on, there is restriction to cumulation (i.e. that those sacrifices have all of them to be performed, not optionally one or the other) although they are different from each other.—True; but the reason for the obligatory cumulation of those sacrifices lies therein that scripture teaches them to be of absolute obligation. No scriptural passage, on the other hand, teaches the absolute obligatoriness of the vidyâs, and it cannot therefore be a rule that they must be cumulated.—Nor can it be a rule that there must be option between them, because a person entitled to one vidyâ cannot be excluded from another vidyâ. It therefore only remains to conclude that one may proceed as one likes.—But—an objection is raised—we must rather conclude that option between them is the rule, because their fruits are non-different. For vidyâs such as 'He who consists of mind, whose body is prâ*n*a;' 'Brahman is Ka, Brahman is Kha;' 'He whose wishes are true, whose purposes are true,' have all of them equally the obtaining of the Lord for their fruit.—This does not affect our conclusion; for we see that it is allowed to proceed as one likes also with regard to certain sacrificial acts which are the means of obtaining the heavenly world, and thus have all of them the same result. It therefore remains a settled conclusion that in the case of vidyâs one may proceed as one likes.

To this we reply as follows. There must be option between the vidyâs, not cumulation, because they have the same fruit. For the fruit of all of them is the intuition of the object meditated upon, and when this object, e.g. the Lord, has once been intuited through one meditation a second meditation would be purposeless. It would, moreover, be impossible even to effect an intuition through the cumulation of several meditations, since that would cause distraction of attention. And that the fruit of a vidyâ is to be effected through intuition various scriptural passages declare; cp. *Kh.* Up. III, 14, 4, 'He who has this faith and no doubt;' B*ri.* Up. IV, 1, 3, 'Having become a god he goes to the gods,' and others. Also Sm*ri*ti-passages such as Bha. Gîtâ VIII, 6, and others.—One therefore has to select one of those vidyâs the fruit of which is the same, and to remain intent on it until, through the intuition of the object to be meditated upon, the fruit of the vidyâ is obtained.

60. But (vidyâs) connected with wishes may, according to one's liking, be cumulated or not; on account of the absence of the former reason.

The above Sûtra supplies a counter-instance to the preceding Sûtra.—We have, on the other hand, vidyâs connected with definite wishes; as e.g. *Kh.* Up. III, 15, 2, 'He who knows that the wind is the child of the regions never weeps for his sons;' *Kh.* Up. VII, 1, 5, 'He who meditates on name as Brahman, walks at will as far as name reaches.' In these vidyâs which, like actions, effect their own special results by means of their 'unseen' Self, there is no reference to any intuition, and one therefore may, according to one's liking, either cumulate them or not cumulate them; 'on account of the absence of the former reason,' i.e. because there is not the reason for option which was stated in the preceding Sûtra.

61. With the (meditations on) members (of sacrificial acts) it is as with their abodes.

Are those meditations—enjoined in the three Vedas—which rest on members of sacrificial actions such as the udgîtha to be superadded to each other, or may we proceed with regard to them as we like?—To this doubt the Sûtra replies, 'it is according to the abodes.' As the abiding-places of those meditations, viz. the Stotra and so on, are combined (for the performance of the sacrifice), so those meditations also. For a meditation is subject to what it rests on.

62. And on account of the teaching.

As the Stotra and the other members of the sacrifice on which the meditations under discussion rest are taught in the three Vedas, so also the meditations resting on them. The meaning of this remark is that also as far as the mode of information is concerned there is no difference between the members of a sacrificial act and the meditations referring to them.

63. On account of the rectification.

The passage, 'From the seat of the Hot*ri* he sets right any mistake committed in the udgîtha' (*Kh*. Up. I, 5, 5), declares that, owing to the might of the meditation on the unity of pra*n*ava and udgîtha, the Hot*ri* sets right any mistake he may commit in his work, by means of the work of the Hot*ri*.

Now, as a meditation mentioned in one Veda is connected (with what is mentioned in another Veda) in the same way as a thing mentioned in another Veda, the above passage suggests the conclusion that all meditations on members of sacrificial acts—in whatever Veda they may be mentioned—have to be combined[1].

64. And because the text states a quality (of the vidyâ) to be common (to the three Vedas).

The text states that the syllable Om which is a quality,

[1] A 'thing' belonging to the *Ri*g-veda, viz. the pra*n*ava, is, according to the *Kh*ândogya-passage, connected with the Sâma-veda meditation on the udgîtha. Hence meditations also which belong to different Vedas may be combined; for there is no difference between them and things as far as connexion is concerned.

i.e. the abode of a meditation, is common to the three Vedas, 'By that syllable the threefold knowledge proceeds. With Om the Adhvaryu gives orders, with Om the Hot*ri* recites, with Om the Udgât*ri* sings.' This suggests that, as the abode of the vidyâ (viz. the O*m*kâra) is common, the vidyâs which abide in it are common also.—Or else the Sûtra may be explained as follows. If the udgîtha and so on, which are matters qualifying the sacrificial action, were not all of them common to all sacrificial performances, the vidyâs resting on them would not go together. But the scriptural passages which teach the sacrificial performances and extend over all subordinate matters, state that the udgîtha and so on are common to all performances. As thus the abodes of the vidyâs go together, the vidyâs abiding in them go together likewise.

65. (The meditations on members of sacrificial actions are) rather not (to be combined), as the text does not state their going together.

The words 'rather not' discard the pûrvapaksha. The meditations resting on members of actions are not to be treated like what they rest on, because scripture does not state their going together. Scripture actually states the going together of the Stotras and other subordinate members of sacrificial action which are enjoined in the three Vedas; cp. passages such as 'After the taking of the graha or the raising of the *k*amasa he performs the Stotra;' 'After the Stotra he recites;' 'Prastot*ri* sing the Sâman;' 'Hot*ri* recite the Yâ*g*yâ for this;' and so on. But, on the other hand, there are no analogous texts expressly teaching the going together of the meditations.—But the going together of the meditations is established by those texts which intimate the successive performance of the different constituent members of a sacrifice!—By no means, we reply. The meditations subserve the end of man, while the texts referred to by you establish only the going together of the udgîtha and the like which subserve the purpose of the sacrifice. That the meditations on the udgîtha and so on—although resting on members of sacrificial acts—yet subserve the end of man only in the same way as the godohana vessel does, we have already explained under III, 3, 42.—And this very difference between members of sacrificial action and the meditations resting on them, viz. that the former subserve the purpose of the sacrifice while the latter subserve the end of man, is founded on the express teaching of scripture[1].—And the further two indicatory marks (pointed out by the pûrvapakshin in Sûtras 63 and 64) supply no reason for the going together of the meditations, because no direct scriptural statement may be constructed from them. Nor[2] does the fact that in each sacrificial performance all foundations of meditations are comprised, enable us to conclude that the meditations founded on them are to be combined also; for the meditations are not caused by what they rest on. The meditations, as resting on their foundations, would, it may be admitted, not exist if those foundations did not exist. But therefrom it does not follow that the going together of the foundations implies a necessary going together of the meditations; for as to this we have no direct scriptural statement.—From all this it results that the meditations may be performed according to one's liking.

66. And because (scripture) shows it.

Scripture moreover shows that the meditations do not go together, viz. in the following passage, 'A Brahman priest who knows this saves the sacrifice, the sacrificer, and all the priests' (*Kh.* Up. IV, 17, 10). For if all meditations were to be combined, all priests would know them all, and the text could not specially announce that the Brahman priest possessing a certain knowledge thereby saves the others.—The meditations may therefore, according to one's liking, be either combined or optionally employed.

[1] A remark refuting the averment made in Sûtra 62.

[2] And this is meant to refute the second interpretation given of Sûtra 64.

FOURTH PÂDA.

Reverence to the highest Self!

1. The purpose of man (is effected) thence (i. e. through the mere knowledge of Brahman), thus Bâdarâyana opines.

The Sûtrakâra at present enters on an inquiry whether the knowledge of the Self which is derived from the Upanishads, is connected with works through him who is entitled to perform the works[1], or is an independent means to accomplish the purpose of man. He begins by stating the final view in the above Sûtra, 'Thence' &c. The teacher Bâdarâyana is of opinion that thence, i. e. through the independent knowledge of Brahman enjoined in the Vedânta-texts, the purpose of man is effected.—Whence is this known?—'From scripture,' which exhibits passages such as the following: 'He who knows the Self overcomes grief' (*Kh.* Up. III, 4, 1); 'He who knows that highest Brahman becomes even Brahman' (Mu. Up. III, 2, 9); 'He who knows Brahman attains the Highest' (Taitt. Up. II, 1); 'For him who has a teacher there is delay only so long as he is not delivered; then he will be perfect' (*Kh.* Up. VI, 14, 2); 'He who has searched out and understands the Self which is free from sin, &c. &c., obtains all worlds and all desires' (*Kh.* Up. VIII, 7, 1); 'The Self is to be seen' &c. up to 'Thus far goes immortality' (B*ri*. Up. IV, 5, 6–15). These and similar texts declare that mere knowledge effects the purpose of man.—Against this the opponent raises his voice as follows.

2. On account of (the Self) standing in a supplementary relation (to action), (the statements as to

[1] The pûrvapakshin (see next Sûtra) maintains that the knowledge of the Self is subordinate to (sacrificial) action through the mediation of the agent, i. e. in so far as it imparts to the agent a certain qualification.

the fruits of the knowledge of the Self) are arthavâdas, as in other cases, thus *G*aimini opines.

As the Self, in consequence of its being the agent, stands in a supplementary relation to action, the knowledge of the Self also is connected with action through the mediation of its object, analogously to the case of the sprinkling of the rice-grains with water; hence as the purpose of the knowledge of the Self is understood thereby, the statements of the text about the fruits of that knowledge are mere arthavâdas. Such is the opinion of the teacher *G*aimini [1]. The case is analogous to that of other textual statements as to the fruits of certain materials, sa*m*skâras and works; which statements have likewise to be understood as arthavâdas. Cp. the passage, 'He whose sacrificial ladle is made of par*n*a-wood hears no evil sound;' 'By anointing his eye he wards off the eye of the enemy;' 'By making the prayâ*g*a and anuyâ*g*a-oblations he makes an armour for the sacrifice, an armour for the sacrificer so that he overcomes his enemies [2].'—But how can it be supposed that

[1] The contention of the pûrvapakshin—*G*aimini—is that the knowledge of the Self has no independent fruit of its own, because it stands in a subordinate relation to sacrificial action. This relation is mediated by the Self—the object of knowledge—which is the agent in all action, and therefore itself stands in a subordinate relation to action. By learning that his Self will outlive the body the agent becomes qualified for actions, the fruit of which will only appear after death. The qualification the Self thus acquires is analogous to that which the rice-grains acquire by being sprinkled with water; for only through this latter act of ceremonial modification (or purification, sa*m*skâra) they become fit to be used in the sacrifice.—As the knowledge of the Self thus has no independent position, it cannot have an independent fruit of its own, and consequently the passages which state such fruits cannot be taken as 'injunctions of fruits,' but merely as arthavâdas, making some additional statement about the fruit of the sacrificial actions to which the knowledge of the Self is auxiliary.

[2] The material, i. e. the ladle made of par*n*a-wood, is auxiliary to the sacrifice, and the fruit which the text ascribes to it (viz. hearing no evil sound) therefore has to be viewed as a fruit of

the knowledge of the Self which the text does not exhibit under any special heading can enter into sacrificial action as a subordinate member, without the presence of any of the means of proof—general subject-matter and so on—which determine such subordinate relation?—The pûrvapakshin may reply that the knowledge of the Self enters into sacrificial action through the mediation of the agent, on the ground of the means of proof called vâkya (sentence; syntactical unity)[1]. But this we deny because in the present case 'sentence' has no force to teach the application (of the knowledge of the Self to the sacrifices, as a subordinate member of the latter). Things which the text states under no particular heading may indeed be connected with the sacrifice on the ground of 'sentence,' through some intermediate link which is not of too wide an application[2]; but the agent is an intermediate link of too wide an application, since it is common to all action whether worldly or based on the Veda. The agent cannot therefore be used as a mediating link to establish the connexion of the knowledge of the Self with the sacrifice.—Your objection is not valid, the pûrvapakshin replies, since the knowledge of a Self different from the body is of no use anywhere but in works based on the Veda. For such knowledge is of no use in worldly works, in all of which the activity may be shown to be guided by visible purposes; with reference to Vedic works, on the other hand, whose fruits manifest themselves only after the death of this body no activity would be possible

the entire sacrifice. Analogously in the case of the sa*m*skâra—the anointing—which fits the sacrificer for performing the sacrifice, and in the case of the prayâ*g*as and anuyâ*g*as which are merely subordinate members of the dar*s*apûr*n*amâsa.

[1] The entire Veda constituting an extended syntactical whole, in which the agent is the same.

[2] Thus the quality of being made of par*n*a-wood is connected with the sacrifices on the ground of the vâkya implied in 'yasya par*n*amayî guhûr bhavati,' because here we have as an intermediate link the guhû, i.e. a special implement which is used at sacrifices only, and therefore is not of too wide an application.

were it not for the knowledge of a Self separate from the body, and such knowledge therefore has its uses there.—But, another objection is raised, from attributes given to the Self, such as 'free from sin,' and the like, it appears that the doctrine of the Upanishads refers to that Self which stands outside the sa*m*sâra and cannot therefore be subordinate to activity.—This objection too is without force; for what the Upanishads teach as the object of cognition is just the transmigrating Self, which is clearly referred to in such terms as 'dear' (B*ri*. Up. II, 4, 5). Attributes such as being free from sin, on the other hand, may be viewed as aiming merely at the glorification of that Self.—But in more than one place Brahman, the cause of the world, which is additional to the transmigrating Self and itself not subject to transmigration has been established, and the Upanishads teach that this very Brahman constitutes the real nature of the transmigrating Self!—True, that has been established; but in order to confirm that doctrine, objections and their refutation are again set forth with reference to the question as to the fruit (of the knowledge of the Self).

3. On account of scripture showing (certain lines of) conduct.

'*G*anaka the king of the Videhas sacrificed with a sacrifice at which many presents were given to the priests' (B*ri*. Up. III, 1, 1); 'Sirs, I am going to perform a sacrifice' (*Kh*. Up. V, 11, 5); these and similar passages—which occur in sections that have another purport—show that those who know Brahman are connected with sacrificial action also. And similarly we apprehend from the fact that according to scripture Uddâlaka and others taught their sons and so on, that they were connected with the condition of life of householders. If mere knowledge could effect the purpose of man, why should the persons mentioned have perforated works troublesome in many respects? 'If a man would find honey in the Arka tree why should he go to the forest?'

4. Because scripture directly states that.

'What a man does with knowledge, faith and the Upanishad is more powerful' (*Kh.* Up. I, 1, 10); this passage directly states that knowledge is subordinate to work [1], and from this it follows that mere knowledge cannot effect the purpose of man.

5. On account of the taking hold together.

'Then both his knowledge and his work take hold of him' (B*ri.* Up. IV, 4, 2); as this passage shows that knowledge and work begin together to manifest their fruits, it follows that knowledge is not independent.

6. And because scripture enjoins (works) for such (only as understand the purport of the Veda).

'He who has learnt (lit. "read") the Veda from a family of teachers, according to the sacred injunction, in the leisure time left from the duties to be performed for the Guru; who after having received his discharge has settled in his own house, studying his sacred texts in some sacred spot' (*Kh.* Up. VIII, 15); such passages also show that those who know the purport of the whole Veda are qualified for sacrificial action, and that hence knowledge does not independently bring about a result.—But the expression 'who has read' directly states only that the Veda is read, not that its purport is understood!—Not so, we reply. The reading of the Veda extends up to the comprehension of its purport, as thus the reading has a visible purpose [2].

7. And on account of definite rules.

'Performing works here (i. e. in this life) let a man wish to live a hundred years; thus work will not cling to thee, man; there is no other way than that' (Î*s*a. Up. 2); 'The

[1] For the instrumental case 'vidyayâ' directly represents knowledge as a means of work.

[2] According to the Mîmâ*m*sâ principle that, wherever possible, actions enjoined must be understood to have a visible purpose (a supersensuous result being admitted only where no visible result can be made out).

Agnihotra is a sattra lasting up to old age and death; for through old age one is freed from it or through death' (*S*at. Brâ. XII, 4, 1, 1); from such definite rules also it follows that knowledge is merely supplementary to works.

Against all these objections the Sûtrakâra upholds his view in the following Sûtra.

8. But on account of (scripture teaching) the additional one (i.e. the Lord), (the view) of Bâdarâya*n*a (is valid); as that is seen thus (in scriptural passages).

The word 'but' discards the pûrvapaksha.—The assertion made in Sûtra 2 cannot be maintained 'on account of the text teaching the additional one.' If the Vedânta-texts taught that the transmigrating embodied Self which is an agent and enjoyer is something different from the mere body, the statements as to the fruit of the knowledge of the Self would, for the reasons indicated above, be mere arthavâdas. But what the Vedânta-texts really teach as the object of knowledge is something different from the embodied Self, viz. the non-transmigrating Lord who is free from all attributes of transmigratory existence such as agency and the like and distinguished by freedom from sin and so on, the highest Self. And the knowledge of that Self does not only not promote action but rather cuts all action short, as will be declared in Sûtra 16. Hence the view of the reverend Bâdarâya*n*a which was stated in Sûtra 1 remains valid and cannot be shaken by fallacious reasoning about the subordination of knowledge to action and the like. That the Lord who is superior to the embodied Self is the Self many scriptural texts declare; compare 'He who perceives all and knows all' (Mu. Up. I, 1, 9); 'From terror of it the wind blows, from terror the sun rises' (Taitt. Up. II, 8); 'It is a great terror, a raised thunderbolt' (Ka. Up. II, 6, 2); 'By the command of that imperishable one, O Gârgî' (B*ri*. Up. III, 8, 9); 'It thought, may I be many, may I grow forth. It sent forth fire' (*Kh*. Up. VI, 2, 3). There are indeed passages in which the transmigrating Self—hinted at by such terms as 'dear'—is referred to as the object of knowledge, such as 'But for the love of the Self everything is dear. Verily the Self is to be seen' (B*ri*. Up. II, 4, 5); 'He who breathes in the up-breathing he is thy Self and within all' (B*ri*. Up. III, 4, 1); 'The person that is seen in the eye that is thy Self,' up to 'But I shall explain him further to you' (*Kh*. Up. VIII, 7 ff.). But as there are at the same time complementary passages connected with the passages quoted above—viz. 'There has been breathed forth from this great Being the *Ri*g-veda, Yagur-veda,' &c. (B*ri*. Up. II, 4, 10); 'He who overcomes hunger and thirst, sorrow, passion, old age and death' (B*ri*. Up. III, 5, 1); 'Having approached the highest light he appears in his own form. That is the highest person' (*Kh*. Up. VIII, 12, 3)—which aim at giving instruction about the superior Self; it follows that the two sets of passages do not mean to teach an absolute difference of the two Selfs and that thus contradiction is avoided. For the Self of the highest Lord is the real nature of the embodied Self, while the state of being embodied is due to the limiting adjuncts, as appears from scriptural passages such as 'Thou art that;' 'There is no other seer but he.' All which has been demonstrated by us at length in the earlier parts of this commentary in more than one place.

9. But the declarations (of scripture) are equal (on the other side).

In reply to the averment made in Sûtra 3, we point out that there are declarations of scripture, of equal weight, in favour of the view that knowledge is not complementary to action. For there are scriptural passages such as, 'Knowing this the *ri*shis descended from Kavasha said: For what purpose should we study the Veda? for what purpose should we sacrifice? Knowing this indeed the Ancient ones did not offer the Agnihotra;' and 'When Brâhma*n*as know that Self and have risen above the desire for sons, wealth, and worlds, they wander about as mendicants' (B*ri*. Up. III, 5). Scripture moreover shows that

Yâ*gñ*avalkya and others who knew Brahman did not take their stand on works. 'Thus far goes immortality. Having said so Yâ*gñ*avalkya went away into the forest' (B*ri*. Up. IV, 5, 15). With reference to the indicatory sign (as to the dependence of knowledge to work) which is implied in the passage, 'Sirs, I am going to perform a sacrifice,' we remark that it belongs to a section which treats of Vai*s*vâ-nara. Now, the text may declare that a vidyâ of Brahman as limited by adjuncts is accompanied by works; but all the same the vidyâ does not stand in a subordinate relation to works since 'leading subject-matter' and the other means of proof are absent.

We now reply to the averment made in Sûtra 4.

10. (The direct statement is) non-comprehensive.

The direct scriptural statement implied in 'What a man does with knowledge' &c. does not refer to all knowledge, as it is connected with the knowledge forming the subject-matter of the section. And the latter is the knowledge of the udgîtha only, 'Let a man meditate on the syllable Om (as) the udgîtha.'

11. There is distribution (of the work and knowledge) as in the case of the hundred.

In reply to the averment (Sûtra 5) that the passage, 'Then both his knowledge and his work take hold of him,' indicates the non-independence of knowledge, we point out that the passage must be understood in a distributed sense, knowledge taking hold of one man and work of another. The case is analogous to that of the 'hundred.' When it is said, 'Let a hundred be given to these two men,' the hundred are divided in that way that fifty are given to one man and fifty to the other.—Moreover what the text says about the laying hold does not refer to him who is about to obtain final release; for the concluding passage, 'So much for the man who desires,' indicates that the whole section refers to the soul implicated in the sa*m*sâra, and a new beginning is made for him who is about to be released, in the clause, 'But as to the man who does not desire.' The clause about the laying hold thus comprises all knowledge which falls within the sphere of the transmigrating soul whether it be enjoined or prohibited[1], since there is no reason for distinction, and to all action whether enjoined or prohibited, the clause embodying a reference to knowledge and work as established elsewhere. And on this interpretation there is room for the clause even without our having recourse to the distribution of knowledge and work.

The next Sûtra replies to the averment made in Sûtra 6.

12. Of him who has merely read the Veda (there is qualification for works).

As the clause, 'Having learnt (read) the Veda from a family of teachers,' speaks only of the reading, we determine that acts are there enjoined for him who has only read the Veda.—But from this it would follow that on account of being destitute of knowledge such a person would not be qualified for works!—Never mind; we do not mean to deny that the understanding of sacrificial acts which springs from the reading of the texts is the cause of qualification for their performance; we only wish to establish that the knowledge of the Self derived from the Upanishads is seen to have an independent purpose of its own and therefore does not supply a reason of qualification for acts. Analogously a person who is qualified for one act does not require the knowledge of another act.

Against the reasoning of Sûtra 7 we make the following remark.

13. There being no specification (the rule does) not (specially apply to him who knows).

In passages such as 'Performing works here let a man live' &c., which state definite rules, there is no specification

[1] Pratishiddhâ *k*a nagnastrîdar*s*anâdirûpâ. Ân. Gi.—Pratishiddhâ *k*a yathâsa*kkh*âstrâdhigamanalaksha*n*â (not 'yathâ sa*kkh*âstra' as in the Biblioth. Indica edition). Bhâmatî.

of him who knows, since the definite rule is enjoined without any such specification.

14. Or else the permission (of works) is for the glorification (of knowledge).

The passage 'Performing works here' may be treated in another way also. Even if, owing to the influence of the general subject-matter, only he who knows is to be viewed as he who performs works, yet the permission to perform works must be viewed as aiming at the glorification of knowledge; as appears from the subsequent clause, 'no work clings to the man.' The meaning of the entire passage thus is: To a man who knows no work will cling, should he perform works during his whole life even, owing to the power of knowledge. And this clearly glorifies knowledge.

15. Some also by proceeding according to their liking (evince their disregard of anything but knowledge).

Moreover some who know, having obtained the intuition of the fruit of knowledge, express, in reliance thereon, the purposelessness of the means of all other results, viz. by proceeding according to their liking (and abandoning those means). A scriptural text of the Vâ*g*asaneyins runs as follows: 'Knowing this the people of old did not wish for offspring. What shall we do with offspring, they said, we who have this Self and this world' (B*ri*. Up. IV, 4, 22). And that the fruit of knowledge, being present to intuition, does not manifest itself at a later time only as the fruits of actions do, we have explained more than once. From this also it follows that knowledge is not subordinate to action, and that the scriptural statements as to the fruit of knowledge cannot be taken in any but their true sense.

16. And (scripture teaches) the destruction (of the qualification for works, by knowledge).

Moreover scripture teaches that this whole apparent world—which springs from Nescience, is characterised by actions, agents and results of actions and is the cause of all qualification for works—is essentially destroyed by the power of knowledge. Compare such passages as 'But when all has become the Self of him, wherewith should he see another, wherewith should he smell another?' (B*ri*. Up. IV, 5, 15). For him now who should teach that the qualification for works has for its necessary antecedent the knowledge of the Self which the Vedânta-texts teach, it would follow that the qualification for works is cut short altogether. From this also it follows that knowledge is independent.

17. And (knowledge belongs) to those who are bound to chastity; for in scripture (that condition of life is mentioned).

Scripture shows that knowledge is valid also for those stages of life for which chastity is prescribed. Now in their case knowledge cannot be subordinate to work because work is absent; for the works prescribed by the Veda such as the Agnihotra are no longer performed by men who have reached those stages.—But, an objection is raised, those stages of life are not even mentioned in the Veda!—This is not so, we reply. Certain Vedic passages clearly intimate them; so e.g. 'There are three branches of the law' (*Kh*. Up. II, 23, 1); 'Those who in the forest practise faith and austerity' (*Kh*. Up. V, 10, 1); 'Those who practise penance and faith in the forest' (Mu. Up. I, 10, 11); 'Wishing for that world only mendicants wander forth' (B*ri*. Up. IV, 4, 22); 'Let him wander forth at once from the state of studentship.'—That the stages requiring chastity are open to men whether they have reached householdership or not, and whether they have paid the debts (of procreating a son, &c.) or not, is known from scripture and Sm*ri*ti. Herefrom also follows the independence of knowledge.

18. *G*aimini (considers that scriptural passages mentioning those stages of life in which chastity is obligatory, contain) a reference (only to those stages);

they are not injunctions; for (other scriptural passages) forbid (those stages).

The Vedic texts which have been quoted to the end of showing the existence of the stages of life on which chastity is binding—such as 'There are three branches of the law' and so on—have no power to establish those stages. For the teacher *G*aimini is of opinion that those passages contain only a reference to the other stages of life, not an injunction (of them).—Why?—Because they contain no words expressive of injunction such as imperative verbal forms, and because each of them is seen to have some other purport. In the passage, 'There are three' &c., the text at first refers to three stages of life ('Sacrifice, study, and charity are the first' &c. &c.), thereupon declares them not to have unbounded results ('All these obtain the world of the blessed'), and finally glorifies 'the state of being grounded on Brahman' as having unbounded results ('the Brahmasa*m*stha obtains immortality').—But is not a mere reference even sufficient to intimate the existence of those stages of life?—True; but they are established (enjoined) not by direct scriptural statements, but only by Sm*ri*ti and custom, and therefore when contradicted by direct scriptural statement[1] are either to be disregarded or else to be viewed as concerning those who (for some reason or other) are disqualified (for active worship, sacrifices and the like).—But together with the stages demanding chastity the text refers to the condition of the householder also[2]. ('Sacrifice, study, and charity are the first.')—True; but the existence of the state of the householder is established (not by that passage but) by other scriptural passages, viz. those which enjoin on the householder certain works such as the Agnihotra. Hence the reference in the passage under discussion aims at glorification only, not at injunction.

---

[1] Such as that concerning the permanent obligation of the Agnihotra and so on.

[2] And we therefore may conclude that those stages are as valid as the—notoriously valid—state of householdership.

Moreover, direct scriptural enunciations forbid other stages of life; cp. 'A murderer of the gods is he who removes the fire;' 'After having brought to thy teacher his proper reward do not cut off the line of children' (Taitt. Up. I, 11, 1); 'To him who is without a son the world does not belong; all beasts even know that.'—Similarly the passages, 'Those who in the forest practise faith and austerity' (*Kh*. Up. V, 10, 1), and the analogous passage (from the Mu*nd*aka), contain instruction not about the other stages of life but about the going on the path of the gods. And of clauses such as 'austerity is the second' it is doubtful whether they speak of a stage of life at all. And a passage like 'Wishing for that world only mendicants wander forth,' does not enjoin the wandering forth but merely glorifies that world.—But there is at any rate one scriptural text which directly and unambiguously enjoins the condition of life of the wandering mendicant, viz. the one of the *G*âbâlas, 'Let him wander forth at once from the state of studentship.'—True, but our discussion is carried on without reference to that passage.

19. (The other stage of life) is to be accomplished, (according to) Bâdarâya*n*a; on account of the scriptural statement of equality.

The teacher Bâdarâya*n*a is of opinion that that other stage of life is something to be accomplished. The view that there is a contradiction because the other stage of life is stated in the Veda and, on the other hand, works such as the Agnihotra must necessarily be performed, and that, in order to remove this contradiction, that other stage of life must be entered upon by those only who are not qualified for active worship, he rejects; being of opinion that that other stage is to be entered upon, in the same way as the state of the householder, even by him who does not wish to do so.—On what ground?—'On account of the scriptural statement of equality.' For we have a passage (viz. 'There are three branches of the law,' &c.) which refers equally to that other stage as to the state of the householder. As the state of the householder which is enjoined in other passages only is here referred to, so also that other stage of life. The case is analogous to the reference made to the wearing of the sacrificial thread round the neck or on the right shoulder—which two modes are established in other scriptural passages—in a passage the purpose of which it is to enjoin the wearing of the thread on the left shoulder. The other stage must therefore be entered upon in the same way as the state of the householder.—Analogously in the passage, 'Wishing for that world only mendicants leave their homes,' the last stage of life is mentioned together with the study of the Veda, sacrifice and so on, and in the passage, 'Those who in the forest,' &c., with the knowledge of the five fires.—The remark, made above by the pûrvapakshin, that in such passages as 'austerity is the second' there is unambiguous reference to a further stage of life, is without force, since there is a reason enabling us to determine what is meant. The text proclaims in the beginning that there are three subdivisions ('There are three branches of the law'). Now the sacrifice and the other duties (which the text enumerates subsequently to the introductory clause) can, because they are more than three, and rest on separate originative injunctions, be comprised within the three branches only if they are connected with one of the stages of life. Now the terms 'sacrifice' and so on indicate that the stage of householdership constitutes one branch of the law, and the term 'Brahma*k*ârin' clearly denotes another stage; what then remains but to assume that the term 'austerity' also denotes a stage of life, viz. the one in which austerity is the chief thing? Analogously the reference to the forest—in the passage, 'Those who in the forest,'—indicates that by the austerity and faith mentioned there we have to understand that stage of life in which austerity and faith are the chief thing.—From all this it follows that the further stage of life has to be gone through, even if the passage under discussion should do nothing but refer to it.

20. Or (the passage rather is) an injunction, as in the case of the carrying (of the firewood).

Or the passage is rather to be understood as containing an injunction, not a mere reference.—But, an objection is raised, if we assume it to be an injunction we thereby oppose the conception of the entire passage as a coherent whole, while yet the passage has clearly to be conceived as constituting such a whole, viz. as meaning that while the three branches of the law have for their result the world of the blessed, the condition of being grounded in Brahman has immortality for its result.—True, but all the same we must set aside the conception of the passage as a whole—well founded as it is—and assume it to be an injunction. For it is a new injunction because no other injunction is observed, and as the conception of the other stage of life clearly arises from the passage it is impossible to interpret it as a coherent whole by means of the assumption that it is a mere gu*n*avâda [1].

The case is analogous to that of the 'carrying.' There is a scriptural text (relating to the Agnihotra which forms part of the mahâpit*ri*yag*ñ*a), 'Let him approach carrying the firewood below (the ladle holding the offering); for above he carries it for the gods.' Now this passage may be conceived as an unbroken whole if we view it as referring to the carrying below only; nevertheless we determine that it enjoins the carrying above because that

---

[1] In the clause 'vidhyantarâdar*s*anât' I can see nothing more than an explanation of—or reason for—the 'apûrvatvât.' If we viewed the passage as glorifying the brahmasa*m*sthatâ compared to the three branches of the law through the statement of its supersensuous results (so that it would constitute an arthavâda of the kind called gu*n*avâda), we should indeed preserve the unity of the passage—which is destroyed if we view it as enjoining the different stages of life. But all the same the latter explanation is the true one; for a glorificatory passage presupposes an injunctive one, and as no such injunctive passage is met with elsewhere, it is simpler to assume that the present passage is itself injunctive than to construe (on the basis of it if viewed as a gu*n*avâda) another injunctive passage. (In Ânanda Giri's gloss on this passage—Biblioth. Indica edition—read 'vihitatvopagamaprasaktyâ' and 'stutilaksha*n*ayaika°.')

is not enjoined anywhere else[1]. This is explained in the chapter treating of 'complement,' in the Sûtra, 'But it is an injunction,' &c. (Pû. Mîm. Sû.). In the same way we assume that our passage referring to the different âsramas is an injunctory passage only.

Even if (to state an alternative conclusion) the passage contains references only to the other âsramas, it must be viewed as enjoining at any rate the condition of being grounded in Brahman, owing to the glorification of that condition. The question here arises whether that state belongs to any one comprised within the four âsramas, or only to the wandering mendicant. If now a reference to the mendicant also is contained within the references to the âsramas up to the Brahma*k*ârin (i.e. the three âsramas the text refers to before the passage about the brahmasa*m*stha); then, as all four âsramas are referred to equally and as somebody not belonging to any âsrama could not possibly be called brahmasa*m*stha, it follows that the term 'brahmasa*m*stha' denotes any one standing within one of the four âsramas. If, on the other hand, the mendicant is not comprised within the references to the three âsramas, he alone remains, and this establishes the conclusion that the brahmasa*m*stha is the mendicant only. (We therefore have to inquire which of the two alternatives stated has to be adopted.)—Here some maintain that the term 'austerity' which denotes the hermit in the woods implies a reference to the mendicant also. But this is wrong. For as long as any other explanation is possible, we must not assume that a term which expresses a distinctive attribute of the hermits living in the forest comprises the wandering mendicants also. Both the Brahma*k*ârin and the householder are

[1] The ekavâkyatâ is preserved if we take the clause from 'above' as an arthavâda meant to give the reason why in sacrifices offered to the Fathers the firewood has to be carried below. Nevertheless the clause must be taken as a vidhi enjoining the carrying above in all sacrifices offered to the gods, because this particular is not enjoined elsewhere.

referred to by distinctive terms applying to them only, and we therefore expect that the mendicant and the hermit also should be referred to by analogous terms. Now 'austerity' is a distinctive attribute of the hermits living in the woods; for the principal conventional meaning of the word 'austerity' is mortification of the body. The distinctive attribute of the mendicant, on the other hand, viz. restraint of the senses and so on, cannot be denoted by the term 'austerity.' Moreover it would be an illegitimate assumption that the âsramas which are known to be four should here be referred to as three. And further the text notifies a distinction, viz. by saying that those three reach the world of the blessed, while one enjoys immortality. Now there is room for such a distinction if the hermits and the mendicants are separate; for we do not say 'Devadatta and Yag*ñ*adatta are stupid, but one of them is clever,' but we say 'Devadatta and Yag*ñ*adatta are stupid, but Vish*n*umitra is clever.' The passage therefore has to be understood in that sense, that those belonging to the three former âsramas obtain the world of the blessed, while the remaining one, i. e. the wandering mendicant, enjoys immortality.—But how can the term 'brahmasa*m*stha,' which according to its etymological meaning may be applied to members of all âsramas, be restricted to the mendicant? and, if we agree to take it in its conventional meaning, it follows that immortality may be reached by merely belonging to an âsrama, and hence that knowledge is useless!—To these objections we make the following reply. The term 'brahmasa*m*stha' denotes fulfilment in Brahman, a state of being grounded in Brahman to the exclusion of all other activity. Now such a state is impossible for persons belonging to the three former âsramas, as scripture declares that they suffer loss through the non-performance of the works enjoined on their âsrama. The mendicant, on the other hand, who has discarded all works can suffer no loss owing to non-performance. Such duties as are incumbent on him, viz. restraint of the senses and the like, are not opposed to the state of being grounded in Brahman, but rather helpful to it. For the only work enjoined on him by his â*s*rama is the state of being firmly grounded in Brahman, wherein he is strengthened by restraint of the senses and so on—just as sacrifices and the like are prescribed for the other â*s*ramas—and loss he incurs only by neglecting that work. In agreement herewith texts from scripture and Sm*ri*ti declare that for him who is grounded in Brahman there are no works. Compare 'Renunciation is Brahman; for Brahman is the highest; for the highest is Brahman; above those lower penances, indeed, there rises renunciation;' 'Those anchorites who have well ascertained the object of the knowledge of the Vedânta and have purified their nature by the Yoga of renunciation' (Mu. Up III, 2, 6); and similar scriptural passages. And Sm*ri*ti-texts to the same effect, such as 'They whose minds are fixed on him, who have their Self in him, their stand on him, their end in him' (Bha. Gîtâ V, 17). All these passages teach that for him who is founded on Brahman there are no works. From this there also follows the non-validity of the second objection raised above, viz. that the mendicant's reaching immortality through the mere stage of life in which he stands would imply the uselessness of knowledge. —In this way we understand that, although there is a reference to the other stages of life, that which is indicated by the quality of being grounded in Brahman is the state of the wandering mendicant.

This whole discussion has been carried on by the teacher without taking into account the text of the *G*âbâlas, which enjoins the other stage of life. But there exists that text which directly enjoins the other stage, 'Having completed his studentship he is to become a householder; having been a householder he is to become a dweller in the forest; having been a dweller in the forest he is to wander forth; or else he may wander forth from the student's state; or from the house; or from the forest.' Nor can this text be interpreted as referring to those who are not qualified for works; for it states no difference, and there is a separate injunction (of the pârivrâ*g*ya-state) for those who are not qualified, viz. in the passage, 'May he have taken vows upon himself or not, may he be a snâtaka or not, may he be one whose fire has gone out or one who has no fire,' &c. That the text does not refer to such only as are not qualified for works, further follows from the fact that the state of the mendicant is meant to subserve the development of the knowledge of Brahman[1], as scripture declares, 'The wandering mendicant, with colourless dress, shaven, wifeless, pure, guileless, living on alms, qualifies himself for the intuition of Brahman.'—From all this it follows that the stages of life for which chastity is obligatory are established by scripture, and that knowledge—because enjoined on persons who have entered on those stages—is independent of works.

21. If it be said that (texts such as the one about the udgîtha are) mere glorification, on account of their reference (to parts of sacrifices); we deny that, on account of the newness (of what they teach, if viewed as injunctions).

'That udgîtha is the best of all essences, the highest, holding the highest place, the eighth' (*Kh.* Up. I, 1, 3); 'This earth is the *Rik*, the fire is Sâman' (*Kh.* Up. I, 6, 1); 'This world in truth is that piled-up fire-altar' (*S*at. Brâ. X, 1, 2, 2); 'That hymn is truly that earth' (Ait. Âr. II, 1, 2, 1); with reference to these and other similar passages a doubt arises whether they are meant to glorify the udgîtha and so on, or to enjoin devout meditations.

The pûrvapakshin maintains that their aim is glorification, because the text exhibits them with reference to subordinate members of sacrificial actions, such as the udgîtha and so on. They are, he says, analogous to passages such as 'This earth is the ladle;' 'the sun is the tortoise;' 'the heavenly world is the Âhavanîya,' whose

[1] Which has to be acquired in the regular prescribed way of Brahmanical studentship.

aim it is to glorify the ladle and so on. To this the Sûtrakâra replies as follows. We have no right to consider the purpose of those passages to be mere glorification, on account of the newness. If they aim at injunction, a new matter is enjoined by them; if, on the other hand, they aimed at glorification they would be devoid of meaning. For, as explained in the Pû. Mîm. Sû., glorificatory passages are of use in so far as entering into a complementary relation to injunctive passages; but the passages under discussion are incapable of entering into such a relation to the udgîtha and so on which are enjoined in altogether different places of the Veda, and would therefore be purposeless as far as glorification is concerned. Passages such as 'This earth is the ladle' are not analogous because they stand in proximity to injunctive passages.—Therefore texts such as those under discussion have an injunctive purpose.

22. And on account of the words expressive of becoming.

Moreover the text exhibits words of clearly injunctive meaning, in connexion with the passages quoted above, viz. 'Let him meditate on the udgîtha' (*Kh.* Up. I, 1, 1); 'Let him meditate on the Sâman' (*Kh.* Up. II, 2, 1); 'Let him think: I am the hymn' (Ait. Âr. II, 1, 6). Now these injunctive forms would be rendered futile by the assumption of the texts under discussion aiming at glorification only. Compare the following saying of those who know Nyâya, 'Let him do, let it be done, it is to be done, let it become, let it be; these forms are in all Vedas the settled signs of injunction.' What they mean thereby is that injunction is the sense of all potential, imperative, &c., verbal forms.—Moreover in each of the sections to which the passages under discussion belong the text states special fruits, 'He becomes indeed a fulfiller of desires' (*Kh.* Up. I, 1, 7); 'He is able to obtain wishes through his song' (*Kh.* Up. I, 7, 9); 'The worlds in an ascending and a descending line belong to him' (*Kh.* Up. II, 2, 3). For this reason also the texts about the udgîtha and so on are meant to enjoin devout meditations.

23. (The stories told in the Upanishads) are for the purpose of the pâriplava; we deny this on account of (certain stories only) being specified.

'Yâ*gñ*avalkya had two wives, Maitreyî and Kâtyâyanî' (B*ri*. Up. IV, 5, 1); 'Pratardana, forsooth, the son of Divodâsa came to the beloved abode of Indra' (Kau. Up. III, 1); 'There lived once upon a time *G*âna*s*ruti Pautrâya*n*a, who was a pious giver, giving much and keeping open house' (*Kh*. Up. IV, 1, 1); with regard to these and similar stories met with in the Vedânta portions of scripture there arises a doubt whether they are meant to subserve the performance of the pâriplava[1], or to introduce the vidyâs standing in proximity to them.

The pûrvapakshin maintains that those scriptural stories subserve the pâriplava because they are stories like others, and because the telling of stories is enjoined for the pâriplava. And from this it follows that the Vedânta-texts do not chiefly aim at knowledge, because like mantras they stand in a complementary relation to sacrificial performances.

This conclusion we deny 'on account of the specification.' Under the heading 'he is to recite the pâriplava,' scripture specifies certain definite stories such as that of 'Manu Vivasvat's son the king.' If, now, for the reason that all tales as such are alike, all tales were admitted for the pâriplava, the mentioned specification would be devoid of meaning. We therefore conclude that those scriptural stories are not meant to be told at the pâriplava.

24. This follows also from the connexion (of the stories with the vidyâs) in one coherent whole.

And as thus the stories do not subserve the pâriplava it

[1] I.e. have to be recited at stated intervals during the year occupied by the a*s*vamedha sacrifice.

is appropriate to assume that they are meant to bring nearer to our understanding the approximate vidyâs with which they are seen to form connected wholes; for they serve to render the latter more acceptable and facilitate their comprehension.

In the Maitreyî-brâhma*n*a we see that the story forms a whole with the vidyâ beginning, 'The Self indeed is to be seen,' &c.; in the account of Pratardana with the vidyâ, 'I am prâ*n*a, the conscious Self;' in the legend of *G*âna*s*ruti with the vidyâ, 'Air indeed is the end of all.' The case of all these stories is analogous to that of stories met with in scriptural texts referring to works, whose purpose is the glorification of injunctions standing in proximity; as e.g. 'He cut out his own omentum.'—The stories under discussion therefore do not subserve the pâriplava.

25. For this very reason there is no need of the lighting of the fire and so on.

The expression 'For this very same reason' must be viewed as taking up Sûtra III, 4, 1, because thus a satisfactory sense is established. For this very same reason, i.e. because knowledge subserves the purpose of man, the lighting of the sacrificial fire and similar works which are enjoined on the different â*s*ramas are not to be observed, since man's purpose is effected through knowledge.

The Sûtrakâra thus sums up the result of the first adhikara*n*a, intending to make some further remarks.

26. And there is need of all (works), on account of the scriptural statement of sacrifices and the like; as in the case of the horse.

We now consider whether knowledge has absolutely no need of the works enjoined on the different â*s*ramas, or whether it has some need of them. Under the preceding Sûtra we have arrived at the conclusion that as knowledge effects its own end the works enjoined on the â*s*ramas are absolutely not required. With reference to this point the present Sûtra now remarks that knowledge has regard for all works enjoined on the â*s*ramas, and that there is not absolute non-regard.—But do not the two Sûtras thus contradict each other?—By no means, we reply. Knowledge having once sprung up requires no help towards the accomplishment of its fruit, but it does stand in need of something else with a view to its own origination.—Why so?—On account of the scriptural statements of sacrifices and so on. For the passage, 'Him Brâhma*n*as seek to know by the study of the Veda, by sacrifice, by gifts, by penance, by fasting' (B*ri*. Up. IV, 4, 22), declares that sacrifices and so on are means of knowledge, and as the text connects them with the 'seeking to know,' we conclude that they are, more especially, means of the origination of knowledge. Similarly the passage, 'What people call sacrifice that is really brahma*k*arya' (*Kh*. Up. VIII, 5, 1), by connecting sacrifices and so on with brahma*k*arya which is a means of knowledge, intimates that sacrifices &c. also are means of knowledge. Again the passage, 'That word which all the Vedas record, which all penances proclaim, desiring which men live as religious students, that word I tell thee briefly, it is Om' (Ka. Up. I, 2, 15), likewise intimates that the works enjoined on the â*s*ramas are means of knowledge. Similarly Sm*ri*ti says, 'Works are the washing away of uncleanliness, but knowledge is the highest way. When the impurity has been removed, then knowledge begins to act.'

The phrase, 'as in the case of the horse,' supplies an illustration on the ground of suitability. As the horse, owing to its specific suitability, is not employed for dragging ploughs but is harnessed to chariots; so the works enjoined on the â*s*ramas are not required by knowledge for bringing about its results, but with a view to its own origination.

27. But all the same he (who is desirous of knowledge) must be possessed of calmness, subjection of the senses, &c., since those (states) are enjoined as auxiliaries to that (viz. knowledge), and must (on that account) necessarily be accomplished.

Perhaps somebody might think that we have no right to look upon sacrifices and the like as means of knowledge because there is no injunction to that effect. For a passage like 'By sacrifice they seek to know' is of the nature of an anuvâda, and therefore does not aim at enjoining sacrifices but rather at glorifying knowledge, 'so glorious is knowledge that they seek to obtain it through sacrifices and the like.'

But even should this be so the seeker for knowledge must possess calmness of mind, must subdue his senses and so on; for all this is enjoined as a means of knowledge in the following scriptural passage, 'Therefore he who knows this, having become calm, subdued, satisfied, patient, and collected, sees self in Self' (B*ri*. Up. IV, 4, 23). And what is enjoined must necessarily be carried out.—But in the above passage also we observe only a statement as to something actually going on—'Having become calm, &c., he sees,' not an injunction!—Not so, we reply. The introductory word 'therefore' which expresses praise of the subject under discussion makes us understand that the passage has an injunctive character[1].

Moreover the text of the Mâdhyandinas directly reads 'let him see' (not 'he sees'). Hence calmness of mind and so on are required even if sacrifices, &c., should not be required.—Sacrifices and so on, however, are required likewise, because (as said in Sûtra 26) scripture teaches them.—But it has been said that in the passage, 'Him they seek to know by sacrifices,' no injunction is observed!—True; but nevertheless we must assume the passage to be an injunction, because the connexion of the search for knowledge with sacrifices and so on is something new; i.e. is not established by another text, and therefore the

[1] For if there were no injunction, the praise would be without meaning. The 'therefore' connects the passage with the preceding clause, 'he is not sullied by any evil deed.' The sense then is, 'Because he who knows the Self as described before is not sullied by any evil deed, therefore let him, after having become calm, &c., see the Self, and so on.'

passage under discussion cannot be an anuvâda referring to it. The case is analogous to that of passages such as 'therefore Pûshan[1] receives a well-crushed share of food, for he is toothless.' There also no injunction is directly stated; but as the matter of the passage is new we assume an injunction and understand that the grains for Pûshan are to be crushed at all vik*ri*tis of the dar*s*apûr*n*amâsa; as was explained in the Pûrva Mîmâ*m*sâ.

An analogous conclusion was arrived at under Sûtra 20.—Sm*ri*tis also such as the Bhagavadgîtâ explain that sacrifices and the like if undertaken without a view to their special results become for him who is desirous of final release a means of knowledge. Hence sacrifices and the like, on the one hand, and calmness of mind and so on, on the other hand, according to the â*s*ramas, i.e. all works enjoined on the â*s*ramas must be had regard to with a view to the springing up of knowledge. Calmness of mind, &c., are, on account of the expression 'he who knows this' connecting them with knowledge, to be viewed as approximate—direct—means of knowledge, while sacrifices and so on which scripture connects with the search of knowledge are to be looked upon as remote—indirect—means.

28. And there is permission of all food, (only) in the case of danger of life; on account of this being shown (by scripture).

In the colloquy of the prâ*n*as the *Kh*andogas record, 'To him who knows this there is nothing which is not food' (*Kh*. Up. V, 1, 2); and the Vâ*g*asaneyins, 'By him nothing is eaten that is not food, nothing is received that is not food' (B*ri*. Up. VI, 1, 14). The sense of the two passages is that anything may be eaten by him.—A doubt here arises whether the texts enjoin the permission of eating anything

[1] The passage quoted occurs in the Veda under the heading of the dar*s*apûr*n*amâsa. But as Pûshan has no share in the fundamental form of that sacrifice, we conclude that the injunction implied in the passage is valid for those vik*ri*tis of the dar*s*apûr*n*amâsa in which offerings are made to Pûshan.

as an auxiliary to knowledge—as calmness of mind, &c., are—or mention them for the purpose of glorification.—The pûrvapakshin maintains that the passages are injunctions because thus we gain an instruction which causes a special kind of activity. What, therefore, the text teaches is the non-operation of a definite rule, in so far as auxiliary to the knowledge of the prâ*n*as in proximity to which it is taught.—But this interpretation implies the sublation of the scriptural rules as to the distinction of lawful and unlawful food!—Such sublation, we reply, is possible, because the present case is one of general rule and special exception. The prohibition of doing harm to any living creature is sublated by the injunction of the killing of the sacrificial animal; the general rule which distinguishes between such women as may be approached and such as may not, is sublated by the text prescribing, with reference to the knowledge of the Vâmadevya, that no woman is to be avoided ('Let him avoid no woman, that is the vow,' *Kh*. Up. II, 13, 2); analogously the passage which enjoins, with reference to the knowledge of the prâ*n*as, the eating of all food may sublate the general rule as to the distinction of lawful and unlawful food.

To this we reply as follows. The permission to eat any food whatever is not enjoined, since the passages do not contain any word of injunctive power; for the clause, 'To him who knows this there is nothing,' &c., expresses only something actually going on. And where the conception of an injunction does not naturally arise we may not assume one from the mere wish of something causing a special line of activity. Moreover the text says that 'for him who knows this there is nothing that is not food,' only after having said that everything even unto dogs and the like is food for the Prâ*n*a. Now food such as dogs and the like cannot be enjoyed by the human body; but all this can be thought of as food of the Prâ*n*a. From this it follows that the passage is an arthavâda meant to glorify the knowledge of the food of the Prâ*n*a, not an injunction of the permission of all food.—This the Sûtra indicates in the words, 'and there is permission of all food in danger of life.' That means: Only in danger of life, in cases of highest need, food of any kind is permitted to be eaten. 'On account of scripture showing this.' For scripture shows that the *ri*shi *K*âkrâya*n*a when in evil plight proceeded to eat unlawful food. In the brâhma*n*a beginning, 'when the Kurus had been destroyed by hailstones,' it is told how the *ri*shi *K*âkrâya*n*a having fallen into great wretchedness ate the beans half eaten by a chief, but refused to drink what had been offered on the ground of its being a mere leaving; and explained his proceeding as follows: 'I should not have lived if I had not eaten them; but water I can drink wherever I like.' And again on the following day he ate the stale beans left by himself and another person. Scripture, in thus showing how the stale leaving of a leaving was eaten, intimates as its principle that in order to preserve one's life when in danger one may eat even unlawful food. That, on the other hand, in normal circumstances not even a man possessing knowledge must do this, appears from *K*âkrâya*n*a's refusing to drink.—From this it follows that the passage, 'For to him who knows this,' &c., is an arthavâda.

29. And on account of the non-sublation.

And thus those scriptural passages which distinguish lawful and unlawful food,—such as *Kh*. Up. VII, 26, 2, 'When the food is pure the whole nature becomes pure,'—are non-sublated.

30. And this is said in Sm*ri*ti also.

That in cases of need both he who knows and he who does not know may eat any food Sm*ri*ti also states; compare e.g. 'He who being in danger of his life eats food from anywhere is stained by sin no more than the lotus leaf by water.'—On the other hand, many passages teach that unlawful food is to be avoided. 'Intoxicating liquor the Brâhma*n*a must permanently forego;' 'Let them pour boiling spirits down the throat of the Brâhma*n*a who drinks spirits;' 'Spirit-drinking worms grow in the mouth of the spirit-drinking man, because he enjoys what is unlawful.'

31. And hence also a scriptural passage as to non-proceeding according to liking.

There is also a scriptural passage prohibiting unlawful food, the purpose of which it is to stop procedure therein according to one's liking, viz. in the Sa*m*hitâ of the Ka*th*as, 'Therefore a Brâhma*n*a is not to drink spirits.' This text also is more appropriate if we take the passage, 'To him who knows this,' as an arthavâda.—Hence passages of that kind are arthavâdas, not injunctions.

32. The works of the â*s*ramas (are incumbent on him) also (who does not desire release); because they are enjoined.

Under Sûtra 26 it has been proved that the works enjoined on the â*s*ramas are means of knowledge. Now we will consider whether those works have to be performed also by him who does not desire final release and therefore takes his stand on his â*s*rama merely without wishing for knowledge.—Here the pûrvapakshin maintains that as the works incumbent on the â*s*ramas are enjoined as means of knowledge by the passage, 'Him the Brâhma*n*as seek to know by the study of the Veda' &c., the works of permanent obligation are not to be performed by him who, not desirous of knowledge, wishes for some other fruit. Or else they are to be performed by him also; but then they cannot be means of knowledge, since it would be contradictory to attribute to them a permanent and a non-permanent connexion[1].

Against this conclusion the Sûtrakâra remarks that the works of permanent obligation are to be performed by

[1] I.e. we must not think that because they enjoin the 'nityatâ' of certain works, other passages may not enjoin the same works as mere means of knowledge.

him only who, not desirous of release, takes his stand on the â*s*ramas merely, because they are enjoined by texts such 'as long as his life lasts he is to offer the agnihotra.' For to such texts no excessive weight must be ascribed.—The next Sûtra replies to the objection raised above in the words, 'but then they cannot be means of knowledge.'

33. And through the co-operativeness (of the works towards the origination of knowledge).

Those works are also co-operative with knowledge just because they are enjoined as such, viz. in passages such as 'Him the Brâhma*n*as seek to know by the study of the Veda,' &c. This has been explained under Sûtra 26. Nor must you think that the texts stating the co-operation of the works of the â*s*ramas towards knowledge refer to the fruit of knowledge, as e.g. the offerings called prayâ*g*as co-operate towards the fruit of the dàr*s*apûr*n*amâsa of which they are auxiliary members; for knowledge is not characterised by injunction, and the fruit of knowledge is not to be effected by means. Means characterised by injunctions such as the dar*s*apûr*n*amâsa-sacrifice which aim at bringing about certain fruits such as the heavenly world require other (subordinate) means co-operating towards the fruit (such as the prayâ*g*as). But not so knowledge. Compare on this point Sûtra 25. Therefore texts stating the co-operation of works (with knowledge) have to be interpreted as stating that works are means for the origination of knowledge.—Nor need we fear that thus there arises a contradiction of permanent and non-permanent connexion. For there may be difference of connexion even where there is no difference of work. One connexion is permanent, resting on the texts about the life-long performance of the agnihotra and so on; of this knowledge is not the result. The other connexion is non-permanent, resting on texts such as 'Him the Brâhma*n*as seek to know,' &c.; of this knowledge is the result. The case is analogous to that of the one khadira, which through a permanent connexion serves the purpose of the sacrifice, and through a non-permanent connexion the purpose of man.

34. In any case the same (duties have to be performed) on account of the twofold indicatory marks.

In any case, i. e. whether viewed as duties incumbent on the âsramas or as co-operating with knowledge, the very same agnihotra and other duties have to be performed.—What, it may be asked, does the teacher wish to preclude by the emphatic expression 'the very same?'—The suspicion, we reply, that those works might be separate works[1]. In the ayana of the Ku*nd*apâyins indeed the injunctive statement, 'They offer the agnihotra for a month[2],' enjoins a sacrifice different from the permanent (ordinary) agnihotra; but in our present case there is no analogous separation of works.—Why?—On account of the twofold indicatory mark; i. e. on account of both scripture and Sm*ri*ti supplying indicatory marks. In the first place, the scriptural passage, 'Him the Brâhma*n*as seek to know through the study of the Veda,' &c., directs that sacrifices and the like—as things already established and the form of which is already in existence (viz. through previous injunctions)—are to be employed as means in the search for knowledge; and does not originate a new form of those works, while the passage quoted above, 'They offer the agnihotra for a month,' does originate a new separate sacrifice.—In the second place the Sm*ri*ti-passage, 'He who performs the work to be done without aiming at the fruit of the work,' shows that the very same work which is already known as something to be performed subserves the origination of knowledge. Moreover the Sm*ri*ti-passage, 'He who is qualified by those forty-eight purifications,' &c., refers to the purifications required for Vedic works, with a view to the origination of knowledge in him who has undergone those purifications.—The Sûtrakâra therefore rightly emphasizes the non-difference of the works.

---

[1] That the works referred to in the Upanishads as means of knowledge, might be works altogether different from those enjoined in the karmakâ*nd*a as means of bringing about certain special results such as the heavenly world.

[2] See above, p. 250.

35. And scripture also declares that (those performing works) are not overpowered (by passion and the like).

This Sûtra points out a further indicatory mark fortifying the conclusion that works co-operate towards knowledge. Scripture also shows that he who is furnished with such means as Brahma*k*arya, &c., is not overpowered by such afflictions as passion and the like. Compare the passage, 'That Self does not perish which they find out by Brahma*k*arya' (*Kh.* Up. VIII, 5, 3).—It is thus a settled conclusion that sacrifices and so on are works incumbent on the â*s*ramas as well as co-operative towards knowledge.

36. But also (persons standing) between (are qualified for knowledge); for that is seen (in scripture).

A doubt arises whether persons in want who do not possess means, &c., and therefore are not able to enter one or the other of the â*s*ramas, standing between as it were, are qualified for knowledge or not.—They are not qualified, the pûrvapakshin maintains. For we have ascertained that the works incumbent on the â*s*ramas are the cause of knowledge, and those persons have no opportunity to perform those works.—To this the Sûtrakâra replies, 'But also between.' Even a person who because he does not belong to an â*s*rama stands between, as it were, is qualified for knowledge. 'For that is seen.' For we meet with scriptural passages declaring that persons of that class—such as Raikva and the daughter of Va*k*aknu—possessed the knowledge of Brahman (*Kh.* Up. IV, 1; B*ri*. Up. III, 6, 8).

37. This is stated in Sm*ri*ti also.

It is recorded in itihâsas also how Sa*m*varta and others who paid no regard to the duties incumbent on the â*s*ramas, in going naked and so on, became great Yogins all the same.—But the instances quoted from scripture and Sm*ri*ti furnish merely indicatory marks; what then is the final conclusion?—That conclusion is stated in the next Sûtra.

38. And the promotion (of knowledge is bestowed on them) through special acts.

Also for widowers, &c., the favour of knowledge is possible through special acts of duty, such as praying, fasting, propitiation of divinities, &c., which are not opposed to their â*s*rama-less condition and may be performed by any man as such. Thus Sm*ri*ti says, 'By mere prayer no doubt the Brâhma*n*a perfects himself. May he perform other works or not, the kindhearted one is called Brâhma*n*a' (Manu Sa*m*h. II, 87), which passage shows that where the works of the â*s*ramas are not possible prayer qualifies for knowledge. Moreover knowledge may be promoted by â*s*rama works performed in previous births. Thus Sm*ri*ti also declares, 'Perfected by many births he finally goes the highest way' (Bha. Gîtâ VI, 45); which passage shows that the aggregate of the different purificatory ceremonies performed in former births promotes knowledge.—Moreover knowledge—as having a seen result (viz. the removal of ignorance)—qualifies any one who is desirous of it for learning and so on, through the mere absence of obstacles[1]. Hence there is no contradiction in admitting qualification for knowledge on the part of widowers and the like.

39. Better than this is the other (state of belonging to an â*s*rama), on account of the indicatory marks.

'Than this,' i.e. 'than standing between,' a better means of knowledge it is to stand within one of the â*s*ramas, since this is confirmed by *S*ruti and Sm*ri*ti. For scripture supplies an indicatory mark in the passage, 'On that path goes whoever knows Brahman and who has done holy

[1] I.e. any one who wishes to learn may do so, if only there is no obstacle in the way. No special injunction is wanted.

works (as prescribed for the âsramas) and obtained splendour' (B*ri*. Up. IV, 4, 9); and Sm*ri*ti in the passage, 'Let a Brâhma*n*a stay not one day even outside the âsrama; having stayed outside for a year he goes to utter ruin.'

40. But of him who has become that (i.e. entered on a higher âsrama) there is no becoming not that (i.e. descending to a lower one), according to *G*aimini also, on account of restrictive rule, absence of such like (i.e. statements of descent), and non-existence (of good custom).

It has been established that there are stages of life for which chastity is obligatory. A doubt here arises whether one who has entered them may for some reason or other fall from them or not.—The pûrvapakshin maintains that as there is no difference a person may descend to a lower stage, either from the wish of well performing the duties of that stage, or influenced by passion and the like.—To this we reply as follows, 'Of him who has become that,' i.e. of him who has reached the stages for which chastity is obligatory, there is no 'becoming not that,' i.e. descending thence.—Why?—'On account of restrictive rule, absence of such like, and non-existence.' That means: there are, in the first place, restrictive rules declaring that a descent may not take place. Compare 'for life mortifying the body in the house of a tutor' (*Kh*. Up. II, 23, 2); 'He is to go into the forest, that is he is not to return thence, that is the Upanishad;' 'Having been dismissed by the teacher he is to follow one of the four âsramas, according to rule, up to release from the body.'—In the second place there are texts teaching the ascent to higher âsramas ('Having completed the Brahma*k*arya state he is to become a householder; he may wander forth from the Brahma*k*arya state'); but there are none teaching the descent to lower âsramas.—And in the third place there exists no good custom of that kind.—The descent to a lower âsrama can in no way be based on the wish of well performing the duties of that âsrama; for

Smriti says, 'One's own duty, however badly performed, is better than another duty well carried out' (Bha. Gîtâ III, 35). And the principle is that whatever is enjoined on a certain person constitutes his duty, not what a person is able to perform well; for all duty is characterised by injunction. Nor is a descent allowed owing to the influence of passion, &c.; for restrictive rules are weightier than passion.—By the word 'also' the Sûtrakâra indicates the consensus of *G*aimini and Bâdarâya*n*a on this point, in order to confirm thereby the view adopted.

41. And not also (can the expiation take place) prescribed in the chapter treating of qualification, because on account of the inference of his lapse from Sm*ri*ti he (the Naish*th*ika) is not capable of it.

If a Brahma*k*ârin for life breaks from inattention the vow of chastity, is he to perform the expiatory sacrifice enjoined by the text, 'A student who has broken the vow of chastity shall sacrifice an ass to Nir*ri*ti[1]' or not?—He is not, the pûrvapakshin says. For although in the chapter which treats of qualification (Pû. Mîm. Sû. VI, 8, 22) that expiatory ceremony has been settled (for Brahma*k*ârins in general), it does not yet hold good for the professed Brahma*k*ârin. For Sm*ri*ti declares that such sins cannot be expiated by him any more than a head once cut off can again be healed on to the body, 'He who having once entered on the duties of a Naish*th*ika again lapses from them, for him—a slayer of the Self—I see no expiation which might make him clean again.' The Upakurvâ*n*a (i.e. he who is a Brahma*k*ârin for a certain time only, not for life) on the other hand, about whose sin Sm*ri*ti makes no similar declaration, may purify himself by the ceremony mentioned.

42. But some (consider the sin) a minor one, (and

[1] Cp. e.g. Âpastamba Dharma-sûtra I, 9, 26, 8. The passage quoted in the text is, however, a scriptural one.

hence claim) the existence (of expiation for the Naishthika also); as in the case of the eating (of unlawful food). This has been explained (in the Pûrva Mîmâmsâ).

Some teachers, however, are of opinion that the transgression of the vow of chastity, even on the part of a professed Brahmakârin, is a minor sin, not a mortal one, excepting cases where the wife of the teacher and so on are concerned. For they plead that that sin is not anywhere enumerated among the deadly ones such as violating a teacher's bed and so on. Accordingly they claim the expiatory ceremony to be valid for the Naishthika as well as the Upakurvâna; both being alike Brahmakârins and having committed the same offence. The case is analogous to that of eating. Just as Brahmakârins (in general) who have broken their vow by eating honey, flesh, and the like may again purify themselves by a ceremony, so here also.—The reason for this decision is that for those who assume the absence of all expiation on the part of the Naishthikas no scriptural passage supporting their view is met with; while those who admit expiation can base their view on the passage quoted above ('A student who has broken the vow' &c.), which makes no distinction between Upakurvânas and Naishthikas. It therefore is more appropriate to assume the validity of the ceremony for Naishthikas also. The principle guiding the decision has been explained in the chapter treating of the means of right knowledge (Pû. Mî. Sû. I, 3, 8).—On this view the Smriti-passage which declares that there is no expiation for the Naishthika must be explained as aiming at the origination of weighty effort on the Naishthika's part.—Similarly in the case of the mendicant and the hermit. The hermit, when he has broken his vows, undergoes the Krikkhra penance for twelve nights and then cultivates a place rich in plants. The mendicant proceeds like the hermit, with the exception of cultivating the Soma-plant, and undergoes the purifications prescribed for his state. The rules given by Smriti for those cases have to be followed.

43. But (they are to be kept outside) in either case, on account of Sm*ri*ti and custom.

But whether lapses from the duties of one's order, committed by those who are bound to chastity, be mortal sins or minor sins, in either case such persons are to be excluded by honourable men (*s*ish*t*as). For Sm*ri*ti refers to them in terms of the highest reproach; cp. passages such as the one quoted under Sûtra 41; and the following one, 'He who touches a Brâhma*n*a that has broken his vow and fallen from his order, or a hanged man or one gnawed by worms must undergo the *K*ândrâya*n*a penance.' And good custom also condemns them; for good men do not sacrifice, study, or attend weddings with such persons.

44. To the lord (of the sacrifice) only (the agentship in meditations belongs), because scripture declares a fruit; this is the view of Âtreya.

With regard to meditations on subordinate members of sacrificial actions there arises a doubt whether they are to be carried out by the sacrificer (i.e. him for whom the sacrifice is performed) or by the officiating priests.—By the sacrificer, the pûrvapakshin maintains, because scripture declares fruits. For a fruit is declared in such texts as the following one, 'There is rain for him, and he brings rain for others who thus knowing meditates on the fivefold Sâman as rain' (*Kh.* Up. II, 3, 2); and we must conclude that that fruit goes to the Lord of the sacrifice, because it is he who is entitled to the sacrificial performance together with its subordinate members, and because such meditations fall within the sphere of that to which he is entitled. And that the fruit belongs to him who carries out the meditations scripture states when saying, 'There is rain for him who meditates.'—But scripture declares a fruit for the priest also, viz. in the passage, 'Whatever desire he may desire either for himself or for the sacrificer he obtains by his singing.'—That passage, we reply, is of no force because it expressly declares the fruit (as belonging to the priest in a special case only). Hence the lord of the sacrifice only is the agent in those meditations which have a fruit, this is the opinion of the teacher Âtreya.

45. (They are) the work of the priest, this is the view of Au*d*ulomi; since for that (i.e. the entire sacrificial work) he is feed.

The assertion that the meditations on subordinate members of the sacrifice are the work of the sacrificer is unfounded. They rather are the work of the priest, as the teacher Au*d*ulomi thinks. For the priest is rewarded for the work together with its subordinate members; and the meditations on the udgîtha and so on fall within the performance of the work since they belong to the sphere of that to which the person entitled (viz. the lord of the sacrifice) is entitled. Hence they are to be carried out by the priests only, the case being analogous to that of the restrictive rule as to the work to be performed by means of the godohana vessel. In agreement herewith scripture declares the udgât*ri* to be the agent in knowledge, in the following passage, 'Him Vaka Dâlbhya knew. He was the udgât*ri* of the Naimishîya-sacrificers' (*Kh*. Up. I, 2, 13). With reference to the circumstance noted by the pûrvapakshin that scripture states the fruit to belong to the agent, we remark that this makes no difference: for with the exception of cases expressly stated the priest cannot be connected with the sacrifice since he subserves the purposes (acts for) another (viz. the lord of the sacrifice).

46. And on account of scriptural statement.

'Whatever blessing the priests pray for at the sacrifice, they pray for the good of the sacrificer; thus he said' (*S*at. Brâ. I, 3, 1, 26); 'Therefore an udgât*ri* who knows this may say: what wish shall I obtain for you by my singing?' (*Kh*. Up. I, 7, 8). These scriptural passages also declare that the fruit of meditations in which the priest is the agent goes to the sacrificer.—All this establishes the conclusion that the meditations on subordinate parts of the sacrifice are the work of the priest.

47. There is the injunction of something else co-operating (towards knowledge) (which is) a third thing (with regard to bâlya and pâ*nd*itya), (which injunction is given) for the case (of perfect knowledge not yet having arisen) to him who is such (i. e. the Sa*m*nyâsin possessing knowledge); as in the case of injunctions and the like.

'Therefore let a Brâhma*n*a after he has done with learning wish to stand by a childlike state; and after he has done with the childlike state and learning (he is, or, may be) a Muni; and after he has done with what constitutes Muniship and non-Muniship (he is, or, may be) a Brâhma*n*a' (B*ri*. Up. III, 5). With reference to this passage a doubt arises whether it enjoins the state of a Muni or not.—The pûrvapakshin maintains that it does not enjoin it, since the injunction is completed with the clause, 'Let him wish to stand by a childlike state.' The following clause 'then a Muni' contains no verbal form of injunctive force and therefore must be viewed as a mere anuvâda (making a remark concerning the state of a Muni which is already established). Should it be asked how this conclusion is reached, we reply that Muniship is established by the clause 'having done with learning' (which forms part of the injunctive portion of the passage), as 'Muni' and 'learned man' both denote knowledge [1]. It is, moreover, clear also that the last clause, 'and after he has done with what constitutes Muniship and non-Muniship (he is) a Brâhma*n*a,' does not enjoin the condition of a Brâhma*n*a, as that state is previously established (independently of that clause); but the words 'then a Brâhma*n*a' are a mere glorificatory anuvâda. Now as the words 'then a Muni' show an analogous form of enunciation (to the clause 'then a Brâhma*n*a'), they also can embody a glorificatory anuvâda only.

[1] The state of a Muni is already enjoined by the clause 'pâ*nd*ítya*m* nirvidya;' the clause 'atha muni*h*,' therefore, may be viewed as an anuvâda (as which it could not be viewed, if there were no previous injunction of mauna).

To all this we reply as follows. 'There is an injunction of something else which co-operates.' The passage must be understood as enjoining the state of a Muni—which co-operates towards knowledge—in the same way as it enjoins learning and a childlike state, because that state is something new (not enjoined before).—But it has been said above that the word 'learning' already intimates Muniship!—This, we reply, does not invalidate our case since the word 'muni' denotes (not only knowledge as the term 'learned man' does, but) pre-eminence of knowledge, on the ground as well of its etymology from 'manana,' i.e. thinking, as of common use, shown in such phrases as 'I am the Vyâsa of Munis also.'—But the term 'Muni' is also seen to denote the last order of life; cp. passages such as 'Householdership, studentship, the order of Munis, the order of hermits in the woods.'—Yes, but it has not that meaning exclusively, as we see that it does not apply to phrases such as 'Valmîki is the foremost among Munis.' In the passage quoted (about the four orders) the last order is referred to, by the term 'Muni,' because there it stands in proximity to the other orders of life, and, as the state of the Ascetic is the only one which remains (after we have assigned the three other terms to the stages of life clearly denoted by them), the last order may be denoted 'mauna' because knowledge is its principal requirement.—We therefore conclude that in the passage under discussion the state of the Muni—whose characteristic mark is pre-eminence of knowledge—is enjoined as something third—with regard to the childlike state and learning.—Against the objection that the injunction terminates with the childlike state, we remark that all the same we must view the Muniship also as something enjoined, as it is something new, so that we have to supplement the clause as follows: 'then *he is to be* a Muni.' That the state of a Muni is something to be enjoined, in the same way as the childlike state and learning, also follows from its being referred to as something to be done with (like bâlya and pâ*nd*itya). It is enjoined 'on him who is such,' i.e. on the Sa*m*nyâsin possessing knowledge.—How do we know this latter point?—Because the Sa*m*nyâsin who possesses knowledge forms the topic, as we see from the preceding passage, 'Having cognized the Self and risen above the desire for sons, &c., they wander about as mendicants.'—But if the Sa*m*nyâsin possesses knowledge, pre-eminence of knowledge is already established thereby; what then is the use of the injunction of Muniship?—To this the Sûtra replies 'in the case of.' That means: in the case of pre-eminence of knowledge not being established owing to the prevailing force of the (erroneous) idea of multiplicity; for that case the injunction (of Muniship, i.e. of pre-eminence of knowledge) is given. 'As in the case of injunctions and the like.' With reference to sacrifices such as are enjoined in the passage, 'He who is desirous of the heavenly world is to offer the dar*s*apûr*n*amâsa-sacrifice,' the aggregate of subordinate members, such as the establishment of the sacred fires, is enjoined as something helpful; similarly in this text whose topic is knowledge and which therefore does not chiefly aim at injunction, Muniship is enjoined as something helpful to knowledge.

As thus the order of the ascetic, as distinguished by a childlike state and so on, is actually established by scripture, for what reason does the *Kh*ândogya Upanishad wind up with the householder, viz. in the passage, 'After having received his discharge from his teacher he settles in his own house,' &c.? For by concluding with the householder, scripture manifests special regard for him.—To this doubt th next Sûtra replies.

48. On aco nt of his being all, however, there is winding up with the householder.

The word 'however' is meant to lay stress on the householder's being everything. For the performance of many works belonging to his own â*s*rama, such as sacrifices and the like, which involve not a little trouble, is enjoined on him by scripture, and at the same time the duties of the other â*s*ramas—such as tenderness for all living creatures, restraint of the senses and so on—are incumbent on him also as far as circumstances allow. There is therefore nothing contradictory in the *Kh*ândogya winding up with the householder.

49. On account of there being injunction of the others also, in the same way as of the state of a Muni.

As the state of the Muni (Sa*m*nyâsin) and the state of the householder are enjoined in scripture, so also the two other orders, viz. that of the hermit and that of the student. For we have already pointed above to passages such as 'Austerity is the second, and to dwell as a student in the house of a teacher is the third.' As thus the four â*s*ramas are equally taught by scripture, they are to be gone through equally, either in the way of option (between them) or in the way of comprehension (of all of them).—That the Sûtra uses a plural form (of 'the others') when speaking of two orders only, is due to its having regard either to the different sub-classes of those two, or to their different duties.

50. (The passage enjoining bâlya means that the ascetic is to live) not manifesting himself; on account of the connexion (thus gained for the passage).

The passage, 'Therefore let a Brâhma*n*a after he has done with learning wish to stand by a childlike state,' speaks of the childlike state as something to be undertaken. Now by the 'childlike state' we have to understand either the nature or the actions of a child. Childhood in so far as it means a period of life cannot be brought about at will, and we therefore must take the 'childlike state' to mean either the behaviour of a child—such as attending to the calls of nature without any respect of place, &c.—or inward purity, i. e. absence of cunning, arrogance, force of the sensual passions, and so on [1].—With regard to the

[1] I am doubtful as to the true reading in this place. The 'va' of the Calcutta edition (p. 1039, last line) has certainly to be struck

doubt thus arising the pûrvapakshin maintains that by 'childlike being' people more commonly understand behaving, talking, and eating according to one's liking, freely attending to the calls of nature and so on, and that therefore the word is to be understood here also in that sense.—But such free conduct is improper, because sinfulness and so on would follow from it!—Not so, the pûrvapakshin replies; for the Sa*m*nyâsin possessing knowledge is, through express scriptural statements, free from all sinfulness thus incurred; just as the sacrificer is declared to be free from the sin he might incur in slaying the sacrificial animal.

To this we reply that it is not so because the statement of the text may be understood in a different sense. For as long as another rational interpretation of the word 'bâlya' is possible we have no right to adopt an interpretation which involves the assumption of another injunction being rendered futile. Moreover subordinate matters are enjoined with a view to the furtherance of the principal matter, and what here is the principal matter is the endeavour after knowledge which ascetics have to take upon themselves. Now if we accepted the entire conduct of a child as what is enjoined here we could in no way show that the endeavour of knowledge is furthered thereby. We therefore understand by 'bâlya' the special inward state of a child, i.e. absence of strong sensual passions and the like. This the Sûtra expresses by saying 'Not manifesting.' The meaning of the clause under discussion thus is: Let him be free from guile, pride, and so on, not manifesting himself by a display of knowledge, learning, and virtuousness, just as a child whose sensual powers have not yet developed themselves does not strive to make a display of himself before others. For thus the passage gains a connexion with the entire chapter on the ground of co-operating towards the principal matter. In agreement herewith Sm*ri*ti-writers have said, 'He whom nobody knows either

out. Some good MSS. read:—bâla*k*aritam antargatâ· bhâvavi*s*uddhir aprarû*dh*endriyatva*m* dambhâdirahitatva*m* vâ.—The 'antargatâ' seems to mean the same as the 'ântara*h*,' p. 1041, ll. 1–2.

as noble or ignoble, as ignorant or learned, as well-conducted or ill-conducted, he is a Brâhma*n*a. Quietly devoted to his duty, let the wise man pass through life unknown; let him step on this earth as if he were blind, unconscious, deaf.' Another similar passage is, 'With hidden nature, hidden conduct,' and so on.

51. In this life also (the origination of knowledge takes place) if there is no obstruction of what is ready at hand; on account of this being seen (in scripture).

Beginning from Sûtra 26 of the present pâda we have discussed the various means of knowledge. We are now to consider whether knowledge—the fruit of those means—when accomplishing itself accomplishes itself only here in this life, or sometimes in the next life only.—The pûrvapakshin maintains that it accomplishes itself here in this life only. For, he argues, knowledge has for its antecedent the learning of scripture and so on, and nobody applies himself to learning, &c., with the intention that knowledge should result therefrom in the next life only; we rather observe that men begin to learn with a view to knowledge already springing up in this life. And also sacrifices and the like produce knowledge only mediately through learning and so on; for knowledge can be produced (directly) through the means of right knowledge only[1]. Hence the origination of knowledge takes place in this life only.—To this we reply, 'The origination of knowledge takes place in this life if there is no obstruction of that which is ready at hand.' That means: When the means of knowledge which is operative is not obstructed by some other work the results of which are just then reaching maturity, knowledge already reaches maturity in this life.

[1] Of which study is one.—Sacrifices indeed may bear their special fruits in the next life only; but in so far as they co-operate towards knowledge they are effective in this life. For their only action in that line is to purify the mind and thus to render it fitter to receive knowledge.

But when such an obstruction takes place, then in the next life. And a work's reaching maturity depends on place, time, and operative cause presenting themselves. Nor is there any binding rule according to which the same time, place, and operative cause which ripen one work should ripen another work also; for there are works the fruits of which are opposed to each other. And scripture also goes only so far as to teach what the fruit of each work is, without teaching the special conditions of place time, and operative cause. And owing to the specific strength of the means employed the supersensuous power of one work manifests itself (i. e. the fruit of that work realizes itself), while that of another is obstructed thereby and comes to a standstill.

Nor is there any reason why a man should not form, with regard to knowledge, an unspecified intention[1]; for we may freely form the intention that knowledge should spring up from us either in this life or in some subsequent life. And knowledge although springing up through the mediation of learning and so on, springs up only in so far as learning destroys the obstacles in the way of knowledge. Thus scripture also declares the difficulty of knowing the Self, 'He of whom many are not even able to hear, whom many even when they hear of him do not comprehend; wonderful is a man when found who is able to teach him; wonderful is he who comprehends him when taught by an able teacher' (Ka. Up. I, 2, 7).—Moreover scripture relates that Vâmadeva already became Brahman in his mother's womb, and thus shows that knowledge may spring up in a later form of existence through m ans procured in a former one; for a child in the womb cannot possibly procure such means in its present state.

The same is shown by Sm*ri*ti. Vâsudeva being asked by Ar*g*una, 'What will be the fate of him O K*ri*sh*n*a, who has not reached perfection?' replies, 'None who performs good works undergoes an evil fate;' declares thereupon

[1] I. e. there is no reason for the assertion made by the pûrvapakshin that men form a specified intention only, viz. that knowledge should spring up in this life only.

that such a man reaches the world of the blessed and is, later on, born again in a good family; and finally states just what we at present maintain in the passage beginning, 'There he obtains that knowledge which corresponds to his former bodily existence,' and closing, 'Perfected by many states of existence he then goes the highest way.'—It therefore is an established conclusion that knowledge originates, either in the present or in a future life, in dependence on the evanescence of obstacles.

52. No such definite rule (exists) as to the fruit which is release, on account of the assertions as to that condition, on account of the assertions as to that condition.

We have seen that in the case of persons desirous of release who rely upon the means of knowledge there exists a definite difference of result. in so far as the knowledge resulting springs up either in this life or a future life according to the degree of strength of the means employed. It might now be supposed that there exists a similar definite difference with regard to the fruit characterised as final release, owing to the superior or inferior qualification of the persons knowing.

With reference to this possible doubt the Sûtra now says, 'No such definite rule as to that fruit which is release.' That means: We must not suppose that in the case of that fruit which is release there exists an analogous definite rule of difference.—Why?—'On account of the assertions (by scripture) about that condition.' For all Vedânta-texts assert the state of final release to be of one kind only. The state of final release is nothing but Brahman, and Brahman cannot be connected with different forms since many scriptural passages assert it to have one nature only. Compare e.g. 'It is neither coarse nor fine' (B*ri*. Up. III, 8, 8); 'That Self is to be described by No, no' (B*ri*. Up. III, 9, 26); 'Where one sees nothing else' (*Kh*. Up. VII, 24, 1); 'That immortal Brahman is before' (Mu. Up. II, 2, 11); 'This everything is that Self' (B*ri*. Up. II, 4, 6);

'This great unborn Self, undecaying, undying, immortal, fearless, is indeed Brahman' (B*ri*. Up. IV, 4, 25); 'When the Self only is all this how should he see another?' (B*ri*. Up. IV, 5, 15).—Moreover the means of knowledge might perhaps, according to their individual strength, impart a higher (or lower) degree to their result, viz. knowledge, but not to the result of knowledge, viz. release; for, as we have explained more than once, release is not something which is to be brought about, but something whose nature is permanently established, and is reached through knowledge. Nor does, in reality, knowledge admit of lower or higher degree; for it is, in its own nature, high only, and would not be knowledge at all if it were low. Although therefore knowledge may differ in so far as it originates after a long or short time, it is impossible that release should be distinguished by a higher or lower degree. And from the absence of difference of knowledge also there follows absence of definite distinction on the part of the result of knowledge (viz. release). The whole case is analogous to that of the results of works. In that knowledge which is the means of release there is no difference as there is between works. In those cognitions, on the other hand, which have the qualified Brahman for its object—such as 'he who consists of mind, whose body is prâ*n*a'—a difference is possible according to the addition or omission of qualities, and hence there may be a definite distinction of results, just as there is between the results of actions. This is also indicated by the passage, 'according as they meditate on him they become.' But in meditations on Brahman devoid of qualities it is otherwise. Thus Sm*ri*ti also says, 'No higher road is possible for any one; for they speak of inequality only where there are qualities.'—The repetition of the clause 'on account of the assertions as to that condition' indicates the termination of the adhyâya.

FOURTH ADHYÂYA.

FIRST PÂDA.

REVERENCE TO THE HIGHEST SELF!

1. Repetition (of the mental functions of knowing, meditating, &c., is required) on account of the text giving instruction more than once.

The third adhyâya was taken up chiefly with a discussion of the means of knowledge as related to the higher and lower vidyâs. In the fourth adhyâya we shall now discuss the fruits of knowledge, and as occasion suggests some other topics also.—In the beginning, however, we shall carry on, in a few adhikara*n*as, a special discussion connected with the means of knowledge. 'Verily the Self is to be seen, to be heard, to be thought, to be reflected on' (B*ri*. Up. II, 4, 5); 'Let a wise Brâhma*n*a after he has discovered him practise wisdom' (B*ri*. Up. IV, 4, 21); 'That it is which we must search out, that it is which we must try to understand' (*Kh*. Up. VIII, 7, 1).

Concerning these and similar passages a doubt arises whether the mental action referred to in them is to be performed once only or repeatedly.—Once only, the pûrvapakshin says; as in the case of the prayâ*g*a-offerings and the like. For thereby the purpose of scripture is accomplished; while to practise repetitions not demanded by scripture would be to accomplish what is not the purpose of scripture.—But passages have been quoted which teach repetition 'it is to be heard, to be thought, to be reflected on,' &c.!—Let us then repeat exactly as scripture says, i. e. let us hear the Self once, let us think it once, let us reflect on it once, and nothing more. But where scripture teaches something once only—viz. in such passages as 'He knows,' 'Let him meditate,' &c.—no repetition has to be practised.—To this we reply as follows. Repetition is to be performed because scripture gives repeated instruction. For the repeated instruction contained in passages such as 'He is to be heard, to be thought, to be reflected on' intimates the repetition of the required mental acts.—But the pûrvapakshin has said above that the repetition is to extend exactly to what scripture says and not to go further!—This is wrong, we reply, because all those mental activities have for their end intuition. For hearing and so on when repeated terminate in intuition, and thus subserve a seen purpose, just as the action of beating, &c., terminates in freeing the rice grains from their husks. Moreover also such terms as 'meditating,' 'being devoted to,' and 'reflecting' denote actions in which repetition is implied as a quality. Thus we say in ordinary life that a person 'is devoted' to a teacher or a king if he follows him with a mind steadily set on him; and of a wife whose husband has gone on a journey we say that she thinks of him, only if she steadily remembers him with longing. And (that also 'knowing' implies repetition, follows from the fact that) in the Vedânta-texts the terms 'knowing' and 'meditating' are seen to be used one in the place of the other. In some passages the term 'knowing' is used in the beginning and the term 'meditating' in the end; thus e.g. 'He who knows what he knows is thus spoken of by me,' and 'Teach me, sir, the deity which you meditate on' (*Kh.* Up. IV, 1, 4; 2, 2). In other places the text at first speaks of 'meditating' and later on of 'knowing;' thus e.g. 'Let a man meditate on mind as Brahman,' and 'He who knows this shines and warms through his celebrity, fame, and glory of countenance' (*Kh.* Up. III, 18, 1; 6).—From this it follows that repetition has to be practised there also, where the text gives instruction once only. Where, again, the text gives repeated instruction, repeated performance of the mental acts is directly intimated.

2. And on account of an indicatory mark.

An indicatory mark also gives to understand that repetition is required. For, in the section treating of meditation on the udgîtha, the text rejects the meditation on the udgîtha viewed as the sun, because its result is one sun only, and (in the clause 'Do thou resolve his rays,' &c.) enjoins a meditation on his manifold rays as leading to the possession of many suns (*Kh*. Up. I, 5, 1; 2); which shows that the repetition of meditations is something well known. Now as other meditations are meditations no less than the one referred to, it follows that repetition holds good for all of them.

Here the following objection may be raised. With regard to those meditations whose fruit is something to be effected repetition may hold good, because thereby superior strength may be imparted to them. But of what use can repetition be with regard to the meditations having for their object the highest Brahman, which present to us Brahman as the universal Self characterised by eternal purity, thought, and freedom? Should it be said that repetition has to be allowed because the knowledge of Brahman being the Self cannot spring up on hearing a text once only, we reply that in that case it will not spring up even when it is heard repeatedly. For if a text such as 'Thou art that' does not originate the true notion of Brahman if heard once, what hope is there that the desired effect should be produced by its repetition?—Perhaps it will be said that a sentence alone is not able to lead to the intuition of a thing; but that a sentence assisted by reasoning may enable us to intuite Brahman as the universal Self. But even in that case repetition would be useless; for the reasoning will lead to the desired intuition even if gone through once only.—Again it will perhaps be said that the sentence and reasoning together effect only a cognition of the generic nature of the object known, not of its specific individual character. When, to exemplify this, a man says that he feels a pain in his heart another person can infer from this statement—and certain accompanying symptoms such as trembling of the limbs—only that there exists a pain in general but is unable to intuite its specific character; all he knows is 'This man suffers a pain.' But what removes ignorance is (not a general knowledge but) the intuitive knowledge of the specific character of something. And repetition serves to produce such knowledge.—This also is not so. For if so much only is done repeatedly even, no specific knowledge can spring up. When a specific character is not cognized through scripture and reasoning being applied once, it will not be cognized through them if applied a hundred times even. Hence whether scripture and reasoning produce specific knowledge or general knowledge, in either case they will do so even if acting once only; and repetition therefore is of no use. Nor can it be laid down as a binding rule that scripture and reasoning, applied once, in no case produce intuitive knowledge; for their effect will after all depend on the various degrees of intelligence of those who wish to learn. Moreover a certain use of repetition may be admitted in the case of worldly things which consist of several parts and possess generic character as well as individual difference; for there the student may grasp by one act of attention one part of the object, and by another act another part; so e.g. in the case of long chapters to be studied. But in order to reach a true knowledge of Brahman whose Self is mere intelligence and which therefore is destitute of generic character as well as specific difference there clearly is no need of repetition.

To this we make the following reply. Repetition would indeed be useless for him who is able to cognize the true nature of Brahman even if enounced once only in the sentence 'Thou art that.' But he who is not able to do that, for him repetition is of use. For this reason the teacher in the *Kh*ândogya, having given instruction in the sentence 'Thou art that, O *S*vetaketu,' and being again and again asked by his pupil—'Please, sir, inform me still more'—removes his pupil's reasons for doubt, and again and again repeats the instruction 'Thou art that.' We have already given an analogous explanation of the passage 'The Self is to be heard, to be thought, to be reflected upon.'—But has not the pûrvapakshin declared that if the first enunciation of the sentence 'Thou art that' is not able to effect an intuition of its sense, repetition will likewise fail of the desired effect?—This objection, we reply, is without force, because the alleged impossibility is not confirmed by observation. For we observe that men by again and again repeating a sentence which they, on the first hearing, had understood imperfectly only, gradually rid themselves of all misconceptions and arrive at a full understanding of the true sense.—Moreover the sentence 'Thou art that' teaches that what is denoted by the term 'thou' is identical with what is denoted by 'that.' Now the latter term denotes the subject of the entire section, viz. the thinking Brahman which is the cause of the origin and so on of the world; which is known from other passages such as 'Brahman which is true knowledge, infinite' (Taitt. Up. II, 1); 'Brahman that is knowledge and bliss' (B*ri*. Up. III, 9, 28); 'That Brahman is unseen, but seeing; unknown, but knowing' (B*ri*. Up. III, 8, 11); 'not produced' (Mu. Up. II, 1, 2); 'not subject to old age, not subject to death' (B*ri*. Up. IV, 4, 25); 'not coarse, not fine; not short, not long' (B*ri*. Up. III, 8, 8). In these passages terms such as 'not produced' deny the different phases of existence such as origination; such terms as 'not coarse' deny of it the qualities of substances such as coarseness; and such terms as 'knowledge' declare that the luminousness of intelligence constitutes its nature. The entity thus described—which is free from all the qualities of transmigratory existence, has consciousness for its Self and is called Brahman—is known, by all students of the Vedânta, as what is denoted by the term 'that.' They likewise know that what is denoted by the term 'thou' is the inward Self (pratyagâtman); which is the agent in seeing and hearing, is (successively) apprehended as the inward Self of all the outward involucra beginning with the gross body (cp. Taitt. Up.), and finally ascertained as of the nature of intelligence. Now in the case of those persons for whom the meaning of these two terms is obstructed by ignorance, doubt, and misconception, the sentence 'Thou art that' cannot produce a right knowledge of its sense, since the knowledge of the sense of a sentence presupposes the knowledge of the sense of the words; for them therefore the repetition of the scriptu text and of reasoning must be assumed to have a purpose, viz. the discernment of the true sense of the words.—And although the object to be known, viz. the Self, does not consist of parts, yet men wrongly superimpose upon it the attribute of being made up of many parts, such as the body, the senses, the manas, the buddhi, the objects of the senses, the sensations, and so on. Now by one act of attention we may discard one of these parts, and by another act of attention another part; so that a successively progressing cognition may very well take place. This however is merely an antecedent of the (true) knowledge of the Self (in which there can be no successive stages).

Those quick-witted persons, on the other hand, in whose mind the sense of the words is not obstructed by ignorance, doubt, and misconception, are able to intuite the sense of the sentence 'Thou art that' on its first enunciation even, and for them therefore repetition is not required. For the knowledge of the Self having once sprung up discards all ignorance; so that in this case no progressive process of cognition can be acknowledged.—All this might be so—an objection is raised—if cognition did spring up in any mind in the way described. (But this is not the case); for the cognition of the Self being subject to pain and so on has such strength that nobody ever reaches the cognition of all absence of pain and so on.—This objection, we reply, is without force; for it can be shown that the conceit of the Self being subject to pain, &c., is a wrong conceit, no less than the conceit of the body being the Self. For we clearly observe that when the body is cut or burned a wrong notion springs up, 'I am being cut,' 'I am being burned;' and similarly we observe that when sons, friends, &c.—who are even more external to the Self than one's own body—suffer affliction, that affliction is wrongly attributed to the Self. Analogous to these cases is the conceit of the Self being subject to pain, &c.; for like the body and so on, the condition of being subject to pain is observed as something external to intelligence. This moreover follows from its not being continued in such states as dreamless sleep and the like; while scripture expressly declares that in deep sleep intelligence suffers no interruption, 'And when there he does not see, yet he is seeing,' &c. (B*ri*. Up. IV, 3, 22). Hence the intuition of the Self consists in the knowledge, 'My Self is pure intelligence free from all pain.' For him who possesses that knowledge there remains no other work. Thus scripture says, 'What shall we do with offspring, we who have this Self and this world' (B*ri*. Up. IV, 4, 22). And Sm*ri*ti also says, 'But that man who loves the Self, is satisfied by the Self and has all his longings stilled by the Self only, for him there is no further work' (Bha. Gîtâ III, 12).—For him, on the other hand, who does not reach that intuition all at once, we admit repetition, in order that the desired intuition may be brought about. He also, however, must not be moved towards repetition in such a way as to make him lose the true sense of the teaching, 'Thou art that.' In the mind of one on whom repetition is enjoined as a duty, there arise infallibly notions opposed to the true notion of Brahman, such as 'I have a claim on this (knowledge of the Self) as an agent; this is to be done by me[1].' But if a learner, naturally slow-minded, is about altogether to dismiss from his mind the purport of the sentence, because it does not reveal itself to him, it is permissible to fortify him in the understanding of that sense by means of reasoning on the texts relative to repetition and so on.—All this establishes the conclusion that, also in the case of cognitions of the highest Brahman, the instruction leading to such cognition may be repeated.

3. But as the Self (scriptural texts) acknowledge and make us comprehend (the Lord).

The Sûtrakâra now considers the question whether the highest Self whose characteristics scripture declares is

[1] Care must be taken not to engender in the mind of such a learner the notion that the repeated acts of reflection are incumbent on him as a duty; for such notions would only obstruct the end aimed at, i. e. the intuition that the Self of the meditating man is identical with Brahman's Self, to which no notions of duty or action apply.

to be understood as the 'I' or as different from me.—But how can a doubt arise, considering that scripture exhibits the term 'Self' whose sphere is the inward Self?—This term 'Self'—a reply may be given—may be taken in its primary sense, provided it be possible to view the individual soul and the Lord as non-different; but in the other case the term has to be taken in a secondary (metaphorical) sense only[1].

The purvapakshin maintains that the term 'Self' is not to be taken as meaning the 'I.' For that which possesses the qualities of being free from all evil, &c., cannot be understood as possessing qualities of a contrary nature, nor can that which possesses those contrary qualities be understood as being free from all evil and so on. But the highest Lord possesses the qualities of being free from all evil, &c., and the embodied Self is characterised by qualities of a contrary nature.—Moreover, if the transmigrating soul constituted the Self of the Lord, it would follow that he is no Lord, and thus scripture would lose its meaning; while, if the Lord constituted the Self of the individual soul, the latter would not be entitled (to works and knowledge), and scripture would thus also lose its meaning. The latter assumption would moreover run counter to perception and the other means of proof.—Should it be said that, although the Lord and the soul are different, they yet must be contemplated as identical, on the basis of scripture, just as Vish*n*u and other divinities are contemplated in images and so on; the answer is that this contemplation may take place, but that therefrom we must not conclude that the Lord is the real Self of the transmigrating soul.

To all this we make the following reply. The highest Lord must be understood as the Self. For in a chapter treating of the highest Lord the *G*âbâlas acknowledge him to be the Self, 'Thou indeed I am, O holy divinity; I indeed thou art, O divinity!'—In the same light other

[1] And in that case the identity of the highest Self and the 'I' would not follow from the term 'Self.'

texts have to be viewed, which also acknowledge the Lord as the Self, such as 'I am Brahman' (B*ri*. Up. I, 4, 10). Moreover certain Vedânta-texts make us comprehend the Lord as the Self, 'Thy Self is this which is within all' (B*ri*. Up. III, 4, 1); 'He is thy Self, the ruler within, the immortal' (B*ri*. Up. III, 7, 3); 'That is the True, that is the Self, thou art that' (*Kh*. Up. VI, 8, 7).—Nor can we admit the truth of the assertion, made by the pûrvapakshin, that all these passages teach merely a contemplation (of the Lord) in certain symbols, analogous to the contemplation of Vish*n*u in an image. For that would firstly involve that the texts have not to be understood in their primary sense[1]; and in the second place there is a difference of syntactical form. For where scripture intends the contemplation of something in a symbol, it conveys its meaning through a single enunciation such as 'Brahman is Mind' (*Kh*. Up. III, 18, 1), or 'Brahman is Âditya' (*Kh*. Up. III, 19, 1). But in the passage quoted above, scripture says, 'I am Thou and thou art I.' As here the form of expression differs from that of texts teaching the contemplation of symbols, the passage must be understood as teaching non-difference. This moreover follows from the express prohibition of the view of difference which a number of scriptural texts convey. Compare e.g. 'Now if a man worships another deity, thinking the deity is one and he another, he does not know' (B*ri*. Up. I, 4, 10); 'From death to death goes he who here perceives any diversity' (B*ri*. Up. IV, 4, 19); 'Whosoever looks for anything elsewhere than in the Self is abandoned by everything' (B*ri*. Up. II, 4, 6).—Nor is there any force in the objection that things with contrary qualities cannot be identical; for this opposition of qualities can be shown to be false.—Nor is it true that from our doctrine it would follow that the Lord is not a Lord. For in these matters scripture alone is authoritative, and we, moreover, do not at all admit that scripture teaches the Lord to be the Self of the transmi-

[1] And this is objectionable as long as it has not been demonstrated that the primary meaning is altogether inadmissible.

grating soul, but maintain that by denying the transmigrating character of the soul it aims at teaching that the soul is the Self of the Lord. From this it follows that the non-dual Lord is free from all evil qualities, and that to ascribe to him contrary qualities is an error.—Nor is it true that the doctrine of identity would imply that nobody is entitled to works, &c., and is contrary to perception and so on. For we admit that before true knowledge springs up, the soul is implicated in the transmigratory state, and that this state constitutes the sphere of the operation of perception and so on. On the other hand texts such as 'But when the Self only has become all this, how should he see another?' &c., teach that as soon as true knowledge springs up, perception, &c., are no longer valid.—Nor do we mind your objecting that if perception, &c., cease to be valid, scripture itself ceases to be so; for this conclusion is just what we assume. For on the ground of the text, 'Then a father is not a father' up to 'Then the Vedas are not Vedas' (B*ri*. Up. IV, 3, 22), we ourselves assume that when knowledge springs up scripture ceases to be valid.—And should you ask who then is characterised by the absence of true knowledge, we reply: You yourself who ask this question!—And if you retort, 'But I am the Lord as declared by scripture,' we reply, 'Very well, if you have arrived at that knowledge, then there is nobody who does not possess such knowledge.'—This also disposes of the objection, urged by some, that a system of non-duality cannot be established because the Self is affected with duality by Nescience.

Hence we must fix our minds on the Lord as being the Self.

4. Not in the symbol (is the Self to be contemplated); for he (the meditating person) (may) not (view symbols as being the Self).

'Let a man meditate on mind as Brahman; this is said with reference to the body. Let a man meditate on ether as Brahman; this is said with reference to the Devas' (*Kh*. Up. III, 18, 1); 'Âditya is Brahman, this is the doctrine'

(*Kh.* Up. III, 19, 1); 'He who meditates on name as Brahman' (*Kh.* Up. VII, 1, 5). With regard to these and similar meditations on symbols a doubt arises whether the Self is to be apprehended in them also, or not.

The pûrvapakshin maintains that it is right to apprehend the Self in them also because Brahman is known from scriptural passages as the (universal) Self. For those symbols also are of the nature of Brahman in so far as they are effects of it, and therefore are of the nature of the Self as well.

We must not, our reply runs, attach to symbols the idea of Brahman. For he, i.e. the meditating person, cannot comprehend the heterogeneous symbols as being of the nature of the Self.—Nor is it true that the symbols are of the nature of the Self, because as being effects of Brahman they are of the nature of Brahman; for (from their being of the nature of Brahman) there results the non-existence of (them as) symbols. For the aggregate of names and so on can be viewed as of the nature of Brahman only in so far as the individual character of those effects of Brahman is sublated; and when that character is sublated how then can they be viewed as symbols, and how can the Self be apprehended in them? Nor does it follow from the fact of Brahman being the Self that a contemplation of the Self can be established on the ground of texts teaching a contemplation on Brahman (in certain symbols), since a contemplation of the latter kind does not do away with agentship and the like. For the instruction that Brahman is the Self depends on the doing away with agentship and all other characteristics of transmigratory existence; the injunction of meditations, on the other hand, depends on the non-removal of those characteristics. Hence we cannot establish the apprehension of the Self (in the symbols) on the ground of the meditating person being the same as the symbols. For golden ornaments and figures made of gold are not identical with each other, but only in so far as gold constitutes the Self of both. And that from that oneness (of symbol and meditating person) which depends on Brahman being the Self of all there results non-existence of the symbols (and hence impossibility of the meditations enjoined), we have explained above.—For these reasons the Self is not contemplated in symbols.

5. A contemplation of Brahman (is to be superinduced on symbols of Brahman), on account of the exaltation (thereby bestowed on the symbols).

With regard to the texts quoted above there arises another doubt, viz. whether the contemplation of Âditya and so on is to be superimposed on Brahman, or the contemplation of Brahman on Âditya and so on [1].—But whence does this doubt arise?—From the absence of a decisive reason, owing to the grammatical co-ordination. For we observe in the sentences quoted a co-ordination of the term 'Brahman' with the terms 'Âditya,' &c. 'Âditya is Brahman,' 'Prâ*n*a is Brahman,' 'Lightning is Brahman;' the text exhibiting the two members of each clause in the same case. And here there is no obvious occasion for co-ordination because the words 'Brahman' on the one hand, and 'Âditya' and so on on the other hand, denote different things; not any more than there exists a relation of co-ordination which could be expressed by the sentence 'The ox is a horse.'—But cannot Brahman and Âditya and so on be viewed as co-ordinated on the basis of the relation connecting a causal substance and its effects, analogously to the case of clay and earthen vessels?—By no means, we reply. For in that case dissolution of the effect would result from its co-ordination with the causal substance, and that—as we have already explained—would imply non-existence of the symbol. Moreover, the scriptural passages would then be statements about the highest Self, and thereby the qualification for meditations would be sublated [2]; and further the mention of a limited effect would be purposeless [3]. It follows herefrom that we have

[1] I. e. whether Brahman is to be meditated upon as Âditya, or Âditya as Brahman.

[2] While, as a matter of fact, scripture enjoins the meditations.

[3] It would serve no purpose to refer to limited things, such as

to do here with the superimposition of the contemplation of one thing on another thing—just as in the case of the text, 'The Brâhma*n*a is Agni Vai*s*vânara,'—and the doubt therefore arises the contemplation of which of the two things is to be superimposed on the other.

The pûrvapakshin maintains that there exists no fixed rule for this case, because we have no scriptural text establishing such a rule.—Or else, he says, contemplations on Âditya and so on are exclusively to be superimposed on Brahman. For in this way Brahman is meditated upon by means of contemplations on Âditya, and scripture decides that meditations on Brahman are what is productive of fruits. Hence contemplations on Brahman are not to be superimposed on Âditya and so on.

To this we make the following reply. The contemplation on Brahman is exclusively to be superimposed on Âditya and so on.—Why?—'On account of exaltation.' For thus Âditya and so on are viewed in an exalted way, the contemplation of something higher than they being superimposed on them. Thereby we also comply with a secular rule, viz. the one enjoining that the idea of something higher is to be superimposed upon something lower, as when we view—and speak of—the king's charioteer as a king. This rule must be observed in worldly matters, because to act contrary to it would be disadvantageous; for should we view a king as a charioteer, we should thereby lower him, and that would be no ways beneficial.—But, an objection is raised, as the whole matter rests on scriptural authority, the suspicion of any disadvantage cannot arise; and it is, further, not appropriate to define contemplations based on scripture by secular rules!—That might be so, we reply, if the sense of scripture were fully ascertained; but as it is liable to doubt, there is no objection to our having recourse to a secular rule whereby to ascertain it. And as by means of that rule we decide that what scripture means

the sun and so on, as being resolved into their causal substance, i.e. Brahman. True knowledge is concerned only with the resolution of the entire world of effects into Brahman.

is the superimposition of a higher contemplation on something lower, we should incur loss by superimposing a lower contemplation upon something higher.—As moreover in the passages under discussion the words 'Âditya' and so on stand first, they must, this being not contradictory, be taken in their primary sense. But, as our thought is thus defined by these words taken in their true literal sense, the word 'Brahman,' which supervenes later on, cannot be co-ordinated with them if it also be taken in its true literal sense, and from this it follows that the purport of the passages can only be to enjoin contemplations on Brahman (superinduced on Âditya and so on).—The same sense follows from the circumstance that the word 'Brahman' is, in all the passages under discussion, followed by the word 'iti,' 'thus[1].' 'He is to meditate (on Âditya, &c.) as Brahman.' The words 'Âditya' and so on, on the other hand, the text exhibits without any such addition. The passages therefore are clearly analogous to such sentences as 'He views the mother o' pearl as silver,' in which the word 'mother o' pearl' denotes mother o' pearl pure and simple, while the word 'silver' denotes, by implication, the idea of silver; for the person in question merely thinks 'this is silver' while there is no real silver. Thus our passages also mean, 'He is to view Âditya and so on as Brahman.'—The complementary clauses, moreover, which belong to the passages under discussion ('He who knowing this meditates (upon) Âditya as Brahman;' 'Who meditates (on) speech as Brahman;' 'Who meditates (on) will as Brahman'), exhibit the words 'Âditya' and so on in the accusative case, and thereby show them to be the direct objects of the action of meditation[2].—Against the remark that in all the mentioned cases Brahman only has to be meditated upon in order that a fruit may result from the meditation, we point out that from the mode of proof used

---

[1] Which in the translations given above of the texts under discussion is mostly rendered by 'as before the words concerned.

[2] While the word 'Brahman' does not stand in the accusative case.

above we infer that (not Brahman but) only Âditya and so on have to be meditated upon. But as in the case of hospitality shown to guests, Brahman, that is the supreme ruler of all, will give the fruit of meditations on Âditya and so on as well. This we have already shown under III, 2, 28. And, after all, Brahman also is meditated upon (in the cases under discussion) in so far as a contemplation on Brahman is superinduced on its symbols, analogously as a contemplation on Vish*n*u is superinduced on his images.

6. And the ideas of Âditya and so on (are to be superimposed) on the members (of the sacrificial action); owing to the effectuation (of the result of the sacrifice).

'He who burns up these, let a man meditate upon him as udgîtha' (*Kh*. Up. I, 3, 1); 'Let a man meditate on the fivefold Sâman in the worlds' (*Kh*. Up. II, 2, 1); 'Let a man meditate on the sevenfold Sâman in speech' (*Kh*. Up. II, 8, 1); 'This earth is the *Rik*, fire is Sâman' (*Kh*. Up. I, 6, 1).—With regard to these and similar meditations limited to members of sacrificial action, there arises a doubt whether the text enjoins contemplations on the udgîtha and so on superinduced on Âditya and so on, or else contemplations on Âditya, &c., superinduced on the udgîtha and so on.

No definite rule can here be established, the pûrvapakshin maintains, since there is no basis for such a rule. For in the present case we are unable to ascertain any special pre-eminence, while we were able to do so in the case of Brahman. Of Brahman, which is the cause of the whole world and free from all evil and so on, we can assert definitively that it is superior to Âditya and so on; the udgîtha and so on, on the other hand, are equally mere effects, and we cannot therefore with certainty ascribe to any of them any pre-eminence.—Or else we may decide that the ideas of the udgîtha and so on are to be superinduced exclusively on Âditya and so on. For the udgîtha and so on are of the nature of sacrificial work, and as it is known that the fruit is attained through the work, Âditya and so on if meditated upon as udgîtha and so on will themselves become of the nature of work and thereby be causes of fruit.—Moreover, the text, 'This earth is the *Rik*, the fire is the Sâman,' is followed by the complementary passage, 'this Sâman is placed upon this *Rik*,' where the word '*Rik*' denotes the earth and the word 'Sâman' the fire. Now this (viz. this calling the earth '*Rik*' and calling the fire 'Sâman') is possible only if the meaning of the passage is that the earth and the fire have to be viewed as *Rik* and Sâman; not if the *Rik* and the Sâman were to be contemplated as earth and fire. For the term 'king' is metaphorically applied to the charioteer—and not the term 'charioteer' to the king—the reason being that the charioteer may be viewed as a king.—Again in the text, 'Let a man meditate upon the fivefold Sâman in the worlds,' the use of the locative case 'in the worlds' intimates that the meditation on the Sâman is to be superimposed on the worlds as its locus. This is also proved by the analogous passage, 'This Gâyatra Sâman is woven on the vital airs' (*Kh*. Up. II, 11, 1).—Moreover (as proved before), in passages such as 'Âditya is Brahman, this is the instruction,' Brahman, which is mentioned last, is superimposed on Âditya, which is mentioned first. In the same way the earth, &c., are mentioned first, and the hiṅkâra, &c., mentioned last in passages such as 'The earth is the hiṅkâra' (*Kh*. Up. II, 2, 1). —For all these reasons the idea of members of sacrificial action has to be transferred to Âditya and so on, which are not such members.

To this we make the following reply. The ideas of Âditya and so on are exclusively to be transferred to members of sacrificial action, such as the udgîtha and so on. For what reason?—'On account of effectuation'—that means: Because thus, through their connexion with the supersensuous result (of the sacrificial work under discussion), when the udgîtha and so on are ceremonially qualified by being viewed as Âditya and so on, the sacrificial work is successful[1]. A scriptural passage—viz. *Kh*.

[1] Certain constituent members of the sacrificial action—such as

Up. I, 1, 10, 'Whatever one performs with knowledge, faith, and the Upanishad is more powerful'—moreover expressly declares that knowledge causes the success of sacrificial work.—Well then, an objection is raised, let this be admitted with regard to those meditations which have for their result the success of certain works; but how is it with meditations that have independent fruits of their own? Of this latter nature is e.g. the meditation referred to in *Kh*. Up. II, 2, 3, 'He who knowing this meditates on the fivefold Sâman in the worlds (to him belong the worlds in an ascending and a descending scale).'—In those cases also, we reply, the meditation falls within the sphere of a person entitled to the performance of a certain work, and therefore it is proper to assume that it has a fruit only through its connexion with the supersensuous result of the work under the heading of which it is mentioned; the case being analogous to that of the godohana-vessel[1].—And as Âditya and so on are of the nature of fruits of action, they may be viewed as superior to the udgîtha and so on which are of the nature of action only. Scriptural texts expressly teach that the reaching of Âditya (the sun) and so on constitutes the fruit of certain works.—Moreover the initial passages, 'Let a man meditate on the syllable Om as the udgîtha,' and 'Of this syllable the full account is this' (*Kh*. Up. I, 1, 1), represent the udgîtha only as the object of meditation, and only after that the

---

the udgîtha—undergo a certain ceremonial purification (sa*m*skâra) by being meditated upon as Âditya and so on. The meditations therefore contribute, through the mediation of the constituent members, towards the apûrva, the supersensuous result of the entire sacrifice.

[1] The sacred text promises a special fruit for the employment of the milking-pail (instead of the ordinary *k*amasa), viz. the obtainment of cattle; nevertheless that fruit is obtained only in so far as the godohana subserves the accomplishment of the apûrva of the sacrifice. Analogously those meditations on members of sacrificial works for which the text promises a separate fruit obtain that fruit only in so far as they effect a mysterious sa*m*skâra in those members, and thereby subserve the apûrva of the sacrifice.

text enjoins the contemplations on Âditya and so on.—Nor can we accept the remark that Âditya and so on being meditated upon as udgîtha, &c., assume thereby the nature of work and thus will be productive of fruit. For pious meditation is in itself of the nature of work, and thus capable of producing a result. And if the udgîtha and so on are meditated upon as Âditya, &c., they do not therefore cease to be of the nature of work.—In the passage, 'This Sâman is placed upon this *Rik*,' the words '*Rik*' and 'Sâman' are employed to denote the earth and Agni by means of implication (laksha*n*â), and implication may be based, according to opportunity, either on a less or more remote connexion of sense. Although, therefore, the intention of the passage is to enjoin the contemplation of the *Rik* and the Sâman as earth and Agni, yet—as the *Rik* and the Sâman are mentioned separately and as the earth and Agni are mentioned close by—we decide that, on the ground of their connexion with the *Rik* and Sâman, the words '*Rik*' and 'Sâman' are employed to denote them (i. e. earth and Agni) only. For we also cannot altogether deny that the word 'charioteer' may, for some reason or other, metaphorically denote a king.—Moreover the position of the words in the clause, 'Just this (earth) is *Rik*,' declares that the *Rik* is of the nature of earth; while if the text wanted to declare that the earth is of the nature of *Rik*, the words would be arranged as follows, 'this earth is just *Rik*.'—Moreover the concluding clause, 'He who knowing this sings the Sâman,' refers only to a cognition based on a subordinate member (of sacrificial action), not to one based on the earth and so on.—Analogously in the passage, 'Let a man meditate (on) the fivefold Sâman in the worlds,' the worlds—although enounced in the locative case—have to be superimposed on the Sâman, as the circumstance of the 'Sâman' being exhibited in the objective case indicates it to be the object of meditation. For if the worlds are superimposed on the Sâman, the Sâman is meditated upon as the Self of the worlds; while in the opposite case the worlds would be meditated upon as the Self of the Sâman.—The same remark applies to the passage, 'This Gâyatra

Sâman is woven on the prâ*n*as' (*Kh*. Up. II, 11, 1).—Where again both members of the sentence are equally exhibited in the objective case, viz. in the passage, 'Let a man meditate on the sevenfold Sâman (as) the sun' (*Kh*. Up. II, 9, 1), we observe that the introductory passages—viz. 'Meditation on the whole Sâman is good;' 'Thus for the fivefold Sâman;' 'Next for the sevenfold Sâman' (*Kh*. Up. II, 1, 1; 7, 2; 8, 1)—represent the Sâman only as the object of meditation, and therefrom conclude that Âditya has to be superinduced on it, and not the reverse.—From this very circumstance of the Sâman being the object of meditation, it follows that even in cases where the two members of the sentence have a reverse position—such as 'The earth (is) the hiṅkâra,' &c.—the hiṅkâra, &c., have to be viewed as earth and so on; and not the reverse.—From all this it follows that reflections based on things not forming constituent members of the sacrifice, such as Âditya and so on, are to be superimposed on the udgîtha and the like which are such constituent members.

7. Sitting (a man is to meditate), on account of the possibility.

As meditations connected with members of sacrificial action depend on action, we need not raise the question whether they are to be carried on in a sitting, or any other posture. The same holds good in the case of perfect intuition, since knowledge depends on its object only. With regard to all other meditations, on the other hand, the author of the Sûtras raises the question whether they may be undertaken indifferently by a person standing, sitting, or lying down, or only by a person sitting.

The pûrvapakshin here maintains that as meditation is something mental there can be no restriction as to the attitude of the body.—No, the author of the Sûtras rejoins; 'Sitting' only a man is to meditate.—Why?—'On account of the possibility.' By meditation we understand the lengthened carrying on of an identical train of thought; and of this a man is capable neither when going nor when running, since the act of going and so on tends to distract the mind.

The mind of a standing man, again, is directed on maintaining the body in an erect position, and therefore incapable of reflection on any subtle matter. A man lying down, finally, is unawares overcome by slumber. A sitting person, on the other hand, may easily avoid these several untoward occurrences, and is therefore in a position to carry on meditations.

8. And on account of thoughtfulness.

Moreover also the word 'thoughtfulness' denotes a lengthened carrying on of the same train of ideas. Now 'thoughtfulness' we ascribe to those whose mind is concentrated on one and the same object, while their look is fixed and their limbs move only very slightly. We say e.g. that the crane is thoughtful, or that a wife whose husband has gone on a journey is thoughtful. Now such thoughtfulness is easy for those who sit; and we therefore conclude herefrom also that meditation is the occupation of a sitting person.

9. And with reference to immobility (scripture ascribes thought to the earth, &c.).

Moreover, in the passage 'The earth thinks as it were' scripture ascribes thought to the earth, with regard to its immobility. This also helps us to infer that meditation is the occupation of one who is sitting.

10. And Sm*ri*ti-passages say the same.

Authoritative authors also teach in their Sm*ri*tis that a sitting posture subserves the act of meditation: cp. e.g. Bha. Gîtâ VI, 11, 'Having made a firm seat for one's self on a pure spot.' For the same reason the Yoga*s*âstra teaches different sitting postures, viz. the so-called lotus position and so on.

11. Where concentration of mind (is possible), there (meditation may be carried on), on account of there being no difference.

A doubt here arises with regard to direction, place, and

time, viz. whether any restrictive rules exist or not.—Against the view of those who maintain that such rules exist because we have analogous rules concerning the locality, &c., of Vedic works, the Sûtrakâra remarks that all rules concerning direction, place, and time depend on the aim merely; that is to say: Let a man meditate at whatever time, in whatever place and facing whatever region, he may with ease manage to concentrate his mind. For while scripture prescribes an easterly direction, the time of forenoon, and a spot sloping towards the east for certain sacrifices, no such specific rules are recorded for meditation, since the requisite concentration may be managed indifferently anywhere.—But, an objection is raised, some passages record such specific rules, as e.g. the following one, 'Let a man apply himself (to meditation) in a level and clean place, free from pebbles, fire and dust, noises, standing water, and the like, favourable to the mind, not infested by what hurts the eyes, full of caves and shelters' (*S*vet. Up. II, 10).—Such particular rules are met with indeed; but the teacher being friendly-minded says that there is no binding rule as to the particulars mentioned therein. The clause 'favourable to the mind' moreover shows that meditation may be carried on wherever concentration of the mind may be attained.

12. Up to death (meditations have to be repeated); for then also it is thus seen in scripture.

The first adhikara*n*a (of the present adhyâya) has established that repetition is to be observed with regard to all meditations. But now a distinction is made. Those meditations which aim at complete knowledge, terminate—in the same way as the beating of the rice grains is terminated by the husks becoming detached from the grains—with their effect being accomplished; for as soon as the effect, i.e. perfect knowledge, has been obtained, no further effort can be commanded, since scriptural instruction does not apply to him who knows that Brahman—which is not the object of injunction—constitutes his Self. On the other hand a doubt arises whether the devotee is to repeat those meditations which aim at certain forms of exaltation for a certain time only and then may stop; or whether he is to repeat them again and again as long as he lives.

Here the pûrvapakshin maintains that such meditations are to be carried on for some time only and then to be given up, since this satisfies the demands of those scriptural passages which teach meditations distinguished by repetition.

To this we make the following reply. The devotee is to reiterate those meditations up to his death, since the supersensuous result (of such meditations) is reached by means of the extreme meditation. For such works also as originate a fruit to be enjoyed in a future state of existence presuppose, at the time of death, a creative cognition analogous to the fruit to be produced; as appears from such passages as, 'Endowed with knowledge (i.e. the conception of the fruit to be obtained) he (i.e. the individual soul) goes after that (viz. the fruit) which is connected with that knowledge' (B*ri*. Up. IV, 4, 2); 'Whatever his thought (at the time of death), with that he goes into Prâ*n*a, and the Prâ*n*a united with light, together with the individual Self, leads on to the world as conceived (at the moment of death)' (Pr. Up. IV, 2, 10). This also follows from the comparison to the caterpillar (B*ri*. Up. IV, 4, 3). But the meditations under discussion do not, at the time of death, require any other creative cognition but a repetition of themselves. Such meditations therefore as consist in the creative conception of a fruit to be obtained must be repeated up to the moment of death. Analogously the scriptural text, *S*at. Brâ. X, 6, 3, 1—'With whatever thought he passes away from this world'—declares that the meditation extends up to the time of death. Similarly *S*m*ri*ti says, 'Remembering whatever form of being he in the end leaves this body, into that same form he ever passes, assimilated to its being' (Bha. Gîtâ VIII, 6); and 'At the time of death with unmoved mind' (Bha. Gîtâ VIII, 10). And that at the moment of death also there remains something to be done, the scriptural passage (*Kh*. Up. III, 17, 6) also proves. 'Let a man, at the time of death, take refuge with this triad.'

13. On the attainment of this (viz. Brahman) (there take place) the non-clinging and the destruction of later and earlier sins; this being declared (by scripture).

The supplement to the third adhyâya is finished herewith, and an inquiry now begins concerning the fruit of the knowledge of Brahman.—The doubt here presents itself whether, on the attainment of Brahman, sins the results of which are opposed in nature to such attainment are extinguished or not. They cannot possibly be extinguished, the pûrvapakshin maintains, before they have given their results, because the purpose of all works is their result. For we understand from scripture that work possesses the power of producing results; if, therefore, the work would perish without the enjoyment of its result, scripture would thereby be rendered nugatory. Sm*ri*ti also declares that 'works do not perish.'—But from this it would follow that all scriptural instruction regarding expiatory ceremonies is meaningless!—This objection is without force, we reply, because expiatory ceremonies may be viewed as merely due to certain special occurrences; as is the case with the offering enjoined on the occasion of the house (of one who has established the sacred fireplace) being burned[1].—Let us moreover admit that expiatory ceremonies, because enjoined on account of a person being afflicted by some mischief, may be meant to extinguish that mischief. But there is no analogous injunction of the knowledge of Brahman.—But if we do not admit that the works of him who knows Brahman are extinguished, it follows that he must necessarily enjoy the fruits of his works and thus cannot obtain release!—This follows by no means; but in the same way as the results of works, release will take place in due dependence on place, time, and special causes.—For these reasons the obtainment of Brahman does not imply the cessation of (the consequences of) misdeeds.

[1] Scripture enjoins the ish*t*i in question merely on the occasion of the house being burned, not as annulling the mischief done.

To this we make the following reply. On the obtainment of Brahman there take place the non-clinging (to the agent) of the posterior sins and the annihilation of anterior ones.—'On account of this being declared.' For in a chapter treating of the knowledge of Brahman scripture expressly declares that future sins which might be presumed to cling to the agent do not cling to him who knows: 'As water does not cling to a lotus-leaf, so no evil deed clings to him who knows this' (*Kh.* Up. IV, 14, 3). Similarly scripture declares the destruction of previously accumulated evil deeds: 'As the fibres of the Ishîkâ reed when thrown into the fire are burned, thus all his sins are burned' (*Kh.* Up. V, 24, 3). The extinction of works the following passage also declares, 'The fetter of the heart is broken, all doubts are solved, extinguished are all his works when He has been beheld who is high and low' (Mu. Up. II, 2, 8).—Nor is there any force in the averment that the assumption of works being extinguished without their fruits having been enjoyed would render scripture futile. For we by no means deny the fruit-producing power of works; this power actually exists; but we maintain that it is counteracted by other causes such as knowledge. Scripture is concerned only with the existence of this power in general, not with its obstruction and non-obstruction. Thus also the Sm*ri*ti passage, 'For work is not extinguished,' expresses the general rule; for as fruition of the result is the purpose of work, work is not extinguished without such fruition. But it is assumed that evil deeds are extinguished through expiatory ceremonies and the like, on account of scriptural and Sm*ri*ti passages such as 'All sins transcends he, the murder of a Brâhma*n*a transcends he who offers the a*s*vamedha-sacrifice and who knows it thus' (Tai. Sa*m*h. V, 3, 12, 1).—Nor is there any truth in the assertion that expiatory ceremonies are due to certain special occurrences (without possessing the power of extinguishing the evil inherent in such occurrences) For as these expiatory acts are enjoined in connexion with evil events, we may assume that they have for their fruit the destruction of such evil, and are therefore not entitled to assume any other fruit.—Against the objection that knowledge is not actually enjoined with reference to the destruction of evil while expiatory acts are so enjoined, we make the following remark. In the case of the meditations on the qualified Brahman there exists such injunction, and the corresponding complementary passages declare that he who possesses such knowledge obtains lordly power and cessation of all sin. Now there is no reason why the passages should not expressly aim at declaring these two things[1], and we therefore conclude that the fruit of those vidyâs is the acquisition of lordly power, preceded by the annulment of all sin. In the case of vidyâs referring to Brahman devoid of qualities we indeed have no corresponding injunction; nevertheless the destruction of all works follows from the cognition that our true Self is not an agent. (With relation to these vidyâs about Brahman as devoid of qualities) the term 'non-clinging' shows that, as far as future works are concerned, he who knows Brahman does not enter at all into the state of agency. And as to works past, although he has entered as it were into that state owing to wrong knowledge, yet those works also are dissolved when, through the power of knowledge, wrong cognition comes to an end; this is conveyed by the term 'destruction.' 'That Brahman whose nature it is to be at all times neither agent nor enjoyer, and which is thus opposed in being to the (soul's) previously established state of agency and enjoyment, that Brahman am I; hence I neither was an agent nor an enjoyer at any previous time, nor am I such at the present time, nor shall I be such at any future time;' this is the cognition of the man who knows Brahman. And in this way only final release is possible; for otherwise, i.e. if the chain of works which have been running on from eternity could not be cut short, release

[1] I. e. there is no reason to assume that those passages mention the acquisition of lordly power and the cessation of sin merely for the purpose of glorifying the injunction, and not for the purpose of stating the result of our compliance with the injunction.

could never take place.—Nor can final release be dependent on locality, time, and special causes, as the fruit of works is; for therefrom it would follow that the fruit of knowledge is non-permanent and cannot be.

It therefore is an established conclusion that on attaining Brahman there results the extinction of all sin.

14. Of the other (i. e. good works) also there is, in the same way, non-clinging; but at death.

In the preceding adhikara*n*a it has been shown that, according to scriptural statements, all natural sin—which is the cause of the soul's bondage—does, owing to the power of knowledge, either not cling to the soul or undergo destruction. One might now think that works of religious duty which are enjoined by scripture are not opposed to knowledge also founded on scripture. In order to dispel this notion the reasoning of the last adhikara*n*a is formally extended to the case under discussion. For him who knows there is 'in the same way,' i.e. as in the case of sin, 'non-clinging' and destruction 'of the other also,' i.e. of good works also; because such works also, as productive of their own results, would be apt to obstruct thereby the result of knowledge. Scripture also—in passages such as 'He overcomes both' (B*ri*. Up. IV, 4, 22)—declares that good works are extinguished no less than evil ones, and the extinction of works which depends on the cognition of the Self not being an agent is the same in the case of good and of evil works, and moreover there is a passage making a general statement without any distinction, viz. 'And his works are extinguished' (Mu. Up. II, 2, 8). And even there where the text mentions evil works only, we must consider good works also to be implied therein, because the results of the latter also are inferior to the result of knowledge. Moreover scripture directly applies the term 'evil works' to good works also, viz. in the passage, *Kh*. Up. VIII, 4, 1, 'Day and night do not pass that bank,' where good works are mentioned together with evil works, and finally the term 'evil' is without any distinction applied to all things mentioned before, 'All evil things turn back from it.'—'But at death.' The word 'but' is meant for emphatical assertion. As it is established that good as well as evil works—which are both causes of bondage—do, owing to the strength of knowledge, on the one hand not cling and on the other hand undergo destruction, there necessarily results final release of him who knows as soon as death takes place.

15. But only those former (works) whose effects have not yet begun (are destroyed by knowledge); because (scripture states) that (i. e. the death of the body) to be the term.

In the two preceding adhikaranas it has been proved that good as well as evil works are annihilated through knowledge. We now have to consider the question whether this annihilation extends, without distinction, to those works whose effects have already begun to operate as well as to those whose effects have not yet begun; or only to works of the latter kind.

Here the pûrvapakshin maintains that on the ground of scriptural passages such as 'He thereby overcomes both,' which refer to all works without any distinction, all works whatever must be considered to undergo destruction.

To this we reply, 'But only those whose effects have not begun.' Former works, i.e. works, whether good or evil, which have been accumulated in previous forms of existence as well as in the current form of existence before the origination of knowledge, are destroyed by the attainment of knowledge only if their fruit has not yet begun to operate. Those works, on the other hand, whose effects have begun and whose results have been half enjoyed—i.e. those very works to which there is due the present state of existence in which the knowledge of Brahman arises—are not destroyed by that knowledge. This opinion is founded on the scriptural passage, 'For him there is delay only as long as he is not delivered (from the body)' (*Kh*. Up. VI, 14, 2), which fixes the death of the body as the term of the attainment of final release. Were it otherwise, i.e. were all works whatever extinguished by knowledge, there would be no reason for the continuance of the current form of existence, and the rise of knowledge would therefore be immediately followed by the state of final release; in which case scripture would not teach that one has to wait for the death of the body.—But, an objection is raised, the knowledge of the Self being essentially non-active does by its intrinsic power destroy (all) works; how then should it destroy some only and leave others unaffected? We certainly have no right to assume that when fire and seeds come into contact the germinative power of some seeds only is destroyed while that of others remains unimpaired!—The origination of knowledge, we reply, cannot take place without dependence on an aggregate of works whose effects have already begun to operate, and when this dependence has once been entered into, we must —as in the case of the potter's wheel—wait until the motion of that which once has begun to move comes to an end, there being nothing to obstruct it in the interim. The knowledge of our Self being essentially non-active destroys all works by means of refuting wrong knowledge; but wrong knowledge—comparable to the appearance of a double moon—lasts for some time even after it has been refuted, owing to the impression it has made.—Moreover it is not a matter for dispute at all whether the body of him who knows Brahman continues to exist for some time or not. For how can one man contest the fact of another possessing the knowledge of Brahman—vouched for by his heart's conviction—and at the same time continuing to enjoy bodily existence? This same point is explained in scripture and Sm*ri*ti, where they describe him who stands firm in the highest knowledge.—The final decision therefore is that knowledge effects the destruction of those works only—whether good or evil—whose effects have not yet begun to operate.

16. But the Agnihotra and the like (tend) towards the same effect; scripture showing this.

The reasoning as to evil deeds has been extended to the

non-clinging and destruction of good deeds also. Against a notion which now might present itself, viz. that this extension comprehends all good works alike, the Sûtrakâra remarks, 'But the Agnihotra and so on.'—The word 'but' is meant to set that notion aside. Works of permanent obligation enjoined by the Veda, such as the Agnihotra, tend 'towards the same effect,' i e. have the same effect as knowledge. For this is declared by texts such as the following one, 'Brâhma*n*as seek to know him by the study of the Veda, by sacrifices, by gifts' (B*ri*. Up. IV, 4, 22).—But, an objection is raised, as knowledge and works have different effects, it is impossible that they should have one and the same effect!—It is observed, we reply, that sour milk and poison whose ordinary effects are fever and death have for their effects satisfaction and a flourishing state of the body, if the sour milk is mixed with sugar and the poison taken while certain mantras are recited; in the same way works if joined with knowledge may effect final release.—But final release is something not to be effected at all; how then can you declare it to be the effect of works?—Works, we reply, may subserve final release mediately. For in so far as furthering knowledge, work may be spoken of as an indirect cause of final release. For the same reason the equality of effect spoken of above extends only to works past (at the time when knowledge springs up). Because for him who knows Brahman no future Agnihotras and the like are possible, since the attainment of the Self of Brahman—which Brahman is not subject to injunction—lies outside the sphere of sacred precept. In those meditations, on the other hand, which refer to the qualified Brahman, the Self does not cease to be an agent, and consequently future Agnihotras and the like are not excluded. Such works also—because they have no other effect if undertaken without a view to reward—may be brought into connexion with knowledge.

To what works then, it may be asked, does the statement refer made above about the non-clinging and the destruction, and to what works the following statement made in some *S*âkhâ about the application of works, 'His sons enter upon his inheritance, his friends on his good works, his enemies upon his evil works?'—To this question the next Sûtra replies.

17. For (there is) also (a class of good works) other than this, according to some. (There is agreement) of both (teachers) (as to the fate of those works.)

'For also one other than this,' i. e. there is also a class of good works different from works of permanent obligation, viz. those good works which are performed with a view to a fruit. Of those latter works the passage quoted above from some *S*âkhâ ('His friends enter on his good works') teaches the application. And first of those works Sûtra 14 teaches that, in the same way as evil deeds, they do not cling to the doer or else are destroyed. Both teachers, *G*aimini as well as Bâdarâya*n*a, are agreed that such works, undertaken for the fulfilment of some special wish, do not contribute towards the origination of true knowledge.

18. For (the text) 'whatever he does with knowledge' (intimates that).

In the preceding adhikara*n*a the following conclusion has been established:—Works of permanent obligation such as the Agnihotra, if performed by a person desirous of release with a view to release, lead to the extinction of evil deeds committed, thus become a means of the purification of the mind, and thereby cause the attainment of Brahman, which leads to final release; they therefore operate towards the same effect as the knowledge of Brahman. Now the Agnihotra and similar works are either connected with a special knowledge based on the constituent members of the sacrificial work, or absolute (non-connected with such knowledge). This appears from scriptural texts such as 'He who knowing this sacrifices; he who knowing this makes an offering; he who knowing this recites; he who knowing this sings; therefore let a man make him who knows this his Brahman-priest

(*Kh*. Up. IV, 17, 1); therefore both perform the work, he who knows this and he who does not know it' (*Kh*. Up. I, 1, 10).—We have now to consider the question whether only such Agnihotras and so on as are connected with knowledge cause knowledge on the part of him who desires release and thus operate towards the same effect as knowledge; or whether both kinds of works—those connected with knowledge and those not so connected—equally act in that way. The doubt concerning this point arises on the one hand from scriptural passages such as 'That Self they seek to know by sacrifice' (B*ri*. Up. IV, 4, 22), which represent sacrifices and the like, without difference, as auxiliary to the knowledge of the Self; and on the other hand from our observing that a superiority is conceded to Agnihotras, &c., if connected with knowledge.

Here the pûrvapakshin maintains that only such sacrificial works as are connected with knowledge are helpful towards the cognition of the Self, since we understand from various scriptural and Sm*ri*ti passages that works connected with knowledge are superior to those destitute of knowledge; cp. e. g. 'On the very day on which he sacrifices on that day he overcomes death again, he who knows this' (B*ri*. Up. I, 5, 2); and 'Possesser of this knowledge thou wilt cast off the bonds of action;' 'Action is far inferior to concentration of mind' (Bha. Gîtâ II, 39; 49).

To this the Sûtrakâra replies, 'For what with knowledge only.' It is true that works such as the Agnihotra if joined with knowledge are superior to works destitute of knowledge, in the same way as a Brâhma*n*a possessed of knowledge is superior to one devoid of knowledge. Nevertheless works such as the Agnihotra even if not connected with knowledge are not altogether ineffective; for certain scriptural texts declare that such works are, all of them without any difference, causes of knowledge; so e. g. the passage, 'That Self they seek to know through sacrifices.'—But, as we understand from scripture that works connected with knowledge are superior to those destitute of knowledge, we must suppose that the Agnihotra and the like if unaccompanied by knowledge are inoperative towards the cognition of the Self!—By no means, we reply. The proper assumption is that the Agnihotra and so on, if accompanied by knowledge, possess a greater capability of originating knowledge and therefore are of superior causal efficiency with regard to the cognition of the Self; while the same works if devoid of knowledge possess no such superiority. We cannot, however, admit that the Agnihotra and similar works which scripture, without making any distinction, declares to subserve knowledge (cp. 'they seek to know through sacrifices') should not subserve it. With this our conclusion agrees the scriptural text, 'Whatever he performs with knowledge, faith, and the Upanishad that is more powerful' (*Kh.* Up. I, 1, 10); for this text—in speaking of the greater power of work joined with knowledge and thus proclaiming the superiority of such work with regard to its effect—intimates thereby that work destitute of knowledge possesses some power towards the same effect. By the 'power' of work we understand its capacity of effecting its purpose. We therefore accept as settled the following conclusion: All works of permanent obligation, such as the Agnihotra—whether joined with or devoid of knowledge—which have been performed before the rise of true knowledge, either in the present state of existence or a former one, by a person desirous of release with a view to release; all such works act, according to their several capacities, as means of the extinction of evil desert which obstructs the attainment of Brahman, and thus become causes of such attainment, subserving the more immediate causes such as the hearing of and reflecting on the sacred texts, faith, meditation, devotion, &c. They therefore operate towards the same effect as the knowledge of Brahman.

19. But having destroyed by fruition the two other (sets of work) he becomes one with Brahman.

It has been shown that all good and evil deeds whose effects have not yet begun are extinguished by the power of knowledge. 'The two others,' on the other hand, i.e. those good and evil works whose effects have begun, a man has at first to exhaust by the fruition of their consequences, and then he becomes one with Brahman. This appears from scriptural passages such as 'For him there is delay so long as he is not delivered (from the body), then he will become one with Brahman' (*Kh.* Up. VI, 14, 2); and 'Being Brahman he goes to Brahman' (B*ri*. Up. IV, 4, 6). —But, an objection is raised, even when perfect intuition has risen the practical intuition of multiplicity may continue after the death of the body, just as it continued before death; analogously to the visual appearance of a double moon (which may continue even after it has been cognized as false).—Not so, we reply. After the death of the body there no longer exists any cause for such continuance; while up to death there is such a cause, viz. the extinction of the remainder of works to be enjoyed.—But a new aggregate of works will originate a new fruition!—Not so, we reply; since the seed of all such fruition is destroyed. What, on the death of the body, could originate a new period of fruition, is only a new set of works, and works depend on false knowledge; but such false knowledge is completely destroyed by perfect intuition. When therefore the works whose effects have begun are destroyed, the man who knows necessarily enters into the state of perfect isolation.

SECOND PÂDA.

Reverence to the Highest Self!

1. Speech (is merged) in mind, on account of this being seen, and of the scriptural statement.

Being about to describe the path of the gods which leads those who possess the lower kind of knowledge towards the attainment of their reward, the Sûtrakâra begins by explaining, on the basis of scriptural statements, the successive steps by which the soul passes out of the body; for, as will be stated later on, the departure of the soul is the same in the case of him who possesses the (lower) knowledge and of him who is devoid of all knowledge.

About the process of dying we have the following passage, 'When a man departs from hence his speech merges in his mind, his mind in his breath, his breath in fire, fire in the highest deity' (*Kh.* Up. VI, 6, 1). A doubt here arises whether the passage means to say that speech itself, together with its function, is merged in the mind, or only the function of speech.

The pûrvapakshin maintains that speech itself is merged in the mind. For this explanation only is in agreement with the direct statement of the sacred text, while the other alternative compels us to have recourse to an implied meaning; now wherever direct enunciation and implied meaning are in conflict the preference has to be given to the former, and we therefore maintain that speech itself is merged in the mind.

To this we reply that only the function of speech is merged in the mind.—But how can this interpretation be maintained, considering that the teacher (in the Sûtra) expressly says 'Speech in the mind?'—True, we reply; but later on he says 'There is non-division, according to scriptural statement' (Sûtra 16), and we therefrom conclude that what is meant in the present Sûtra is merely cessation of the function of speech. For if the intention were to express absorption of the thing (i.e. the organ of speech) itself, there would be 'non-division' in all cases, and for what reason then should 'non-division' be specially stated in another case (i.e. in the case of which Sûtra 16 treats)? The meaning therefore is that the different functions are retracted, and that while the function of the mind continues to go on the function of speech is retracted first.—Why so?—'Because this is seen.' It is a matter of observation that while the mind continues to act the function of speech comes to an end; nobody, on the other hand, is able to see that the organ of speech itself, together with its function, is merged in the mind.—But are we not justified in assuming such a merging of speech in the mind, on the ground of scriptural statement?—This is impossible, we reply, since mind is not the causal substance of speech. We are entitled to assume only that a thing is merged in what is its causal substance; a pot e.g. (when destroyed) is merged in clay. But there is no proof whatever for speech originating from mind. On the other hand we observe that functions originate and are retracted even where they do not inhere in causal substances. The function of fire, e.g. which is of the nature of heat, springs from fuel which is of the nature of earth, and it is extinguished in water.—But how do you, on this interpretation, account for the scriptural statement that 'speech is merged in the mind?'—'And on account of the scriptural statement,' the Sûtrakâra replies. The scriptural statement also may be reconciled with our interpretation, in so far as the function and the thing to which the function belongs are viewed as non-different.

2. And for the same reason all (sense-organs) (follow) after (mind).

'Therefore he whose light has gone out comes to a new birth with his senses merged in the mind' (Pr. Up. III, 9); this passage states that all senses without difference are merged in the mind. 'For the same reason,' i.e. because there also as in the case of speech, it is observed that the eye and so on discontinue their functions, while the mind together with its functions persists, and because the organs themselves cannot be absorbed, and because the text admits of that interpretation; we conclude that the different organs follow after, i.e. are merged in, the mind only as far as their functions are concerned.—As all organs[1] without difference are merged in the mind, the special mention made of speech (in Sûtra 1) must be viewed as made in agreement with the special example referred to by scripture, 'Speech is merged in mind.'

3. That mind (is merged) in breath, owing to the subsequent clause.

It has been shown that the passage, 'Speech is merged in mind,' means a merging of the function only.--A doubt here arises whether the subsequent clause, 'mind in breath,' also means to intimate a merging of the function only or of that to which the function belongs.—The pûrvapakshin maintains the latter alternative. For that, he says, agrees with scripture, and moreover breath may be viewed as the causal substance of mind. For scripture—'Mind is made of earth, breath of water' (*Kh.* Up. VI, 6, 5)—states that mind comes from earth and breath from water, and scripture further states that 'Water sent forth earth' (*Kh.* Up. VI, 2, 4). When mind therefore is merged in breath, it is the same as earth being merged in water; for mind is earth and breath is water, causal substance and effect being non-different.

To this we reply as follows. 'The subsequent clause' intimates that the mind, after having absorbed within itself the functions of the outer senses, is merged in breath only in the way of its function being so merged. For we observe in the case of persons lying in deep sleep or about to die that, while the function of breath persists, the functions of the mind are stopped. Nor is the mind capable of being itself merged in breath, since breath does not constitute its causal substance.—But it has been shown above that breath is the causal substance of mind!—This is not valid,

[1] I. e. the functions of all organs.

we reply. For the relation of causality, made out in such an indirect way, does not suffice to show that mind is really merged in breath. Were it so, then mind would also be merged in earth, earth in water, breath in water. Nor is there, on the alternative contemplated, any proof of mind having originated from that water which had passed over into breath.—Mind cannot therefore, in itself, be merged in breath. And that the scriptural statement is satisfied by a mere merging of the function—the function and that to which the function belongs being viewed as identical—has been shown already under the preceding Sûtra.

4. That (viz. breath) (is merged) in the ruler (i.e. the individual soul), on account of the (statements as to the prâ*n*as) coming to it and so on.

We have ascertained that a thing which has not originated from another is not itself merged in the latter, but only through its functions. A doubt now arises whether, according to the word of scripture, the function of breath is merged in heat, or in the individual soul which is the ruler of the body and senses.—According to the pûrvapakshin we must conclude that the breath is merged in heat only, since the scriptural statement allows no room for doubt and we are not entitled to assume something not declared by scripture. The breath under discussion persists 'in the ruler,' i.e. the intelligent Self (the individual soul) which possesses nescience, work, and former knowledge as limiting adjuncts; i.e. the function of breath has that soul for its substratum. —Why so?—'On account of (the prâ*n*as) going towards him,' &c.—Another scriptural passage declares that all prâ*n*as without any difference go to the soul, 'All the prâ*n*as go to the Self at the time of death when a man is thus going to expire' (B*ri*. Up. IV, 3, 38). Another passage again specially declares that the prâ*n*a with its five functions follows the individual soul, 'After him thus departing the prâ*n*a departs,' and that the other prâ*n*as follow that prâ*n*a, 'And after the prâ*n*a thus departing all the other prâ*n*as depart' (B*ri*. Up. IV, 4, 2). And the text, 'He is furnished with intelligence' (ibid.), by declaring the individual soul to be of intimately intelligent nature, suggests that in it, viz. the soul, the prâ*n*a—into which the different organs of knowledge have been merged—has taken its abode.—But scripture also says, 'The prâ*n*a (is merged) in heat;' why then make the addition implied in the doctrine—that breath is merged in the individual soul?—We must make that addition, we reply, because in the process of departure &c. the soul is the chief agent, and because we must pay regard to specifications contained in other scriptural passages also.—How then do you explain the statement, 'Breath is merged in heat?'—To this question the next Sûtra replies.

5. To the elements (the soul, with prâ*n*a, goes), on account of the subsequent scriptural clause.

The soul joined by the prâ*n*a takes up its abode within the subtle elements which accompany heat and form the seed of the (gross) body. This we conclude from the clause, 'Breath in heat.'—But this passage declares, not that the soul together with the prâ*n*a takes up its abode in heat, but only that the prâ*n*a takes up its abode!—No matter, we reply; since the preceding Sûtra intercalates the soul in the interval (between prâ*n*a and te*g*as). Of a man who first travels from *S*rughna to Mathurâ and then from Mathurâ to Pâ*t*aliputra, we may say shortly that he travels from *S*rughna to Pâ*t*aliputra. The passage under discussion therefore means that the soul together with the prâ*n*a abides in the elements associated with heat.—But how are you entitled to draw in the other elements also, while the text only speaks of heat?—To this question the next Sûtra replies.

6. Not to one (element) (the soul goes); for both (i. e. scripture and Sm*ri*ti) declare this.

At the time of passing over into another body the individual soul does not abide in the one element of heat only; for we see that the new body consists of various elements. This matter is declared in the question and answer about the waters called man (*Kh*. Up. V, 3, 3); as explained by us in III, 1, 2.—Scripture and Sm*ri*ti alike teach this doctrine; compare e.g. 'Consisting of earth, water, wind, ether, heat' (B*ri*. Up. IV, 4, 5); and 'The subtle perishable parts of the five (elements) from them all this is produced in due succession' (Manu I, 27).—But is there not another scriptural text—beginning 'Where then is that person?'—which teaches that at the time of the soul attaining a new body, after speech and the other organs have been withdrawn within the soul, work constitutes the soul's abode, 'What those two said, as work they said it; what they praised, as work they praised it' (B*ri*. Up. III, 2, 13)?—That passage, we reply, describes the operation of bondage consisting of the senses and their objects—there called grahas and atigrahas—and therefore work is spoken of as the abode; here on the other hand the elements are said to be the abode because we have to do with the origination of a new body out of the matter of the elements. The expression 'they prayed' moreover intimates only that work occupies the chief place in the process, and does not exclude another abode. The two passages therefore do not contradict each other.

7. And common (to him who knows and him who does not know) (is the departure) up to the beginning of the way; and the immortality (of him who knows) (is relative only) without having burned (nescience and so on).

The question here arises whether the departure of the soul, as described hitherto, is the same in the case of him who knows and him who is destitute of knowledge; or whether there is any difference.—There is a difference, the pûrvapakshin maintains. For the departure as described has for its abode the elements, and this abiding in the elements is for the purpose of a new birth. But he who possesses true knowledge cannot be born again, since scripture declares that 'He who knows reaches immortality.' Hence only he who is devoid of knowledge departs in the way described.—But as that departure is described in chapters treating of knowledge it can belong only to him who knows!—Not so, the pûrvapakshin replies. In the same way as sleep and the like, the departure of the soul is only referred to in the texts as something established elsewhere (not as something to be taught as part of true knowledge). Passages such as 'When a man sleeps,—is hungry,—is thirsty' (*Kh.* Up. VI, 8), although forming part of chapters concerned with true knowledge, mention sleep and so on which are common to all living beings, because they assist the comprehension of the matter to be taught, but do not aim at enjoining them specially for those who know. Analogously the texts about the soul's departure refer to that departure only in order to teach that 'that highest deity in which the heat of the dying man is merged, that is the Self, that art thou.' Now that departure is (in other scriptural passages) specially denied of him who knows; it therefore belongs to him only who does not know.

To this we make the following reply. That departure which is described in the passage, 'speech is merged in mind,' &c., must be 'common' to him who knows and him who does not know 'up to the beginning of the way;' because scripture records no distinction. The soul destitute of true knowledge having taken its abode in the subtle elements which constitute the seed of the body and being impelled by its works, migrates into a new body; while the soul of him who knows passes into the vein, revealed by true knowledge, which is the door of release. In this sense the Sûtra says 'up to the beginning of the way.'—But he who knows reaches immortality, and immortality does not depend on a change of place; why then should the soul take its abode in the elements or set out on a journey?—That immortality, we reply, is 'without having burned' i. e. for him who, without having altogether burned nescience and the other afflictions, is about to obtain, through the power of the lower knowledge, a relative immortality only, there take place the entering on the way and the abiding in the elements. For without a substratum the prâ*n*as could not move. There is thus no difficulty.

8. This (aggregate of the elements) (continues to exist) up to the (final absolute) union (with Brahman); on account of the declarations of the saṁsâra state (made by scripture).

With regard to the final clause, 'Heat in the highest deity,' the force of its connexion with what precedes shows that the meaning is 'the heat of the dying man is—together with the individual soul, the prâṇa, the aggregate of the organs and the other elements—merged in Brahman.'—We now have to consider of what kind that merging is.—The pûrvapakshin maintains that it is an absolute absorption of the things merged, since it is proved that those things have the highest deity for their causal matter. For it has been established that the deity is the causal substance of all things that have an origin. Hence that passing into the state of non-separation is an absolute one.

To this we reply as follows. Those subtle elements—heat and so on—which constitute the abode of hearing and the other organs persist up to the 'union,' i. e. up to final release from the saṁsâra, which is caused by perfect knowledge. 'On account of the declarations of the saṁsâra state' made in passages such as 'Some enter the womb, for embodied existence as organic beings; others go into inorganic matter, according to their work and according to their knowledge' (Ka. Up. II, 5, 7). Otherwise the limiting adjuncts of every soul would, at the time of death, be absorbed and the soul would enter into absolute union with Brahman; which would render all scriptural injunction and scriptural doctrine equally purportless. Moreover bondage, which is due to wrong knowledge, cannot be dissolved but through perfect knowledge. Hence, although Brahman is the causal substance of those elements, they are at the time of death—as in the case of deep sleep and a pralaya of the world—merged in it only in such a way as to continue to exist in a seminal condition.

9. And (heat is) subtle in measure; as this is thus observed.

The elementary matter of heat and the other elements

which form the substratum for the soul when passing out of this body, must be subtle in its nature and extent. This follows from the scriptural passages, which declare that it passes out by the veins and so on. Their thinness renders them capable of passing out, and their transparency (permeability) is the cause of their not being stopped by any gross substance. For these reasons they, when passing out of the body, are not perceived by bystanders.

10. For this reason (it is) not (destroyed) by the destruction (of the gross body).

On account of this very subtlety the subtle body is not destroyed by what destroys the gross body, viz. burning and the like.

11. And to that same (subtle body) that warmth (belongs), on account of the proof (which observation furnishes).

To that same subtle body belongs the warmth which we perceive in the living body by means of touch. That warmth is not felt in the body after death, while such qualities as form, colour and so on continue to be perceived; it is, on the other hand, observed as long as there is life. From this it follows that the warmth resides in something different from the body as ordinarily known. Scripture also says, 'He is warm if going to live, cold if going to die.'

12. Should you say that on account of the denial (made by scripture) (the soul of him who knows Brahman does not depart); we deny this, (because scripture means to say that the prâ*n*as do not depart) from the embodied soul.

From the distinction conveyed by the clause, 'and (relative) immortality without having burned' (Sûtra 7), it follows that in the case of absolute immortality being reached there is no going and no departure of the soul from the body.—The idea that for some reason or other a departure of the soul might take place in this latter case also, is precluded by the following scriptural passage, 'But as to the man who does not desire, who, not desiring, freed from desires, is satisfied in his desires, or desires the Self only, of him the vital spirits do not depart,—being Brahman, he goes to Brahman' (*Bri.* Up. IV, 4, 6). From this express denial—forming part of the higher knowledge—it follows that the prâ*n*as do not pass out of the body of him who knows Brahman.

This conclusion the pûrvapakshin denies. For, he says, the passage quoted does not deny the departure of the prâ*n*as from the body, but from the embodied (individual) soul.—How is this known?—From the fact that in another *S*âkhâ we have (not the sixth, genitive, case 'of him,' but) the fifth, ablative, case 'from him'—'From him the vital spirits do not depart' (Mâdhyandina *S*âkhâ). For the sixth case which expresses only relation in general is determined towards some special relation by the fifth case met with in another *S*âkhâ. And as the embodied soul which has a claim on exaltation and bliss is the chief topic of the chapter, we construe the words 'from him' to mean not the body but the embodied soul. The sense therefore is 'from that soul when about to depart the prâ*n*as do not depart, but remain with it.' The soul of him who dies therefore passes out of the body, together with the prâ*n*as. This view the next Sûtra refutes.

13. For (in the text) of some (the denial of the soul's departure) is clear.

The assertion that also the soul of him who knows Brahman departs from the body, because the denial states the soul (not the body) to be the point of departure, cannot be upheld. For we observe that in the sacred text of some there is a clear denial of a departure, the starting-point of which is the body.—The text meant at first records the question asked by Ârtabhâga, 'When this man dies, do the vital spirits depart from him or not?' then embraces the alternative of non-departure, in the words, No, replied Yâ*gñ*avalkya; thereupon—anticipating the objection that a man cannot be dead as long as his vital spirits have not departed—teaches the resolution of the prâ*n*as in the body 'in that very same place they are merged;' and finally, in confirmation thereof, remarks, 'he swells, he is inflated, inflated the dead man lies.' This last clause states that swelling, &c., affect the subject under discussion, viz. that from which the departure takes place (the 'tasmât' of the former clause), which subject is, in this last clause, referred to by means of the word 'He.' Now swelling and so on can belong to the body only, not to the embodied soul. And owing to its equality thereto[1] also the passages, 'from him the vital spirits do not depart;' 'in that very same place they are resolved,' have to be taken as denying a departure starting from the body, although the chief subject of the passage is the embodied soul. This may be done by the embodied soul and the body being viewed as non-different[2]. In this way we have to explain the passage if read with the fifth case.—If again the passage is read with the sixth case ('of him the vital spirits do not depart'), it must be understood as denying the departure of him who knows, as its purport manifestly is to deny a departure established elsewhere. But what it denies can only be a departure from the body; for what is established (viz. for ordinary men not possessing the highest knowledge) is only the departure (of the soul, &c.) from the body, not the departure (of the prâ*n*as, &c.) from the embodied soul.—Moreover, after the passage, 'Either through the eye or through the skull or through other places of the body, him thus departing the prâ*n*a departs after, and after the departing prâ*n*a all prâ*n*as depart,' &c., has at length described the departure and transmigration of the soul as belonging to him who does not know, and after the account of him

[1] I. e. its belonging to the same chapter and treating of the same subject.

[2] The two being viewed as non-different, the pronoun (tasmât), which properly denotes the soul, the person, may be used to denote the body.—Abhedopa*k*âre*n*a dehadehinor dehiparâmar*s*inâ sarvanâmnâ deha eva parâm*r*ish*t*a iti. Bhâ.

who does not know has been concluded with the words. 'So much for the man who has desires,' the text designates him who knows as 'he who has no desires;' a designation which would be altogether inappropriate if the text wanted to establish departure, &c., for that person also. The passage therefore has to be explained as denying of him who knows the going and departing which are established for him who does not know. For thus only the designation employed by the text has a sense.—And for him who knowing Brahman has become the Self of that omnipresent Brahman, and in whom all desires and works have become extinct, departing and going are not even possible, as there is not any occasion for them. And such texts as 'there he reaches Brahman' (B*ri*. Up. IV, 4, 7) indicate the absence of all going and departing.

14. And Sm*ri*ti also says that.

In the Mahâbhârata also it is said that those who know do not go or depart, 'He who has become the Self of all beings and has a complete intuition of all, at his way the gods themselves are perplexed, seeking for the path of him who has no path.'—But, an objection is raised, other passages speak of men knowing Brahman as going, so e.g. '*S*uka the son of Vyâsa being desirous of release travelled to the sphere of the sun; being called by his father who had followed him, he gave an answering shout.'—That passage, we reply, describes (not the effects of the highest knowledge but only) how an embodied person, through the power of Yoga (which is of the nature of the lower knowledge), reached some special place and freed himself from the body. This appears from it being mentioned that he was seen by all beings; for the beings could not see a person moving without a body. The conclusion of the story makes all this clear, '*S*uka having moved through the air more rapidly than wind, and having shown his power, was known by all beings.'—It thus follows that he who knows Brahman neither moves nor departs. To what sphere the scriptural texts about going and so on refer we shall explain later on.

15. Those (elements, &c.) (are merged) in the highest Brahman; for thus (scripture) says.

Those, i. e. the sense organs—denoted by the term 'prâ*n*a'—and the elements of him who knows the highest Brahman, are merged in that same highest Brahman.—Why?—Because scripture declares that 'Thus these sixteen parts of the spectator that go towards the person, when they have reached the person, sink into him' (Pr. Up. VI, 5).—But another text which refers to him who knows teaches that the parts also are merged in something different from the highest Self, 'The fifteen parts enter into their elements' (Mu. Up. III, 2, 7).—No, we reply. This latter passage is concerned with the ordinary view of the matter, according to which the parts of the body which consist of earth and so on are merged in their causal substances, earth and so on. The former passage, on the other hand, expresses the view of him who knows; according to which the whole aggregate of the parts of him who knows the highest Brahman is merged in Brahman only.—There is thus no contradiction.

16. (There is absolute) non-division (from Brahman, of the parts merged in it); according to scriptural declaration.

When the parts of him who knows are merged in Brahman, is there a remainder (which is not so merged), as in the case of other men; or is there no such remainder? As the merging of him also who knows falls under the general heading of merging, it might be assumed that of him also there remains a potential body, and the Sûtrakâra therefore teaches expressly that the elements, &c., of him who knows enter into the relation of (absolute) non-division from Brahman.—On what ground?—Because scripture declares this. For after having taught the dissolution of the parts, the text continues, 'Their name and form are broken, and people speak of the person only; and he becomes without parts and immortal' (Pr. Up. VI, 5). And when parts that are due to nescience are dissolved through knowledge it is not possible that a remainder should be left. The parts therefore enter into absolute non-division from Brahman.

17. (There takes place) a lighting up of the point of its (the soul's) abode (viz. the heart); the door (of its egress) being illuminated thereby; owing to the power of knowledge and the application of meditation to the way which is part of that (knowledge); (the soul) favoured by him in the heart (viz. Brahman) (passes upwards) by the one that exceeds a hundred (i. e. by the hundred and first vein).

Having absolved the inquiry into a point of the higher knowledge into which we were led by a special occasion, we now continue the discussion connected with the lower knowledge.—It has been stated that up to the beginning of the way the departure of him who knows and him who does not know is the same. The present Sûtra now describes the soul's entering on the way. The abode of the soul, when—having taken within itself speech and the other powers—it is about to depart, is the heart, according to the text, 'He taking with him those elements of light descends into the heart' (B*ri*. Up. IV, 4, 1). Of the heart the point becomes lighted up, and subsequent to that is the departure of the soul, starting from the eye or some other place, according to the passage, 'The point of his heart becomes lighted up, and by that light the Self departs, either through the eye or through the skull or through other places of the body' (B*ri*. Up. IV, 4, 2). The question here arises whether that departure is the same for him who knows and him who does not know, or if there is a special limitation in the case of the former; and the primâ facie view might be upheld that there is no such limitation since scripture records no difference. Against this the teacher states that although, equally for him who does know and him who does not know, the point of the heart becomes shining and the door of egress thereby is lighted up, yet he who knows departs through the skull only, while the others depart from other places.—Why so?—'On account of the power of knowledge.' If also he who knows departed, like all others, from any place of the body, he would be unable to reach an exalted sphere; and then all knowledge would be purportless. 'And on account of the application of meditation on the way forming a part of that.' That means: in different vidyâs there is enjoined meditation on the soul's travelling on the way connected with the vein that passes through the skull;—which way forms a part of those vidyâs. Now it is proper to conclude that he who meditates on that way should after death proceed on it[1]. Hence he who knows, being favoured by Brahman abiding in the heart on which he had meditated, and thus becoming like it in nature departs by the vein which passes through the skull and 'exceeds the hundred,' i. e. is the hundred and first. The souls of other men pass out by other veins. For thus scripture says, in a chapter treating of the knowledge of Brahman dwelling in the heart, 'There are a hundred and one veins of the heart; one of them penetrates the crown of the head; by that moving upwards a man reaches immortality; the others serve for departing in different directions' (*Kh.* Up. VIII, 6, 5).

18. (The soul after having passed forth from the body) follows the rays.

There is the vidyâ of him within the heart which begins, 'There is this city of Brahman and in it the palace, the small lotus, and in it that small ether' (*Kh.* Up. VIII, 1, 1). A subsequent section of that chapter—beginning with the words, 'Now these veins of the heart'—describes at length the connexion of the veins and the rays, and the text then continues, 'When he departs from this body, he departs upwards by those very rays,' and further on, 'By that

[1] For otherwise the meditation enjoined would be 'ad*ri*sh*t*ârtha' only; an alternative not to be admitted anywhere as long as a 'seen' purpose can be demonstrated.

moving upwards he reaches immortality.' From this we understand that the soul passing out by the hundred and first vein follows the rays.—A doubt here arises as to whether the soul of him who dies by night as well as of him who dies by day follows the rays, or the soul of the latter only.—Since scripture mentions no difference, the Sûtra teaches that the souls follow the rays in both cases.

19. (Should it be said that the soul does) not (follow the rays) by night; (we reply) not so, because the connexion (of veins and rays) exists as long as the body; and (scripture) also declares this.

It might perhaps be said that the veins and rays are connected during the day, so that the soul of a person who dies during the day may follow those rays; but not the soul of one who dies by night when the connexion of the veins and rays is broken.—But this is a mistaken assumption, because the connexion of rays and veins lasts as long as the body exists. This scripture also declares, 'They (the rays) stretch out from yonder sun and slip into these veins; they stretch from these veins and slip into yonder sun' (*Kh.* Up. VIII, 6, 2). We moreover observe that the rays of the sun continue to exist in the nights of the summer season; for we feel their warmth and other effects. During the nights of the other seasons they are difficult to perceive because then few only continue to exist; just as during the cloudy days of the cold season.—This the following scriptural passage also shows, 'Day he makes in the night.'—If, moreover, he who dies at night mounted upwards without following the rays, the following of the rays would be generally meaningless. For the text gives no special direction to the effect that he who dies by day mounts upwards by means of the rays, while he who dies by night mounts without them.—Should, on the other hand, even he who knows be prevented from mounting upwards, by the mere mischance of dying by night, knowledge would in that case produce its fruit eventually only, and the consequence would be that—as the time of death is not fixed—nobody would apply himself to knowledge.—If, again, a man dying at night should wait for the dawn (to mount upwards), it might happen that, owing to the action of the funeral fire, &c., his body would, at the time of daybreak, not be capable of entering into connexion with the rays. Scripture moreover expressly says that he does not wait, 'As quickly as he sends off the mind he goes to the sun' (*Kh.* Up. VIII, 6, 5).—For all these reasons the soul follows the rays by night as well as by day.

20. And for the same reason (the departed soul follows the rays) also during the southern progress of the sun.

For the same reason, viz. because waiting is impossible, and because the fruit of knowledge is not a merely eventual one, and because the time of death is not fixed, also that possessor of true knowledge who dies during the southern progress of the sun obtains the fruit of his knowledge. Because dying during the northern progress of the sun is more excellent, and because Bhîshma is known to have waited for that period, and because scripture says, 'From the light half of the month (they go) to the six months when the sun goes to the north,' it might be thought that the northern progress of the sun is needful for dying. This notion the Sûtra refutes. The greater excellence of the sun's northern progress applies to those only who do not possess the highest knowledge.—Bhîshma's waiting for the sun's northern progress was due to his wish of upholding good customs and of showing that by the favour of his father he could choose the time of his death.—And the sense of the scriptural passage quoted will be explained under IV, 3, 4.—But we have the following Sm*ri*ti-text, 'At what times the Yogins depart either not to return or to return, those times I will declare to thee' (Bha. Gîtâ VIII, 23), which determines specially that to die by day and so on causes the soul not to return. How then can he who dies by night or during the sun's southern progress depart not to return? Concerning this point the next Sûtra remarks:

21. (These details) are recorded by Smriti with reference to the Yogins; and both (Sâṅkhya and Yoga) are Smriti (only).

The rules as to dying by day and so on in order not to return are given by Smriti for the Yogins only. And those two, viz. Yoga and Sâṅkhya are mere Smriti, not of scriptural character. As thus it has a different sphere of application and is based on a special kind of authority, the Smriti rule as to the time of dying has no influence on knowledge based on scripture.—But, an objection is raised, we have such passages as the following one, 'Fire, light, the day, the light half of the month, the six months of the northern progress; smoke, night, the dark half of the month, the six months of the southern progress' (Bha. Gîtâ VIII, 24; 25); in which though belonging to Smriti we recognise the path of the gods and the path of the fathers just as determined by scripture!—Our refutation, we reply, of the claims of Smriti applies only to the contradiction which may arise from the teaching of Smriti regarding the legitimate time of dying. 'I will tell you the time,' &c. In so far as Smriti also mentions Agni and the other divinities which lead on the departed soul, there is no contradiction whatever.

THIRD PÂDA.

Reverence to the highest Self!

1. On the road beginning with light (the departed soul proceeds), on account of that being widely known.

It has been explained that up to the beginning of the way, the departure is the same. About the way itself, however, different texts make different declarations. One passage describes it as constituted by the junction of the veins and rays, 'Then he mounts upwards by just those rays' (*Kh.* Up. VIII, 6, 5). Another passage describes it as beginning with light, 'They go to the light, from light to day' (*Kh.* Up. V, 10, 1). Another way is described, Kau. Up. I, 3, 'Having reached the path of the gods, he comes to the world of Agni.' Another, B*ri*. Up. V, 10, 1, 'When the person goes away from this world, he comes to the wind.' Another again, Mu. Up. I, 2, 11, 'Free from passions they depart through the gate of the sun.' A doubt here arises whether these ways are different from each other, or whether there is only one road of which the different texts mention different particulars.—The pûrvapakshin embraces the former alternative, for the reason that those roads are referred to in different chapters and form parts of different meditations. If, moreover, we regarded the statements about light and so on, the emphatical assertion [1] made in the first of the passages quoted above would be contradicted; and the statement about the quickness of mounting, 'As quickly as he sends off the mind he goes to the sun,' would also be interfered with. We therefore conclude that the roads described are different roads. To this we reply, 'On the road beginning with light;'

[1] The emphasis lies in the word 'eva,' i.e. 'just' or 'only,' which seems to exclude any stages of the way but those rays.

i.e. we maintain that every one who desires to reach Brahman moves on the road beginning with light.—Why so?—'On account of its being widely known.' That road is known to all who possess knowledge. Thus the chapter of the vidyâ of the five fires ('And those also who in the forest meditate on the True as faith,' &c., B*ri*. Up. VI, 2, 15) expressly states that the road beginning with the light belongs to those also who practise other meditations.—That road, an objection is raised, may present itself to the mind in the case of those meditations which do not mention any road of their own; but why should it be accepted for such meditations as mention different roads of their own?—This objection would be valid, we reply, if the various roads mentioned were entirely different; but as a matter of fact there is only one road leading to the world of Brahman and possessing different attributes; and this road is designated in one place by one attribute and in another place by another attribute. For this relation of attributes and what possesses attributes is established by the circumstance that we recognise, in all the passages quoted, some part of the road[1]. And if the chapters which mention the roads are different, we, as long as the meditation is one, have to combine the different attributes of the road (mentioned separately in the different chapters), in the same way as (in general) the different particulars of one meditation (which are stated in different chapters) have to be combined. And even if the meditations (in which the particulars of the road are mentioned) are different, the road must be viewed as one and the same, because we recognise everywhere some part of the road and because the goal is everywhere the same. For all the following passages declare one and the same result, viz. the obtainment of the world of Brahman: 'In these worlds of Brahman they dwell for ever and ever' (B*ri*. Up. VI, 2, 15); 'There he dwells eternal years' (B*ri*.

[1] Each passage mentions at least one of the stages of the road leading to the world of Brahman, and we thus conclude that the same road—of which the stations are the attributes—is meant everywhere.

Up. V, 10, 1); 'Whatever victory, whatever greatness belongs to Brahman, that victory he gives, that greatness he reaches' (Kau. Up. I, 2); 'Those who find the world of Brahman by Brahma*k*arya' (*Kh*. Up. VIII, 4, 3).—To the remark that the emphatical assertion (made in the passage, 'Just by those rays,' &c.) would be contradicted by our admitting light and so on as stages of the road, we reply that no such difficulty exists, because that passage aims only at establishing the rays (as part of the road). For the one word 'just' cannot at the same time establish the rays and discard light and so on. The passage therefore must be understood as only emphasising the connexion with the rays.—Nor does the regard paid by us to the statements about light and so on being stages of the way contradict what one passage says about speed; for that passage means to say that one goes (to the world of Brahman) more quickly than anywhere else, so that its sense is, 'In the twinkling of an eye one goes there[1].'—Moreover the passage, 'On neither of these two ways' (*Kh*. Up. V, 10, 8)—in teaching that there is a third inferior road for those who have missed the other two roads—shows that besides the road of the fathers there is only one further road, viz. the road of the gods, of which light and so on are stages. The text about light and so on mentioning a greater number of stages while other texts mention a smaller number, it stands to reason that the less numerous should be explained in conformity with the more numerous. For this reason also the Sûtra says, 'On the road beginning with light, on account of its being widely known.'

2. From the year to Vâyu; on account of the absence and presence of specification.

But by what special combination can we establish between

[1] Read in the text—tvarâva*k*ana*m* tv ar*k*irâdyapekshâyâm api gantavyântarâpekshayâ kshaipryârtha°.—Ânandagiri comments—tvareti, ar*k*irâdimârgasyaikye*-*pi kuta*s*kid anyato gantavyâd anenopâyena satyaloka*m* ga*t* iti ga*kkh*antîti gantavyabhedâpekshayâ va*k*ana*m* yuktam ity artha*h*.

the different attributes of the road the relation of what is determined by attributes and of determining attributes? The teacher out of kindness to us connects them as follows.—The Kaushîtakins describe the road of the gods as follows, 'Having reached the path of the gods he comes to the world of Agni, to the world of Vâyu, to the world of Varu*n*a, to the world of Indra, to the world of Pra*g*âpati, to the world of Brahman' (Kau. Up. I, 3). Now the world of Agni means the same as light, since both terms denote burning, and we therefore need not, with regard to them, search for the order in which they are to be combined. Vâyu, on the other hand, is not mentioned in the road beginning with light; in what place then is he to be inserted?—We read, *Kh*. Up. V, 10, 1, 'They go to the light, from light to day, from day to the waxing half of the moon, from the waxing half of the moon to the six months when the sun goes to the north, from those months to the year, from the year to Âditya.' Here they reach Vâyu after the year and before Âditya.—Why so?—'On account of the absence and presence of specification.' About Vâyu—concerning whom the passage, 'He goes to the world of Vâyu,' contains no specification—another passage does state such a specification, viz. B*ri*. Up. V, 10, 1, 'When the person goes away from this world he comes to Vâyu. Then Vâyu makes room for him like the hole of a wheel, and through it he mounts higher, he comes to Âditya.' On account of this specification which shows Vâyu to come before Âditya, Vâyu must be inserted between the year and Âditya.—But as there is a specification showing that Vâyu comes after Agni, why is he not inserted after the light?—There is no such specification, we reply.—But a scriptural passage has been quoted which runs as follows, 'Having reached the path of the gods he comes to the world of Agni, to the world of Vâyu.'—In that passage, we reply, we have only two clauses, of which the text exhibits one before the other, but there is no word expressing order of succession. We have there only a simple statement of facts, 'He goes to this and to that.' But in the other text we perceive a regular order of succession;

for it intimates that after having mounted on high through an opening as large as the wheel of a chariot, granted by Vâyu, he approaches the sun. The Sûtra therefore rightly says, 'On account of the absence and presence of specification.'—The Vâgasaneyins in their text record that he proceeds 'from the months to the world of the gods, from the world of the gods to the sun' (B*ri*. Up. VI, 2, 15). Here, in order to maintain the immediate succession of Vâyu and Âditya, we must suppose the souls to go from the world of the gods to Vâyu. What the Sûtra says about the soul going to Vâyu from the year has reference to the text of the *Kh*ândogya. As between the Vâgasaneyaka and the *Kh*ândogya, the world of the gods is absent from one, the year from the other. As both texts are authoritative, both stages have to be inserted in each, and the distinction has to be made that, owing to its connexion with the months, the year has the first place (i.e. after the months and before the world of the gods), and the world of the gods the second place.

3. Beyond lightning (there is) Varu*n*a, on account of the connexion (of the two).

The *Kh*ândogya continues, 'From Âditya to the moon, from the moon to lightning.' Here Varu*n*a (mentioned in the Kaushîtaki-upan.) has to be brought in so that above that lightning he goes to the world of Varu*n*a. For there is a connexion between lightning and Varu*n*a; the broad lightnings dance forth from the womb of the clouds with the sound of deep thunder, and then water falls down. And a Brâhma*n*a also says, 'It lightens, it thunders, it will rain' (*Kh*. Up. VII, 11, 1). But the lord of all water is Varu*n*a, as known from *S*ruti and Sm*ri*ti.—And above Varu*n*a there come Indra and Pragâpati, as there is no other place for them, and according to the force of the text, as it stands. Varu*n*a and so on should be inserted at the end, for that reason also that they are merely additional, no particular place being assigned to them. And lightning is the end of the road beginning with light[1].

[1] So that Varu*n*a and so on are to be placed after lightning.

4. (They are) conductors, this being indicated.

With regard to those beginning with light a doubt arises whether they are marks of the road, or places of enjoyment, or leaders of the travelling souls.—The first possible view of the question is that light and so on are marks of the road, because the instruction has that character. For as in ordinary life a man wishing to go to a village or a town is told, 'Go from here to that hill, from there to a fig-tree, from that to a river, from that to a village; after that you will reach the town;' so here the text also says, 'from light to day, from day to the waxing half of the month,' &c.—Or else light and so on may be viewed as places of enjoyment. For the text connects Agni and so on with the word 'world'; 'He comes to the world of Agni,' &c. Now the term 'world' is used to denote places of enjoyment of living beings, as when we say, 'The world of men; the world of the Fathers; the world of the gods.' A Brâhma*n*a passage also says, 'They remain attached to the worlds which consist of day and night' (*S*at. Brâ. X, 2, 6, 8). Therefore light and the rest are not conductors. Moreover, they cannot be conductors because they are without intelligence. For in ordinary life intelligent men only are appointed by the king to conduct travellers over difficult roads.

To all this we reply as follows. They must be conductors, because the text indicates this. For we read, 'From the moon to the lightning; there a person that is not a man leads them to Brahman;' which shows their conductorship to be something settled. Should it be objected that this last sentence exhausts itself in conveying its own purport[1]; we say No; for the attribute ('that is not a man') has only the meaning of excluding his previously established humanity. Only if in the case of the light and the rest personal conductors are settled, and those of human nature, it is appropriate to use the attribute

[1] And has not the additional power of indicating, i.e. enabling us to infer that also the beings previously mentioned are 'leaders' of the soul.

'amânava,' to the end of excluding this (previously established) humanity[1].

But mere indication has no force, as there is nothing to prove (that there must be such personal conductors).—To this objection the next Sûtra replies.

5. (There are personal conductors) because that is established on the ground of both (i. e. road and travellers) being bewildered (i. e. unconscious).

As, owing to their separation from a body, the organs of those who go on the road beginning with light are wrapped up, they are incapable of ruling themselves; and the light &c., as they are without intelligence, are equally incapable. Hence it follows that the particular intelligent deities who represent light and the rest are appointed to the conductorship. For in ordinary life also drunken or senseless people whose sense-organs are wrapped up follow a road as commanded by others.—Again light and the rest cannot be taken for marks of the road because they are not always present. A man who dies in the night cannot come to day in its true (physical) nature; and he cannot wait (for the break of day), as we have already explained above (IV, 2, 19). But this objection does not apply to gods who are permanent. And gods may be called light and so on, because they represent light and so on. Nor is the expression, 'From light to day,' &c. objectionable, even if we adopt the sense of conductorship; for it means, through the light as cause they come to the day; through the day as cause, to the waxing half of the moon. And such instruction is seen also in the case of conductors known in ordinary life, for they say, Go hence to Balavarman, thence (i.e. Balavarman conducting you) to *G*ayasi*m*ha, thence to

[1] Why should it be specially stated that this last 'conducting person' is amânava? Only, because it is a settled matter that the previously mentioned beings are also 'conducting persons,' and at the same time 'mânava.' The last clause therefore does not only directly teach that a person conducts the souls to Brahman, but at the same time 'indicates' that the beings mentioned before in connexion with the road are also 'personal conductors.'

K*ri*sh*n*agupta. Moreover, in the beginning where the text says that they go to the light, a relation in general only is expressed, not a special relation; at the end, however. where it is said he leads them to Brahman, a special relation is expressed, viz. that between conducted and conductor. Therefore this is accepted for the beginning also.—And as the organs of the wandering souls are wrapped up together there is no possibility of their enjoying anything. Although, however, the wanderers do not enjoy anything, the word 'world' may be explained on the ground that those worlds are places of enjoyment for other beings dwelling there—The conclusion therefore is that he who has reached the world of Agni is led on by Agni, and he who has reached the world ruled by Vâyu, by Vâyu.

But how, if we adopt the view of conductorship, can this apply to Varu*n*a and the rest? Varu*n*a and the rest were inserted above the lightning; but scripture states that after the lightning until Brahman is reached a person leads who is not a man.—To this doubt the next Sûtra replies.

6. From thence (the souls are led) by him only who belongs to the lightning; the sacred text stating that.

From thence, i. e. after they have come to the lightning they go to the world of Brahman, being led through the worlds of Varu*n*a and the rest by the person, not a man, who follows immediately after the lightning. For that that person leads them is stated in the following passage, 'When they have reached the place of lightning a person, not a man, leads them to the world of Brahman' (B*ri*. Up. VI, 2, 15). Varu*n*a and the rest, we must understand, favour them either by not hindering or somehow assisting them.—Therefore it is well said that light and so on are the gods who act as conductors.

7. To the effected (Brahman) (the souls are led); (thus opines) Bâdari; because going to him is possible.

With regard to the passage, 'He leads them to Brahman,'

the doubt arises whether that person leads the souls to the effected, lower, Brahman, or to the highest, non-modified, chief Brahman.—Whence the doubt?—Because the (ambiguous) word Brahman is used, and because scripture speaks of going.—The opinion of the teacher Bâdari is that the person, who is not a man, leads them to the lower, qualified, effected Brahman; because it is possible to go to that. For the effected Brahman which occupies a definite place can be the goal of a journey. With the highest Brahman, on the other hand, we cannot connect the ideas of one who goes, or object of going, or act of going; for that Brahman is present everywhere and is the inner Self of all.

8. And on account of (the Brahman to which the souls are led) being qualified (in another passage).

That the soul's going has for its object the effected Brahman, we conclude from another scriptural passage also which qualifies Brahman in a certain way, 'He leads them to the worlds of Brahman; in these worlds of Brahman they live for ever and ever' (B*ri*. Up. VI, 2, 15). For it would be impossible to qualify the highest Brahman by means of the plural number ('worlds'); while the plural number may be applied to the lower Brahman which may abide in different conditions.—The term 'world' also can directly denote only some place of enjoyment falling within the sphere of effects and possessing the quality of being entered into, while it must be understood in a metaphorical sense in passages[1] such as 'Brahman is that world' (B*ri*. Up. IV, 4, 23).—And also what the text says concerning an abode and some one abiding within it ('in these worlds of Brahman,' &c.), cannot be directly understood of the highest Brahman.—For all these reasons the leading of the souls has the lower Brahman for its goal.

But even on this interpretation the word 'Brahman' is inappropriate, as it has been proved that Brahman is the

[1] Where the term 'world' is applied to the highest Brahman.

cause of the origination and so on of the entire world.—To this objection the next Sûtra replies.

9. But on account of its proximity (to the higher Brahman) there is designation (of the lower Brahman) as that.

The word 'but' indicates the setting aside of the doubt.—As the lower Brahman is in proximity to the higher one, there is nothing unreasonable in the word 'Brahman' being applied to the former also. For when the higher Brahman is, for the purposes of pious meditation, described as possessing certain effected qualities—such as consisting of mind and the rest—which qualities depend on its connexion with certain pure limiting adjuncts; then it is what we call the lower Brahman.—But with the assumption of the lower Brahman there does not agree what scripture says about the souls not returning; for there is no permanence anywhere apart from the highest Brahman. And scripture declares that those who have set out on the road of the gods do not return, 'They who proceed on that path do not return to the life of man' (*Kh.* Up. IV, 15, 6); 'For them there is no return here' (B*ri.* Up. VI, 2, 15); 'Moving upwards by that a man reaches immortality' (*Kh.* Up. VIII, 6, 5).

To this objection we make the following reply.

10. On the passing away of the effected (world of Brahman) (the souls go) together with the ruler of that (world) to what is higher than that; on account of scriptural declaration.

When the reabsorption of the effected Brahman world draws near, the souls in which meanwhile perfect knowledge has sprung up proceed, together with Hira*n*yagarbha the ruler of that world, to 'what is higher than that,' i.e. to the pure highest place of Vish*n*u. This is the release by successive steps which we have to accept on the basis of the scriptural declarations about the non-return of the souls. For we have shown that the Highest cannot be directly reached by the act of going.

11. And on account of Sm*ri*ti.

Sm*ri*ti also agrees with this view; cp. the following passage, 'When the pralaya has come and the end of the highest (i.e. Hira*n*yagarbha), then they all, together with Brahman, with purified minds enter the highest place.'—The final conclusion (siddhânta) therefore is that the going of the souls, of which scripture speaks, has for its goal the effected Brahman.—But what is the primâ facie view, with regard to which this final conclusion has been established in Sûtras 7–11?—This required primâ facie view is now set forth in the following Sûtras.

12. To the highest (Brahman) (the souls are led); *G*aimini (opines); owing to this being the principal sense (of the word 'Brahman').

The teacher *G*aimini is of opinion that the passage, 'He leads them to Brahman,' refers to the highest Brahman. For the highest Brahman constitutes the principal, primary sense, of the word 'Brahman,' which denotes the lower Brahman only in a secondary, metaphorical way. And where both senses are possible, the primary sense has to be preferred.

13. And because scripture declares that.

The text, 'Going upwards by that he reaches immortality,' declares that immortality is reached by going. But immortality is possible only in the highest Brahman, not in the effected one, because the latter is transitory. So scripture says, 'Where one sees something else, that is little, that is mortal' (*Kh*. Up. VII, 24, 1). According to the text of the Ka*th*a-upanishad also the going of the soul is towards the highest Brahman; for after the highest Brahman has been introduced there as general subject-matter—in the passage, 'That which thou seest,' &c., I, 2, 14, no other kind of knowledge is taken up later on.

14. And the intention of entering (can) not (be referred) to the effected (Brahman).

Moreover the intention of entering into which is expressed

in the passage, 'I enter the hall of Pra*g*âpati, the house' (*Kh*. Up. VIII, 14, 1), cannot have the lower Brahman for its object. For the immediately preceding passage, 'That within which these forms and names are contained is the Brahman,' shows that the highest Brahman, different in nature from the effected one, is the general subject-matter; and the subsequent passage, 'I am the glory of the Brâhmans,' represents the soul as the Self of all; it being known from another scriptural passage that 'Glory' is a name of the highest Brahman, 'There is no likeness of him whose name is great glory' (Vâ*g*. Sa*m*h. XXXII, 3). And in the vidyâ of Brahman within the heart it is said of this same entering the house that it is preceded by going [1], 'There is the city of Brahman Aparâ*g*itâ, and the golden hall built by Prabhu' (*Kh*. Up. VIII, 5, 3). And that the performing of a journey is intended follows also from the use of the verb 'pad,' which denotes going (prapadye, I enter).—The other (primâ facie) view therefore is that all the passages about the soul's going refer to the highest Brahman.

These two views have been embodied by the teacher in the Sûtras; one in the Sûtras 7–11, the other in the Sûtras 12–14. Now the arguments contained in the former set are capable of proving the fallaciousness of the arguments in the latter set, but not vice versâ; from which it follows that the former set states the final view and the latter set the primâ facie view only.—For nobody can compel us to accept the primary sense of a word (such as Brahman) even where it is impossible to do so.—And although met with in a chapter that treats of the highest knowledge, the reference to the going to Brahman—which belongs to another kind of knowledge—may be explained as aiming merely at the glorification of the highest knowledge (not at teaching that the going to Brahman is the result of higher

[1] I am not quite sure which passage in the daharavidyâ is supposed to prove that the entering of Brahman's house is preceded by going. Probably VIII, 6, 5, 'He departs upwards; he is going to the sun.'

knowledge).—And with reference to the passage, 'I enter the hall of Pra*g*âpati, the house,' there is no reason why we should not separate that passage from what precedes and refer the intention of entering to the effected Brahman. And the qualified Brahman also may be spoken of as being the Self of all, as shown by other passages such as 'He to whom all works, all desires belong,' &c. (*Kh*. Up. III, 14, 2). The texts about the going therefore all belong to the lower knowledge.—Others again, in accordance with the general principle that the earlier Sûtras set forth the primâ facie view, while the later ones contain the siddhânta view, maintain that the passages about the soul's going fall within the sphere of the higher knowledge. But this is impossible, because nothing may go to the highest Brahman. 'Omnipresent and eternal like the ether;' 'The Brahman which is visible, not invisible, the Self that is within all' (B*ri*. Up. III, 4, 1); 'Self only is all this' (*Kh*. Up. VII, 25, 2); 'Brahman only is all this, it is the best' (Mu. Up. II, 2, 11): from all these passages we ascertain that the highest Brahman is present everywhere, within everything, the Self of everything, and of such a Brahman it is altogether impossible that it ever should be the goal of going. For we do not go to what is already reached; ordinary experience rather tells us that a person goes to something different from him.—But we observe in ordinary experience also that something already reached may become an object of going, in so far as qualified by a different place; a man living on the earth, e. g. goes to the earth, in so far as he goes to another place on the earth. In the same way we see that a child reaches the adult state which in reality belongs to the child's identical Self, but is qualified by a difference of time. Analogously Brahman also may be an object of going in so far as it is possessed of all kinds of powers.—This may not be, we reply, because scripture expressly negatives Brahman's possessing any distinctive qualities.—'Without parts, without actions, tranquil, without fault, without taint' (*S*vet. Up. VI, 19); 'Neither coarse nor fine, neither short nor long' (B*ri*. Up. III, 8, 8); 'He who is without and within, unproduced' (Mu. Up. II, 1, 2);

'This great, unborn Self, undecaying, undying, immortal, fearless, is indeed Brahman' (B*ri*. Up. IV, 4, 25); 'He is to be described by No, no!' (B*ri*. Up. III, 9, 26); from all these scriptural texts, as well as from Sm*ri*ti and reasoning, it follows that the highest Self cannot be assumed to possess any differences depending on time or space or anything else, and cannot therefore become the object of going. The cases of places on the earth and of the different ages of man are by no means analogous; for they are affected by differences of locality and so on, and therefore can be gone to or reached.—Nor will it avail our opponent to say that Brahman possesses manifold powers, because scripture declares it to be the cause of the world's origination, sustentation, and final retractation; for those passages which deny difference have no other sense (but just the absolute denial of all difference).—But in the same way also those passages which state the origination and so on of the world have no other sense! (i. e. cannot be understood to teach anything but just the origination and so on of the world).—This is not so, we reply; for what they aim at teaching is the absolute oneness of Brahman. For texts which by means of the simile of the lump of clay, &c., teach that only that which is, viz. Brahman, is true, while everything effected is untrue, cannot aim at teaching the origination, &c. of the world.—But why should the passages about the origination, &c. of the world be subordinate to those which deny all difference, and not vice versâ?—Because, we reply, the texts which negative all difference effect the cessation of all desire. For when the absolute oneness, permanence, and purity of the Self have once been apprehended, we cognize that the highest aim of man has been attained, and therefore conceive no further desires. Compare the following texts: 'What trouble, what sorrow can there be to him who beholds that unity?' (Î*s*â-up. 7); 'Thou hast reached fearlessness, O *G*anaka' (B*ri*. Up. IV, 2, 4); 'He who knows does not fear anything; he does not distress himself with the thought, Why did I not do what is good? Why did I do what is bad?' (Taitt. Up. II, 9.) This also follows from our observing that those who know realise contentment of mind; and from the fact that scripture blames the false notion of (the reality of) effects, 'From death to death goes he who sees here any difference' (Ka. Up. II, 4, 10). The texts negativing all difference cannot therefore be understood as subordinate to other texts. Those texts, on the other hand, which speak of the origination of the world and so on have no similar power of conveying a sense which effects cessation of all desire. At the same time it is manifest that they have another (than their literal) meaning. For the text, after having said at first, 'Of this shoot sprung up know that it cannot be without a root' (*Kh.* Up. VI, 8, 3), declares in the end that Being which is the root of the world is the only object of cognition. Similarly Taitt. Up. III, 1, 'That from which these beings are born, that by which when born they live, that into which they enter at their death, seek to know that; that is Brahman.' As thus the passages about origination and so on aim at teaching the unity of the Self, Brahman cannot be viewed as possessing manifold powers, and cannot therefore be the object of the action of going.—And, as already explained under IV, 2, 13, also the text B*ri*. Up. IV, 4, 6 ('Of him the prâ*n*as do not depart; being Brahman he goes to Brahman'), denies any going to the highest Brahman.

Moreover, on the hypothesis of going, that which goes, i.e. the individual soul, must be either a part of Brahman to which it goes, or an effect of Brahman, or different from Brahman; for if the two were absolutely identical no going could take place.—Well, what then?—We reply as follows. If, in the first place, the soul is a part of Brahman, it cannot go to it, since the whole is permanently reached by the part. Besides, the hypothesis of whole and parts cannot be applied to Brahman, which is acknowledged to be without parts.—The same objection lies against the hypothesis of the soul being an effect of Brahman; for also that which passes over into an effect is permanently reached by the effect. A jar made of clay does not exist apart from the clay which constitutes its Self; were it so apart it would cease to be. And on both hypotheses, as that to which the parts or the effects would belong, i. e. Brahman is altogether unchanging, its entering into the Sa*m*sâra state could not be accounted for.—Let then, in the third place, the soul be different from Brahman. In that case it must be either of atomic size, or infinite, or of some intervening extent. If it is omnipresent, it cannot go anywhere. If it is of some middling extent, it cannot be permanent. If it is of atomic size, the fact of sensation extending over the whole body cannot be accounted for. The two hypotheses of atomic and middling extent have moreover been refuted at length in a former part of this work (II, 3, 19 ff.). And from the soul's being different from the highest Brahman it also would follow that such texts as 'Thou art that' are futile. This latter objection also lies against the theories of the soul being a part or an effect of Brahman. Nor can the difficulty be got over by it being pleaded that a part and an effect are not different from the whole and the causal substance; for that kind of oneness is not oneness in the true literal sense—From all those three theories it moreover equally follows that the soul cannot obtain final release, because its Sa*m*sâra condition could never come to an end. Or else, if that condition should come to an end, it would follow that the very essence of the soul perishes; for those theories do not admit that the (imperishable) Brahman constitutes the Self of the soul.

Here now some come forward with the following contention. Works of permanent obligation and works to be performed on special occasions are undertaken to the end that harm may not spring up; such works as are due to special desires, and such as are forbidden, are eschewed, in order that neither the heavenly world nor hell may be obtained, and those works whose fruits are to be enjoyed in the current bodily existence are exhausted by just that fruition. Hence, as after the death of the present body, there is no cause for the origination of a new body, that blessed isolation which consists in the soul's abiding within its own nature will accomplish itself for a man acting in the way described above, even without the cognition of his

Self being identical with Brahman's Self.—All this is inadmissible, we reply, because there is no proof of it. For scripture nowhere teaches that he who desires release should conduct himself in the way described. To say that because the Sa*m*sâra state depends on works, it will cease when works are absent, is an altogether arbitrary style of reasoning. And (whether arbitrary or not) this reasoning falls to the ground, because the absence of the cause is something that cannot be ascertained. It may be supposed that each living being has, in its former states of existence, accumulated many works which have part of them pleasant, part of them unpleasant results. As these works are such as to lead to contrary results, which cannot be enjoyed all of them at the same time, some works whose opportunity has come, build up the present state of existence; others sit inactive waiting for a place, a time, and operative causes (favourable to them). As these latter works cannot thus be exhausted in the present state of existence, we cannot definitely assert, even in the case of a man who conducts himself as described above, that at the end of his present bodily existence all cause for a new bodily existence will be absent. The existence of a remainder of works is, moreover, established by scriptural and Sm*ri*ti passages, such as, 'Those whose conduct has been good' (*Kh.* Up. V, 10, 7); 'Then with the remainder.'—But may not, an objection is raised, those remaining works be wiped out (even in the present existence) by the performance of works of permanent obligation and such works as are due to special occasions?—This may not be, we reply, because the two sets of works are not of contrary nature. Where there is contrariety of nature, one thing may be wiped out by another; but good deeds performed in previous states of existence, and works of permanent obligation and so on (performed in the present life), are both of them equally pure and therefore not of opposite nature. Bad works indeed, as being of impure nature, are opposed to works of permanent obligation, &c., and therefore may be extinguished by the latter. But even from this admission it does not follow that the causes for a new embodied existence are altogether absent; for those causes may be supplied by good deeds, and we do not know that the evil works have been extinguished without a remainder. Nor is there anything to prove that the performance of works of permanent obligation, &c., leads only to the non-origination of harm, and not at the same time to the origination of new results (to be extinguished in future states of existence); for it may happen that such new results spring up collaterally. Thus Âpastamba says, 'When a mango tree is planted for the sake of its fruits, it in addition gives shade and fragrance; thus additional advantages spring from the performance of religious duty.'—Nor can anybody who has not reached perfect knowledge promise to refrain altogether, from birth to death, from all actions either forbidden or aiming at the fulfilment of special wishes: for we observe that even the most perfect men commit faults, however minute. This may be a matter of doubt; all the same it remains true that the absence of causes for a new existence cannot be known with certainty.—If, further, the soul's unity with Brahman's Self—which is to be realised through knowledge—is not acknowledged, the soul whose essential nature it is to be an agent and enjoyer cannot even desire the state of blissful isolation; for a being cannot divorce itself from its true essence, not any more than fire can cease to be hot.—But, an objection is raised, what is of disadvantage to the soul is the state of agentship and fruition in so far as actually produced, not its mere potentiality. Release of the soul may, therefore, take place if only that actual condition is avoided while its potentiality remains. —This also, we reply, is not true; for as long as the potentiality exists it will inevitably produce the actuality. —But, our opponent resumes, potentiality alone, without other co-operative causes, does not produce its effect; as long therefore as it is alone it cannot, though continuing to exist, do any harm!—This also, we reply, is not valid; for the co-operative causes also are, potentially, permanently connected (with the acting and enjoying soul). If, therefore, the soul whose essence is acting and enjoying is not considered to possess fundamental identity with Brahman

—an identity to be realised by knowledge—there is not any chance of its obtaining final release. Scripture, moreover (in the passage, 'There is no other way to go,' *S*vet. Up. III, 8), denies that there is any other way to release but knowledge.—But if the soul is non-different from the highest Brahman, all practical existence comes to an end, because then perception and the other means of right knowledge no longer act!—Not so, we reply. Practical life will hold its place even then, just as dreamlife holds its place up to the moment of waking. Scripture, after having said that perception and the rest are operative in the sphere of those who have not reached true knowledge ('For where there is duality, as it were, there one sees the other,' &c.; B*ri*. Up. IV, 5, 15), goes on to show that those means of knowledge do not exist for those who possess that knowledge ('But when the whole of him has become the Self, whereby should he see another,' &c.). As thus for him who knows the highest Brahman all cognition of something to be gone to, &c. is sublated, his going cannot in any way be shown to be possible.

To what sphere then belong the scriptural texts about the soul's going?—To the sphere of qualified knowledge, we reply. Accordingly the soul's going is mentioned in the chapter treating of the knowledge of the five fires, in the chapter treating of the knowledge of Brahman's couch, in the chapter treating of the knowledge of Agni Vais*v*ânara (*Kh*. Up. V, 3–10; Kau. Up. I; *Kh*. Up. V, 11–24). And where the soul's going is spoken of in a chapter treating of Brahman—(as e.g. in the passages, 'He leads them to Brahman,' &c., *Kh*. Up. IV, 15, 6, in a chapter treating of Brahman, as shown by 'Breath is Brahman,' &c., IV, 10, 5; and 'He departs upward,' &c., *Kh*. Up. VIII, 6, 5, in the chapter beginning 'There is this city of Brahman,' VIII, 1, 1)—such attributes as 'vâmanî,' i.e. Leader of blessings (*Kh*. Up. IV, 15, 3), and 'satyakâma,' i.e. having true wishes, show that there the qualified Brahman has to be meditated upon, and to that Brahman the soul can go. No passage, on the other hand, speaks of the soul's going to the highest Brahman; while such going is specially denied in the passage, 'Of him the prâ*n*as do not depart.' In passages, again, such as 'He who knows Brahman obtains the Highest' (Taitt. Up. II, 1), we indeed meet with the verb 'to reach,' which has the sense of going; but because, as explained before, the reaching of another place is out of question, 'reaching' there denotes only the obtainment (realisation) of one's own nature, in so far as (through true knowledge) the expanse of names and forms which Nescience superimposes (on Brahman) is dissolved. Such passages are to be understood analogously to the text, 'Being Brahman he enters into Brahman' (B*ri*. Up. IV, 4, 6).—Besides, if the going were understood as connected with the highest Brahman, it could only subserve the purpose either of satisfying (the mind of him who knows) or of reflection. Now, a statement of the soul's going cannot produce any satisfaction in him who knows Brahman, since satisfaction is already fully accomplished through his perfect condition, bestowed on him by knowledge, of which he is immediately conscious. Nor, on the other hand, can it be shown that reflection on the soul's going in any way subserves knowledge, which is conscious of eternally perfect blessedness, and has not for its fruit something to be accomplished.—For all these reasons the soul's going falls within the sphere of the lower knowledge. And only in consequence of the distinction of the higher and lower Brahman not being ascertained, statements about the soul's going which apply to the lower Brahman are wrongly put in connexion with the higher Brahman.

But are there really two Brahmans, a higher one and a lower one?—Certainly there are two! For scripture declares this, as e.g. in the passage, 'O Satyakâma, the syllable Om is the higher and also the lower Brahman' (Pr. Up. V, 2).—What then is the higher Brahman, and what the lower?—Listen! Where the texts, negativing all distinctions founded on name, form, and the like, designate Brahman by such terms as that which is not coarse and so on, the higher Brahman is spoken of. Where, again, for the purpose of pious meditation, the texts teach Brahman as qualified by some distinction depending on name, form, and so on, using terms such as

'He who consists of mind, whose body is prâ*n*a, whose shape is light' (*Kh*. Up. III, 14, 2), that is the lower Brahman.—But is there not room here for the objection that this distinction of a higher and a lower Brahman stultifies the scriptural texts asserting aduality?—Not so, we reply. That objection is removed by the consideration that name and form, the adjuncts (of the one real Brahman), are due to Nescience. Passages such as 'If he desires the world of the fathers' (*Kh*. Up. VIII, 2, 1), which the text exhibits in proximity to a meditation on the lower Brahman, show that the fruit of such meditation is lordship over the worlds; a fruit falling within the sphere of the Sa*m*sâra, Nescience having not as yet been discarded. And as that fruit is bound to a special locality, there is nothing contradictory in the soul's going there in order to reach it. That the soul, although all-pervading, is viewed as going because it enters into connexion with the buddhi and the rest of its adjuncts, just as general space enters into connexion with jars and the like, we have explained under II, 3, 29.

For all these reasons the view of Bâdari as set forth in Sûtra 7 is the final one; while Sûtra 12, which states *G*aimini's opinion, merely sets forth another view, to the end of the illumination of the learner's understanding.

15. Those who do not take their stand on symbols he leads, thus Bâdarâya*n*a (opines); there being no fault in the twofold relation (resulting from this opinion); and the meditation on that (i.e. Brahman) (is the reason of this twofold relation).

It is a settled conclusion that all going has reference to the effected Brahman, not to the highest Brahman. Another doubt now arises here. Does that person who is not a man lead to the world of Brahman all those who take their stand on the effected Brahman, without any difference; or only some of them?

The pûrvapakshin maintains that all those who possess knowledge—provided that knowledge be not of the highest Brahman—go to the world of Brahman. For in Sûtra III,

3, 31 that going was put in connexion with all the different vidyâs (of the qualified Brahmans), without any distinction.

To this the Sûtrakâra replies, 'Those who do not take their stand on symbols.' That means: Excepting those who take their stand on symbols (i.e. who meditate on certain things as symbolically representing Brahman), that person who is not a man leads all others who take their stand (i.e. who meditate) on the effected Brahman to the world of Brahman; this is the opinion of the teacher Bâdarâya*n*a. For in acknowledging in this way a twofold relation there is no fault; since the argumentation as to the non-restriction of going (Sûtra III, 3, 31) may be understood as referring to all meditations with the exception of those on symbols. The words, 'and the meditation on that,' state the reason for this twofold relation. For he whose meditation is fixed on Brahman reaches lordship like that of Brahman, according to the scriptural relation, 'In whatever form they meditate on him, that they become themselves.' In the case of symbols, on the other hand, the meditation is not fixed on Brahman, the symbol being the chief element in the meditation.—But scripture says also that persons whose mind is not fixed on Brahman go to it; so in the knowledge of the five fires, 'He leads them to Brahman' (*Kh.* Up. V, 10, 2).—This may be so where we observe a direct scriptural declaration. We only mean to say that where there is no such declaration the general rule is that those only whose purpose is Brahman go to it, not any others.

16. And scripture declares a difference (in the case of meditations on symbols).

With reference to the meditations on symbols, such as name and so on, scripture declares that each following meditation has a different result from the preceding one, 'As far as name reaches he is lord and master;—speech is greater than name;—as far as speech reaches he is lord and master;—mind is greater than speech' (*Kh.* Up. VII, 1, ff.).

Now this distinction of rewards is possible because the meditations depend on symbols, while there could be no such distinction if they depended on the one non-different Brahman.—Hence those who take their stand on symbols cannot have the same reward as others.

FOURTH PÂDA.

REVERENCE TO THE HIGHEST SELF!

1. (On the soul's) having entered (into the highest light), there is manifestation (of its own nature); (as we infer) from the word 'own.'

'Thus does that serene being, having risen out of this body and entered into the highest light, manifest itself by its own nature' (*Kh.* Up. VII, 12, 3). Regarding this text a doubt arises whether the Self[1] manifests itself through some adventitious distinction—as the Self (of him who possesses the lower knowledge only) does in the world of the gods and other abodes of enjoyment—or only through its own Self.—The pûrvapakshin maintains that, as in other places, here also the manifestation takes place through some adventitious characteristic; because release also is a fruit (like other fruits, e.g. svarga), and because 'manifestation' means as much as origination. If the manifestation took place only through the Self's own nature, it would already appear in the Self's former states; for a thing's own nature is never absent from it. The Self therefore manifests itself by means of some adventitious distinction.

To this we make the following reply. It manifests itself through its Self only, not through any other attribute.—Why so?—On account of the word 'own' in the clause 'by its own nature.' For on the other view the qualification conveyed by 'own' would be unmeaning.—But may not the term 'own' merely indicate that that form belongs to that which manifests itself?—Not so, we reply. This is a point which would not require to be stated. For as in

[1] Sa*m*prati *k*aturthe pâde paravidyâphalaikade*s*o brahmabhâvâvirbhâva*h*, sagu*n*avidyâphala*m* *k*a sarve*s*varatulyabhogatvam avadhârayishyate, tatrâparavidyâprâpyam uktvâ paravidyâprâpyam âha sa*m*padyeti. Ân. Gi.

whatever form a thing manifests itself that form necessarily belongs to it, the qualification 'own' would be devoid of purport. It has a meaning, on the other hand, if it denotes the Self, the sense conveyed then being that the manifestation takes place only through the nature of the Self, not through any other, adventitious, nature.—But, as a thing cannot be without its own nature, what difference is there between the Self's former states and its present state (after the manifestation)?—To this question the next Sûtra replies.

2. (The Self whose true nature has manifested itself is) released; according to the promise (made by scripture).

That soul, of which the text says that it manifests itself, is released from its former bondage and abides in its own pure Self; while previously its Self was stained by the three states (i. e the state of waking, dreaming, and dreamless sleep), according to *Kh.* Up. VIII, 9–11, 'It is blind;'—'it weeps as it were;'—'it goes to utter annihilation.' This is the difference.—But how is it known that in its present condition the soul is released?—'On account of the promise,' the Sûtra says. For after the teacher has promised to give further instruction about the Self as free from the imperfections of the three states ('I shall explain him further to you,' *Kh.* Up. VIII, 11, 3), he introduces the topic (of the released Self) in the words, 'Him being free from the body neither pleasure nor pain touches,' and concludes, 'By his own nature he manifests himself; that is the highest Person.' The words at the beginning of the tale also, 'The Self which is free from sin' (VIII, 7, 1), make a promise regarding the released Self. And release is a fruit in so far only as it is a cessation of all bondage, not as implying the accession of something new. And with reference to the assertion that manifestation is the origination of something new we remark that it is so only with regard to a former condition (which ceases to be), as when we say of a convalescent person that he now manifests himself free from sickness. Hence there is no room for objections.

3. (The light into which the soul enters is) the Self; owing to the subject-matter of the chapter.

But how can the soul be called 'released,' considering that the clause 'having entered into the highest light' speaks of it as within the sphere of what is a mere effect? For the word 'light,' according to general usage, denotes physical light. And none who has not passed beyond the sphere of what is effected can be released, it being known that whatever is an effect is tainted with evil.—This objection is without force, we reply; because in the passage referred to the word 'light' denotes the Self, in accordance with the subject-matter of the chapter. For as such the highest Self is introduced in the words, 'The Self which is free from sin, old age, death,' &c., and we therefore may not all at once pass over to physical light; incurring thereby the fault of abandoning the topic under discussion and introducing a new one. Besides, the word 'light' sometimes denotes the Self, as e.g. in the passage, 'That the gods meditate on as the light of lights' (B*ri*. Up. IV, 4, 16). We have discussed this at length under I, 3, 40.

4. (The released soul abides) in non-division (from the highest Self); because that is seen from scripture.

A doubt here arises whether that soul of which the text says, 'Having entered the highest light it manifests itself by its true nature,' remains separate from the highest Self, or abides in the state of non-division from it.—Somebody might be inclined to think that—because in the passage, 'He moves about there,' a distinction is made between the abode and him who abides; and because the clause, 'Having entered the highest light,' mentions an agent and an object (of the agent's activity)—the soul remains distinct from the highest Self.—This view the Sûtra sets aside. The released soul is non-separate from the highest Self.—Why so?—Because that is seen from scripture. For passages such as 'Thou art that' (*Kh.* Up. VI, 8, 7); 'I am Brahman' (B*ri.* Up. I, 4, 10); 'Where he sees nothing else' (*Kh.* Up. VII, 24, 1); 'But there is then nothing second, nothing else different that he could see' (B*ri.* Up. IV, 3, 23), show that the highest Self abides in the state of non-division. And the fruit must be assumed to correspond to the cognition, according to what was explained under IV, 3, 15. And also such passages as 'Just as pure water poured into pure water remains the same, thus, O Gautama, is the Self of a thinker who knows' (Ka. Up. II, 4, 15), whose object it is to describe the nature of the released soul, declare that there is non-separation only. The same follows from the comparisons (of the soul entering Brahman) to rivers falling into the sea. Passages where separation (of abode and abiding thing, &c.) is expressed, may be explained as, in a secondary sense, expressing non-separation; so e.g. *Kh.* Up. VII, 24, 1, 'In what does the Infinite rest?—In its own greatness;' and *Kh.* Up. VII, 25, 2, 'Loving the Self, playing with the Self.'

5. By (a nature) like that of Brahman (the soul manifests itself); (thus) *G*aimini (opines); on account of reference and the rest.

It has been concluded that the clause, 'by its own nature,' means that the soul manifests itself by its own Self only, not by some other adventitious character. What has now to be inquired into is the specific qualities of that nature. Here the Sûtra at first states the opinion of the teacher *G*aimini. According to him the soul's own nature is 'like that of Brahman,' i.e. it comprises all the qualities beginning with freeness from sin and concluding with truthfulness of conception (i. e. the qualities enumerated in *Kh.* Up. VIII, 7, 1), and also omniscience and omnipotence; and in this nature the soul manifests itself.—Why so?—Because this is known from reference[1] and the rest. For the reference

[1] The commentators say that the 'and the rest' of the Sûtra comprises vidhi and vyapadesa, and give the following definitions.

to certain qualities made in VIII, 7, 1, teaches that the Selfhood of the Self is such (i.e. such as made up of those qualities).—Again, the passage, 'He there moves about eating, playing, rejoicing,' shows that the Self possesses lordly power; so also the passage, 'For him there is free movement in all worlds' (*Kh.* Up. VIII, 1, 6).—And thus also there is justification for such designations as 'All-knowing; all-powerful.'

6. By the sole nature of intelligence (the soul manifests itself), as that is its Self; thus Au*d*ulomi (opines).

Although the text enumerates different qualities, such as freeness from sin, &c., these qualities rest only on fanciful conceptions due to difference of words; for what the text intimates is only absence in general of all qualities such as sin and the rest. Intelligence alone constitutes the nature of the Self, and hence it is proper to conclude that it manifests itself in a nature consisting of that only. This conclusion will also agree with other scriptural texts, such as B*ri*. Up. IV, 5, 13, 'Thus this Self has neither inside nor outside, but is altogether a mass of knowledge.'—Qualities, on the other hand, such as having true wishes, are indeed mentioned by the text as real (positive) attributes, the meaning being that his wishes are true, i.e. truly existent; but all the same they, as depending on the connexion with limiting adjuncts, cannot constitute the true nature of the

Upanyâsa is the reference to something known (established elsewhere), which reference is made with a view to a vidhi, i.e. the establishing of something not yet known (upanyâso nâmoddes*ah* sa *k*â*nyatra *g*ñ*â*tasyâ*nyavidhânâyânuvâda*h*). Thus here the qualities —freeness from sin—are referred to as known, for the purpose of establishing the vidhi, 'That it is which we must search out.'—The passage, 'He there wanders about,' &c., is a vidhi; for it teaches what is not already known from elsewhere.—The mentioning of such qualities as omniscience and omnipotence is vyapades*a*, i.e. simple expression of something known without reference to a vidhi.

Self, as intelligence does. For all manifoldness of character has to be denied of Brahman, as we have shown under III, 2, 11. For the same reason the mention made of eating and so on, means only the absence of all pain in general, and aims at glorification, just as the passage about 'loving the Self' (*Kh*. Up. VII, 25, 2). For love, play, and the like cannot in their literal sense be ascribed to the action of the Self, because they presuppose something second (beyond the Self). Hence the soul manifests itself in the nature of pure intelligence, free from all manifoldness, calm, not capable of being expressed by any terms. This is the view of the teacher Au*d*ulomi.

7. Thus also, on account of the existence of the former (qualities), (admitted) owing to reference and so on, there is absence of contradiction, (as) Bâdarâya*n*a (thinks).

Thus also, i. e. although it be admitted that intelligence only constitutes the true nature of the Self, also the former nature, i.e. lordly power like that of Brahman, which is intimated by reference and the rest, is—with a view to the world of appearances—not rejected; and hence there is no contradiction. This is the opinion of the teacher Bâdarâya*n*a.

8. But by mere will (the released effect their purposes); because scripture states that.

In the meditation on Brahman within the heart we read as follows: 'If he desires the world of the fathers, by his mere will the fathers rise,' &c. (*Kh*. Up. VIII, 2, 1).—A doubt here presents itself whether the will alone is the cause of the rising of the fathers, or the will joined with some other operative cause.—The pûrvapakshin maintains that although scripture says 'by his mere will,' some other cause must be supposed to co-operate, as in ordinary life. For as in our ordinary experience the meeting with one's father is caused by one's will, and, in addition, by the act of going and so on, so it will be in the case of the released soul also; and thus we do not assume something contrary to observation. When the text says 'by his mere will,' it implies, as in the case of a king, the whole apparatus of other easily procurable instrumental causes by which the desired object is obtained. Besides, if the fathers and so on rose owing to a mere wish, they would be of unstable nature, like the imaginary representation of some desired object, and thus not be able to procure any solid enjoyment.—To this we reply that the rising of the fathers and so on is due to the will only.—Why so?—Because scripture declares this. If any other cause were required, the direct scriptural statement 'by his will only' would thereby be contradicted. And even if we admit some other cause accompanying the act of will, it cannot be a cause to be realised by an effort; for therefrom it would follow that before the realisation of that cause the will would be barren. Nor can the analogies of ordinary experience be applied to something to be learned from scripture. For as the will of the released differs in nature from the will of ordinary men, it may have the power of effecting something that possesses as much stability as the special purpose requires.

9. And for this very same reason (the released soul is) without another lord.

For this very same reason, i. e. owing to the fact of the will of the released person not being barren, he who knows has no other lord over himself. For not even an ordinary person when forming wishes will, if he can help it, wish himself to be subject to another master. And scripture also declares this when saying, 'Those who depart from hence, after having discovered the Self and those true desires, for them there is freedom in all worlds' (*Kh.* Up. VIII, 1, 6).

10. The absence (of a body and sense-organs, on the part of the released) Bâdari (asserts); for thus scripture says.

The passage, 'By his mere wish the fathers rise,' shows that the released possesses a mind (internal organ, manas) whereby he wills. A question however arises whether he who knows, after having reached lordly power, possesses a body and senses, or not. Here the teacher Bâdari is of opinion that the glorified possessor of knowledge is without body and sense-organs.—Why so?—Because scripture declares this, 'With the mind seeing those wishes he rejoices' (*Kh.* Up. VIII, 12, 5). If he rejoiced with the mind, the body, and the senses, scripture would not specially say 'with the mind.' Hence there are neither body nor sense-organs in the state of release.

11. The presence (of a body and senses) *G*aimini (asserts); because the text records option (of the released person multiplying himself).

The teacher *G*aimini is of opinion that the released person possesses a body and sense-organs as well as a mind. For passages like 'He is onefold, he is threefold' (*Kh.* Up. VII, 26, 2) declare that the Self has the option of manifold existence which cannot be brought about without manifoldness of body.—The capability of optionally multiplying one's self is, indeed, mentioned in the knowledge of plenitude (bhûman) which refers to Brahman as devoid of qualities, but this lordly power which is valid only for the qualified state is there mentioned only in order to glorify the knowledge of the (unqualified) plenitude; and it therefore presents itself as constituting the fruit of qualified knowledge[1].

12. For this reason Bâdarâya*n*a (opines that the released person is) of both kinds; as in the case of the twelve days' sacrifice.

The teacher Bâdarâya*n*a, again, thinks that for this reason, i.e. because scripture contains indications of both kinds, the proper conclusion is that the released person exists in both

[1] Manifoldness of the Self is mentioned in a vidyâ referring to the highest Brahman; but its introduction there is not due to the wish of teaching something about that state, but merely of, rhetorically, glorifying it. We, therefore, are entitled to view that passage as teaching something about him who possesses the lower knowledge.

conditions. When he wishes to have a body, he appears with one; when he wishes to be disembodied, he is without one. For he has various wishes, and all his wishes are realised.—'As in the case of the twelve days' sacrifice.' As the soma sacrifice extending over twelve days may be viewed either as a sattra or as an ahîna sacrifice, because both alternatives are indicated by scriptural passages[1]; so it is here also.

13. When there is no body, (the process) may take place as in the dreaming state.

When there is no body and no sense-organs, the process in the state of release may be viewed as analogous to that in the state of dream, when objects wished, such as a father and so on, have a perceptional existence only while body, senses, and objects do not really exist.

14. When there is (a body), (it may be) as in the waking state.

When, on the other hand, the released person has a body, then the objects of his wishes—fathers and so on—may have real existence, as in the waking state.

15. The entering (of one soul into several bodies) is like (the multiplication of) the flame of a lamp; for thus scripture declares.

Under Sûtra 11 it has been shown that the released person is embodied. The question now arises whether the bodies which the released create for themselves when rendering themselves threefold and so on are soulless like wooden figures, or animated by souls like the bodies of us men.—The pûrvapakshin maintains that as neither the soul nor the manas can be divided they are joined with one body only, while the other bodies are soulless.—To this the Sûtrakâra replies, 'Like the flame of a lamp is their entering,' i. e. just as the one flame of a lamp can pass over into several flames (lighted at the original flame), because it possesses

[1] See Pûrva Mîmâmsâ-sûtras II, 3, 5th adhikarana.

the power of modifying itself, thus the soul of him who knows, although one only, multiplying itself through its lordly power, enters into all those bodies. For scripture declares that in this way one may become many, 'He is onefold, he is threefold, fivefold, sevenfold' (*Kh.* Up. VII, 26, 2). And this is not possible, if we should accept the simile of the wooden puppets, or the entering of other souls into those additional bodies[1]. Nor again can there be any motion on the part of bodies destitute of souls.—Nor is there any force in the objection that, because the Self and the Manas cannot be divided, they cannot be in connexion with more than one body. For the Self, because possessing the quality of having true wishes (i. e. wishes which become real), may be supposed to create other bodies with internal organs, conformable to the original one organ; and, the Self dividing itself through the division of its limiting adjuncts, it may be possible to give a soul to each created body. This is the topic which the books on Yoga treat, in the chapters explaining the connexion of one soul with several bodies.—But how can lordly power, enabling the released soul to enter into several bodies, be admitted, if we consider that different scriptural texts declare that the soul in that state has not any specific cognition? so e.g. 'Whereby should he know another?' 'For there is then no second, nothing else different from him that he could know;' 'An ocean is that one seer, without any duality' (B*ri.* Up. II, 4, 14; IV, 3, 30; 32).

To this objection the next Sûtra replies.

16. (What scripture says about absence of all specific cognition) refers either to deep sleep or union (release); for this is manifested (by the texts).

By 'entering into one's own Self' is meant dreamless

[1] I. e. the scriptural statement about one Self rendering itself manifold can neither be reconciled with the hypothesis of the other bodies being moved by the one soul as puppets are moved by one person through strings, nor with the hypothesis of a new separate soul entering each new body.

sleep; according to the text, 'He is gone to his own Self, he sleeps they say' (*Kh*. Up. VI, 8, 1). 'Union' means blissful isolation (final release), according to the text, 'Being Brahman he goes to Brahman' (B*ri*. Up. IV, 4, 6). What the texts say about absence of specific cognition is said with reference to either of those two states, dreamless sleep or final release.—How do we know this?—Because this is 'manifest,' owing to the fact that those two states form the topic there (where absence of all cognition is mentioned). Compare the passages, 'Having risen from out of these elements it perishes again after them. Having departed there is no more knowledge;' 'But where the Self only is all this;' 'Where when asleep he desires no more desires, and dreams no more dreams' (B*ri*. Up. II, 4, 12; IV, 5, 15; IV, 3, 19). —Those passages, on the other hand, which describe lordly power refer to an altogether different condition, which—like the heavenly world and so on—is an abode where qualified knowledge produces its results.—Thus there is no contradiction.

17. With the exception of world-business (the released possess all lordly power), (the Lord) being the topic (where world-business is referred to), and (the souls) not being near (to such business).

The following doubt here presents itself. Do those who through meditations on the qualified Brahman enter, together with their manas, into a condition of equality with the Lord, possess unlimited lordly power, or power limited to some extent?—The pûrvapakshin maintains that their power must be unlimited, because we meet with texts such as 'He obtains Self-lordship' (Taitt. Sa*m*h. I, 6, 2); 'All the gods bring an offering for him' (Taitt. Sa*m*h. I, 5, 3); 'For them there is freedom in all worlds' (*Kh*. Up. VIII, 1, 6).—To this the Sûtra replies, 'Excepting the world-business.' With the exception of the origination and so on of the world all other lordly powers, as e. g. rendering one's self of atomic size, must belong to the released. The world-business, on the other hand, can belong to the everlastingly perfect Lord only.—Why so?—Because there (where the origination and so on of the world are referred to) the Lord forms the general topic, and because the other (souls) do not stand near (to the world-business). The highest Lord only is appointed to do all work referring to the entire world; for the world's origination and so on are taught only where he constitutes the general subject-matter, and moreover he (only) is eternal, and described in scripture (as the creator, &c. of the world)[1]. The lordly power of the other souls, on the contrary, scripture shows to have a beginning, because it depends on their searching for and striving to know the Lord. They are therefore remote from all world-business. And just because they have minds, they might be of different minds, and one might have the intention of preserving the world while another might wish to destroy it. Such conflicts can only be avoided by assuming that the wishes of one should conform to those of another, and from this it follows that all other souls (but the Lord) depend on the highest Lord.

18. (Should it be said that the souls must possess unlimited power) on account of manifest teaching; we reply No, because scripture states him who, entrusted with office, abides in the spheres (of the sun and so on), (to be that one on whom the soul's obtaining lordly power depends).

It remains to refute the remark, made by the pûrvapakshin, that absolute power on the part of those who know must be inferred from texts directly asserting such power, as e.g. 'He obtains self-lordship.'—This refutation the above Sûtra undertakes. Scripture declares that the obtainment of rulership on the soul's part, depends on the

[1] Ki*m* *k*a paraisyaiva nityatvena svahetvanapeksha*n*asya k*l*ipta*s*aktitvâ*g* *g*agatsar*g*ana*m* prati kalpyasâmarthyâ*k* *k*a vidushâm î*s*vara-vishayaiva *g*agats*ri*sh*t*ir esh*t*avyâ, ki*m* *k*a paurvâparyâlo*k*anâyâm î*s*varasyaiva *g*agatsarga*h* *s*abdâd gamyate *g*anmâdisûtram ârabhya *k*aitad upapâditam. Ân. Gi.

highest Lord who, as entrusted with definite offices, abides in certain definite abodes, such as the sphere of the sun, &c. This is shown by the text going on to say (after the clause quoted above), 'He obtains the lord of Mind.' For that means that he obtains the lord known to be the lord of all minds. In accordance herewith the text later on says that he becomes lord of speech, lord of the eye, lord of the ear, lord of understanding.—Similarly in other passages also the lordly power of the other souls has to be viewed, according to circumstances, as depending on the eternally perfect Lord.

19. And (there is also a form of the highest Lord) not abiding in effected things; for thus scripture declares his abiding.

Moreover, according to scripture, there is also an eternal form of the highest Lord which does not abide in effects; he is not only the ruling soul of the spheres of the sun and so on which lie within the sphere of what is effected. For the text declares his abiding in a twofold form, as follows: 'Such is the greatness of it; greater than it is the Person. One foot of him are all beings; three feet of him is what is immortal in heaven' (*Kh.* Up. III, 12, 6). And it cannot be maintained that that form of him which is divorced from all effects is reached by those who put their trust on his other form; for their minds are not set on the former. Hence as he who does not reach that form of the double-natured highest Lord which is divorced from all qualities stops at that form which is distinguished by qualities, so also, unable to reach unlimited power within the latter form, he stops at limited lordly power.

20. And thus perception and inference show.

Scripture and Sm*ri*ti both declare that the highest light does not abide within effected things, 'The sun does not shine there, nor the moon and the stars, nor these lightnings, and much less this fire' (Mu. Up. II, 2, 10). 'The sun does not illume it, nor the moon, nor fire' (Bha. Gîtâ XV, 6). —The Sûtra is meant to show that the non-abiding of the highest light within effected things is a well-known circumstance.

21. And on account of the indications of equality of enjoyment only.

The lordly power of those who take their stand on the effected Brahman is not absolute, for that reason also that scripture teaches that their enjoyment only is equal to that of the eternally perfect Lord. For scripture contains statements and indications of the difference (of the Lord and the released soul); compare 'To him he says, Water indeed is enjoyed[1] (by me); that world (is to be enjoyed by thee also)' (Kau. Up. I, 7); 'As all beings honour that deity, so do all beings honour him who knows that' (B*ri*. Up. I, 5, 20); 'He obtains through it equality (in body) and sameness of abode with that deity' (B*ri*. Up. I, 5, 23). But from the circumstance of the lordly power of the released souls not being absolute it follows that it comes to an end, and then they will have to return from the world of Brahman!—To this objection the reverend Bâdarâya*n*a replies in the following Sûtra.

22. (Of them) there is non-return, according to scripture; non-return, according to scripture.

Those who, in following the road of the gods, to which the vein and the ray are leading, and on which light is the first stage, reach the world of Brahman as described by scripture—where 'there are the two lakes Ara and *N*ya in the world of Brahman, in the third heaven from hence,' and where 'there is the lake Airammadîya and the A*s*vattha tree showering down Soma, and the city of Brahman Aparâ*g*itâ and the golden hall built by Prabhu' (*Kh*. Up. VIII, 5, 3)—and set forth at length in mantras,

[1] All the commentators explain the reading 'mîyante.'—Ân. Gi. says—ta*m* brahmalokagatam upâsaka*m* hira*n*yagarbha*h* svasamîpam upâgata*m* sânunayam âha mayâ khalv âpa evâm*ri*tamayyo mîyante d*ris*yante bhu*g*yante tavâpy asâv am*ri*tarûpodakalaksha*n*o loko bhogyo yathâsukha*m* bhu*g*yatâm.

arthavâdas, and so on; those, we say, who reach that world do not return from there after having finished the enjoyment of their deeds; as those do who have gone to the world of the moon and other places.—Why so?—Because scriptural passages teach that they do not so return. Compare 'Moving upwards by it he reaches the immortal' (*Kh.* Up. VIII, 6, 6); 'For them there is no return' (B*ri.* Up. VI, 2, 15); 'Those who proceed on that path do not return to the life of man' (*Kh.* Up. IV, 15, 6); 'He reaches the world of Brahman and does not return' (*Kh.* Up. VIII, 15, 1). That the finality of their lordly power does not imply their return to the life of man, we have shown under IV, 3, 10. It is a settled matter that those who through perfect knowledge have dispelled all mental darkness and are devoted to the eternally perfect Nirvâ*n*a do not return. And as those also who rely on the knowledge of the qualified Brahman in the end have recourse to that (Nirvâ*n*a), it follows that they also do not return.—The repetition of the words, 'Non-return, according to scripture,' indicates the conclusion of this body of doctrine.

INDEX OF QUOTATIONS

TO

VOLUMES XXXIV (i) AND XXXVIII (ii).

INDEX OF SANSKRIT WORDS

TO

VOLUMES XXXIV (i) AND XXXVIII (ii).

GENERAL INDEX

TO

VOLUMES XXXIV (i) AND XXXVIII (ii).

[1] Arranged in the following order:—(1) names, definitions, and symbols of B.; (2) nature, qualities, powers, forms, parts, abodes of B.; (3) higher and lower B.; (4) unity of, and oneness with B.; (5) B. is everything; (6) B. and the world; (7) B. and the soul; (8) B. and Scripture; (9) knowledge of B.; (10) meditation on B.; (11) B. and final release; (12) world of B.

[1] Arranged in the following order:—(1) different designations and notions of different schools about it; (2) its nature and characteristics; (3) its size; (4) s. and body; (5) s. and Brahman, the Lord, the highest Self; (6) its states of dream, sleep, swoon; (7) its fate after death; (8) the released s.

CORRIGENDA.

VOLUME XXXIV.

Page lxi, line 25, *read* (10) *for* (9
„ lxiv, „ 32, *read* prakritaitâvattva
„ cxvi, „ 3, *read* I, 1, 4 *for* I, 4
„ 34, „ 20, *read* I, 3, 4 *for* III, 1, 4
„ 172, „ 6 from below, *read* or *for* on
„ 191, „ 22, *read* nâdîs *for* nadîs
„ 246, last line, *read* Ka. Up. I, 3, 15
„ 282, line 23, *read* IV, 4, 24 *for* IV, 24
„ 402, „ 13, and line 8 from below, *read* samgñâ° *for* samgñâ°
„ 440, „ 26, *read* igyâ *for* îgyâ

VOLUME XXXVIII.

Page 154, line 12, *read* Vaisvânara *for* °svanara
„ 182, „ 4 from below, *read* Bâdarâyana *for* Bâdârayana
„ 190, last line, *read* Up. II, 6, 2
„ 221, line 7, *read* Avabhritha- *for* Avabritha-
„ 236, „ 9 } *read* Aparântaratamas *for* Aparântamas
„ „ „ 23 }
„ 287, „ 2 from below, *read* guhû *for* guhû
„ 295, „ 11 „ „ *read* 2, 11 *for* 10, 11
„ 319, „ 6 „ „ *read* Krikkhra *for* Krikkhra
„ 330, „ 13 „ „ *read* their *for* its
„ 352, „ 18 „ „ *read* Pr. Up. III, 10 *for* Pr. Up. IV, 2, 10

TRANSLITERATION OF ORIENTAL ALPHABETS ADOPTED FOR THE TRANSLATIONS OF THE SACRED BOOKS OF THE EAST.

CONSONANTS.	MISSIONARY ALPHABET. I Class.	II Class.	III Class.	Sanskrit.	Zend.	Pehlevi.	Persian.	Arabic.	Hebrew.	Chinese.
Gutturales.										
1 Tenuis	k	...	....	क	𐬐	𐭪	ک	ك	כּ	k
2 „ aspirata	kh	...	....	ख	𐬑	𐭧	...	...	כ	kh
3 Media	g	...	....	ग	𐬔	𐭢	گ	...	גּ	...
4 „ aspirata	gh	...	....	घ	𐬖	𐭢	...	...	ג	...
5 Gutturo-labialis	q	...	....	...	....	...	ق	ق	ק	...
6 Nasalis	ṅ (ng)	...	....	ङ	{𐬧 (ng) / 𐬣 (N)}	...	...	...	...	...
7 Spiritus asper	h	...	....	ह	𐬵 (𐬸 hv)	𐭧	ه	ه	ה	h, hs
8 „ lenis	’	...	....	...	....	...	ا	ا	א	...
9 „ asper faucalis	‘h	...	....	...	....	...	ح	ح	ח	...
10 „ lenis faucalis	’h	...	....	...	....	...	ع	ع	ע	...
11 „ asper fricatus	...	*‘h*	....	...	....	...	خ	خ	ח	...
12 „ lenis fricatus	...	*’h*	....	...	....	...	...	...	...	...
Gutturales modificatae (palatales, &c.)										
13 Tenuis	...	*k*	....	च	𐬗	𐭰	چ	...	...	*k*
14 „ aspirata	...	*kh*	....	छ	....	...	...	...	...	*kh*
15 Media	...	*g*	....	ज	𐬘	𐭰	ج	ج	...	...
16 „ aspirata	...	*gh*	....	झ	....	...	غ	غ	...	...
17 „ Nasalis	...	*ñ*	....	ञ	....	...	...	...	...	...

CONSONANTS (*continued*).	MISSIONARY ALPHABET. I Class.	II Class.	III Class.	Sanskrit.	Zend.	Pehlevi.	Persian.	Arabic.	Hebrew.	Chinese.
18 Semivocalis	y	...	...	य	𐬫; 𐬪, [illegible] init.	[illegible]	ي	ي	י	y
19 Spiritus asper	...	(ʿy)	...	...	...	...	...	...	...	...
20 „ lenis	...	(ʾy)	...	...	...	...	...	...	...	...
21 „ asper assibilatus	...	*s*	...	श	𐬱	[illegible]	ش	ش	...	...
22 „ lenis assibilatus	...	*z*	...	...	𐬲	[illegible]	ژ	...	...	*z*
Dentales.										
23 Tenuis	t	...	...	त	𐬙	[illegible]	ت	ت	תּ	t
24 „ aspirata	th	...	...	थ	𐬚	...	...	...	ת	th
25 „ assibilata	...	...	TH	...	...	...	ث	ث	...	...
26 Media	d	...	...	द	𐬛	[illegible]	د	د	דּ	...
27 „ aspirata	dh	...	...	ध	𐬜	...	...	...	ד	...
28 „ assibilata	...	...	DH	...	...	...	ذ	ذ	...	...
29 Nasalis	n	...	...	न	𐬥	[illegible]	ن	ن	נ	n
30 Semivocalis	l	...	...	ल	...	[illegible], [illegible], [illegible]	ل	ل	ל	l
31 „ mollis 1	...	*l*	...	ळ	...	...	...	...	...	...
32 „ mollis 2	...	...	L	...	...	...	...	...	...	...
33 Spiritus asper 1	s	...	...	स	𐬯	[illegible]	س (ث)	س	שׂ	s
34 „ asper 2	...	...	s (ʃ)	...	...	...	...	...	ס	...
35 „ lenis	z	...	...	...	𐬰	[illegible]	ز (ذ)	ز	ז	z
36 „ asperrimus 1	...	...	z (ʒ)	...	...	...	ص	ص	צ	ʒ, ʒh
37 „ asperrimus 2	...	...	ẓ (ʒ̣)	...	...	...	ض	...	...	...

Dentales modificatae (linguales, &c.)										
38 Tenuis	. . .	*t*	. . . .	ट	. . . .	. . .	ط	ط	ט	. . .
39 „ aspirata	. . .	*th*	. . . .	ठ	. . . .	. . .	ط	ط	. . .	. . .
40 Media	. . .	*d*	. . . .	ड	[illegible]	[illegible]	. . .	. . .	. . .	. . .
41 „ aspirata	. . .	*dh*	. . . .	ढ	. . . .	. . .	. . .	ض	. . .	. . .
42 Nasalis	. . .	*n*	. . . .	ण	[illegible]	. . .	. . .	. . .	. . .	. . .
43 Semivocalis	r	. . .	. . . .	र	[illegible]	[illegible]	ر	ر	ר	. . .
44 „ fricata	. . .	*r*	. . . .	. . .	. . . .	. . .	. . .	. . .	. . .	r
45 „ diacritica	. . .	. . .	R	. . .	. . . .	. . .	. . .	. . .	. . .	. . .
46 Spiritus asper	sh	. . .	. . . .	ष	[illegible]	[illegible]	. . .	. . .	. . .	sh
47 „ lenis	zh	. . .	. . . .	. . .	. . . .	. . .	. . .	. . .	. . .	. . .
Labiales.										
48 Tenuis	p	. . .	. . . .	प	[illegible]	[illegible]	پ	. . .	פּ	p
49 „ aspirata	ph	. . .	. . . .	फ	. . . .	. . .	. . .	. . .	פ	ph
50 Media	b	. . .	. . . .	ब	[illegible]	[illegible]	ب	ب	בּ	. . .
51 „ aspirata	bh	. . .	. . . .	भ	. . . .	. . .	. . .	. . .	ב	. . .
52 Tenuissima	. . .	*p*	. . . .	. . .	. . . .	. . .	. . .	. . .	. . .	. . .
53 Nasalis	m	. . .	. . . .	म	[illegible]	[illegible]	م	م	מ	m
54 Semivocalis	w	. . .	. . . .	. . .	[illegible]	. . .	. . .	. . .	. . .	w
55 „ aspirata	hw	. . .	. . . .	. . .	. . . .	. . .	. . .	. . .	. . .	. . .
56 Spiritus asper	f	. . .	. . . .	. . .	[illegible]	[illegible]	ف	ف	. . .	f
57 „ lenis	v	. . .	. . . .	व	[illegible]	[illegible]	و	و	ו	. . .
58 Anusvâra	. . .	*m̃*	. . . .	अं	[illegible]	. . .	. . .	. . .	. . .	. . .
59 Visarga	. . .	*h*	. . . .	अः	. . . .	. . .	. . .	. . .	. . .	. . .

VOWELS	MISSIONARY ALPHABET. I Class.	II Class.	III Class.	Sanskrit.	Zend.	Pehlevi.	Persian.	Arabic.	Hebrew.	Chinese.
1 Neutralis	0	...	...	...	...	...	...	...	ְ	ă
2 Laryngo-palatalis	ĕ	...	...	...	...	...	...	...	...	...
3 „ labialis	ŏ	...	...	...	...	ו fin.	...	...	...	...
4 Gutturalis brevis	a	...	...	अ	𐬀	𐬀 init.	ـَ	ـَ	ַ	a
5 „ longa	â	(*a*)	...	आ	𐬁	𐬀	ـَا	ـَا	ָ	â
6 Palatalis brevis	i	...	...	इ	𐬌	...	ـِ	ـِ	ִ	i
7 „ longa	î	(*i*)	...	ई	𐬍	ى	ـِي	ـِي	ִי	î
8 Dentalis brevis	*li*	...	...	ऌ	...	...	...	...	...	...
9 „ longa	*lî*	...	...	ॡ	...	...	...	...	...	...
10 Lingualis brevis	*ri*	...	...	ऋ	...	...	...	...	...	...
11 „ longa	*rî*	...	...	ॠ	...	...	...	...	...	...
12 Labialis brevis	u	...	...	उ	𐬎	...	ـُ	ـُ	ֻ	u
13 „ longa	û	(*u*)	...	ऊ	𐬏	ו	ـُو	ـُو	וּ	û
14 Gutturo-palatalis brevis	e	...	...	...	𐬆(e) 𐬈(*e*)	...	...	...	ֶ	e
15 „ longa	ê (ai)	(*e*)	...	ए	𐬇, 𐬉	ى	...	...	ֵ	ê
16 Diphthongus gutturo-palatalis	âi	(*ai*)	...	ऐ	...	...	ـَيْ	ـَيْ	...	âi
17 „ „	ei (ĕi)	...	...	...	...	...	...	...	...	ei, êi
18 „ „	oi (ŏu)	...	...	...	...	...	...	...	...	...
19 Gutturo-labialis brevis	o	...	...	...	𐬊	...	...	...	ָ	o
20 „ longa	ô (au)	(*o*)	...	ओ	𐬋	ו	...	...	וֹ	...
21 Diphthongus gutturo-labialis	âu	(*au*)	...	औ	𐬆𐬎 (*au*)	...	ـَوْ	ـَوْ	...	âu
22 „ „	eu (ĕu)	...	...	...	...	...	...	...	...	...
23 „ „	ou (ŏu)	...	...	...	...	...	...	...	...	...
24 Gutturalis fracta	ä	...	...	...	...	...	...	...	...	...
25 Palatalis fracta	ï	...	...	...	...	...	...	...	...	...
26 Labialis fracta	ü	...	...	...	...	...	...	...	...	ü
27 Gutturo-labialis fracta	o	...	...	...	...	...	...	...	...	...